Acclaim for *City of Oranges*

"The curious reader with no ideological axe to grind, but an interest in the people and their fate, could do no better than start here. . . . Only by hearing the other's story can there be any hope of human reconciliation. It is in the stories that the future lies, and Adam LeBor has magnificently, and sympathetically, told them."   —*The Independent*

"Outstanding. . . . A clear-eyed study of one of the great cities of the eastern Mediterranean. . . . LeBor easily sustains what might have been a rather fragmented tale, intercutting with great skill the numerous voices that recount his narrative. . . . An excellent and courageous book."   —*The Guardian*

"We have heard the story from politicians and generals, heard the last words of suicide bombers and the howls of their victims. But *City of Oranges* brings us something quite different: the sound of ordinary people trying to get on with their lives in the middle of interminable conflict."
—*The Sunday Times* (London)

"LeBor delivers a strong tale that leads us through the winding streets of Jaffa. It becomes so evocative that one can almost see the bakeries, smell the souks, see the seaside cafés, the Italianate apartments and the buzzing piazza known as Clock Tower Square. . . . If one can't get to Palestine today, then the next best thing is to read *City of Oranges*. . . . This book is for anyone who loves the Middle East, but also for those who do not yet know it and have been too timid to take on a weighty and more political book. LeBor succeeds in telling the story of ordinary people living in extraordinary times, and by doing that, tells us the painful story of Palestine itself."
—*The Independent on Sunday*

"An astute and balanced history." —*The Times* (London)

"Happily, and unusually, this book approaches the conflict from a far more even-handed perspective. In tracing the story of the bitter division of Israeli and Palestinian territories . . . Adam LeBor not only avoids academic dryness, but also manages to tell each of their stories without condemnation." —*The Observer*

"LeBor is an unusually skillful collector of tales, an abundantly empathetic listener. Like a good saga, *City of Oranges* draws the reader in to know the fate of each of the families." —Esther Solomon, *Haaretz*

"This is an enjoyable and useful book for everyone browsing through the hitherto unknown pages of the life of Jaffa's Arab society." —*Asharq Alawsat*

"Engrossing. . . . LeBor uses the deeply moving experience of individuals as a lens through which to explore the complex history of Israel and Palestine in the twentieth century." —*Financial Times*, Summer Reads 2006

"Honest, direct narrative, based on scrupulous reporting with real historical depth." —*Prospect* magazine, Books of the Year, 2006

"Some writers have a way with words, others an unerring nose for research. LeBor has both—plus compassion for the sufferings on all sides." —*The Jewish Chronicle*

CITY

of

ORANGES

ALSO BY ADAM LEBOR

NONFICTION

A Heart Turned East: Among the Muslims of Europe and America

Hitler's Secret Bankers: The Myth of Swiss Neutrality During the Holocaust

Seduced by Hitler: The Choices of a Nation and the Ethics of Survival
(with Roger Boyes)

Milosevic: A Biography

"Complicity with Evil": The United Nations in the Age of Modern Genocide

FICTION

Night Hotel

CITY

of

ORANGES

AN INTIMATE HISTORY
OF ARABS AND JEWS IN JAFFA

ADAM LeBor

W. W. NORTON & COMPANY
New York • London

Copyright © 2007, 2006 by Adam LeBor

First American edition 2007

First published in Great Britain 2006 by Bloomsbury under the title *City of Oranges: Arabs and Jews in Jaffa*

Maps by Reginald Piggott, 2006

All rights reserved

Printed in the United States of America

For information about permission to reproduce selections from this book, write to Permissions, W. W. Norton & Company, Inc., 500 Fifth Avenue, New York, NY 10110

Manufacturing by Courier Westford

Book design by Chris Welch

Production manager: Anna Oler

Library of Congress Cataloging-in-Publication Data

LeBor, Adam.
City of oranges: an intimate history of Arabs and Jews in Jaffa / Adam LeBor.
p. cm.
Includes bibliographical references and index.
ISBN 978-0-393-32984-1 (pbk.)
1. Jews—Israel—Tel Aviv—Social life and customs. 2. Arabs—Israel—Tel Aviv—Social life and customs. 3. Jaffa (Tel Aviv, Israel)—Social life and customs. 4. Jaffa (Tel Aviv, Israel)—History. 5. Tel Aviv (Israel)—Social life and customs. I. Title.
DS110.T357L415 2007
956.94'8—dc22
2007002389

W. W. Norton & Company, Inc., 500 Fifth Avenue, New York, N.Y. 10110
www.wwnorton.com

W. W. Norton & Company Ltd., Castle House, 75/76 Wells Street, London W1T 3QT

1 2 3 4 5 6 7 8 9 0

For my mother, Brenda LeBor

Two important phenomena, of the same nature but opposed, are emerging at this moment in Asiatic Turkey. They are the awakening of the Arab nation and the latent efforts of the Jews to reconstitute on a very large scale the ancient kingdom of Israel. These movements are destined to fight each other continually until one of them wins.

Arab writer Najib Azouri,
LE REVEIL DE LA NATION ARABE, 1905

Contents

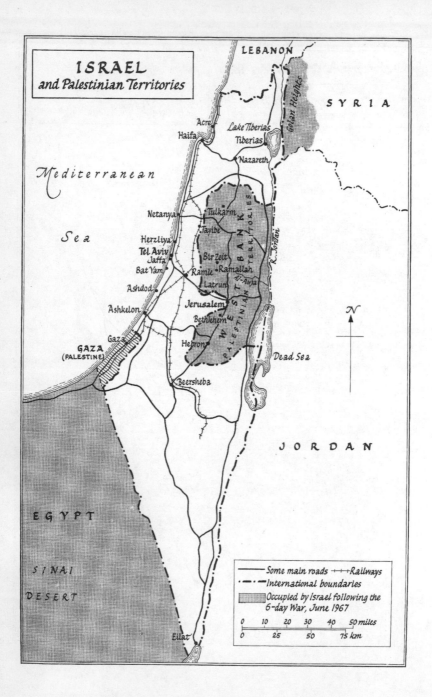

ISRAEL
and Palestinian Territories

LEBANON

SYRIA

Mediterranean

Sea

Acre
Haifa
Lake Tiberias
Tiberias
Golan Heights
Nazareth

Netanya
Tulkarm
Jayibe
Herzliya
Tel Aviv
Jaffa
Bat Yam
Bir Zeit
Ramle
Ramallah
Latrun
R. Jordan
W. Auja

WEST BANK
PALESTINIAN TERRITORIES

Ashdod

Ashkelon
Jerusalem
Bethlehem

GAZA
(PALESTINE)
Gaza
Hebron
Dead Sea

N

Beersheba

JORDAN

EGYPT

SINAI
DESERT

——— Some main roads +++ Railways
—·—· International boundaries
▨ Occupied by Israel following the
6-day War, June 1967

0   10   20   30   40   50 miles
0   25   50   75 km

Eilat

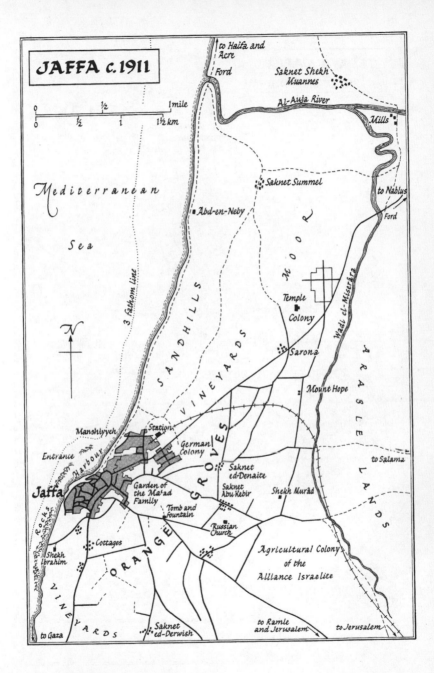

JAFFA c. 1911

to Haifa and Acre

Ford

Saknet Shekh Muannes

Al-Auja River

Mills

½ 1mile
0 ½ 1 1½ km

Mediterranean

Sea

Saknet Summel

Abd-en-Neby

to Nablus

Ford

M O O R

Temple Colony

Wadi el-Miserâre

3 Fathom Line

N

S A N D H I L L S

V I N E Y A R D S

Sarona

Mount Hope

A R A B L E   L A N D S

Manshiyyeh

Station

German Colony

Saknet ed-Denaite

Entrance

Harbour

Garden of the Ma'ad Family

Saknet Abu Kebir

Shekh Murâd

to Salama

Jaffa

O R A N G E   G R O V E S

Tomb and Fountain

Russian Church

Rocks

Cottages

Shekh Ibrahim

V I N E Y A R D S

Agricultural Colony of the Alliance Israelite

to Gaza

Saknet ed-Derwish

to Ramle and Jerusalem

to Jerusalem

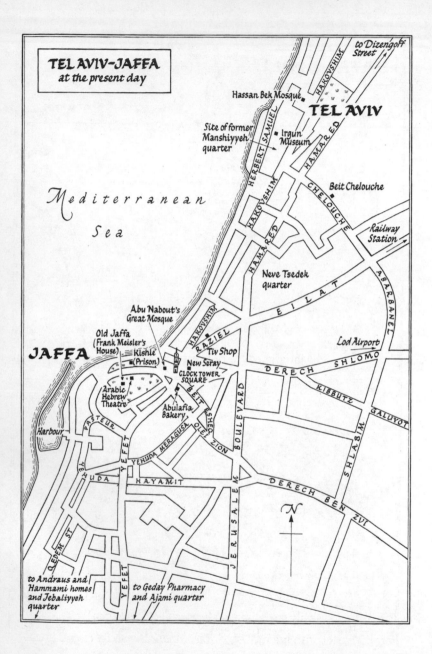

Illustrations

Frank Meisler and his father, Misha. (*Meisler family collection*)
The Hammami family in 1947. (*Hammami family collection*)
Two of the Hammami brothers with friends. (*Hammami family collection*)

THE FAMILIES THEN

Aharon Chelouche, the great family patriarch, and his wife, Sarah. (*Chelouche family collection*)
Avraham Haim Chelouche, his wife, Sarina, and their family. (*Chelouche family collection*)
Julia Chelouche (*née* Bohbout), wife of David Chelouche. (*Chelouche family collection*)
Zaki Chelouche. (*Chelouche family collection*)
Yosef Pomrock and his wife, Simha, daughter of Avraham Haim Chelouche. (*Pomrock family collection*)

THE MANDATE BEGINS TO CRACK

Arab demonstrators in Jaffa's Central Square, October 1933. (*Palestine Remembered*)
British military engineers blow up a large swath of Old Jaffa during the Arab Revolt in 1936. (*Palestine Remembered: picture 1215*)
Amin Andraus leans against a pillar of his former car showroom, the morning after the British blew it up as a punishment. (*Andraus family collection*)

BUSINESSMEN ...

Yaakov Chelouche sitting at his desk in the Anglo-Palestine Company bank in Jaffa, c. 1900. (*Chelouche family collection*)

The door of the first branch of the Anglo-Palestine Company. (*Adam LeBor/Northfoto*)

Amin Andraus and several of his friends on a shooting party in the 1930s. (*Andraus family collection*)

... AND SHOPKEEPERS

Dr Fakhri Geday at the counter of his pharmacy shop at 65 Yefet Street. (*Adam LeBor/Northfoto*)

Yoram Aharoni in Tiv, his spice and coffee shop on Raziel Street. (*Aharoni family collection*)

The Abulafia bakery, by Clock Tower Square. (*Adam LeBor/Northfoto*)

AL-NAKBA—THE CATASTROPHE

The wreckage of Jaffa's New Seray after it was blown up by the Stern Group in January 1948. (*Palestine Remembered*)

Hasan Hammami with his classmates on a course in first aid. (*Hammami family collection*)

Two members of the Haganah in action on the border between Jaffa and Tel Aviv. (*Getty Images*)

Palestinian refugees fleeing from Jaffa to Gaza in May 1948. (*Palestine Remembered*)

INDEPENDENCE

Yoram and Rina Aharoni, 1947. (*Aharoni family collection*)

Youssef Kamel Geday, father of Dr Fakhri Geday. (*Geday family collection*)

David Ben-Gurion, the first prime minister of Israel. (*Zoltan Kluger, Israeli Government Press Office*)

Cheering citizens gather in Tel Aviv as the State of Israel is declared. (*Hans Pinn, Israeli Government Press Office*)

EXILE, WAR AND INTIFADA

Suad Andraus standing next to Kamal Nasser, a Palestinian poet, in the village of Bir Zeit. (*Andraus family collection*)

Hasan Hammami on his wedding day in 1956. (*Hammami family collection*)

Tank crews in southern Israel during the Six Day War. (*Moshe Milner, Israeli Government Press Office*)

Ofer Aharoni as a young conscript at the Suez Canal, c. 1970. (*Aharoni family collection*)

Egyptian Mig shot down during the Yom Kippur War. (*Ron Ilan, Israeli Government Press Office*)

Israeli units moving into battle on the Golan Heights during the Yom Kippur War, 1973. (*David Rubinger, Israeli Government Press Office*)

Palestinian youths hurl rocks and stones at Israeli troops during the Al-Aqsa Intifada. (*Getty Images*)

JAFFA TODAY

The Clock Tower. (*Adam LeBor/Northfoto*)

The Old Seray. (*Adam LeBor/Northfoto*)

The façade of the New Seray being rebuilt in the summer of 2003. (*Adam LeBor/Northfoto*)

A row of shops and houses on Raziel Street, formerly Nagib Bustros Street. (*Adam LeBor/Northfoto*)

Neve Tsedek as seen from the roof of Beit Chelouche. (*Adam LeBor/Northfoto*)

The alley known in the nineteenth century as Sharia Serafeen, street of the money-changers. (*Adam LeBor/Northfoto*)

THE FAMILIES TODAY

The Andraus family. (*Adam LeBor/Northfoto*)

Julia Chelouche. (*Chelouche family collection*)

Frank Meisler, with his sculpture of King David and Bathsheba. (*Meisler family collection*)

Hasan Hammami, his sister, Fadwa, and daughter, Rema, on the beach at Jaffa in 1993. (*Hammami family collection*)

Yoram and Rina Aharoni. (*Adam LeBor/Northfoto*)

Sami Abou-Shehade and his grandfather Ismail. (*Adam LeBor/Northfoto*)

Shlomo Chelouche at home in Tel Aviv. (*Adam LeBor/Northfoto*)

JAFFA AND TEL AVIV TODAY

The hotels and urban sprawl of Tel Aviv, looking north from Jaffa. (*Adam LeBor/Northfoto*)

The view of Jaffa from the promenade above Tel Aviv's beach. (*Adam LeBor/Northfoto*)

Dramatis Personae

ABULAFIA

Khamis   Director of the Abulafia bakery, journalist

ABOU-SHEHADE

Ismail   Fisherman in Jaffa port during the 1960s

Sami   Grandson of Ismail, postgraduate student at Tel Aviv University

AHARONI

Yoram   Born Yaakov Yosefov in Bulgaria, former member of the Stern Group, owner of Tiv spice and coffee shop, father of Ofer

Rina   Wife of Yoram, former Stern Group member
Ofer   Lives in Jaffa, veteran of 1973 and 1982 wars

ALBO

Sami   Born in Turkey, Jaffa Jewish community activist

ANDRAUS

Amin (elder)   Leader of Jaffa's Arabs after 1948, businessman
Leila   Eldest daughter of Amin Andraus, administrator at
                    Tabeetha School
Salim   Son of Amin Andraus, retired accountant
Wedad   Middle daughter of Amin Andraus, teacher at
                    Tabeetha School
Suad   Youngest daughter of Amin Andraus, British pro-
                    consul
Amin (younger)   Grandson of above, lawyer in Tel Aviv
Robyn (Amina)   Sister of Amin (younger), teacher in Jaffa

CHELOUCHE

Avraham   Founder of the Chelouche dynasty in Jaffa. Father of
                    Aharon, Rica, Hannah
Aharon (elder)   Jeweller and money-changer in late nineteenth-
                    century Jaffa. Father of Yaakov, Yosef Eliyahu and
                    Avraham Haim
Aharon   Former dean of students at Tel Aviv University,
                    great-grandson of above
Avraham Haim   Father of David, Marco, Zaki and Simha
David   Son of Avraham Haim Chelouche, husband of Julia

Edith	Daughter of David and Julia Chelouche
Jacob	Son of Shlomo, lives in Tel Aviv
Julia (*née* Bohbout)	Wife of David Chelouche, mother of Edith
Yaakov	Treasurer of Anglo-Palestine Bank in early twentieth century, father of Shlomo and Gabriel
Yosef Eliyahu	Brother of Yaakov and Avraham Haim, husband of Freha, father of seven children. Businessman and community leader.
Shlomo	Organiser of emigration to Israel of Moroccan Jews, son of Yaakov
Mary (*née* Hayon)	Wife of Shlomo
Zaki	Architect in 1930s Tel Aviv
Marco	Brother of Zaki
Pomrock, Simha (*née* Chelouche)	Wife of Yosef, mother of Zvi
Pomrock, Yosef	Husband of Simha Chelouche, father of Zvi
Pomrock, Zvi	Chelouche family archivist

GEDAY

Youssef Kamel	Pharmacist from old Jaffa family, father of Fakhri
Fakhri	Pharmacist, son of Youssef Kamel

HAMMAMI

Shaker	Textile merchant in early twentieth-century Jaffa, father of Ahmad, grandfather of Hasan

Ahmad Shaker	Worked in citrus industry, left Jaffa in 1948 with wife, Nafise, and nine children, including Hasan, Mustafa and Fadwa
Nafise (*née* Shattila)	Wife of Ahmad
Hasan	Former manager with Procter & Gamble, lives in Florida, father of Rema
Mustafa	Brother of Hasan, lives in Toronto
Hasna, Fadwa (*née* Hammami)	Sister of Hasan, widow of Suleiman Fadwa, lives in East Jerusalem
Rema	Professor of anthropology at Bir Zeit University, Palestinian Territories
Said	PLO ambassador to London, assassinated 1978, cousin of Hasan

Meisler

Frank	Born in Danzig, architect and sculptor
Michal	Daughter of Frank

Others

Moyal, Mazal	Grandmother of Julia Chelouche
Nachmias, Yoseph	Irgun veteran of the April 1948 battle for Jaffa
Topaz, Moris	Doctor, treats victims of suicide bombings
Buchbinder, Behira	Jewish resident of Ajami, community activist
Bohbout, Josef	Jewish businessman in early twentieth-century

Jaffa, father of Julia Chelouche

Ezraty, Igal	Director of Local Theatre, Hebrew language company at Jaffa's Arabic-Hebrew Theatre
Jahashan, Adib	Director of El-Saraya, Arabic theatre company at Jaffa's Arabic-Hebrew Theatre
Goughti, Ali	Teacher in Jaffa
Kaldes, Yaron	Chief of Jaffa's detectives
Lahat, Shlomo	Mayor of Tel Aviv–Jaffa 1974–93

NB: To ease the reader's path through the narrative, not all children, siblings and wives are included above, only those who play a part in the book.

Author's Note

This book is based on hours of interviews with several generations of Jaffa families, their recollections of parents and grandparents and their memoirs, letters and personal archives, reaching back to the early twentieth century. These are their stories of their lives, as they remember them. This is what they want to say, and the quotes of every interviewee have been checked back with them for accuracy.

Two caveats should be noted here. Firstly, no contemporary issue arouses such furious passions as Israel and Palestine. The authorial opinions and analysis expressed in the book are mine alone. The inclusion of a named person does not mean that they necessarily agree with, or approve of, my observations and conclusions. Nor, of course, does it automatically exclude that possibility. Secondly, in the Middle East, terminology is always a source of dispute. There is an ongoing debate in Israel about the term for the country's ethnic Arab minority, who are full citizens, in contrast to the Palestinians living beyond the 1967 borders. Jewish Israelis tend to prefer 'Israeli Arab' or 'Arab Israeli'. Nationally conscious Arabs prefer 'Palestinian citizens of Israel', or even just 'Palestinian'. I have used the first three interchangeably, to prevent ungainly repetition, while reserving 'Palestinian' for those outside the state's current borders. The areas under Palestinian rule I refer to as Palestinian territories, for ease of understanding. I also sometimes refer to Israeli Jews as simply 'Jews'. I hope it will be clear from the context that this means Jews in Israel, and not all Jews living around the world.

Introduction

One of my favourite places in Jaffa is a bench on the walkway overlooking the beach. To the right stretches the expanse of Tel Aviv—a jumble of tower block hotels shimmering in the summer heat, the city sprawling inland behind them. To the left, an older and more soothing vista: the sandstone buildings of the Jaffa seafront, the minaret of the Jami'a al-bahr, the mosque by the sea, and the tree-lined slopes that stretch from the top of Old Jaffa down to the water. There is always something to watch: the turquoise waves topped with white as they break on the sand and rocks; a flotilla of small fishing boats bobbing in the distance; the slim man practising tai-chi for hours; a class of Arab schoolgirls wearing modest headscarves, traipsing across the sand, past the archaeological excavation of the Old Ottoman seawall.

Was I sitting in Jaffa or Tel Aviv? I couldn't be sure. There is no formal boundary or demarcation. The two cities are neighbours, and Jaffa has now been absorbed into Tel Aviv. But history and memory are more enduring than the decision of municipal bureaucrats. The relationship between ancient Jaffa and twentieth-century Tel Aviv is a metaphor for that between Israel and the Palestinians. As much as and perhaps even more than Jerusalem, Jaffa has played a central role in the history of Israel and Palestine. Jerusalem was Palestine's spiritual capital, but Jaffa, known as the 'Bride of Palestine', was its political and cultural centre. It is ironic then that Tel Aviv, the modern Hebrew city, was founded as a suburb of Jaffa in the early twentieth century. The early Zionist pioneers saw Jaffa as crumbling and unhygienic. The answer, they decided, was to build new European-style settlements on its fringes to house the Jewish immigrants pouring in from Russia and eastern Europe. By the 1920s the new Jewish suburbs of Neve Tsedek, Neve Shalom, Ahuzat Bayit and others had evolved into a fully-fledged city. Tel Aviv was no longer the child of Jaffa, but its sibling rival. Its very architecture was a political statement. The 'White City' soon enjoyed the largest concentration of Bauhaus buildings in the world. Their clean, ascetic lines and open-plan design were a response, even a challenge, to the oriental maze of Old Jaffa—a statement that in the heart of the Levant it was possible to live a 'modern', European lifestyle.

But Tel Aviv did not have the only claim on modernity. Jaffa too boasted newspapers, cinemas, theatres, a radio station, cultural and literary associations, even boxing and other sports champions that were the pride of Palestine. Its oranges, especially the sweet and juicy Shamouti, were famed the world over, and kept many thousands in gainful employment, including the Jewish traders who bought and sold the fruit. All that came to an end in a few days in April 1948, when the Irgun launched a ferocious mortar bombardment against Jaffa. By 13 May, when Jaffa surrendered, just a few thousand of its original population of about a hundred thousand remained. Almost the entire city had fled, either on land to the West Bank or Jordan or by boat to Gaza and Lebanon.

The Bride of Palestine was swiftly abandoned. Most of Jaffa's inhabitants believed they would be back in a couple of weeks, once the fighting was over and the Jews defeated. They were wrong, and few have ever returned. Jaffa herself has paid the price. The beautiful Ottoman villas of the Ajami and Jebaliyyeh quarters crumbled into disrepair. Hundreds of homes were eventually demolished and the rubble dumped on the beach. Tel Aviv thrived and expanded many miles inland and up the coast, while Jaffa decayed. At least the ancient heart of the city, dating back to the Biblical era, was saved from the wreckers' balls and restored. Old Jaffa is now home to trendy art galleries and smart jewellery shops. Better renovated than demolished— yet even Old Jaffa's inhabitants admit there is something unreal about its spotless, shiny alleys, bereft of their original inhabitants.

THERE ARE LIBRARIES full of books on the Israeli-Arab conflict. But none so far has focused primarily on the human story, on the lives of real people from both sides. Of course no single work can capture the intricacy of a century-old struggle, but I hope the people featured in this book give a sense of its complexity and its human dimension. They are Muslim, Christian and Jewish. They are middle class and working class. They are artisans and intellectuals, artists and businessmen. Some are left-wing, others right—wing in short, human beings, in all their variety and contradictions.

Jaffa is a comparatively small place, with a population of just over

45,000, of whom about two thirds are Israeli Jews and one third Israeli Arabs. It can be walked from end to end in an hour. As I explained what I was attempting to do, friends introduced me to friends, and many doors opened in both communities. On the Arab side, my starting point was to find families who had lived in Jaffa since before 1948. Almost all of Jaffa's once prosperous middle class had fled, but the Geday and Andraus families had remained. Fakhri Geday's pharmacy shop on Yefet Street is a Jaffa institution. The Gedays can trace back their roots in Jaffa for eight generations. Fakhri, born in 1927, still lives in the spacious stone house built by his ancestors in the nineteenth century, and is a fount of memories of pre-1948 Jaffa. A short drive away, on the outskirts of the city, live the Andraus sisters, Suad, Leila and Wedad, in a beautiful 1930s villa overlooking the sea, built by their late father, Amin. Stepping inside the Andraus home is like travelling back in time to the days of Mandate Palestine. Courteous and welcoming, the Andraus sisters, all in their sixties, are living testimony to the legacy of their father. Amin was born in 1898 and educated at the Schneller German boarding school in Jerusalem, and his self-reliance and strong moral sense helped him take on the role of community leader after 1948. Amin sent his children to Jordan for sanctuary but stayed on in his house, together with his mother, Haya, surrounded by sandbags. When Jaffa finally capitulated, he was one of those who signed the surrender agreement with the new Israeli authorities and negotiated supplies of food and water, as well as security, for the few remaining Arabs.

Most of those who stayed were not part of Jaffa's *haute bourgeoisie*. Ismail Abou-Shehade, born in 1924, was a mechanic. In fact he had originally wanted to be a *qadi*, an Islamic judge, but the outbreak of war in 1939 prevented him from studying in Cairo. Ismail later thrived financially, and opened a fishing business in Jaffa's port. I found Ismail after I had read about his grandson Sami, a student at Tel Aviv University, in the Israeli press. Sami is part of the new generation of Arab Israelis who call themselves Palestinians. Eloquent and confident, he uses the freedoms of Israeli democracy to articulate the Palestinian national cause. Sami is now a fixture in Jaffa, as he organises regular walking tours, recounting the city's story from the Palestinian perspective.

Here, then, were those who stayed. But most of Jaffa's Arab population did not, and the experience of exile and dispossession is central to Palestinian history. My search for a family who fled in 1948 led me, through various journalist contacts in Jerusalem, to Rema Hammami, a professor of anthropology at Bir Zeit University. Rema sent me first to her aunt, Fadwa. As Rema promised, Fadwa was 'full of Jaffa lore' and told me much about her childhood before 1948, the trauma of the *Nakba*—the Palestinian catastrophe—and the years afterwards. Fadwa in turn led me to her brother, Hasan, Rema's father. After a successful career at Procter & Gamble, Hasan had retired to Florida. We began a lengthy correspondence by email and eventually met in Budapest. Hasan's moving memories range from those of his days as a small boy in Jaffa—when the Andraus sisters were forbidden from playing with him as he was thought too boisterous—to his years working across the Arab world, studying in Britain and eventually settling in the United States. They include a fascinating, if depressing, interlude in Gaza, when he tried unsuccessfully to bring his business expertise to the Arafat regime.

The Geday and Andraus families are Christian, the Hammamis and Abou-Shehades Muslim. For the Jewish families I also sought a mix that represented different aspects of Jewish and Israeli history: Ashkenazi, eastern European Jews who had fled the Holocaust; Sephardic and Arabic-speaking Jews; those rooted in Ottoman-era Palestine and comparatively recent arrivals. I began with the Chelouches, one of the founding families of Tel Aviv. Together with his family, Avraham Chelouche arrived in Jaffa from north Africa in the mid-nineteenth century. The Chelouches soon prospered. They used the profits from their jewellery and money-changing business to finance the building of the first Jewish suburbs of Jaffa, which eventually led to the establishment of Tel Aviv. Arabic-speaking, oriental in their culture, the Chelouches were an organic part of the Middle East. Avraham's descendants, such as Aharon and Shlomo, helped to build up both the *Yishuv*—the Zionist state-in-waiting—and Israel itself after 1948, becoming part of the country's civic and business elite. In many ways, their story encapsulates that of Israel and its relations with both its Arab minority and its neighbours.

Like Fakhri Geday's pharmacy, Yoram Aharoni's coffee and spice shop Tiv—'quality'—was also a Jaffa institution, open for fifty years. Yoram fled Bulgaria in March 1941, the night the Nazis invaded, arriving in Palestine after a perilous voyage. Arrested immediately by the British authorities, he joined the extremist Stern Group on his release in 1942, and lived underground for almost six years, fighting the British. With the war over, Yoram and his father, Shabat, opened their shop. Tiv's stocks of coffee and spices reflected Jaffa's waves of Jewish immigrants after 1948. The Balkan Jews who poured into Jaffa bought paprika and black pepper, but when the Jews from north Africa began arriving in the 1950s, Yoram soon became expert in grading cumin, cinnamon and the fiery red peppers used in Moroccan cuisine. Decades later, Yoram's son Ofer returned to Jaffa, not to work but to live, one of a pioneering wave of renovators who rebuilt the crumbling houses from the Ottoman era.

Frank Meisler, too, is a renovator. He arrived in Britain as a schoolboy in 1939, on one of the last *Kindertransports* from Nazi Germany. After the war, in the 1950s, with his parents dead at Auschwitz and his hometown, Danzig, renamed Gdansk and occupied by the Soviets, Frank decided to emigrate to Israel. His memories of the young state, with all its nervous insecurity, populated by traumatised Holocaust survivors, portray a very different place from today's regional and military power. An artist and an architect, Frank spent his Saturdays sketching the Old City. When in the 1960s the decision was taken to renovate Old Jaffa and not demolish it, Frank was one of the first to move into the new 'artists' quarter'. Yet for all Old Jaffa's beauty, he knows that something has been lost for ever with the disappearance of its Arab inhabitants.

It is now barely remembered that many Jewish emigrants from Arab countries and Turkey did not want to come to Israel. The educated elites of those communities relocated to France, Britain or North America. The less well-off Jews were dumped in dismal 'development towns' in the middle of the desert by an uncaring and often racist Ashkenazi elite. Israel in the 1950s was not quite the promised land the Jews had longed for. Sami Albo arrived in 1957 at the age of six. In Istanbul his family had lived in a spacious apartment. In Jaffa, three generations shared one and a half rooms in a draughty Arab villa. Perhaps the hardships of his youth helped shape Sami's outlook today as a community activist. But his main concerns now are no longer Ashkenazi bureaucrats but the increasing radicalisation and Islamisation of his Arab neighbours.

Sami Albo could usefully discuss these concerns with Khamis

Abulafia, one of the directors of the Abulafia bakery. It was there that my journey into Jaffa's past and present began. Founded in 1879 and open twenty-four hours a day, Abulafia is an institution. The display cabinets are crowded with breads and delicacies stuffed with cheese or mushrooms, baked with eggs or topped with salty Arab cheese and *zataar*, a mix of olive oil and hyssop. The Abulafias are Muslim Arabs, but pride themselves on their good relations with their Jewish customers. The bakery even closes for eight days during the Jewish festival of Passover, when it is forbidden to eat leavened bread or cakes.

'They call our bakery the gate of Jaffa. Jaffa is a special model for co-existence between Muslims, Jews and Christians. Our bakery is a meeting point for all three, a special place. We have deep connections and relations with Jewish people,' explains Khamis. The fifth child of his late parents, Khamis takes his name from the Arabic word for five. He is a friendly, intelligent man in his mid-forties, with shrewd eyes and grey hair—a good choice for the public face of the Abulafia business empire. Khamis studied Hebrew literature at university and speaks the language fluently. The Abulafias have prospered; the family also owns a restaurant nearby in the restored quarter of Old Jaffa, another bakery in Tel Aviv and a property company.

A well-known figure in Jaffa, Khamis often mediates in disputes. The backdrop of the political conflict adds an extra layer of rancour to neighbours' arguments if one is Jewish and the other Arab. His favourite film is *Gandhi*, he says, which he has seen more than twenty times. Sitting in the bakery's office, he recounts several episodes of his one-man peace mission. A friend of his brought a young woman to see him who openly said she hated Arabs. 'What she knew of Arabs she read in the newspapers, and we only appear in bad news, not good,' says Khamis. They talked for a while, and the woman said she was having difficulties with her examinations, especially with Biblical Hebrew. 'We met every day for two weeks, and I coached her. She passed, with 88 per cent. Now she is one of my best friends and she is sorry that she judged us like that.'

One day in Tel Aviv, near the bus station, a young woman asked Khamis for help. 'She was about sixteen, and she said that three guys were bothering her. I told her to come with me, and told them to leave her, that she was my daughter. They apologised. She was from Beer-sheba, in the south. I took her to sit down, brought her a drink and some pizza, and said nobody would disturb her while I was with her. After a while she asked me if I was an Arab. I told her yes, and she didn't want to believe me. I asked her why, and she said, "Because Arabs are always bothering us, even killing us." For me this was a golden opportunity. I said, "Those who were bothering you were Jewish. That doesn't mean all Jews are potential rapists. Maybe you met or saw bad Arabs. Now you met a good one."' The girl asked Khamis for his telephone number. The next day her father telephoned to thank him, and invited him to visit the family.

I ask Khamis how much effect his one-man campaign can have. He smiles wryly. 'I don't want to sound like Don Quixote. But these are small contributions to make the world a better and more pleasant place. I believe a journey of one thousand miles starts with a single step. I support the Jewish people's right to live here, but they have to understand, and to believe, that I also have that same right.' I nod my agreement. This is our first meeting, but during the many weeks I spent in Jaffa I would talk with Khamis several times. For now, he is still sounding me out. The legend of Jaffa as a 'special model for co-existence', where Jews and Arabs live together in peace and mutual respect, is a bland, safe starting point. Like the shiny, renovated alleys of Old Jaffa, it has a superficial appeal. Our later discussions would be more serious, even provocative. For Khamis and I both know that Jaffa's reality, its present and its past, is far more complex than either the tourist myth or the media coverage would lead us to believe.

PART ONE

I

A Battered Bride

1921

The fundamental cause of the Jaffa riots and the subsequent
acts of violence was a feeling among the Arabs of
discontent with, and hostility to, the Jews.

*Summary of the findings of the Haycraft
Commission into the 1921 Jaffa riots*[1]

I n Jaffa, in the spring of 1921, a young Jewish woman called Julia
Bohbout was planning her wedding. Julia was twenty-one, dark-
haired and vivacious with lively eyes, a popular girl who made
friends easily. She was fluent in Arabic and French, played the piano
and was gifted at needlework. Julia danced the waltz and even a daring new import from South America, the tango. The Bohbout family
lived on Nagib Bustros Street, the heart of Jaffa's commercial centre,
which drew shoppers from across the Levant. The shop windows displayed the latest European fashions and household goods, while
neighbouring cafés were crowded with customers drinking coffee,
smoking and eating ice cream. Spacious Italianate apartments were
built above the shops and overlooked the street. The flats had stone
floors, high ceilings to let the sea breeze flow through, arched windows and long balconies decorated with fine ironwork.

Julia had just returned from a two-month trip to Cairo to see her relatives and prepare her trousseau. Her fiancé was David Chelouche, who was considered quite a catch. David was ten years older, tall and pleasant looking with dark eyes, but good looks were secondary to the fact that the Chelouche family was one of the most respected dynasties in Jaffa, if not in all Palestine. The Chelouches were leaders of Jaffa's Jewish community, and they had helped found neighbouring Tel Aviv. Like the Bohbouts, they were Sephardim from north Africa, Jews who could trace their ancestry back to the expulsion from Spain in 1492, known in Hebrew as *sepharad*. At home, the Chelouches and Bohbouts usually spoke Arabic, not Hebrew. Jaffa's Sephardic families were linked together by marriage, blood and business. David's uncles owned a thriving shop on Nagib Bustros Street that sold building materials and beautifully patterned tiles. The Chelouche brothers' pipes, bricks and ironwork were designed for modern European-style homes, but the brightly coloured symmetrical patterns on the tiles were rooted in the Orient. Jaffa's profitable commercial life was testimony to the web of social and business links that still bound together Arab and Jew.

JERUSALEM WAS PALESTINE'S religious capital, but Jaffa was its cultural and commercial centre. With its English, French, Italian and Arab language schools, artists and writers, three newspapers and many printing houses, the city was proud of its vigorous intellectual life. The Near East radio station broadcast from Jaffa, and much of the Palestinian political elite came from the city. Its cinemas offered romance and adventure films from Cairo as well as the latest Hollywood releases. Its sports clubs produced boxers such as Al-Dasuqi, the national champion, who triumphed across the Levant, and also two soccer teams, one Muslim and one Christian. The city was scented by its orange groves, the fruit of which was famed across the world for its quality. Jaffa's mosques, synagogues and churches dated back centuries.

Jaffa in the 1920s was an integral part of the Middle East: taxis left for Beirut and Damascus, a day or so away by car; trains departed for Haifa and Jerusalem, Gaza and Cairo, and even Khartoum; ships left Jaffa for Europe, taking away oranges and bringing back Jewish immigrants. The sea at Jaffa was too shallow for ocean-going boats to lay anchor. Ships moored offshore, while a fleet of pilot boats set out to bring the cargo and passengers ashore, as they had done for centuries. Like medieval pilgrims before them, the Jewish immigrants were carried on the backs of Arab porters through the waves and onto dry land, there to be assailed by a wall of heat, dust and Jaffa's own smell of oranges, mixed with black tobacco, cardamom-scented coffee and sweat.

Despite the depredations of the First World War, when Jaffa had been bombed, shelled, plagued by locusts, and its Jews deported by the Turks, the 'Bride of the Sea' (as it was known) looked better than ever. The heart of the modern city was Clock Tower Square, a long octagonal piazza flanked by rows of shops. Nearby were Jaffa's famous markets, including the Souk el-Balabseh (textile bazaar) and the Souk el-Attarin (sweets bazaar). The centerpiece was the Clock Tower itself, built by Sultan Abdul Hamid II at the start of the twentieth century, one of more than a hundred across the Ottoman Empire. Tall and unadorned by images of people, in keeping with the precepts of Islam, the clock towers symbolised modernisation. The empire would evolve with the times, its days properly divided into hours and minutes. None of this prevented Abdul Hamid II from being toppled in the Young Turk revolution of 1908, and the Ottoman Empire itself was dismembered in 1917. Now, the old Ottoman *kishle* (prison) by the sea was home to Britain's Palestine Police. Palestine was administered by Britain, under a League of Nations mandate to facilitate a Jewish 'national home'—a mandate that caused fury among its Arabs. In 1920, nine people were killed and more than two hundred wounded when Arab demonstrators attacked Jerusalem's Jewish quarter. Jaffa's turn would soon come.

Jaffa's heart was the Old City, dating back three millennia, with its winding lanes and stepped rows of yellow sandstone buildings built on top of each other. It was here that waves of conquerors had stormed ashore: Canaanites and ancient Egyptians, Romans and Hebrew rebels, Greeks and Byzantines, Crusaders and Saracens, Mamlukes and the Ottomans, who took Jaffa in 1517. Peter the apostle had raised Dorcas from the dead in Jaffa, at the house of Simon the Tanner, Christians believed. Nearby, Richard the Lionheart had accepted the surrender of Salah ad-Din or Saladdin, the mighty Kurdish leader. Even Napoleon had briefly taken the city, in 1799.

Down by the port it really did seem as if little had changed since the Biblical era. Hawkers and peddlers sold vegetables and fruits, spices and trinkets. Overloaded donkeys struggled down narrow alleys. Camels strode disdainfully, their riders swaying as the animals negotiated the potholed roads, past women wrapped in the *habra* (black cloak), their heads veiled and covered. Bedouin traders sipped tiny cups of black coffee, puffing on water-pipes, while small boys fetched humous and pitta bread for their lunch. When it rained the streets filled with sticky mud, but in the dry season they were hot and dusty. Drinking water was drawn from wells; sewage systems were rudimentary at best. It was a miracle that the houses did not simply all tumble into the sea. A miracle, and the legacy of Abou Nabout, the *kaymakam* (governor) of Jaffa a century earlier. Abou Nabout means 'father of the camel whip'. He earned his title, and exercised droit de seigneur with any young woman he liked. But Abou Nabout also reinforced the sea walls, constructed new markets and two *sibils* (public fountains) to dispense clean water and built the Great Mosque, a serene complex of courtyard and prayer space reminiscent of the Al-Azhar mosque in Cairo. When he finally retired he was well provided for—more than two hundred camels transported his riches out of the city.

Julia's engagement had begun with a visit by David Chelouche's father, Avraham Haim, to her father at his textile shop. Josef Bohbout had travelled back and forth for years between Jaffa and Manchester, England, where he owned a wholesale shop at 14 Albert Square. Despite his repeated entreaties, his wife, Esther, had refused to accompany him, as she was scared of sea travel. In Manchester Josef set up not only a business but a whole other family— he had a mistress and two daughters there. But with his health failing, he eventually decided to return to Jaffa for good. It seems neither Josef's family nor Avraham Haim Chelouche knew anything of his double life.

Avraham Haim Chelouche explained that he wanted to marry one of his sons, Marco, to Julia. Julia's father nodded. Few families were offered such an opportunity. Sephardic marriages, like Arab betrothals, were usually arranged; and the bond was based on mutual suitability and social standing. Hopefully, love and romance would follow later. Avraham Haim himself had originally been engaged to a young woman called Rina Elbaz. Two weeks before the wedding, Rina fell ill and died. After a month of mourning her father went to see Avraham's father. He asked if Avraham would like to meet Rina's sister, Serena. They met and were married soon after. Avraham's brother, Yosef Eliyahu, had been betrothed at the age of seventeen and been called home from school in Beirut to be married. If a couple were really opposed, a union would not be forced. But the moral pressure was enormous, for the dynasties must continue.

Julia had her portrait taken and the picture was sent to Paris, where Marco and his brother Zaki were studying. Marco wrote back and thanked his father, but explained that he did not want to marry Julia. Avraham wrote then to Zaki and ordered him home to Jaffa immediately. But Zaki was having the time of his life in Paris. With his romantic eyes and easy charm, Zaki resembled the actor Tyrone Power, and he made the most of his looks. The last thing he wanted was to go back to the suffocating demands of a traditional Sephardic family. Zaki was less tactful than his brother. He wrote back, saying he had fallen in love with an actress. When Zaki's letter reached Jaffa his father was first scandalised, then enraged. An actress! Avraham stormed around the room, waving the letter. His eyes fell on his third son, David. 'You will marry this girl,' he instructed his son. 'Which girl?' asked David, who did not know what his father was talking about. Once Avraham had calmed down and explained, David did not argue. He had already met Julia at a party and liked her, and anyway he had not so far had much luck with women. He had fallen in love with a young woman called Leah and proposed to her. Leah had refused him, telling him she wanted to marry a doctor. David duly enrolled at medical school in Beirut. The first year went reasonably well, but the second proved difficult. Every time there was a dissection class and the corpse was opened, David fainted. He gave up and went back to Jaffa. The next time he saw Leah she told him she was married to a doctor.

David was keen to marry Julia. She was not swept off her feet—another Chelouche would do that—but nevertheless David was a fine young man. He had spent the war in Cairo, working at a bank. He came back to Jaffa by train, with a belt of gold coins hidden under his trousers. He now worked alongside his uncle Yaakov Chelouche at the Anglo-Palestine Company, which financed the Zionist settlements. 'He was a dark boy, friendly,' Julia wrote in her memoir *The Tree and the Roots*, an evocative portrait of a cosmopolitan world long since vanished. Julia records that before her engagement she had dreamt she was standing on Nagib Bustros Street, outside the Chelouche Brothers' construction company's office. In her dream Yaakov Chelouche had placed a necklace of jewels around her neck. Now it seemed that her dream had come true, for the necklace that Yaakov Chelouche gave her symbolised his nephew, her fiancé, David.

For David and Julia these were idyllic days. There were parties, picnics on the beach and trips by horse-drawn buggy to the Eden cinema, the first in Tel Aviv. In that same year, 1920, Aharon, the great patriarch of the Chelouche dynasty and David's grandfather, died. The family sat *shiva*, the Jewish mourning ritual, for a week. Every mirror was turned to the wall, while Aharon's sons sat on low stools. They prayed every evening and received the stream of visitors of all faiths who offered their condolences. Aharon Chelouche had lived to the age of ninety-three. His death marked the end of an era, not only for the Chelouches but also for the old Jaffa, where Jews and Arabs lived side by side—if not always in harmony, then at least mostly in peace. That world was about to be turned upside down, and would never be righted.

. . .

ON 1 MAY 1921 Julia was alone at home with the maid when she heard the mob outside. She heard hundreds of voices chanting in Arabic, 'Aleyhum, aleyhum, to them, to them,' meaning to the Jews. The street was full of Arab men, many of them holding clubs. The Christian-Arab family that lived opposite signalled to Julia to close all the windows and lock the door. She moved quickly. She locked up the house and waited silently while the mob rampaged outside. She could hear the marauders smashing down the doors of the Jewish shops, the splintering of the wood, the sound of glass breaking and shouts of delight as piles of clothes, shoes and rolls of cloth were plundered.

The Arabs' anger was fuelled both by a sense that their country was being stolen from under them by the Jews and by a profound feeling of betrayal. During the First World War the Arabs fought with the British against the Turks. Encouraged by T. E. Lawrence, they launched the Arab revolt, believing that once the Ottoman Empire had been defeated, the western powers would grant them independence. But the Arabs were deceived. The real future of the Middle East, at least as the Allies saw it, was set out in 1916 in the secret Sykes-Picot Agreement. The empire would be carved up, and the Arab nations would form either a confederated Arab state or one single independent state, to be divided into British and French zones of influence. Palestine, apart from Haifa and Acre, would be internationalised, although in the end it came under British rule.

Worse still, from the Arabs' perspective, was the November 1917 letter from Arthur Balfour, the British foreign secretary, to British Zionist leader Lord Rothschild: 'His Majesty's government views with favour the establishment of a national home for the Jewish people and will use their best endeavours to facilitate the achievement of this object, it being clearly understood that nothing shall be done which may prejudice the civil and political rights of existing non-Jewish communities or the rights and political status enjoyed by Jews in any other country.' Not only would there be no independent Arab state, but Palestine was to be handed over to the Jews. The anger caused by the Balfour declaration only intensified with the passage of time.

It is ironic that the violence in Jaffa started as a clash not between Jews and Arabs but between rival groups of Jewish leftists—the Communists and the mainstream socialist Labour Party. Both planned to hold marches in Tel Aviv on May Day. Although much of the Zionist movement was strongly left-wing and sympathetic to Soviet Russia, it was a national, not international, liberation movement. The left-wing Zionists aimed to build a *Jewish* workers' state. For the Communists such ideas were anathema, and they aimed to unite Jewish and Arab workers. At a time of increasing national polarisation, the Communists remained a marginal grouping on the Palestinian political spectrum.

Despite the lack of interest in a Soviet-style Palestine, and a police warning that they had no permit to march, about sixty Communists set off from Jaffa to Tel Aviv. As soon as they ran into the Labour Party demonstration, a giant brawl erupted. The British Palestine Police chased the Communists back to Jaffa. When Jaffa's Arabs saw the fighting between the rival groups of left-wing Jews, they wrongly believed themselves to be under attack and began to fight against the Jews. But whatever the immediate cause of this second round of violence, it was merely a trigger for the Palestinians to vent their anger over far deeper, long-term historical grievances. The struggle for control of Palestine, fury over Jewish immigration, the rivalry between

Jaffa and Tel Aviv—decades of pent-up resentment quickly exploded. The Arabs gathered guns, staves and clubs and attacked the Jews. The police fired into the air to disperse the mobs. The Arabs believed the Jews were shooting at them. Arab marauders, many armed with guns and clubs, broke into Jewish homes. They swiftly killed the families inside, and when the Jews lay dead, Arab women came and looted their belongings. In Ajami a mob attacked a hostel housing Jewish immigrants. Bombs exploded and shots were fired. Arab police arrived and joined in the frenzy. The rioters smashed their way into the hostel. One man was beaten to death with wooden boards. Another was pulled to the ground, stomped on and hit with iron rods. In many places Arabs hid their Jewish friends and neighbours from the rioting mob. Despite having ruled Palestine for almost four years, the British authorities had not yet managed to take proper control, and in fact they never would. Jaffa itself had just ten trained police officers.

The Jewish response was swift and violent, as vigilante groups armed with guns and staves took revenge. Ibrahim Khalil el-Asmar was a baker who worked in Manshiyyeh, the northernmost quarter of Jaffa, which bordered Tel Aviv. The bakery was downstairs, the family flat above. As the fighting spread, Ibrahim locked himself into the shop and stayed indoors. At about three o'clock in the afternoon he heard a huge commotion, and when he looked through the window the streets outside were crowded with rampaging Jews, beating Arabs and breaking into shops and homes. Ibrahim shut the window and hid upstairs. Soon afterwards a gang of Russian Jews smashed the door down and came into the bakery. The Jews were carrying heavy sticks, and one was armed with a revolver. The gunman pointed his pistol at Ibrahim, while the others beat him with sticks. Ibrahim protested in Yiddish, the Jewish-German dialect spoken by Ashkenazi Jews. 'I was a man always at work, I have not been out, I have not done anything,' he proclaimed. It worked. The Jews stopped beating him. They put the broken door back on its hinges. One of the gang advised him to stay in 'and do not go out'.

The next day three British soldiers arrived, accompanied by two Jews and two Jewish policemen. They smashed the door down again and beat Ibrahim with their rifle butts. The soldiers went upstairs and brought down Ibrahim's father, son, wife and daughter. They demanded that the women appear without their veils, a great dishonour for Muslims; the women begged to be allowed to veil themselves. The British group stayed downstairs guarding Ibrahim and his family, while the others searched the house, looking for weapons or stolen property. Nothing was found. Ibrahim and his family were taken to a British military post and held under arrest. Eventually they were released and found refuge at the home of a relative, where they stayed for two weeks. When Ibrahim returned home, some of his furniture had been stolen, together with thirty-six British pounds.[2]

The British declared martial law, but by then it was too late. The violence had spread throughout central Palestine. The final death toll was 95—47 Jews and 48 Arabs—with 140 Jews and 73 Arabs wounded.

When the rioting finally came to an end, Julia ventured outside and picked a path through the debris of the looting: smashed glass, half-destroyed goods and ripped fabrics. Her father's shop was completely destroyed, she wrote in her diary: 'The Arabs had stolen everything, the mahogany desk was broken and the drawer was open, the money stolen. . . . Father returned and became sick with grief over his property which had disappeared in a moment.' Josef Bohbout had a heart attack when he saw his shop.

The Jaffa riots were not planned, but for the Jews, they were reminiscent of the tsarist pogroms, a bitter confirmation of the fears that for centuries had shaped their collective subconscious. The violence triggered a massive and permanent exodus of many Jews from Jaffa to Tel Aviv, and was a powerful blow to any hopes that Palestine could be shared between the two peoples. For the Arabs, the riots proved that the settlers were ready to kill to achieve their eventual aim of appropriating Palestine. The Arab leadership condemned the violence and petitioned Britain for independence and democracy. It achieved nothing. Herbert Samuel, the British high commissioner for Palestine, told the Zionist leader Nahum Sokolow that Palestine was now at war.

2

Tel Aviv Is Born

1920S

*It grew in hectic jumps according to each new wave
of immigration—an inland tide of asphalt and
concrete advancing over the dunes.*
Arthur Koestler on Tel Aviv in the 1920s[1]

What Jaffa needed after the riots, decided Herbert Samuel, was a celebration—something non-political, to bring together Jews, Christians and Muslims. Avraham Haim Chelouche's preparations were well under way for the marriage of his son David to Julia Bohbout. The date was set for 16 October 1921. The Chelouches cultivated good relations with the British authorities, just as their predecessors had with the Ottoman Empire. An ancestral sixth sense, and more particularly an astute business sense, demanded no less. More than thirty years earlier, after David's grandfather Aharon Chelouche had moved to Jaffa's new Jewish quarter of Neve Tsedek, his carriage had overturned in a *wadi*, a dried-up riverbed. The *kaymakam*, concerned for Aharon's wellbeing—and his own financial health—had an iron bridge built across the *wadi* for Aharon's comfort and convenience, and named it the

Chelouche Bridge, after him. Unlike the Ottoman governors, though, the British did not demand constant bribes and 'gifts'.

Jaffa's damaged houses could be repaired, the looted shops restocked. Even broken bones and bruises eventually healed. But both Jews and Arabs knew that a line had been crossed. The dead could not be brought back to life, and a wall of fear and suspicion now separated the two communities. Herbert Samuel appointed the chief justice for Palestine, Sir Thomas Haycraft, to head a commission of enquiry into the Jaffa riots. Its conclusion was that 'the racial strife was begun by the Arabs, and rapidly developed into a conflict of great violence between Arabs and Jews, in which the Arab majority, who were generally the aggressors, inflicted most of the casualties.'[2] Even so, the report claimed, the Zionist leadership needed to do much more to deal with the Arabs' concerns. However emollient the recommendations of the Haycraft Commission, the deep-rooted cause of the 1921 violence was simple: the conflict between two peoples who both claimed ownership of a narrow strip of land on the coast of the Levant—Jewish Zionists and Palestinian Arab nationalists.

The idea of the return to Israel, or spiritual Zionism, is an integral part of Judaism. Every Passover festival is marked by the phrase 'Next year in Jerusalem'. Small, often impoverished Jewish communities had survived across Palestine since the Roman exile in the first century AD. But most Jews lived in the Levant, north Africa, Europe and Russia. 'Next year in Jerusalem' was more a spiritual wish than a real prospect. Jaffa's own ancient Jewish community seems to have faded away by the early nineteenth century, until the arrival of a new wave of Jewish immigrants in the 1830s. The rise of *political* Zionism, and of one man in particular, changed Jewish history for ever.

Theodor Herzl was born in 1860 to a middle-class Jewish family in Budapest. He worked as a journalist and playwright in Vienna before moving to Paris. French anti-Semitism, and in particular the Dreyfus case—in which a Jewish army officer was falsely accused of spying for Germany and imprisoned—convinced him that assimilation would never provide the Jews with a secure future. In 1896 Herzl published his manifesto, *The Jewish State*, the central text of political Zionism.[3] Its businesslike tone argued that the 'Jewish question' would be solved only with the establishment of a Jewish state in Palestine. 'We have sincerely tried everywhere to merge with the national communities in which we live, seeking only to preserve the faith of our fathers. It is not permitted us,' he wrote. 'I consider the Jewish question neither a social nor a religious one, even though it sometimes takes these and other forms. It is a national question, and to solve it we must first of all establish it as an international political problem to be discussed and settled by the civilized nations of the world in council.'[4]

Zionism was not universally popular among Herzl's co-religionists. Religious Jews believed that only when the Messiah arrives can the Temple, and the Jewish state, be rebuilt. Anything else is a man-made blasphemy. Assimilated Jews considered themselves citizens of their states first and Jews second. But Herzl knew the power of words, and that the days of empires, whether Ottoman or Austro-Hungarian, were ending. Serbs and Czechs, Hungarians and Greeks and the Arab nations were all demanding control of their destinies, their writers and poets declaiming the virtues of their oppressed homelands in newly codified languages. The Jews too were a nation, scattered and oppressed, with the right of self-determination. They already had a language—Hebrew, the ancient language of prayer, had been developed into an everyday tongue of commerce, law and love. They had an ancient homeland, Palestine. Statehood, Herzl argued, was the only answer to the strange anomaly of the Jewish people, scattered across the world but still one nation. From Vienna, at least, it all seemed quite straightforward.

All Herzl needed was a solid constituency among Jewry. If that did not quite yet exist, he would invent it. In August 1897, 250 delegates attended Herzl's first Zionist congress in Basel, Switzerland. Herzl wrote in his dairy: 'The fact is—which I conceal from everyone—that I have only an army of *schnorrers* [scroungers]. I am in command only of youths, beggars and sensation mongers.' But thanks to Herzl's dynamism and powers of organisation, the congress was a triumph. When Herzl finally took his place on the podium, the delegates clapped and cheered for fifteen minutes before he could speak. Each delegate wore a badge proclaiming: 'The establishment of a Jewish state is the only possible solution to the Jewish question.' Herzl wrote: 'Were I to sum up the Basel Congress in a word—which I shall guard against pronouncing publicly—it would be this. At Basel I founded the Jewish state. If I said this out loud today, I would be answered by universal laughter. Perhaps in five years, and certainly in fifty, everyone will know it.' Herzl never wavered in his belief: 'If you will it,' he wrote, 'it is no dream.'[5]

Herzl's journey to Palestine in 1898, however, was disappointing. 'Poverty, pain and chaos, all in wonderful colours,' he wrote of Jaffa. Jerusalem was even more of a disappointment. 'If Jerusalem is ever ours, and if I were still able to do anything about it, I would begin by cleaning it up. I would clear out everything that is not sacred, set up workers' houses beyond the city, empty and tear down the filthy rat-holes, burn all the non-sacred ruins, and put the bazaars elsewhere.' Even the Western Wall of the Temple did not move him. 'We have been to the Wailing Wall. Any deep emotion is rendered impossible by the hideous, miserable, scrambling beggary pervading the place.'[6]

Herzl and his disciples believed that Palestine's Arabs would welcome European modernisation. The Zionist slogan, coined by the British writer Israel Zangwill, described Palestine as 'a land without a people for a people without a land.' Reality indicated otherwise. In the late 1880s, Palestine's population numbered about 600,000 people, of whom perhaps just 25,000 were Jews. In 1896, the year that Herzl published *The Jewish State*, Jaffa was home to more than 11,000 Muslims, about 3,000 Christians and the same number of Jews. Parts of Palestine's countryside were indeed barren and had fallen into decline under Ottoman rule, but the land was certainly not empty. Two rabbis sent by the Viennese Jewish community to Palestine after the Basel conference cabled back that 'the bride is beautiful, but she is married to another man'.[7]

This first husband was the country's indigenous Arab population. Palestinian society was divided between landowner and peasant, city and village, Muslim, Christian and Jew, religious believers and secular intellectuals. Greeks, Armenians, Egyptians, Italians, Bosnians, Circassians, Africans, even Germans had settled there. The country's ethnic mosaic was testament to its cosmopolitan vitality. Palestinians too met the requirement for nationhood. They had lived on their land for centuries; they shared a common language and culture and, certainly by the late 1800s, a growing sense of Arab national identity as part of the *nahda*, or intellectual renaissance. Palestine then was a province of Ottoman Syria. Just as in the Balkans, another part of the Ottoman Empire experiencing a nationalist awakening, intellectuals proposed different solutions to the 'national question'. The theoreticians in Belgrade and Beirut often mirrored one another's ideas—a

Greater Serbia or a Greater Syria; a federation of Balkan states or a pan-Arab revival; an Orthodox union or a new Islamic caliphate. But whatever the Palestinian thinkers' differences, they agreed on one point: the land was not to be handed to the Jews but must remain Arab.

The Austro-Hungarian writer Joseph Roth saw things more clearly than Herzl and Zangwill. The Zionist pioneer, he wrote in *The Wandering Jews*, 'brings the Arabs electricity, fountain pens, engineers, machine guns, shallow philosophies and all the other things that come out of England. Of course the Arabs ought to be grateful for those fine new roads. But the instincts of a people close to nature quite rightly rebel against the onslaught of an Anglo-American civilisation, all in the name of national rebirth.'[8] Debate still continues as to when a specifically Palestinian nationalism first appeared, but the establishment in 1911 in Jaffa of the newspaper *Falastin* (Palestine), which addressed its readers as Palestinians, was a defining moment.

FOR THE MIDDLE-CLASS Palestinian, life was very comfortable, apart from the political turmoil. Shaker Hammami owned a shop in Jaffa's Souk el-Balabseh, the clothing and textile market, which supplied the fabric for his own traditional *umbaz* (long robe) and tailored coat. A handsome patriarch with a carefully trimmed white beard, Shaker was always well dressed and neatly barbered. But he usually had a mischievous glint in his eye, especially when his grandchildren piled into his lap, struggling for pride of place. Shaker had four sons and three daughters. His youngest son, Ahmad, was twenty years old in 1924. Ahmad was well built, with dark hair and brown eyes, and his solidity was rooted in his principles: he was a modern, forward-looking man, interested in business, sports and education, but one proud of his Palestinian heritage. Still unmarried, he had graduated from secondary school and started working in the citrus business.

Agriculture was the mainstay of Jaffa's economy. Its farmers grew figs, peaches, apricots, watermelons, almonds, grapes, vegetables, sugar cane and tobacco. The arrival of steamships had brought prosperity to the city, as Jaffa's crops could now be exported to Europe. But Jaffa was most famed for its oranges. There were two main varieties: the Shamouti, thick-skinned and seedless, with a very high juice yield, and the Baladi, with a thinner skin and seeds but also very juicy. The orange groves around Jaffa stretched inland for many kilometres; the air was filled with the scent of blossom in the spring and the scent of fruit in the summer. In a good year, over a million and a half crates were exported, each containing up to 150 oranges. Jaffa's sunny climate, sandy soil, and the care the workers lavished on the citrus groves brought forth a crop famed around the world. The Palestinian farmers were especially skilled in grafting cuttings to produce the most productive and hardy strains. The larger groves were owned by companies that also bought fruit from other groves at a pre-arranged price before harvesting and export.

The citrus industry, then, was a natural career choice for a bright young man. But Ahmad knew there was more to life than work. He was also a keen sportsman and an expert ping-pong and billiards player at the *Al-Nadi al-Islami*, Jaffa's Islamic club. Jaffa's social clubs, attached to its mosques and churches, offered something for every generation: children played ping-pong and adults billiards and backgammon, or they perused the books in the well-stocked libraries. Families sat on the terrace, drinking lemonade and eating ice cream. Soon it came time for Ahmad to start his own family. A particular young woman in her late teens, whom he often saw going home from the Italian nuns' school, had caught his eye. He could not approach her directly, as it would not have been acceptable for her to talk to an unknown man. Ahmad embarked on a little detective work.

He had chosen well. Her name was Nafise Shattila, and she was a couple of years younger than Ahmad, a good age. Usually an Arab man would take a wife eight or ten years younger than himself, to be sure that she would have many years of child-bearing ahead. But Ahmad was more modern-minded. He did not want to wait, and he liked the idea of a wife his own age. Nafise had an independent streak. She had been engaged once already, but had changed her mind and broken it off. Nafise knew knitting, embroidery, painting and the arts of house-keeping. But she had started school late, and even though she could speak fluent Italian, she was illiterate, like many Arab women of her generation. When Nafise had children of her own, she would ensure they were properly educated and would never suffer the same stigma.

Ahmad and Nafise's wedding was a great celebration, and family, friends and dignitaries attended from all over Jaffa. Weddings were the biggest events in Palestinian family life. The groom would leave the mosque with his male friends, and they would dance down the street in a procession, sometimes the length of Jaffa, from Hasan Bey mosque, in Manshiyyeh, through Clock Tower Square, down into Ajami, accompanied by musicians. Wedding guests gave the groom's family sweetmeats and chocolates, rice and sugar and a golden British pound, or even a whole sheep. The women would cook a special wedding dish of rice with mutton, and it was not uncommon for the feasting and celebration to last three or four days, or even a week.

Ahmad built a new house in Jebaliyyeh, on Jaffa's southern edge, not far from the sea. The house had high ceilings, stone floors and wooden shutters. There was a spacious veranda and a garden full of fruit trees—whose crops of custard apples, pomegranates, lemons, pears and persimmons Nafise turned into delicious jam—as well as a separate, smaller rose garden at the front of the house. Nafise had three daughters in quick succession: Nahida, Faizeh and Fatimah. Ahmad loved them very much, but in his heart, he longed for a son.

LIKE HIS FATHER, Shaker, Ahmad Hammami was profoundly disturbed by the 1921 violence. Muslims, Christians and Jews had always lived as neighbours in Palestine. All three religions were respected in the Hammami household—that was an iron rule. Certainly there was room for some Jewish immigrants who wanted to live in harmony with the Arabs. Palestine and Jaffa had always welcomed immigrants, such as Greeks and Italians. Ahmad himself sometimes leased orange groves from Jewish growers. But Palestine was a small country, and their numbers, he and Shaker agreed, should be limited. Many of the Jewish immigrants seemed to have a more fundamental aim: the *a'yan*, the Arab notables, sold them large tracts of land where they established their own Zionist colonies. Ahmad and Shaker were especially angry that the Arab tenant farmers were then thrown off their former holdings, with no provision for their families.

The biggest Zionist colony was Tel Aviv, adjacent to Jaffa. Palestinians often felt uncomfortable in Tel Aviv. The city was an unsettling European implant, where brazen women went unveiled and wore shorts, whose inhabitants spoke Hebrew or German and sat in cafés eating cake, plotting their steady takeover of Palestine. It was not an entirely inaccurate assessment. 'In daylight it looks like Whitechapel, and at night like Monte Carlo,' Arthur Koestler wrote of Tel Aviv in his semi-autobiographical novel *Thieves in the Night*. 'It was a frantic, maddening city which gripped the traveller by his buttonhole as soon as he entered it, tugged and dragged him around like a whirlpool, and left him after a few days faint and limp, not knowing whether he should laugh or cry, love or hate it.'⁹ Even its name was misleading: Tel Aviv means 'Hill of Spring', but the city is almost completely flat, and there is hardly any spring—wet, cold winters jump straight to hot, sticky summers.

In one sense, Tel Aviv's whole rationale was that it was not Jaffa. It was founded in 1909 by the Ahuzat Bayit society, composed of Jaffa's Jewish notables, including Aharon Chelouche. The society wanted to build another new suburb for the Jewish immigrants from Russia and eastern Europe known as the Second Aliyah.¹⁰ After lengthy negotiations with the Ottoman authorities, Ahuzat Bayit bought land for sixty houses on the sand dunes north of Jaffa. The finances were handled by the first Zionist bank, the Anglo-Palestine Company, founded in Jaffa in 1902. Its treasurer was Aharon's son Yaakov. The houses were built by Yaakov's brothers, Avraham Haim and Yosef Eliyahu, who owned a construction company. Ahuzat Bayit would become the nucleus of the future Tel Aviv. A photograph showing its members standing on the bare sand dunes, preparing to divide up the land, is an iconic symbol of Zionism. The message is clear: Palestine was an empty desert, truly 'a land without a people for a people without a land'.

In fact the first settlers outside old Jaffa were not Jews but American millennarian Christians, led by George Washington Adams, a preacher from Maine. Adams, together with forty-three families, landed in Jaffa in September 1866. The venture quickly collapsed in tragedy and farce. Thirteen died, the crops failed, the supplies ran out and Adams drank away the funds. He was actually an out-of-work actor, well known for impersonating clergymen. The *New York Herald* reported that he was 'seen lying in the streets of Jaffa in a state of the most degrading, beastly drunkenness'. The colonists went home. The German Templars, another Christian sect, had more success. They took over some of the American houses and founded two new quarters, called Sarona and Walhalla. By 1870 more than one hundred Templars were running a sawmill, olive press, steam-powered mill, hospital and pharmacy. Sarona and Walhalla had attractive European homes, with tidy, tree-lined streets. 'Their homes are built in an orderly sequence as in all European cities,' noted one observer. 'With its broad streets and elegant buildings, a person might forget he was walking in a desolate land and imagine himself in one of the civilised cities of Europe.'[11]

IN HIS SHOP by the port Aharon Chelouche watched the arrival of the Americans and Germans with interest. Aharon had arrived in Palestine in 1838, together with his parents and two sisters. Their journey from Oran, in Algeria, had been marked by tragedy. The boat bringing two of Aharon's brothers into Haifa harbour had overturned, and Yosef and Eliyahu had drowned. His father, Avraham, had settled in Jaffa and opened a money-changer's and jeweller's business. Both father and son looked like Biblical patriarchs. They had full beards, dressed in long striped robes held in place with wide belts and wore rectangular hats. Jewellery and money-changing had a profitable synergy. Coins were often composed wholly or partly of silver or gold. Aharon knew precisely how much precious metal each contained, when to melt them down and when to sell them. He used his profits to buy large tracts of land around Jaffa. The price of a plot was set in the throw of a stone. The buyer would accompany the seller to the site and hurl the first rock. The two men would then go to the point where it fell, and the buyer would throw the stone again. Aharon quickly became an expert in throwing stones and built up sizeable holdings. The family were rich and respected members of Jaffa's growing Jewish community. Like many of Jaffa's prosperous Jews, the Chelouches took foreign citizenship—in their case French—as a means of protection against the mercurial Ottoman authorities. The provisions of the Capitulations, dating back to the sixteenth century, granted special privileges to foreign citizens in Ottoman lands.[12]

In the mid-1880s Aharon sold around fourteen *dunams* (square kilometres) for the construction of Jaffa's first Jewish quarter, Neve Tsedek. All Ottoman cities were divided into different quarters for each minority: Jaffa already had Armenian, Egyptian, Greek and Maronite areas. But the foundation of Neve Tsedek would later be seen as a political statement: that the Jews were literally staking their own claim to the land. Aharon Chelouche also built a new family house on the sand dunes. When it was finally finished he told his wife, Sara, to prepare the family's move. But Sara and her daughter-in-law Sarina flatly refused to leave. Neve Tsedek was in the middle of nowhere, they said. There were no shops, and they would have no friends there. It was completely open and easy to attack. Aharon's arguments that Jaffa's Jews would soon follow them were ignored. Weeks went by, and the new house began to fill with sand. Only when other families started measuring up to build houses nearby did the Chelouche women relent. By spring 1887, the 'women's rebellion' was over. The family packed up their worldly goods, and a long caravan stretched over the sand dunes as they trekked to Neve Tsedek.

Neve Tsedek inspired more Jewish quarters, such as Neve Shalom. The new communities soon bordered Manshiyyeh, the northernmost tip of Jaffa. Many had Levantine, not European, houses. Beit Chelouche, 'Chelouche House', was typical: a single-storey building with

six large rooms around a communal hall. In short, a classical Arab
villa, surrounded by high walls with an enclosed courtyard. The
houses were built at the back of the courtyard, the toilets at the front.
For Ashkenazi Jews from Europe, Neve Tsedek and Neve Shalom
were an oriental mess. One indignant visitor recorded: 'Someone
who never saw the filth of those neighbourhoods inhabited solely by
our Jewish brethren, someone who never smelled the perfumed
odours of those narrow, dark alleyways can have no idea what squalor,
mire and filth are.'[13]

Despite sharing the same faith, the Ashkenazim and Sephardim
were sharply divided. Many European Jews regarded the Sephardim
with scorn, as old-fashioned, conservative and 'oriental' in their
fealty to the Ottoman authorities. They spoke Arabic rather than
Hebrew and were socially conservative, like the Arabs. Women married young and stayed at home, while the men went out to work.
Julia Chelouche's grandmother Mazal had been engaged at the age of
eleven and gave birth to her first child at fifteen. The Sephardim were
an organic part of the Middle East. The great Jewish communities of
Baghdad, Cairo and Damascus traced their lineage not in centuries
but in millennia, long before the arrival of Islam. In turn the
Sephardim viewed the Ashkenazim as ignorant *arrivistes*, arrogant in
their refusal to learn Arabic, with none of the subtle skills needed to
survive under Muslim rule. At one stage there were even plans for
two separate Jewish councils in Jaffa. Eventually both communities
agreed to work together, to build the new settlement of Ahuzat Bayit
in 1909.

Unlike Neve Tsedek, Ahuzat Bayit was thoroughly planned. By-
laws governed sanitation, building codes, security and even the size
of gardens—three metres wide, facing the street, with a properly

maintained fence. Streets would be six metres wide, with two metres of pavement, and there would be four metres between each house. The settlement, soon renamed Tel Aviv, was the very antithesis of chaotic Jaffa. It was also a huge commercial success. Property values soared. In 1913 two rooms in Neve Tsedek might have cost 250 francs a year, but they cost double that in Tel Aviv. By 1925, Tel Aviv's population had soared to 34,000. The city was booming. It had schools, shops, Hebrew newspapers, an orchestra, a theatre company and its own buses. An electric power station was built. Avraham Haim and Yosef Eliyahu Chelouche travelled to Marseilles, bought a standard house plan and loaded up the boat with building materials. There would be no more stone-carved Arab villas. The houses they built at 30 and 32 Pines Street were precise copies of French provincial homes, with a European layout. For many Jews the appeal of Tel Aviv was as much to do with comfort as with politics. Water was no longer delivered in leather bags from Abou Nabout's fountains but came out of a tap. The houses were European, with a sewage system and gardens where children could play in safety. The streets were clean and there was a sense of municipal order.

Jaffa also had a European-style quarter, around Nagib Bustros Street, named for the Lebanese businessman who had financed its construction. The buildings were designed for maximum security. The ground-floor shop or commercial property was locked and chained at night. A steep staircase led up from the street door to the living quarters on the first floor. A sharp right turn brought visitors to the front door, using the same security principle as the design of medieval castles and city gates, to prevent a frontal attack. A narrow vertical slit in the first-floor wall gave a view down the staircase. In the early years of Jaffa's expansion, at the end of the nineteenth century, a guard stood watch with a rifle so any intruders could be shot down on the steps.

Around this time a man called Alexander Howard lived at number 15 Nagib Bustros Street. His home boasted a magnificent entrance façade, flanked by two columns and topped with Masonic symbols, an arch and a small tabernacle inscribed in Hebrew *Shalom al-Yisrael*, peace unto Israel. Howard's real name was Iskander Awad. A Lebanese Christian from Beirut, Awad worked for Thomas Cook when the travel agent was organising his first tours to the Middle East. He thought that Iskander Awad sounded too Arabic for the British tourists who were beginning to travel to the Levant, so he anglicised his name and persuaded Cook to take him on as a drago-man, a translator and 'fixer' who arranges everything from donkeys to clean drinking water. Howard quickly came to manage the whole eastern section of Cook's tours, which started in London and lasted 105 days, including 30 days in Palestine, for the price of £170, 'first class all the way'. Within a few years, it seems, Cook and Howard had some kind of falling out. In 1876 Thomas Cook advertised his 'New and Improved Arrangements' for his Palestine tours, but there was no mention of Alexander Howard. Howard soon bounced back, though. He opened a hotel in Jerusalem opposite the Jaffa Gate, which adver-tised itself as being able to 'accommodate 125 world-class travellers', with 'hot and cold baths ready at all times'.

The increasingly prosperous Arab merchants of Jaffa built villas to the south, in two new areas called Ajami and Jebaliyyeh. The Levan-tine answer to Tel Aviv was a modern avenue of shops and flats at the bottom of Nagib Bustros, with a line of palm trees in the centre of the road. Built by the *kaymakam* Hasan Bey, it was named Jamal Pasha Boulevard, for the Turks' military governor, better known as Jamal the

Butcher. Hasan Bey also built a new mosque, with an especially tall minaret, by the beach in Manshiyyeh, which had been founded by Egyptian immigrants in the middle of the nineteenth century. The quarter was a maze of shops, bazaars and stately villas that looked out onto the nearby seashore, home to freed slaves, Africans, Gypsies, Persians, Indians and Baluchis. The mosque, named for him, was not popular. Locals said it was built with forced labour and paid for with 'voluntary' contributions. The Hasan Bey mosque had temporal as well as spiritual purposes: it marked the northernmost edge of Jaffa, and prevented Tel Aviv from spreading south. Throughout the following decades, it would be a flashpoint for clashes between Jews and Arabs.

Yet Manshiyyeh also showed the fluidity of relations between Arabs and Jews and the web of connections between Jaffa and Tel Aviv. Both Jews and Arabs lived in Manshiyyeh, attracted by its cheap housing and markets, central position and long sandy beach. There were slums but fine Ottoman villas too, with shady verandas that opened onto the seafront. The Jewish Communists had their headquarters there. Many Arab workers commuted from Manshiyyeh to the construction sites of Tel Aviv. Some of the richer, more westernised Jaffa Arabs found Tel Aviv congenial for other reasons. In Jaffa it was impossible to meet single, unchaperoned women, but in Tel Aviv's liberal atmosphere it was easy, in cafés or even on the beach. The sight of Arab men mixing freely with Jewish women was shocking to some. L. M. Jeune, a Jewish resident of Jaffa, wrote to Meir Dizengoff, the first mayor of Tel Aviv, in June 1922, protesting that not only were 'Arabs of a very inferior class frequenting the Casino', but 'Mixed bathing is drawing the natives to the Bathing Resort, and to my knowledge, three Arabs have bathed there. They will spread the news that they are allowed to mix with the ladies, and there will surely be trouble.'[14]

Tel Aviv was also renowned for its brothels, which catered to both Arabs and Jews, straight and gay.[15] The bed was one of the only places in Palestine where the national question was not a factor. One Jaffa man active in the Arab underground wrote in his memoirs that, after killing a Mandate policeman, he had his record wiped clean by paying off the British military governor with an expensive meal and a night with two of the most skilled prostitutes at the Akarakhaneh brothel on Dizengoff Street.[16] Gay relationships between Arab and Jewish men—and British officials—were not uncommon, notes the historian Mark Levine. Immigrant women from Europe were often thought dangerously licentious. One report noted: 'Suddenly we began to see in the different streets of Tel Aviv cars of the wealthy Arabs and Christians arrive in the middle of the evenings, and parked alongside the houses in which lived the new female immigrants, the wild debauchery continued until the wee hours of the night.'[17] Jews and Arabs shared more than wild parties. The newspaper *Falastin* reported that there was a school for pickpockets operating in Tel Aviv, with both Arab and Jewish students.

Yet despite the pickpockets and parties, tension rose steadily as the *Yishuv*, the Jewish community in Palestine, grew and strengthened. The word *Yishuv* is Hebrew for settlement, but its real meaning was 'state-in-waiting'. The *Yishuv* had its own education system, banks, trade unions, newspapers and medical services. It was not homogenous but reflected the differing strands of Zionist thought from right to left. Some sought separation from the Arabs, others accommodation. The Histradrut, the Zionist trade union organisation, even published two newspapers in Arabic to build bridges with Arab workers. Articles praised Tel Aviv as a successful example of modernising the Middle East. As Joseph Roth had noted, however, Arabs did not want to be modernised by Jews. If the Arab rioters' intention was to slow, or halt, the Zionist project, though, they failed. Jewish settlements became villages, the villages towns and the towns cities. In May 1921 Tel Aviv gained 'town council' status. This anodyne decision had important consequences. A splinter settlement of Jaffa, barely thirteen years old, now had its own law court, fire station and police force. In 1922 six areas of Jaffa were annexed to Tel Aviv, including Neve Tsedek. The Scottish town planner Patrick Geddes, who had revitalised Edinburgh, drew up a comprehensive plan for a modern city. Tel Aviv, it was understood by all, was more than a conurbation. It was the centre of the Hebrew state-in-waiting.

AVRAHAM HAIM CHELOUCHE would have invited Jaffa's Muslim and Christian dignitaries to Julia's wedding that October of 1921 regardless. They had been friends for generations. The wedding invitations were printed in French and Arabic, and the gifts for the guests were imported from Egypt: boxes franked with David and Julia's initials, filled with sugared almonds. The wedding took place at the Eden cinema in Tel Aviv. 'My dress was long and white, with lace to the bottom and a white veil. The buds were arranged nicely. When I went down the stairs and started to walk, the owner of the nearby café stopped me, and threw a jug of sweet Turkish coffee on the ground, as a good omen,' wrote Julia. The cinema entrance was covered in Persian rugs and carpets, lent by Julia's relatives. Flowers spelt out WELCOME at the door. Julia travelled in the high commissioner's Packard convertible with her father, Yosef, and grandmother Mazal. Still the day was tinged with sadness: Julia's mother, Esther, had died not long before.

When the wedding car arrived, the British band struck up and the bridesmaids scattered flowers on the path in front of David and Julia. That evening there was a family dinner at the nearby Palatin Hotel. Afterwards David and Julia set off on honeymoon, going by train to Cairo, Venice and Paris, where his brothers Zaki and Marco lived. The Muslim and Christian guests told Avraham Haim: 'We came for you, Mr Chelouche. This is the first time our feet have touched the ground in Tel Aviv since the disturbances.' Just as Herbert Samuel had hoped, the wedding had brought together Jews and Arabs. But it was for one evening only; within a few years Jaffa would once again explode into violence.

3

Jaffa Strikes

1920s–1930s

There is no choice but to rouse ourselves, there is no choice
but to shake ourselves, there is no choice but to act.

Palestinian diarist Khalil al-Sakakini
on Jewish immigration, 1935

Shlomo Chelouche was getting ready for his favourite excursion, going out with his father, Yaakov, as he did his rounds. The family lived on Rothschild Boulevard, one of the first streets in Tel Aviv. Shlomo, born in 1916, went to school at the Herzliya Gymnasium and was a happy boy, adored and just a bit spoiled. When Yaakov and his wife, Pearla, travelled to Europe each year, they brought Shlomo sailor suits from Paris. He proudly strutted about the house in his new uniform and appointed himself boss of the stable. When Meir Dizengoff came to visit Shlomo's father, Shlomo was watering the garden. After Dizengoff had tied up his horse and gone inside to speak to Yaakov, Shlomo liberally watered the horse.

Life was good and the family prospered. The Anglo-Palestine Company was now the Anglo-Palestine Bank, a mainstay of Palestine's economy. Yaakov Chelouche's counsel and friendship were sought by many. Yaakov was a stylish and charismatic man, with strong features and clear eyes. He wore a tailored three-piece suit with a freshly-starched wing collar, and a carefully trimmed moustache and goatee. Yaakov was preceded on his rounds by his *kawas* (bearer), an imposing figure dressed in a special uniform, who held a polished baton. 'The *kawas* walked in front of my father, with an expression that said, "I am here, leading Mr Chelouche,"' remembered Shlomo, who lived in central Tel Aviv until his death in 2006. A lively raconteur, with a ready laugh and a love of storytelling, he shares the family's sense of history. 'The *kawas* hit the ground with the baton, warning passers-by to make way, that his master was following. He never needed to mention my father's name. Everyone knew who it was when he passed by with his fellow. They all greeted my father—they wanted to prove that they knew him.'

Like all the Chelouches, Yaakov was fluent in Arabic, and he even wrote poetry in the language. Yaakov Chelouche also understood the subtleties of Levantine commerce and the importance of both face and respect. 'My father was loved and respected in Jaffa,' said Shlomo. 'We went to a textile shop where they owed money. They came to the entrance to greet him, brought chairs and coffee. My father sat down and they talked, about the weather, the fruits, the oranges, how they were good this season, better than last, about how Muhammad Ali had bought a new house and Ibn Dahab had just sold his orange grove. They drank the coffee and I had juice.' There was no need for Yaakov to discuss the purpose of his visit. It was understood by all. 'My father finished his coffee, he finished talking shop and thanked the owner. He stood up, called for Mohammad, the *kawas*, and said it was time to go. The *kawas* ushered away the people who had come to watch, and we left. When my father had gone ten metres, the shop owner shouted, "Mr Chelouche, I'll come tomorrow to see you." The money was not mentioned. There was no need. Nobody said, "You owe me this." My father knew he would be paid—that was the delicacy of it.'

Despite the legacy of the May 1921 riots and the increasing polarisation between the two peoples, both communities were still inextricably linked by mutual interests. The Chelouches prided themselves on their cordial business and social relations with their Arab partners. Politics, and the clash between Zionism and Palestinian nationalism, was a backdrop, ever present. But human interaction continued, both social and commercial. Often both were mixed. The elaborate Levantine codes of hospitality and courtesy meant it was impossible to disentangle them. Yaakov wanted his Arab bank customers to prosper, and they in turn wanted their Jewish bank manager to feel secure, explained Shlomo. 'We were neighbours. We lived together and we wanted to succeed together. It meant you give me money and I will develop my business, make money and pay you interest. On the holidays I will not forget to send you sheep, turkeys, oil, wine and goods for your house.'

These arrived regularly at the Chelouche household. But one consignment was always awaited with particular pleasure: half a dozen camels, each loaded with sacks of olives, oranges, watermelons, chicken, lamb and jars of olive oil. The foods were welcome, but more important was the human connection they represented, one that stretched back decades, to the era of the family patriarch, Aharon Chelouche—a friendship that showed that perhaps Arab and Jew, Jaffa and Tel Aviv, could live together and share the land of Palestine and its riches. The story, which begins in the late nineteenth century, is told at length by Julia Chelouche in her memoir:

One morning Aharon Chelouche saw a young Arab boy, aged around sixteen, next to his money changing shop. The boy was crying bitterly. 'What's wrong, why are you crying?' Aharon Chelouche asked him. The young man told Aharon, tears choking his throat, 'I came from my village yesterday. My father Sheikh Samarra sent me to Jaffa to sell a camel and gave me a packet of coins for the trip. Last night I slept at the inn. Robbers came and stole the camel and the money. I was left in my shirt and skin. How can I show my face to my father? And how can I return to my village with no money?'

Aharon Chelouche took a *majida*, a silver coin, out of his pocket and told the boy, 'Take it, my son and do not worry. Your father will forgive you, because what happened was not your fault.' A *majida* was a considerable amount of money in those days, when the Turks ruled Israel.

'Who are you?' stuttered the youngster. 'You do not know me at all, and I am a resident of a distant village, how can I return your money to you?'

'My name is Aharon Chelouche,' the old man said. 'Return to your village and Allah will bless you.'

No more was heard of the Samarras until spring 1917. The Turkish authorities, fearful that the Allies were about to invade Palestine from the sea, expelled Jaffa's Jews inland. Many were foreign citizens, who eagerly awaited the arrival of the British and were regarded as spies or a potential fifth column. The war had brought fear, destruction and near famine to Jaffa. Locusts destroyed the harvests. The economy collapsed, and the Anglo-Palestine Company, registered in Britain, was forced to close. A British warship shelled Jaffa, destroying part of

the staircase of Beit Chelouche. Aharon was wounded in the head and
hand by shrapnel, his daughter Jamila in an eye. The Chelouches and
the Bohbouts relocated to Petach Tikva, a Jewish settlement in central
Palestine. Yaakov Chelouche, the banker, tried to revitalise the local
economy, which had collapsed. Yaakov wrote out promissory notes
and signed and guaranteed them.

But after heavy fighting in the area, the Jews were forced out once
again. The Chelouches moved to Kfar Jamal, near Tayibeh in north-
east Palestine. Their situation deteriorated rapidly. Their funds ran
out, and there was nothing to eat. Aharon's wife, Sara, died. Aharon
was now ninety years old. His son Yaakov was arrested, together with
Yaakov's nephew Moshe. Both were accused of spying for the NILI
espionage ring, which worked for Britain. NILI, an acronym for the
Hebrew words meaning 'The strength of Israel will not lie', was run
by Aaron Aaronsohn and his sister Sarah from the northern town of
Zichron Yaakov. Yaakov and Moshe Chelouche were imprisoned in
Damascus, together with Na'aman Belkind, one of NILI's leaders,
who had been captured by the Turks while attempting to reach Egypt.
Yaakov and Moshe Chelouche were eventually released, but Na'aman
Belkind was hanged in 1917. Yaakov's brothers, Yosef Eliyahu and
Avraham Haim, were now the heads of the family. These were terrible
days for the Chelouches, but help came from an unexpected quarter,
writes Julia:

> The family numbered some forty people, all of whom lived by
> their wits, without money, they peddled rags which they
> brought from the city.... One day, a pair of camels preceded by
> a donkey appeared on the path. The rider got down from the
> donkey and asked, 'Is the refugee Aharon Chelouche here?'

When he was brought to the old man he said, 'You do not know me. My name is Hajj Ibrahim Samarra.[1] I am the youth to whom you once gave a *majida* in Jaffa. Your benevolence will never be forgotten. And I heard that you are refugees here.' And Hajj Ibrahim Samarra unloaded all sorts of good things from the camels, sacks of flour and beans, and leather bags of oil, treasures the likes of which the refugees had forgotten.

There was more to come. Whatever debt Hajj Ibrahim owed to Aharon Chelouche was repaid many times over. The young boy who had lost his money and his father's camel was now a rich man, the Sheikh of three villages.

He invited Yosef Eliyahu [Chelouche] to his home, brought an axe and a rope, measured the length of one of the walls of the room and chopped off the plaster with the axe. When the plaster fell off, a plate was revealed on the wall. From the hole behind it, Hajj Ibrahim removed a red handkerchief holding 500 gold pounds, handed the money to Yosef Eliyahu and said, 'Take it, I have enough. Return it when the war ends, *Inshallah*.[2] It will be my shame if you do not take the money.'

Yosef Eliyahu thanked him from the bottom of his heart and suggested that he give the Sheikh a promissory note. 'Why?' asked Hajj Ibrahim. 'What if we all die in the war?' explained Yosef Eliyahu. 'Then neither of us will need the money,' protested Sheikh Ibrahim.

The hospitality shown by the villagers of Kfar Jamal to the displaced Jews made a profound impression on Yosef Eliyahu Chelouche. A prolific essayist, he had published many articles in Palestine's Arabic press before the start of the war arguing that there was no inherent clash of interests between Jewish settlement in Palestine and Arab aspirations for the land. With mutual respect and tolerance, Jews and Arabs could live together. 'The days of our stay in Kfar Jamal were good,' he wrote in his autobiography, *Reminiscences of My Life*. 'The villagers treated us with great respect. The relations between the Jews and the local people were characterised by kindness and love. There were no disturbances, except a few petty quarrels between the children. Then I used to make peace, by handing out candies.'

Yosef Eliyahu and his brother Avraham Haim were not sure where to bury their mother, Sara, after she died in Kfar Jamal. The nearest Jewish town was five hours' walk away, and travel was impossible without a permit in any case. The sheiks of Kfar Jamal insisted that Sara Chelouche be buried in the village graveyard, to make things easier for the distressed family. Yosef Eliyahu was particularly touched by the many local Arabs who asked if they could attend her funeral. 'It seemed that all of them were standing behind my house, waiting for my permission, and they all came, from youngsters to the village elders. We accompanied her to the grave to the sounds of crying of both Jews and Arabs. . . . During the days of mourning groups of local Arabs came to console us. Their kindness gave us strength from our sorrow and we emerged from our grief, except my sister Jamila, who could not find comfort even for a long time after our mother's death.'

Year after year, the Samarra camel trains arrived at Rothschild Boulevard from Kfar Jamal. Personal relations between Arabs and Jews endured, but with no political solution in sight the violence worsened. In August 1929, the Arabs of Hebron rioted and killed sixty-seven Jews, butchering babies, children and old people. Many of Hebron's Jews were saved by their Arab neighbours, who hid them in their houses, but they all left Hebron soon after—the end of one of the world's oldest Jewish communities. In Jaffa and across Palestine the Jews counter-attacked. Just as in 1921, the worst clashes in Jaffa erupted in Manshiyyeh. Secret detachments of the Haganah, the underground Jewish militia founded in 1920, patrolled the area around the Hasan Bey mosque. Its members were well trained and organised, armed with guns stolen or bought from the British. Arab youths congregated in their own self-defence groups. The two sides were kept 500 yards apart by the Palestine Police.

The chasm between the two sides was far wider than that. The Arabs felt profoundly betrayed, and their protests languished unread on desks in Whitehall. 'Arabs after the Great War lost all the political rights they enjoyed under Turkey and witnessed Jewish riff-raff being introduced from all parts to their country to build a non-existent nation,' wrote Musa Kazim Pasha, president of the Arab Executive of Palestine, to London.[3] The Zionists took a different view. Maurice Samuel, a witness to the 1929 violence, used language highly telling of the ideological and cultural chasm between the two sides: 'On the one side Tel Aviv with its poets, painters and thinkers. On the other, backward Jaffa, in which education is a fantastic luxury, and modern intellectuality—in a *levantised* form at that—the possession of a handful. . . . Only yesterday, too, we had got along so well. The young bloods of Jaffa used to come on Fridays to Tel Aviv. This was their taste of "Europe", of the "civilised world".'[4]

When calm was finally restored, 133 Jews and 116 Arabs were dead across Palestine. The killings further polarised both sides. The minority of Zionists who called for a bi-national or confederal Arab-Hebrew entity rather than a fully fledged Hebrew state were even more marginalised. So were those Arabs prepared to countenance a Jewish 'canton' in a future independent Palestine. The Jewish writer S. Y. Agnon spoke for many when he wrote of the Arabs: 'I do not hate them and I do not love them; I do not wish to see their faces. In my humble opinion we should now build a large ghetto of half a million Jews in Palestine, because if we do not we will, God forbid, be lost.'[5]

In 1933, Adolf Hitler came to power in Germany, the triumph of Nazism providing the final vindication of Herzl's argument that the Jews needed their own state. The Third Reich triggered the Fifth Aliyah. The German Jewish bourgeoisie, known as *yekkes*, poured into Palestine. Dressed in three-piece suits, they sat sweating and drinking coffee in Tel Aviv's cafés, pining for Vienna and Berlin, but they were at least out of the Nazis' reach. By 1935, Tel Aviv's population had reached 120,000. Officially recognised as a city in 1934, Tel Aviv was now the de facto capital of the *Yishuv*, complete with its own philharmonic orchestra.

Not all its inhabitants were Jews. Amin Andraus, a Christian Arab from Nazareth, rented a flat in Tel Aviv from a Turkish Jewish family while he looked for a piece of land on which to build a house in Jaffa. Amin worked in the car business, and was a strikingly attractive man, with high cheekbones and dark eyes that looked out at the world with ironic amusement. After his father, Salim, died in 1907, his mother, Haya, sent him to the German Schneller School in Jerusalem. It was a spartan regime, based on plain food, cold water, hard work and a strong moral sense. One school holiday, he and several friends were about to set off from Jerusalem to Nazareth by horse-drawn coach when several young girls arrived from the Blind School. There was not enough room for all of them, so Amin told his friends that they all had to give up their places. It took them three days to walk home.

Amin was fluent in German, Turkish and Arabic, and during the war was drafted into an Austrian army unit as a translator. In 1917 Amin was captured by the British army, and fortune smiled on him. He was sent home to Nazareth to work at army headquarters translating letters from Turkish or Arabic into English. In truth Amin's English was not very good. But he enlisted an English teacher to help, and they managed very well. Amin was allowed to go home every night with a packet of army rations for himself, his mother, Haya, and his sister, Fahima, riches when Palestine was in a state of near famine.

Amin outgrew Nazareth, which was a sleepy provincial town, less cosmopolitan and more traditional than Jaffa. Some of its residents looked askance at Amin's drive and ambition. Amin loved to hunt, and the story of the shooting trip to Mount Tabor entered the Andraus family folklore. Andraus had set off at a brisk pace, the dogs in front. The Nazarenes with him soon flagged. Their vision of a pleasant stroll was somewhat different from Amin's, which seemed more like a route march. They asked Amin for some water. 'Why didn't you bring any?' he asked, annoyed at their lack of preparation. They asked again for some of his. 'No, this water is for the dogs. You can look after yourselves, but the dogs need me to look after them,' he replied, striding off into the distance.

In 1933, Amin married Hanneh Azzam, a Greek Orthodox Christian from Haifa. Amin wanted a quiet and dignified wedding and declared that there would be no ululating. Should any guest or relative start to make the rhythmic wailing sounds, Amin announced, he would walk out. Nobody ululated at the wedding. Amin and Hanneh went on honeymoon to Egypt, before he took his bride back to Jaffa.

THAT SAME YEAR, 1933, Arab demonstrators fought with police in Jaffa, Jerusalem, Nablus and Haifa. Thirty people were killed and more than two hundred wounded. Across Palestine sniping and bombings were ever more frequent, and the lack of any political solution accelerated the violence. In November 1935 British officials checked a consignment of cement that arrived in Jaffa. It concealed 800 rifles and 400,000 rounds of ammunition for the Jewish underground. In protest the Arab leadership called a one-day general strike and demanded that Britain stop all Jewish immigration, halt land sales and set up a democratic government for Palestine which would automatically have an Arab majority. The demands were refused.

The following spring Arab political leaders established the Arab Higher Committee (AHC) to unite the fractious political groupings. Its leader was the mufti of Jerusalem, Hajj Amin al-Husseini, head of Palestine's Muslims and a great admirer of Hitler. Others included Ragheb al-Nashashibi, the mayor of Jerusalem, and Alfred Rock, a Jaffa Christian grandee. The al-Husseinis had for years been engaged in a bitter feud with the al-Nashashibis. The Jewish Agency, the Zionist organisation that was the government-in-waiting of the Jewish state, deftly exploited this intra-Arab enmity. It facilitated secret 'loans' to al-Nashashibi, keeping him in its debt. Behind its nationalist bluster, the Arab leadership was one of the Jewish Agency's greatest allies. The *a'yan*, the notables, had been selling off Palestine for decades.

One of the oldest Zionist settlements, Rishon Le-Zion, was established on land sold by the Jaffan Dajani family. Together with the mufti of Jaffa, Tawfik al-Dajani, Alfred Rock sold off holdings south of Jebaliyyeh, now the Israeli town of Bat Yam. Arthur Rock, his brother, sold land to the Jewish National Fund. Omar el-Bitar, mayor of Jaffa at various times, sold the land where the religious Jewish settlement of Bnei Brak was founded. Ragheb al-Nashashibi sold the site on which the Hebrew University was built. Relatives of Hajj Amin

al-Husseini also sold land to the Jewish National Fund.[6] Only a fraction of the *fellahin*, the Palestinian Arab farmers, were prepared to part
with their holdings. But at times so much land owned by the *a'yan*
was for sale that the Zionists lacked enough funds to buy it all.

Under the direction of the mufti of Jerusalem, the Arab Revolt
began on 15 April 1936, when militants set up a roadblock outside the
northern city of Tulkarm and shot dead three Jews. In response, Jewish gunmen killed two Arabs near Petach Tikva. On 17 April a Jewish
victim was buried in Tel Aviv, triggering a violent demonstration. The
next day Jewish extremists beat up Arab street traders and shoeshine
boys. That in turn triggered a rampage through Jaffa by a mob of peas-
ants and immigrant workers from Syria, who killed nine Jews and
injured sixty.[7] Once again Jews fled Jaffa for Tel Aviv. Once again
fighting raged through the border quarters between Jaffa and Tel Aviv
as rival mobs looted and burnt shops. The lack of political progress
meant that the cycle of violence was condemned to repeat itself end-
lessly, over the same causes, between the same protagonists, even
around the same buildings.

Arab leaders called a general strike and a boycott of Jewish businesses. By the summer of 1936, a low-intensity guerrilla war was raging across Palestine. 17 June was an average night. Arab riflemen
opened fire on a police patrol from the outskirts of Jaffa, and the
police returned fire, killing one and wounding several, reported *The
Times of London*. Two bombs exploded by the railway line, causing little damage, while 'ineffective shots were fired at police and Jewish
colonies in various localities.'[8] In Jaffa that summer the Old City
echoed almost daily with the sound of shootings. Two Jewish nurses
were murdered and Arab gunmen sniped at Jewish homes and cars.
Crops were burnt and trees cut down. Jewish farmers travelled only in

convoys, with British troops protecting them. In response, Zionist militants bombed the Jaffa train, attacked a Bedouin encampment north of Tel Aviv and sniped at houses in Manshiyyeh, killing several civilians.

Parallel with the fighting, the economic line of separation was drawn ever more clearly. Jews launched the Product Loyalist Alliance (PLA) to boycott Arab goods. PLA zealots inspected Tel Aviv's shops, and 'traitors' were denounced by public announcement or graffiti. Among the Arabs, strong-arm men demanded 'donations' to the national struggle, while business rivals denounced each other to the Jews. In June 1936, Khalil Yousif Rizk informed the Jewish Agency that one George Abou Alice was 'dealing in the smuggling of arms, ammunitions, etc. for the rioters in the districts of Ramleh and Jaffa.' Elias Sasson, head of the Jewish Agency's Arab Affairs department, received the letter with surprise, as they had 'never had any connections whatsoever' with Rizk.[9]

With Jaffa's port shut down, Tel Aviv decided to build its own. 'I want a Jewish sea,' David Ben-Gurion, chairman of the Jewish Agency, proclaimed, for 'the sea is a continuation of Palestine.'[10] The Zionists' confidence was unshakeable. The Anglo-Palestine Bank founded a new company, the Marine Trust, and issued shares to finance the port's construction. When building started, Tel Aviv's mayor, Meir Dizengoff, dropped a stone in the sea to symbolise the port's foundations. He announced: 'I remember when Tel Aviv did not have a harbour,' as though it had already been built and had been there as long as the city itself.

Arab newspapers mirrored the separatist rhetoric of the Zionists. *Falastin* sneered: 'If the Jews think they can do without Jaffa they are wrong, but Jaffa can do without Jews and their city. . . . We are the ones who will proclaim economic war on them, cutting them off for ever.'[11] *Ad-Difaa* declared: 'We here repeat and state over and over again, that this port has been Arab since time immemorial and that it will keep its Arab feature until the end of time.'[12]

Yet everyday life continued. Amin Andraus bought land in Jebaliyyeh, not far from the Hammami house. There he built a stylish cream-coloured 1930s art-deco villa overlooking the sea. It was surrounded by a large curved terrace and garden in the front and the rear, and there was plenty of land to raise chickens and rabbits. Every visitor praised its beauty and location, and Hanneh's industriousness in keeping such a wonderful home. On days when politics did not intrude, life was good. Amin's business was thriving. He had his own car showroom in Jaffa, by the old German colonies. He was a freemason, and the Jaffa lodge brought useful commercial contacts as well as good connections with British officials. Amin had the franchise for Nash cars and Kelvinator refrigerators for Palestine, Jordan and Egypt. Amin and Hanneh's first child was born in 1934: Salim, named in memory of his grandfather. Two years later came a sister for Salim, Leila. The nights were mostly quiet, as the waves lapped at the beach. There was only occasional gunfire.

4

A Widening Divide

1936

*The most important immediate effect of the explosions,
however, has been on the morale of the inhabitants of Jaffa.
They are docile again.*

Report in The Times of London on British army demolitions
of parts of the Old City, datelined Jaffa, 6 July 1936

By summer 1936 Jaffa was under curfew and the Arab Revolt had erupted. The winding lanes of the Old City offered the perfect cover for snipers and gunmen to attack Tel Aviv, or Jewish vehicles. 'This oldest quarter of the town is a maze of sunless and insanitary lanes with congested tenements and catacomb-like cellars,' reported *The Times*, which was why British planes were flying over Jaffa, dropping leaflets onto the city. The authorities planned to demolish at least forty-five houses, and probably twice that number would have to be evacuated. Few believed the British claims that the work was to be carried out in the name of 'urban improvement'. About five hundred people would need new homes, *The Times* opined, 'chiefly of the poorest class of lightermen and hawkers'.

The Royal Engineers used ten tons of gelignite to clear a T-shaped space in the heart of the Old City, blasting a path through the ancient warren for armoured and military vehicles. Dozens of centuries-old buildings were blown to bits, while others were so badly damaged they had to be demolished. Thousands were made homeless. It was far worse than anyone had imagined. 'Onlooker', an anonymous pamphleteer, published a coruscating English-language account of the demolitions, describing them as 'official terrorisation, despotically enforced and ruthlessly promulgated'. The residents were given just twenty-four hours to vacate their homes. 'Great fissures run like flashes of black lightning the whole height of thick stone walls. Half-demolished vaults hang perilously in the air. Arches, unkeyed by the detonations, have slipped into sad mis-shape. The privacy of humble bedrooms is laid bare, the simple furniture, battered and broken, standing pathetically exposed to the public gaze. The lower chambers and little streets are filled with fallen masonry from above.' The homeless were re-housed in schools, huts, basements, the boats in the harbour or tents in the cemetery. Mandate officials offered compensation of about three shillings per person. 'What would the Jews in Europe have to say if this had been done to members of *their* race?' demanded Onlooker.'

Arab homeowners applied for a court order to stop a second wave of demolitions. But the chief justice, Sir Michael McDonnel, could only reject the application, as there were no legal grounds to stop the demolitions, which were taking place under emergency powers. Sir Michael was deeply unhappy about the whole affair, noting the 'singularly disingenuous lack of moral courage displayed by the [Mandate] Administration in the whole matter', and strongly criticised the Mandate leadership. *The Times* newspaper—then the voice of the British establishment—took a different view. Its correspondent wrote: 'The results have certainly justified the Government's decision.

Since the demolitions began sniping and bomb-throwing have entirely ceased in Old Jaffa, and I was able to wander freely about the tortuous alleys of this ancient labyrinth where a fortnight ago no policeman could go.' Even better, he noted, while on his strolls he 'received cheerful greetings from the inhabitants'.[2] As for Sir Michael, he was sacked and left Palestine.

As the Royal Engineers prepared their charges, three excited young Arab boys ran through the Old City to watch the destruction: Fakhri Geday and his friends, the Damiani brothers. The Damianis, like the Gedays, were Christians, and the families were so close they were almost relatives. Both had lived in Jaffa for many generations. When Napoleon had invaded in 1799, the Damianis' diplomacy had helped prevent a massacre of Muslim civilians. The family owned a soap factory in the heart of the Old City, a Jaffa landmark. Would it survive the demolitions? 'The British had blown up a lot of houses by the factory. The boys came to me and said, "Come on, let's go and watch them destroy the buildings. Don't say anything, let's just go", so we ran down into the Old City,' recalls Fakhri. 'Their father was sitting there when we arrived, watching that the British did not destroy his factory. I always remember what he said, that your money is the equal of your life. When he saw us, he sent us straight back home.'

Born in 1927, Fakhri still works at the green-painted pharmacy at 65 Yefet Street that he inherited from his father, Youssef Kamel. The Ajami shop is a Jaffa institution, and customers pop in all day for medicines, salves and treatment for minor ailments. Dressed in his white coat, Fakhri deals with them all with courtesy, effortlessly switching between Hebrew, Arabic and English. With his lively eyes and courteous manner, he has the appearance of a favourite uncle. But beneath his jocular exterior are anger and regret. The Jaffa where he grew up is gone for ever, and Palestine with it. 'I always say it was something exceptional, in all aspects: education, social, cultural. Even in politics, as many of the national figures in the nationalist leadership came from Jaffa. Now the only thing that remains of Jaffa is the name. There is nothing left of the old Jaffa. The glorious days, the peace of mind, the people, they are all lost. Christian or Muslim, we were all Palestinians before 1948, and we were proud of it. When we travelled abroad, we said we were Palestinians. Palestine then was the jewel of the Middle East. People lived in every corner. This is our country and I don't believe that God promised it to anyone else.'

The Gedays were related to the Rock family, which sold substantial tracts of land to the Zionists. Youssef Kamel Geday refused to sell his holdings, despite attempts by Arthur Rock to persuade him to part with them. The Gedays were rooted in Jaffa and would never leave. During the Ottoman era, in the early nineteenth century, Fakhri's forebears lived in the city's heart, behind the city walls. Once Jaffa spread south along the coast, down the Gaza road—now Yefet Street—Fakhri's grandfather Dimitri bought land in Ajami. There he built the family house, where Fakhri and his family still live, a spacious stone villa with a garden of flowers and jasmine trees. Fakhri went to school at nearby St Joseph's, founded in 1882 by French monks. It enjoyed an excellent reputation, in both Jaffa and Tel Aviv. 'We learned Arabic, English and French. It was a wonderful life—we had school every day, and half-days on Sundays and Thursdays. We had our club at St Anthony's church, the most famous club in Jaffa. It was a family place, you could play billiards, ping-pong, backgammon. We met our friends there, drank lemonade and ate ice cream. There was a big library, even a small pharmacy.'

The foreign mission schools were also popular with Jewish families. Over twenty years earlier Julia Chelouche had studied at Tabeetha, which had been founded by two Scottish missionaries in the late 1860s, on the edge of Ajami, not far from the Geday pharmacy. Julia's father had wanted her to learn English, the language in which the curriculum was, and still is, taught. But only a minority of Arab families could afford to send their children to one of the foreign schools. Many Arab boys and girls received at best a rudimentary schooling or remained illiterate. Arab girls were often not allowed to attend school at all by their parents. Yet a lack of formal education did not reduce the hunger for knowledge about Palestine's situation and the conflict between Jew and Arab. Newspaper articles were read aloud in cafés while listeners gathered around in a circle. This was less profitable for Palestine's publishers, as they sold fewer papers, but it gave each writer's view a wide audience. The most popular articles were even memorised and recited by heart.

The Arab press did not always serve its readers well, as Mark Levine notes. *Falastin* often propagated hoary old clichés about Jews. One cartoon showed two women, one Jewish and one Palestinian. The Jewish woman stands provocatively, representing a dangerous, forbidden sexuality. She wears shorts and a revealing blouse, and she is smoking. The Palestinian woman wears traditional dress and sits meekly. As in eastern Europe, Jews were portrayed as simultaneously representing the twin threats of rapacious capitalism and godless Communism. In July 1936 *Falastin* demanded to know 'who harbours, maintains and pays Communism and the Communists. Does Mr Dizengoff not know that a Communist and a Jew are synonymous in this country and throughout the Levant?'[3] The Communists were a tiny minority of the Jewish left. Jews had lived in Palestine and Jaffa for centuries, long before the Arab Muslim conquest in the seventh century, yet they were relentlessly portrayed as outsiders, intruders, bringers of foreign vices. Both Christianity and Islam were rooted in Judaism, but *Al-jamia al-Islamiyyah* advised its readers to wear a tar-boosh whenever they visited Tel Aviv, as the traditional Ottoman headgear would be a symbol of 'holding onto our eastness'.

Literature, too, was highly politicised. The new generation of Palestinian writers and their works were avidly discussed at Jaffa's literary clubs. *The Angel and the Land Broker*, by Muhammed Izzat Darwazah, recounts how a *fellah*, a peasant farmer, is enticed to visit Tel Aviv. There he meets an attractive Jewish girl, the archetypal sexual temptress, who encourages him to spend money he does not have. Once in debt, he is forced to mortgage his land. He cannot meet the payments and sells the land for a fraction of its worth. The farmer leaves his family, becomes a beggar and eventually goes insane. Arab literature (and contemporary Palestinian life) might have been better served had Darwazah dealt with the uncomfortable truth that it was the *a'yan*, rather than the *fellahin*, who were selling off Palestine to the Jews.

Jaffa's cafés offered more secular enjoyments as well: gambling, alcohol and hashish, even the company of women. Many were crowded with young men who had migrated from the villages, where there was little or no work. The countryside boys were lonely, impoverished and bewildered in the anonymous city. Café Baghdadi, on Shabazi Street in Manshiyyeh, was typical. 'All hours of the day it is crowded with very shady characters, who sit and gamble, playing all manner of card games and dominoes. Many women, undoubtedly prostitutes, gather in this café, and hang about, passing from table to table,' noted one Mandate police report.[4]

The political turmoil radicalised many educated Palestinian

women. No longer were they prepared to sit meekly in traditional dress. Many spoke foreign languages and were active in the network of social and charitable organisations such as the YMCA and YWCA. They began to articulate their own voice. As early as the 1920s *Falastin* published a series of articles on women's issues, many of them actually written by women. Headlines included 'The Veil and the Duty to Lift It' and 'The Veil is an Obstacle to Girls' Education'. *Falastin's* pages hosted a lively debate on women and Islam, with correspondents from both the conservative and the progressive side quoting from the Quran to back up their arguments. One article explained 'The Necessity to Liberate Women', although it was written by a man. The Arab Women's Association gathered different women's groups across Palestine into one organisation. Members demanded, and obtained, meetings with Mandate officials, wrote letters and petitions and even demonstrated on the streets, to the consternation of both British and Arab men.

Jaffa's women, Muslim and Christian, also had their own space at home. They organised 'receiving days', known as *istiqbal*, an opportunity to gossip and show off their culinary skills. The hostess served drinks made from pomegranates or almonds, tiny cups of Turkish coffee, sweets and savoury snacks such as *bureks*, tiny pastries stuffed with cheese, meat or potato. The delicacies were consumed, and the hostess's cooking expertise was suitably praised. The women then discussed potential matchmaking among eligible young people. They would plot happily, and a family outing or a picnic would be arranged. The two young people would be left alone—but within sight—to get to know each other. Sometimes the little push worked, sometimes not. Either way there would be something new to discuss at the next *istiqbal*, away from the ears of prying males.

. . .

BY 1936 JULIA and David Chelouche no longer lived in Tel Aviv. They had moved to Haifa in 1930 after a sharp reversal in the family fortunes. During the 1920s Julia's father-in-law, Avraham Haim, and his brother Yosef Eliyahu had overstretched themselves. Taxes were high on their land holdings, the banks were increasing their pressure and the land market collapsed. The brothers were forced to sell substantial areas for a fraction of their worth. Two years later the market jumped back up by 600 or 700 per cent, but by then it was too late. In 1925 Avraham Haim died. David's brothers, Marco and Zaki, returned from Paris and joined the family construction company, which had helped build Neve Tsedek and Ahuzat Bayit. Some time later the firm was closed down, and David and his brothers and cousins were sent to make their own way in the world. David found a job in Haifa, at a flour mill owned by the Rothschilds. Marco opened an estate agency, and Zaki practised as an architect, building blocks of flats in the International Style, otherwise known as Bauhaus. Haifa was just up the coast, only a couple of hours away. But like the Chelouche women in the 1880s who did not want to leave Jaffa for Neve Tsedek, Julia wanted to stay among her family and friends. Saying goodbye to Tel Aviv was heart-rending, she wrote in her memoir: 'I found it difficult to leave family and friends and move to Haifa. I remember the day we left, we stood on the steps and tears streamed from my eyes. My mother in law said to me, "Come and visit us at every opportunity. And on holidays we will all celebrate here."'

Like Jaffa, Haifa was a beautiful city overlooking the sea. Julia and David rented a large flat owned by a Muslim, Hasan Dik. It had nine rooms and two balconies, one overlooking the port and the other Mount Carmel. There was a historic family link to Haifa. It was here

that David's great-grandfather Avraham Chelouche had first arrived
in 1838. Julia and David contributed four children, a further generation, to the dynasty: a son, Aharon, and three daughters, Edith, Rina
and Haya. Aharon, Edith and Rina enrolled at Haifa's Reali School,
one of the most prestigious in all of Palestine, but Haya had reacted
badly to a smallpox vaccination and did not go to school. Eventually
Julia sent her to a children's home in Beirut.

With the borders with Lebanon and Syria open, it was easy to
travel to the neighbouring Arab states. Each summer Julia, her children and other relatives would decamp to the mountains in Lebanon,
where the air was cooler, staying in a different village or small town
each year. David would travel up each weekend from Haifa, a journey
of about three hours, one that cannot now be made. Palestine was
then still part of the Levant. Jaffa's Nagib Bustros Street was crowded
with shoppers from Cairo, Beirut, even Baghdad. Despite the violence
and tension between Jews and Arabs, the old Sephardic families were
still close to their friends among the Arab *a'yan*. Julia, David and their
relatives were friends with the Arab elite families, such as the Rocks,
and a man called Ali Mustakim who would, after 1948, reappear in
the Chelouche family history. One year Julia and David went to a New
Year's ball at the Rock home, in Ajami. 'At midnight they turned off
the lights, then lit them again and wished "Happy New Year" to
everyone. The table was set with all sorts of wonderful foods, the
liquor flowed and we danced until very late,' she wrote.

'We lived in the Middle East, and we were part of the Middle East,'
recalls Julia's daughter Edith Krygier, who was born in 1925. Edith
now lives in a stylish, elegant house north of Tel Aviv and is proud of
her family name and its rich history. 'I remember my grandfather
Avraham Haim and his friends talking about their good Arab friends

in Jaffa. They had a real relationship with them. They would be invited to their homes, and they would invite them back. It was easy for us to make friends with the Arabs, since we spoke their language and were familiar with their culture and customs. The Arabs were not tolerant towards people from other cultures. I was raised learning this from my mother instinctively.' When Edith and Rina were a little older, Julia and David sent them to the American School in Beirut. Those were happy days, she recalls: 'I grew up with children from all over the Middle East—there were girls from the Iraqi royal family and from Egypt. We had wonderful American teachers.'

Yet Edith felt there were some things about the Middle East she would never understand. When her parents' Arab landlord, Hasan Dik, married, the wedding feast lasted for a week. 'They fed the poor Arab people from the back of our house. They were lining up for lamb, rice, fruit and vegetables. Then one day after the wedding Dik decided to deepen the well for his houses. They started digging, and we heard screams. They had lowered a worker down, but he had died because of the poisonous gases inside the well. Hasan Dik knew he died but still ordered his workers to continue digging, so they lowered another one. He died, and then another one was lowered. They all died, all in front of my eyes. They did not have any respect for human life. I will never forget this. On the one hand they fed all the poor people with delicious food, on the other they were very cruel.'

Haifa was a train ride away from Jaffa, and Julia and her family returned to Tel Aviv every year to celebrate *Pesach* (Passover), in the spring. Travelling in the 1930s was a stylish affair, recalls Edith. 'My mother and father both had special suits for the journey. She wore a tweed two-piece, while he had a white linen jacket, with a straw hat. There was an African porter at the station, who wore a long white robe. He took the luggage and you never carried a thing. The train was so clean that the window glass was sparkling. The family made a big fuss about Pesach. They made us new dresses and bought us new shoes. It was a big occasion.'

By the 1930s the kind of relationships the Chelouches enjoyed with their Arab friends were increasingly rare. The leadership of the *Yishuv* was dominated by Ashkenazi Jews from central and eastern Europe. Most could not speak Arabic, did not understand Arab culture or customs and had little or no interest in trying to do so. Many were ardent socialists and distrusted businessmen such as the Chelouches. Instead the Ashkenazi elite preferred to work through their own agencies and ignored the decades-old, carefully nurtured relationships between the Sephardic families and the Arab landowners. Sephardic grandees such as Yosef Eliyahu Chelouche did their best to mediate between the Arabs of Jaffa and the Jews of Tel Aviv. But Chelouche despaired at the insular attitudes of the Jewish immigrants, who seemed not to understand that they were no longer in Europe but were living in the Middle East. The *Yishuv* had been established, he wrote in his autobiography, taking every factor into consideration except one: the Arabs who already lived in Palestine. 'The bitter and terrible truth is that our leaders and many of the founders of the *Yishuv* did not understand the high value of good relations between neighbours. . . . During this period of building our country, we knew nothing about Arab customs, habits, manners, tribes and social trends, their economic and cultural situation and more. In all the Zionist literature there is not even one book that would describe these people's lives accurately or contain genuine information about their situation.'

The Chelouches' business experience and foresight brought them great respect and influence among both peoples. With tact and cau-

tion it would be possible to create a relationship of mutual understanding between Jews and Arabs, wrote Yosef Eliyahu. He was a
revered and respected figure in Palestine, but in later years few among
the *Yishuv* leadership acted on his advice about relations with the
Palestinians. Yosef Eliyahu died in July 1934, just three months after
his beloved wife, Freha. Mourned by his family and his multitude of
friends of all faiths, he was remembered as someone whose life was a
testimony to the possibility of co-existence between Arabs and Jews.
His words still ring true today: 'We have to build a bridge between us
and them.'

MEANWHILE JULIA CHELOUCHE had a new brother-in-law:
an Ashkenazi Jew called Yosef Pomrock, who had married her husband David's sister, Simha. Yosef, a graduate of Warsaw University
and a qualified dentist, had arrived in Palestine in 1921, at the age of
twenty-seven. He had been despatched by his parents to find his
meshugga (crazy) Zionist brother Moshe and take him back to his
hometown of Radom, 100 kilometres south of Warsaw. Moshe was
living in a tent somewhere near Haifa, working with a road-building
group, and he had contracted malaria.

The story of Yosef's mission has entered Chelouche family folklore. Once he arrived in Palestine, he headed straight for Haifa to find
his brother. He took an Arab bus, which dropped him off near a hill.
Yosef trudged up the road until he reached the camp, where he asked
about his brother. 'Moshe is in his tent today, as he does not feel well,'
one of the workers said.

In fact Moshe had begun to feel a little better. He went to the flap
of his tent to take some air, which he hoped might revive him. As he
stood at the tent's opening, he saw in the distance a man coming

towards him, dressed in a suit, holding a dentist's bag. The man looked exactly like his brother Yosef. Moshe shook his head. The man continued to walk towards him. 'I must be very sick,' Moshe told himself. 'I am hallucinating about my brother.' He went back into his tent and took to his bed. When he woke up his brother was beside him, not a hallucination at all. They embraced, and Yosef explained his mission. Moshe nodded. 'It's true, I do have malaria. But at least let's stay here tonight. You can see how we live. We have a campfire, we bake eggs and potatoes, we sing songs. And then tomorrow we can decide what to do.'

Yosef nodded. Why not—what difference could one night make? And he had come a long way. He took off his jacket and made himself comfortable. Later that day, when dusk fell, the workers came back to camp. Young, sun-bronzed, lively and enthusiastic, they were an attractive group, especially the women. They were not like Warsaw girls. They wore shorts. They looked Yosef up and down with frank and confident interest.

Moshe addressed the group as they prepared the evening meal. 'This is my brother, Yosef. He has come to take me home to Poland,' he proclaimed, with a particular tone in his voice. The group understood what he meant and nodded. The camp was especially enjoyable that evening. The fire burned brighter; the food was more plentiful than usual; the Hebrew songs were sung with greater gusto. The young pioneers explained how they were building a new world by hand, a home for the Jews, where they no longer need be afraid or at the mercy of kings and prime ministers. A world where nobody would persecute them because of their faith. They sacrificed much, it was true. There were no cafés or cinemas up here on the hill. They lived in tents. There were wolves, malaria, the risk of attack by Arabs. But there was no other life like this.

Yosef watched and listened, nodding thoughtfully. The next morning he went to the nearest post office and sent a telegram home to Radom: Moshe is not coming back and I am staying. And he did, some time afterwards meeting and marrying Simha Chelouche, sister of David. Yosef Pomrock, the Ashkenazi dentist from Warsaw, 'straight as a cedar tree' as Julia Chelouche described him in her memoir, was made welcome by the Chelouches. He in turn was entranced by their Mediterranean warmth and the spicy, exotic food they prepared, quite unlike anything he had ever eaten in Poland. Yosef and Simha lived in a house that Avraham Haim and Yosef Eliyahu Chelouche had built for their daughters on Herzl Street, one of Tel Aviv's oldest thoroughfares. Yosef and Simha had a daughter, Anina, and a son, Zvi Avraham. The Sephardim and the Ashkenazim were finally intermarrying, and out of the two communities would come a new nation: Israel.

5

Palestine Beckons

1930s

When Jaffa falls into hell I will not be among the mourners.
The diary of David Ben-Gurion, 11 July 1936[1]

asan Hammami was playing happily with his new toys at home in Jebaliyyeh. His favourite was a white rocking horse with a black tail and a splendid red, white and black saddle. The horse was one of several fine gifts he had received lately. He was surprised that his parents had given him so many presents at once, seemingly out of the blue. Then everything suddenly became clear. Hasan spotted a man walking up the street carrying a small case. Every small boy was terrified of him. 'As you can imagine, we were aware of the man carrying a small case, with his name and profession artistically painted on it. My brother Hussein and I smelled blood and ran to hide in the corner of the veranda,' recalls Hasan. It was 1937 and Hasan was five years old, Hussein three. The man with the case was the *mtahher*, the ritual circumciser.

Unlike Jews, who circumcise their sons after eight days, Muslims do not have a set time for the ceremony. Some families arrange it soon after birth, while others leave it until the boy reaches his teens, when, like a Jewish bar-mitzvah, the ceremony is a (rather more painful) rite of passage into adulthood. The ceremonies are virtually identical, although the Jewish blessings are in Hebrew and the Muslim ones in Arabic. The boy is dressed in a white silk or cotton gown. The flap of skin that is removed is buried in the garden, as both faiths hold that body parts should be properly interred. The family and friends then celebrate with a festive meal.

'Hiding did not help and they soon found us,' says Hasan, who, like his father, Ahmad, and grandfather Shaker before him, exudes the old-world elegance and charm of the Palestinian middle class. Hasan now lives in Florida with his English wife, Barbara, but his rich store of memories of life in Jaffa has helped sustain him through the decades of exile. 'The act did not take long. The *mtahher* was an artist. The whole thing was over in a minute. He made sure that there was no bleeding, sprayed on some antiseptic powder and wrapped our penises in white gauze. He left before we'd realised what had happened.' After the operation, Hasan and Hussein changed their usual clothes for a traditional white *jellabiyeh* (robe) without underpants, to prevent any chafing. Within a week or two everything had healed up.

Hasan's father, Ahmad, kept Muslim traditions and prayed regularly. There was no alcohol in the Hammami house, and he gave *zakat*—the charitable donations that are incumbent on Muslims—generously. Ahmad often took Hasan to Jaffa's mosque overlooking the beach, known as the Jami'a al-Bahr, the Mosque of the Sea. It was smaller and more intimate than Abu Nabout's nearby Great Mosque. There was something very special about praying while the waves washed over the beach nearby and the sea breeze blew in, cooling the

prayer hall. 'It was cool in the summer and warm in the winter,' says
Hasan. Ahmad was also a modern man. He and his brothers wore western suits and ties, although sometimes they donned a tarboosh. 'Whenever new technology was launched, my father was the head of the wave.
He bought one of the first deep-well water pumps, an HMV radio and
record player, a telephone exchange that could link a dozen branch lines
for his business and the latest model of car,' says Hasan. 'He had a balanced view of family, business, sports, innovation, modernisation and
community. He had clear ideas about the future and was a strict disci-
plinarian, to ensure especially that we boys did not stray too far. He
worked hard to provide for us, and rarely showed love in the modern
manner of hugging and kissing, but gave it without limit in his care for
us, the time he gave us and everything that he knew.'

Ahmad Hammami was very keen on cars. Shortly before the Second World War broke out, he bought a navy-blue Mercedes with
jump seats, and hired a driver. One day Ahmad took Hasan with him
and briefly left him alone in the car, which still had keys in the ignition. A little knowledge proved to be a dangerous thing. 'I had my first
driving and accident all at once, when I was six years old. I had been
observing what the driver did. I turned the ignition key, pressed the
starter button, and lo and behold, the car started in gear and moved
slowly forward. I began to panic because I had no idea what to do
next. The wall solved the problem, as the car ran into it. But luckily no
harm was done. I did not try this again for a long time.'

Hasan was always an adventurous boy. Once he climbed on the
gardener's horse, which was fun until his cousin Ihsan poked a stick
into the horse's rear. 'It galloped off until it almost ran into the number five bus, and then stopped suddenly. I slid over its neck and
scraped my nose and cheek, which both bled profusely.'

For the children of Jebaliyyeh and neighbouring Ajami, these were idyllic days of playing happily, of swimming and picnics on the beach. Hasan and his brothers swam in a small cove, just a couple of hundred yards from the house, although his sisters were not allowed to go to the beach. 'I learnt to swim at an early age. My father encouraged us to practise, and when he was confident I was ready, he took me out about two hundred yards into the sea on a *hasakeh*, a flat-topped canoe, and tipped me over. The panic I felt in the deep water did not last long. I found I really could swim, not just stay afloat in the water, and I swam back to shore.'

The Andraus house was not far from the Hammamis' home, although Amin and Hanneh told their children not to play with the Hammami boys, who were judged too naughty. Still, Hasan had plenty of playmates. Apart from his own brothers and sisters, there were his many cousins, the children of Ahmad's brothers Mohammad and Adel. The brothers' houses were all built on the same plot of land, surrounded by a walled garden full of flowers and fruit trees. The children even had their own small patch of land which they kept free of weeds, and they grew their own flowers. Hasan's younger sister Fadwa carefully tended a pink rosebush. Every day the ice-man came to deliver the frozen block for the Hammamis' refrigerator, causing great excitement among the children. He arrived on his donkey cart, with great slabs of ice strapped inside, and broke off a large piece. The boys ran after the donkey, picking up the ice chips that were always left behind. In the orange season, the children helped to soak the branches of the pomegranate tree in the pool. Once they were softened by the water, they were woven into boxes to pack oranges.

There was sadness too. The family patriarch, Shaker Hammami, died in his seventies. Shaker had raised his seven children and sent them all to school. They too had children, and he had lived to see a houseful of grandchildren. The cycle of the generations continued, but the Hammamis would always be part of Jaffa, he believed, and that was how it should be. After Shaker died, his sons set up two tents by their houses. Several lambs were prepared and cooked, and a banquet was laid out. 'The place was full of people from all walks of life, many of whom I had never seen before. The atmosphere was not sombre, but reflected a quiet celebration of his memory,' recalls Hasan. Shaker Hammami was laid to rest in a white marble grave, next to his wife, Umm Shaker, in the Muslim cemetery overlooking the sea.

WHEN THE ARAB Revolt began in 1936, Shlomo Chelouche was twenty years old and studying law at London University. He monitored the news from Palestine with growing concern. The riots and violence were getting worse and worse. He was torn between his new home and that of his family. Shlomo loved London, and many of his friends from Tel Aviv and Jerusalem were also studying there. He was an engaging young man, and like his cousin Zaki in Paris, Shlomo did not lack for female company. He was always a popular guest among the Jewish families, who invited him for meals on the Sabbath and Jewish holidays.

Shlomo lived in a bed-and-breakfast by Marble Arch in the heart of London's West End. He went running in Hyde Park and on Sunday spoke at Speakers' Corner, then, as now, a verbal battleground between Zionists and Palestinians. 'The Arabs talked about Palestine, how we were nasty to them, made life difficult and made them suffer. They proclaimed that everything the Jews said about them was untrue. I listened to this, but I couldn't stand it. This was their answer to everything that the Arabs were doing to the Jews.' Eventually, as the violence worsened, Shlomo knew he would have to go home. He explained his plans to his parents, Yaakov and Pearla. They were horrified. 'I decided to go back on the spur of the moment. I was fed up. It was against their will and they did not give me permission. They told me, "We have given you the best opportunity to better yourself, for a good education, and now you want to throw it all away. Finish your studies," they pleaded, "and then do what you must."'

But Shlomo's mind was made up. Beneath the jovial exterior, he was a passionate Zionist. Shlomo had joined the Haganah, the Zionist underground military movement, when he was twelve. Then he was a runner between different units, smuggling notes and orders. As a teenage schoolboy he had trained in the use of weapons and studied basic military techniques. If there was going to be a war between the Jews and the Arabs, he would do his duty. Shlomo left London and returned to Palestine. His older brother Gabriel found him a day job as a tax collector in Netanya, a settlement on the coast to the north of Tel Aviv. In the evenings and at weekends Shlomo continued his training.

The Arab attacks were increasingly ferocious. In September 1937 nineteen people were killed in a raid on the Jewish quarter of Tiberias, eleven of the victims children. The massacres presented Ben-Gurion, the de facto leader of the *Yishuv*, with a dilemma. The Haganah was now working with the British, and if it responded with equal force it would be condemned. The Zionists would lose both their moral authority and the support of the British administration. But neither could they do nothing while Jews were dying. Perhaps the answer lay with the hardline Revisionist Zionists. The Revisionists' leader was Vladimir Jabotinsky, a former Russian journalist and an old rival of Ben-Gurion. Ben-Gurion was more inclined to compromise with the

Arabs, but Jabotinsky stood for confrontation. Jabotinsky had split off from the mainstream Zionist movement in 1925, in protest at its more moderate policies. The Revisionists demanded the rapid establish-ment of a Jewish state on both banks of the Jordan, with a Jewish majority and a Jewish army, to be achieved by a campaign of relentless political pressure on Britain. By 1937 the Revisionists had their own military wing, called the Irgun Zvai Leumi, the National Military Organisation. The Irgun rejected the Haganah's policy of restraint towards the Arabs and believed in pre-emptive strikes. Irgun fighters threw bombs and grenades into crowded Arab shops and markets. They hid by the road and opened fire on Arab vehicles. The Irgun soon had its own martyr when one of its members was hanged for shooting at an Arab bus. The Irgun then carried out the operations the Haganah could not. Many in the Haganah were appalled by their acts and fist-fights broke out between the two sides, but other Haganah members silently applauded. Eventually Ben-Gurion set up a Haganah Special Operations Unit. It too carried out revenge attacks against the Arabs. Innocent civilians were killed in these operations, and Jewish inform-ers and traitors were violently interrogated. The making of a state, both Zionists and Arabs learnt, was a brutal and bloody business.

Arab nationalists circulated leaflets in a 'hearts and minds' cam-paign to win over the British soldiers, calling on them not to sacrifice their lives for Jewish interests. 'Politicians cheaply sell your blood for Jewish money, thus depriving mothers and wives from their children and husbands, without attaining anything to England or to them-selves,' one leaflet proclaimed.[2] The soldiers on patrol, and a good proportion of their officers, may have sympathised, but much of the Mandate political leadership was firmly pro-Zionist. Britain declared martial law and introduced a severe security regime. The Arab Higher

Committee was disbanded, all political parties were banned and several Palestinian leaders were deported to the Seychelles. 'Palestine has become a prison and a detention center,' proclaimed one headline in *Falastin*. The mufti of Jerusalem fled to Beirut. British officers revived the old Turkish practice of *bastinado*, beating the soles of the feet. Arab suspects also had water forced down their noses or were made to stand under icy showers. Thousand of Arabs were held in detention, in camps with harsh regimes. Sometimes prisoners died after being forced to sit in the hot sun for hours without water. British troops raided villages and rounded up the men before laying waste to their houses and humiliating the women. Homes were wrecked, winter food supplies destroyed, furniture smashed.

In 1938 tragedy struck the Chelouche family. Gabriel Chelouche was killed on the road to Jerusalem. He was travelling by taxi when Arab gunmen opened fire on the vehicle from an olive grove. The car was hit and Gabriel was shot dead. Both Arab and Jewish papers carried obituaries, mourning the loss of a talented young man, an engineer and a gifted violinist. Shlomo, his parents and his sisters were devastated. Jaffa's Arab dignitaries came to pay their respects to the family, as custom demanded. When the mourning period was over, Gabriel's room in the family house on Rothschild Boulevard was leased to the Haganah's military intelligence department. They were made welcome, and each day Pearla brought them tea and cakes. There were no more camel caravans from Hajj Ibrahim Samarra, and the two families lost contact.

THE VIOLENCE BRUTALISED all three sides, Arab, British and Jewish. One evening Amin Andraus was working late in his office at the car showroom near the German colony when he looked out of the window. 'He saw a prisoner with his hands handcuffed behind his back, being led by a British policeman. Then the policeman shot the prisoner dead,' recalls Amin's daughter Suad, who still lives in Amin's house together with her sisters, Wedad and Leila. 'The news reports the next morning said a prisoner was shot trying to escape. But being the man he was, my father went to the police to report what he saw. He said that the prisoner was not trying to escape, he had been hand-cuffed, and then he was shot from the back, and he had seen it happen.'

There was no common ground between the Jews and the Arabs, and it became increasingly clear to the British that the Mandate was unworkable. The Peel Commission, set up after the 1936 unrest, pro-posed that Jewish immigration be frozen at 12,000 per year for five years. Palestine would be divided into three zones: an Arab state, a Jewish state and a neutral territory which would stretch from Jaffa to Jerusalem. Most Palestinians rejected the plan. A minority were pre-pared to accept, but backed down under pressure from the mufti of Jerusalem. The Zionists were divided: Britain was now conceding the inevitability of a Jewish state, but the area offered to the Jews was so very small. Buried in the small print of the Peel Commission report was an ominous principle. Several thousand Arabs living in the Jew-ish area would be 'transferred' to the Arab one. If necessary, the trans-fer would be compulsory. The Peel Commission cited the population exchanges between Greece and Turkey in 1923. It was an ill-omened comparison—there, hundreds of thousands of people had been forced to uproot from the homes where their families had lived for centuries, in scenes of great chaos and brutality.

Eventually the Zionists decided to reject the Peel Commission's proposed borders for the Jewish area but agreed to partition. The Woodhead Commission was then despatched to Palestine to work out the practicalities of the Peel Commission's proposals. It concluded that they were unworkable and instead proposed two new sets of boundaries for the two statelets known as Plan B and Plan C, both of which reduced the Jewish area. Events descended into farce. Some members of the Woodhead Commission favoured Plan B, others Plan C. Partition, the British government eventually decided, was impracticable. Meanwhile, the fighting continued.

In Jaffa the British authorities launched an investigation into the death of the prisoner Amin Andraus had seen executed. Some time afterwards, friends of Amin were having a drink at Spinney's, a bar near Jaffa's Clock Tower. 'They overheard some British police plotting to kill my father, so that he would not be able to testify about what he had seen,' says Suad. 'They warned him to leave immediately. He packed his things and took his family to the Lebanon, where they stayed for about a year. When the investigation came to court, my father was the only witness. He came back under protection, in the archbishop of Jerusalem's car.' Amin's moral integrity was vindicated: the policemen were convicted and sentenced.

LIKE SHLOMO CHELOUCHE, Yaakov Yosefov avidly followed the news from Palestine. Yaakov was born in 1924 and lived in the small town of Pazardjik, in southern Bulgaria. The Yosefov family, like most Bulgarian Jews, were Sephardim. In contrast to the grand Sephardic families like the Chelouches, most were artisans, tradesmen and manual workers. They spoke Bulgarian and Ladino, the medieval Judeo-Spanish dialect that their ancestors had brought from Spain. The Yosefov family were richer than most and lived a comfortable, middle-class life. Yaakov's father, Shabat, co-owned a factory that processed paprika and tobacco. Three generations of the

Yosefovs lived in one large house with a maid, but there was no electricity or running water.

Shabat employed five hundred workers and owned several warehouses. He was a well-known figure in the countryside around Pazardjik, jovial and friendly but with a sharp eye for the right price. Shabat had a Bulgarian business partner, with whom he developed the paprika business, and all the villages around Pazardjik grew peppers for the company. The villagers brought their crop to Shabat's factory, where the peppers were dried out, de-seeded and ground up. Shabat's factory processed one hundred tons of paprika a year and exported it across Europe. The tobacco was harvested in the summer, left to dry for several months and then sold in the winter.

Partly because of its Ottoman legacy, there was little anti-Semitism in Bulgaria before the 1930s. Like Turkey, the country was a mosaic of different ethnic minorities and religions. Bulgaria's constitution guaranteed political equality. The Jewish community, about 50,000 strong, mostly lived in peace. The several hundred Jews in Pazardjik, like almost all their co-religionists, were strongly Zionist. Ben-Gurion and Vladimir Jabotinsky both visited Bulgaria; Shabat had kept a paper napkin signed by Ben-Gurion. Like his sons, Shabat was an ardent Zionist. Young pioneers learnt agriculture on his holdings before going to Palestine. Shabat also took practical steps towards future immigration: he went to Palestine as a tourist in 1933 and bought some land near Latrun, in the centre of the country.

There were a dozen Zionist organisations in Bulgaria, for youth and women, for sport and philanthropic activities. The Zionists were split between Ben-Gurion's labour movement and other leftist groups, and Jabotinsky's Revisionists, whose youth movement was called Betar.[3] Yaakov was a member of Maccabee, the labour Zionist youth group. He spent all his free time there with his friends. The Zionists organised summer camps and social and political events in the evenings. Once a year they organised the Day of the Shekel, when supporters donated money and the young people paraded down the street. Long before CNN and the Internet, news travelled quickly from Tel Aviv to Pazardjik and the Yosefov household. 'My brother Yosef was in Betar, but I was in Maccabee. There were many discussions in our family when we heard what was happening in Israel in 1936,' says Yaakov, who now lives north of Tel Aviv with his wife, Rina. White-haired and still trim, Yaakov has a steady gaze. A man who is used to having to stand by what he says, he weighs his words carefully before he speaks. 'My brother said that Chaim Weitzman was a traitor, that the left was soft. They just believed in defence when the Arabs attacked. They did not take the initiative, but only reacted. Betar was more active. They said we should take the fight to the Arabs.'

Yaakov left Maccabee and joined Betar. In Pazardjik, too, Betar prepared to strike back. By the late 1930s the far-right groups in Bulgaria had grown in strength and confidence; pro-Nazi newspapers poured out anti-Semitic propaganda. As the violence worsened, Yaakov and his friends fought back. When the fascists got a Jewish boy on his own and badly beat him up, Yaakov and his friends took an equivalent revenge. But as the tension rose, Yaakov could not concentrate at school and his grades deteriorated. The fascists threw stones at his father's house and broke the windows of the Jewish club in Pazardjik. If Yaakov had any doubts, a visit with his classmates to a Bulgarian military camp made his mind up for him. 'There was an officer lecturing on the machine gun in front of him. He told us that the Bulgarians have two historical enemies, the Turks and the Greeks. "If you are at the front and you see a Turk, then shoot him in the stomach," he said. "If you see a Greek, then shoot him in the head. But if you see a Jew, then don't waste your bullets, and kill him with your knife." I felt angry, and ashamed.' Yaakov went home and told his father that he was leaving for Palestine.

6

Days of Hunger

Early 1940s

*We shall fight the war against Hitler as if there was no White
Paper, and we shall fight the White Paper as if
there was no war.*

*David Ben-Gurion on the 1939 British White Paper,
which limited Jewish immigration to Palestine to
75,000 over the next five years*

L
ike Fakhri Geday before him, Hasan Hammami was a pupil at
St Joseph's College. The curriculum was as rigorous as ever,
with nine-hour days, and French was the only language permitted. 'We had to speak French even during the breaks and when we
were playing, or the monks would give us the "mark", meaning the
blackboard eraser. We had to hand the mark to the friar at the start of
the next class, and take our punishment. It was usually a smack on
the palm of our hand, with the flat side of a ruler,' says Hasan. Regular miscreants were more seriously chastised. 'Frère Kotska meted out
the strongest discipline, with a thin reed, usually on the side of the
legs or on the buttocks. This happened in public, in the classroom.
That was a rare event, and the threat of the pain and humiliation was
enough to prevent us straying.'

Hasan was growing into a confident boy and was developing a

taste for public appearances. He starred in a school play, where he played a child prince of the Abbasid dynasty, which ruled the Muslim caliphate until the thirteenth century. Hasan's character was to be executed after a palace coup. His key line of dialogue was a moment of high drama: 'Shall I die without seeing my mother?' he thundered. 'It was more poetic than gory,' he says. 'My parents came to the first night at the school auditorium. They must have been proud—they were dressed up to the nines.'

But darker currents were running through Jaffa. The Muslim Brotherhood, an Islamic political movement, had arrived. The Brotherhood, founded in Egypt in 1928, called for a return to a pure Islamic life, based on its strict interpretation of the Quran and the *hadith*, the sayings of Muhammad. By the late 1930s and early 1940s it was active throughout north Africa, Syria and Palestine. Jaffa's educated, moderate Muslims like the Hammamis were strongly opposed to the Brotherhood. In those times, the personal became intensely political. 'It was an important occasion when my mother came to the school play without her head or face being covered. I realised later what a stand my parents, like other enlightened families in Jaffa, were taking,' says Hasan. 'The Brotherhood toughs had thrown dirty water over women shopping in the market without their heads covered, and once even battery acid, to try and scare them into submission. The educated men in Jaffa decided this must stop. They took a variety of steps, including going to the market with their wives and making public statements. The Brotherhood did not get much support.'

With the end of the Arab Revolt in 1939, Palestine settled down to a period of relative peace. The uprising had been quashed by the British and the Haganah, considerably aided by the factional infighting that bedevilled Palestinian politics. But the Zionists were not rewarded. After the failure of the Peel and Woodhead Commissions, Jewish and Arab leaders were summoned to London for the St James Conference. It was doomed from the start. The Arabs refused to talk directly to the Jews. The British hosts negotiated with each side separately. The discussions led nowhere. The British issued the 1939 White Paper, which stated that Jewish immigration to Palestine would be limited to 75,000 permits over the next five years. Any subsequent increases would require the permission of the Arabs, but it was highly unlikely that this would be granted. The White Paper also stated that it was not British policy that Palestine should become a Jewish state. Rather, within ten years an independent Palestinian state should be established in which Jews and Arabs would share government.

The White Paper was certainly in breach of the spirit of the Mandate, if not the letter. But with the outbreak of war, Britain believed it could not afford to alienate the Arabs. Palestine was the gateway to Syria and Iraq, and these were of vital strategic importance. The short-lived British love affair with Zionism faded, and the Foreign Office grandees returned to their old love: 'If we must offend one side, let us offend the Jews rather than the Arabs,' said Neville Chamberlain.[1] The Zionists were outraged. 'Satan himself could not have created a more distressing and horrible nightmare,' wrote Ben-Gurion. Nevertheless they believed they had no choice but to stay allied with the British. The Jewish Agency gave the British authorities a list of 134,000 men who wanted to fight in the Allied armies—one out of every two men of military age—and 20,000 women. The struggle for statehood continued: the Agency launched Aliyah Bet, a clandestine international rescue operation to bring Jews from Europe to Palestine.

. . .

IN THE BALTIC PORT of Danzig, far from Jaffa, Zionism and Palestine all seemed very remote to the twelve-year-old schoolboy Frank Meisler. Danzig was a medieval Hanseatic port, a free city-state carved out of Prussia's coast after the First World War. Like Jaffa, Danzig had once been captured by Napoleon—some of Frank's ancestors had served guard duty on the city walls—and was now ruled under a mandate from the League of Nations. And like the Jews of Jaffa, those of Danzig were also divided by language and culture. The German speakers came from old and established families and regarded their Polish co-religionists as uncultured *Ostjuden*, eastern Jews, or even 'Black Jews'. Most of the German Jews were not very observant and were opposed to Zionism. The Polish Jews were much more religious and strongly Zionist.

Frank's parents were a mix of both. His mother, Meta Boss, was a German speaker descended from Sephardim. In later years, an ancestral memory of the Mediterranean and a love of light and sunshine would help steer Frank to Jaffa. Meta's father, Franz, was a rich landowner and horse-dealer who drove a silver Mercedes and sent his daughters to finishing schools in Switzerland. As the Polish Jews poured into Danzig, Franz Boss was often asked to contribute to their well-being. 'Give them double what they ask—that way they will go further,' he proclaimed. Misha Meisler, Frank's father, had arrived in Danzig in the 1920s from Warsaw. Like David Chelouche, Misha had initially enrolled in medical school. He too had fainted every time a corpse was cut open. Misha switched to economics, but his real passion was the tango. One day he saw Meta Boss at the glamorous Casino Hotel, in the Baltic resort of Sopot. He asked her to dance. A year later he asked for her hand, a brave act, considering he was a Polish *Ostjude*. Franz Boss hired private detectives to probe his background. Misha was approved, and the newlyweds went on honeymoon to Vienna, Budapest and Istanbul. Somewhere along the way Frank was conceived.

In 1933 the Nazis won Danzig's municipal elections. Danzig's special status and League of Nations mandate initially gave the Jews some protection. But the moderate façade soon slipped. Jews were removed from public office and professional associations, and some were attacked and beaten in the street. Frank was expelled from his German primary school, so he learnt Polish and enrolled in a Polish secondary school. 'The anti-Semitism there was awful, all-pervasive. They called you a "dirty Jew" or a "perfidious Jew". Nazism was imposed on the Germans, but with the Poles you didn't have to bother with encouraging anti-Semitism. Whatever happened, it was all the Jews' fault,' says Frank, who now lives in Tel Aviv. After a decades-long career as one of Israel's most famous sculptors, he still oversees operations at his studio and foundry in Old Jaffa. The Danzig where Frank grew up no longer exists, but the sharp wit and dry sense of humour that every port city seems to breed live on: 'Actually I always got good marks in school, even though I was Jewish. This may have been because I once caught the teacher kissing a schoolboy.'

In 1935 Frank's father, Misha, and his uncle Fimek fled Danzig, after being tipped off by a friendly Nazi that they were about to be arrested, and they settled in Warsaw. Frank and his mother visited Misha, but she refused to move to Poland. In Danzig Frank joined a youth group called the *Jung-Jüdischer Bund*, the Young Jewish Union. The JJB was not a Zionist group but a middle-of-the-road social and educational organisation. 'Usually there was no talk of Palestine or Zionism. The only time I heard it mentioned was when a friend of my mother's family came to lecture on her experiences there. I heard about sun and beaches and that you float in the Dead Sea,' says Frank. 'My father and his brother once announced in their youth that they were going to Palestine and my grandmother became hysterical. We had some political consciousness because we once hid a young man trying to get to the Soviet Union, who had been in a Nazi camp.'

The JJB were aware enough to strongly dislike the Danzig branch of Betar: 'They were supposed to be our sworn enemies. There was an innate hostility in our club towards Betar. They modelled themselves on the Italian fascists, but to me their uniform was closer to the Nazi one.' The leader of the Revisionists was a man called Hermann Segal, known to the Danzig Jews as 'Lord Almighty'. Segal had murky relations with several high-ranking Nazi officials. When a wealthy Jew was imprisoned, Segal acted as the middleman, somehow facilitating his release by using the jailed man's Swiss bank accounts. Not everyone liked Hermann Segal. But he would help save Frank's life.

By the summer of 1939, as war approached, the Zionist *Ostjuden* and the liberal German speakers had finally ended their squabbling. News came that Britain was accepting Jewish children as refugees. Segal negotiated the sale of a collection of Judaica which had been willed to Danzig's synagogue by Lesser Gielinski, one of Frank's relatives. The collection was purchased by the Jewish Theological Seminary in New York. As Danzig's Jewish community collapsed, the Nazis offered a pittance for the land on which the synagogue stood. It was accepted. Both sets of funds were used to finance the *Kindertransport* to England and to pay for several ships crammed with illegal Jewish immigrants that made their way to Palestine. Everything then happened very quickly. Misha Meisler sent some money to London, where his wife had relatives. Frank went to Warsaw to see his father and have a set of clothes made. His uncle Fimek designed him a blazer, blue with yellow stripes. Frank returned to Danzig and received a British visa.

One sunny afternoon in August 1939, Frank went to the bus station in Danzig, accompanied by his mother and cousin Erich, to start his journey to London. He joined fifteen other Jewish boys and girls, two Jewish officials, and a Gestapo officer wearing knickerbockers, who shook hands with all the children and sat down with them on the bus. 'There was not much drama, or crying and weeping. As children you don't see it as a drama, it's only in retrospect. It was a bit like going on holiday, a strange kind of holiday. Children perceive some events more deeply and others in a more shallow way.' Frank watched from the window as the bus pulled out. 'I waved at my mother and Erich. I watched them become smaller and smaller until they disappeared from view.'

The bus crossed the Polish corridor, and the children then boarded a train for Berlin, where the Nazis were testing air-raid sirens. From Berlin the *Kindertransport* went by train to the Hook of Holland. The Gestapo officer left the party at the Dutch border, wishing the children a *'gute Reise'*, a pleasant journey. Frank arrived safely in London. There the British, like the Nazis, were testing air-raid sirens. A few letters came from Danzig, then nothing. Misha and Meta Meisler were reunited in the Warsaw Ghetto and deported to Auschwitz. Frank Meisler never saw his parents again.

IN JANUARY 1941 the Bulgarian government implemented racial laws against the Jews which were modelled on Nazi Germany's Nuremberg laws. But Yaakov Yosefov would never wear a yellow star. He left Pazardjik for the Bulgarian port of Varna, on the Black Sea.

Varna was the departure point for Palestine. Ships sailed from there to Istanbul and on to the Mediterranean. The journey was extremely dangerous. Most of the vessels were vastly overloaded and barely sea-worthy. The previous December the Uruguayan-registered SS *Salvador* had left for Palestine with more than 300 refugees on board a ship designed for a few dozen passengers. The ship sank, with the loss of more than 200 lives. When Yaakov arrived in Varna, he found that a Romanian vessel called *Dorian II* had docked, carrying 160 refugees from Poland and Romania, including the survivors of the *Salvador*. A substantial bribe was paid to the Bulgarian officials to let almost 200 Bulgarian Jews on board.

The *Dorian II* set sail for Palestine at the end of February. 'The journey was very difficult. The ship was a wreck. The sanitary conditions were terrible, there was nowhere to sleep and if you found a bunk it was tiny,' he says. 'But I did not care at all about any of that. I was very, very happy. We were all singing songs, and we were going to Palestine.' The following night, on 1 March, as the *Dorian II* stopped at Istanbul, the German army entered Bulgaria. The borders were sealed. The *Dorian II* spent a week in harbour in Istanbul, but its passengers were not allowed to go ashore. 'By the time we got to Istanbul most of the coal and water had already been used up. The Jewish community sent out a small boat with water, and we loaded it on board in buckets.'

Six days later the *Dorian II* set sail again into the Mediterranean. This was the most perilous stage of the journey. At night the ship laid anchor and the crew shone all the lights onto the Panamanian flag, hoping that would protect it from the Allied warships and Nazi submarines that crowded the sea lanes of the Mediterranean. Yaakov and the other passengers spent the night on deck, sharing what little food

there was and singing songs. Conditions on board steadily deteriorated. 'Sometimes there was barely any water and so only the children
received some. Then the crew said we had to hand over all our jewellery and valuables or they would not continue. So we tied them up,
and the Swedish captain and a single engineer kept the ship going. I
was shovelling coal into the boilers. When the fuel oil ran out, we
used cooking oil. When the coal ran out, we burnt packing crates and
furniture.' Still the *Dorian II* chugged its way towards Palestine.

On 25 March the ship approached Haifa. A Royal Navy vessel came
alongside. The Jews on board did not have immigration certificates or
permits. Under the terms of the White Paper they were illegal immigrants. But the *Dorian II* presented the British authorities with a
dilemma. In November 1940 the ageing liner *Patria* had been inter-
cepted by the British. The *Patria* was held at Haifa port with 1,900
refugees on board. The British planned to deport them to detention
camps in Mauritius, where other Jews were being held. The Haganah
sabotaged *Patria*. Its aim was to prevent the Jews' deportation, but the
operation went horribly wrong. The ship sank, and 267 Jews were
killed. In addition, sending the *Dorian II*'s passengers to Mauritius, or
anywhere else, would demand considerable British resources. The
vessel would have to be escorted in a guarded convoy, putting British
seamen's lives at risk.

The *Dorian II* was towed into Haifa port. Two British boats moored
alongside, to thwart any potential rescue or sabotage attempts by the
Haganah. Yaakov, like all the passengers, was exhausted, filthy and
hungry. They had been on board for over a month. Every day a fresh
rumour swept the boat: they would be deported to Cyprus, they would
be imprisoned, they would be sent back to Bulgaria. But on 2 April
1941, Yaakov Yosefov stepped down onto the soil of Palestine. 'It was a

very happy day. We all went through a lot and we were exhausted, but I felt my dream had finally come true.' It was not quite the reception for which he had hoped. Bulgaria was at war with Britain, so Yaakov was an enemy alien. He was washed down with disinfectant, immediately arrested and taken to Mizra prison, near the northern port of Acre.

There Yaakov learnt about the new Stern Group, or Lehi, as it was known in Hebrew. In 1940 the Revisionist Zionists had split after their militia, the Irgun, suspended its struggle against the British until the war's end. A minority faction, led by Avraham Stern, a young, charismatic Polish Jew, vehemently opposed the ceasefire. Lehi declared war on Britain, whom they believed was the greatest obstacle to a Jewish state. Lehi even sent out unsuccessful feelers to the Axis powers, on the old Middle East principle that 'the enemy of my enemy is my friend'. Lehi also had good relations with anti-British Arab extremists, from whom they bought explosives and weapons. Both groups saw themselves as fighters against western imperialism. These apparently arcane schisms on Zionism's right wing would have a profound effect on the development of both the *Yishuv* and the Israeli state—most of all, on Yaakov Yosefov's future life. At Mizra he talked long into the night with Bulgarian Lehi members. He was already a member of Betar, but Betar was no longer radical enough for Yaakov. 'Prison is the best place to learn about these things. Everyone chose the side they wanted to belong to. I chose Lehi.'

After six months Yaakov was transferred to Atlit detention camp, near Haifa. It was a forbidding-looking place, surrounded by razor wire and high fences and patrolled by British soldiers. Men, women and children were housed in spartan army barracks. But they were fed three times a day, and Jewish medical staff, social workers and teachers were allowed in.

When two Jews escaped and morale soared among the prisoners, the camp authorities ordered every barracks searched. They found nothing, but one man was taken away. Yaakov and his comrades marched out to the camp's offices to rescue their friend, a brave but hopeless gesture. The commander demanded that they return to barracks. They refused and stood their ground. Two vans appeared, carrying special police units trained to break up demonstrations. 'We all linked arms and began to sing the Hatikvah, the Zionist anthem,' recalls Yaakov. 'They came at us with wooden staves and beat us. The injured ones were sent to hospital. The rest of us were sent to Acre prison. We were the only Jews there, and our conditions were very bad. It was January and very cold, but there were no blankets, mattresses or showers. Our food was three pitta breads a day.' Twice a day the prisoners were let out to exercise. Rommel was advancing across north Africa, and many in Palestine feared the Nazis would soon take Cairo and break through to Palestine. In the prison yard, the Arab prisoners whispered to Yaakov and his comrades that the Germans were coming soon, and then the Jews would all be done for. Yaakov spent sixty-two days in Acre prison before he was taken back to Atlit.

Many Arabs supported the Nazis, who they believed would defeat the treacherous British and French and finally grant them independence. Hajj Amin al-Husseini, the mufti of Jerusalem (and uncle of Yasser Arafat), greatly admired Hitler. Soon after the outbreak of war he fled, disguised as a woman, to Iraq. There he issued a call for *jihad* against Britain. The subsequent Iraqi uprising was put down with the help of David Raziel, the commander of the Irgun, who was killed in the process. The mufti travelled to Berlin, to meet Hitler and be received as an honoured guest. Hitler was ambiguous about promising an independent Palestine but agreed to set up two Muslim SS divi-

sions in the Balkans, the Bosnian Handzar and the Albanian Skender-
beg divisions. The mufti stayed in Berlin until the end of the war.

Al-Husseini was a divisive, hard-line figure, driven by a visceral
hatred of Jews. But *Falastin*, and many of its readers, took a different
view. Palestinian Arab leaders published a statement declaring their
absolute support for the Allies and calling on the Arab population to
do the same. They also asked the British government to re-assess its
position over Palestine and grant the Arabs their 'natural and political rights in their own country'.[2] But for now, they stated, the under-
standable anger of the Palestinian people should be redirected to
assist the poor and the needy. *Falastin*'s editorials took the same position, using arguments drawn from the Quran to explain that despite
the British oppression of the Palestinian leadership and betrayal of
the Palestinian cause, Arab and Islamic values prevented the Palestinians from supporting the Nazis. Like many Jews, *Falastin* also
attacked the American government for its hypocrisy over Jewish
refugees, in that it decried Nazi persecution but kept the door firmly
shut. The newspaper appointed itself Jaffa's civic voice and conscience. Its articles called on the Mandate authorities to organise civil
defence training, compensate orange-grove owners who had lost
money and also ensure work for Jaffa's labourers.[3]

The war brought great hardship to the Hammami family. Jaffa's citrus industry collapsed, and Ahmad closed down his company. Before
1939 much of the fruit had been exported to Europe, but this was now
impossible. The orange farmers sold a small amount locally, and
some was turned into jam or marmalade. But this amounted to a fraction of their former sales. Thousands of tons of oranges were dumped
and buried. The stench of rotting fruit hung over the city. 'My father's
income dropped drastically, and our lives were greatly disrupted.

Everything was rationed and there were severe shortages. All the cars and trucks were taken away for the war effort,' recalls Hasan. 'My father became a wholesaler of dried goods. It was all right for one or two years, but then it became more difficult, as the supplies began to dry up and rationing was more severe.' Ahmad then took a drastic, foolhardy and very brave decision. 'My father showed what he was really made of. He went into a trade of which he had no experience. He organised a sheep drive. He got together a crew, found an old small truck—and vehicles were very hard to come by then—and set off for northern Iraq,' explains Hasan. Ahmad said goodbye to his family, hugged and kissed Nafise and the children and set off for the desert. Each feared that they would never see the other again. Ahmad made it to Iraq and purchased several thousand sheep. Now all he had to do was get them, and himself, back to Palestine in one piece.

7

The White City Shines

1940s

*I was in the newest place in the world . . . a place
where everything was new and everything was possible,
including a kind of rebirth of the human spirit.*

Evelyn Sert, heroine of the novel
When I Lived in Modern Times, *by Linda Grant,*
set in Mandate Tel Aviv

Yosef Pomrock, husband of Simha Chelouche, died in April 1942, when he was just forty-eight years old. He had stayed on in Palestine, just as he had told his parents he would— even though they had sent him there from Radom to bring his brother Moshe home. Yosef loved his life there, had risen high in Tel Aviv society and sat on the municipal council. Meir Dizengoff had been the *sandak*, the man who holds the baby, at Yosef's son Zvi's circumcision. 'May Zvi too one day be the mayor of Tel Aviv,' proclaimed Dizengoff, before the celebrations began. Although Yosef was an Ashkenazi, he rapidly adapted to the Sephardic lifestyle, even learning Arabic, the language usually spoken by the Chelouches. 'My father fell in love with my mother, and with the oriental way of life,' Zvi recalls. 'He loved to visit all my mother's old aunts and eat there. The Chelouches were a very charming family, with wonderful food and traditions that he had never seen in Poland. They were very warm people, very close, always hugging and kissing each other.' An engaging silver-haired lawyer in his early seventies, Zvi Pomrock is the chief historian of the Chelouche family. He is a walking encyclopaedia of both his hometown, Tel Aviv, and Chelouche lore, which he expounds with great enthusiasm.

Zvi was eleven years old when his father, Yosef, died. His uncles Zaki and Marco took him under their wing. Two years later they presided over Zvi's bar mitzvah, the ceremony marking his passage to adulthood. Zaki was then one of the city's most renowned architects and sat on the municipal design committee. Zaki and Marco took Zvi to Jaffa and explained the history of the Chelouches. Zvi loved Jaffa, the feel of the smooth sandstone buildings, the blue of the sea and the powerful sense of history reaching back through the generations. 'Zaki and Marco were substitute fathers to me and we met almost every day. That's why I know so much about Jaffa and the founding of Tel Aviv. In Jaffa they took me to the street of the money-changers, where Aharon Chelouche had his shop. They showed me where the old Arab coffee house was that had a cannon that was fired to mark the end of Ramadan. Marco was born in Jaffa itself, and Zaki was the first grandson of Aharon Chelouche to be born in the Beit Chelouche.'

Zaki was commissioned to draw up plans for a new market for Tel Aviv. Jewish women were increasingly uneasy about shopping in Jaffa, partly because they did not feel safe any more, but also for ideological reasons. 'Jaffa was Jaffa, it was far away and they believed in Tel Aviv,' explains Zvi. 'It was also not pleasant for Jewish women to shop in Jaffa. In Arab families often the men went to the market, while the women stayed at home. But the Jewish women were much more modern, and they went shopping alone. It was an uncomfortable situation.' Zaki's plans were accepted. The new Souk Chelouche—'Che-louche Market'—bordered Manshiyyeh, Neve Tsedek and the Yemenite quarter. 'You could buy everything at the Souk Chelouche,' recalls Zvi. 'I still remember the smell. There were all kinds of foods set out on the stalls: fish, meat, bread, chicken, vegetables. There was even a small slaughterhouse.'

Zaki had studied art nouveau architecture in Paris. But there would be no fussy peacock motifs or decorative swirls and curls in this modern Hebrew city. Tel Aviv's architects chose the Bauhaus model as a foundation for their own school, known as the International Style, which adapted Bauhaus principles to the Mediterranean. The Bauhaus school, founded in Weimar, Germany, in 1919, aimed to synthesise simple, elegant design with modern mass production. Its open, democratic ethos embodied the spirit of Tel Aviv. Tel Aviv's Jews were more likely to wear simple shirts, shorts and sandals than tuxedos or ball gowns. The city was modern and forward-looking. The apartment blocks were run as co-operatives. Each had its own laundry, kindergarten, grocery shop, post office and plot of land, where residents could grow vegetables to keep alive the pioneering spirit of connection to the land. The city soon had the greatest concentration of Bauhaus-influenced buildings in the world.

'Choosing Bauhaus was a rebellion against the old society and the old ways. Tel Aviv is a city that started a new life, a new society. In Beit Chelouche the family lived together like a tribe, but when Zaki came back from Paris, the atmosphere here was that everyone was building the new state. Nobody was building art nouveau buildings with flowers. They wanted functional modern houses to live in,' says Zvi. 'Also, it is very hot here, with a lot of sunlight, and that goes with the Bauhaus style.' Tel Aviv's residential buildings were almost all three or four storeys high. The architects all had their own style, but the overall uniformity in design was intentional: Tel Aviv was a community, and it flowed horizontally, radiating a sense of equality, openness, even optimism. 'We drove through the orange groves until we reached the White City and it was white, then,' exclaims Evelyn Sert, the fictional heroine of *When I Lived in Modern Times*. 'They were houses like machines, built of concrete and glass, not houses at all, they were ideas. I saw walls erected not just for privacy, but as barriers against the blinding light; windows small and recessed, each with a balcony and each shaded by the shadow cast by the balcony above it; stairwells lit by portholes, reminding me that we were by the sea.'[1]

The International Style was suited to Tel Aviv for practical as well as ethical and artistic reasons. By the early 1940s Tel Aviv had grown to almost 200,000 inhabitants. One in three of Palestine's Jewish population lived there. Buildings were constructed in concrete, which is comparatively cheap and easy to use. Several of Tel Aviv's architects studied with Le Corbusier. They incorporated his innovation of building apartment blocks on stilts, known as pilotis. The space underneath the building was used as a green garden area, and also allowed for air flow. The flat roofs were a social space. In the summer sun the White City was dazzling. Tel Aviv prided itself especially on its cultural life, accessible to all. The Mann Auditorium, built in the 1950s, was designed to embody the values of an egalitarian society: its entrance was on the ground floor, without a grand, imposing staircase; the foyer was simple and open, and many of the walls were made of glass. Culture was to be de-mystified and democratised.

Zvi and his mother, Simha, lived in one of Zaki's buildings, at 56 Ahad Ha'am Street—still home to his law office.[2] It was a model Bauhaus construction: sparse and angular with large corner windows and a winding iron staircase. The flats were light, if spare in their design. Zvi's mother did not like the building. She thought the flat, with its long corridor, looked like a train. From the simple door handles to the window frames, everything matched. A few doors away, at number 49, stood what many acclaim as Zaki's masterpiece: a curved, almost voluptuous cream-coloured apartment house whose feminine lines and L-shaped balconies seemed to blend both art deco and Bauhaus into a new style of its own. The influence of the Chelouche family on Tel Aviv was indisputable. Back in the 1880s Zaki's grandfather Aharon had built Beit Chelouche in Neve Tsedek. Thirty years later his father, Avraham Haim, had constructed houses in the French provincial style. Then Zaki designed Bauhaus buildings, the three generations embodying the departure from Jaffa and the foundation and evolution of Tel Aviv. 'Zaki was very old-fashioned, and he personally took care of every detail. He would not compromise with the owners. He built the house as he believed it should be built. If he wanted to add another floor, it would have to be exactly the same as the others,' says Zvi.

Simha kept herself busy after her husband died. Every Friday she invited her friends over, sometimes for a simple social occasion, at others to promote a new young musician she had discovered. Simha never remarried. 'I had one husband, and now he's gone,' she said. Simha's brothers, Zaki and Marco, were also unlucky in love, even though both were married. Their dark good looks and old-world charm especially entranced the Ashkenazi women, and both had plenty of admirers. 'All the Chelouche men loved women very much,' says Zvi. 'They were attractive, educated and cultured, and they liked the good life.' Only the third brother, David, married to Julia, enjoyed a happy domestic life.

One day Marco's wife, Paulette, was swimming at Tel Aviv's beach when she was stung in the face by an insect. Her face swelled up and the doctors were unable to help. After three days Paulette died. Stricken with grief, Marco moved back home to his parents' house. Zaki had married a girl from Jerusalem, Mafleda Abujdid. Mafleda was a modern young woman, poised and elegant, educated in London. She rode horses, spoke foreign languages and played tennis. 'Mafleda was very different from Zaki. She was very open-minded, and she was not constant. She went to the beach in very daring swimsuits, and at parties she used to dance with other men,' says Zvi. Zaki too considered himself a sophisticated person. He spoke Hebrew, Arabic, French and German. He was well-mannered, sophisticated and cultured and always well dressed in a perfectly-tailored suit. He owned a beautiful open-topped car. He could not drive but had his own personal chauffeur, Yaakov, who took him everywhere. But Mafleda's behaviour was too much, says Zvi. 'Zaki was old-fashioned and he could not accept this, and so they divorced.'

Some time later, Zaki married his second wife, Mira. There he fared no better; they argued incessantly. Zaki admitted to Zvi that he was difficult. When he had a migraine attack he had to lie down in a cold, dark room with a slice of potato on each eye. And at home everything had to be in the right place. The perfectionism that was tolerable in an architect was less so in a husband. His diary had a fixed day for everything, all planned in advance, from work appointments to social outings. Once fixed, the times would not be altered.

Despite his idiosyncrasies, Zaki had one devoted female admirer: his sister-in-law, Julia. 'My mother did not fall in love with my father as much as with the idea of getting married, and the honeymoon, making a home, and going to Venice and Paris,' explains Julia's daughter Edith Krygier. 'When they got to Paris, they met David's brothers, Zaki and Marco. Marco was a merchant, while Zaki was an architect and a playboy. He was very handsome and charismatic. My mother once told me that she adored him at first sight, but when she got to know him better she found out that he had a negative side as well.' Zaki sometimes behaved badly towards women and could be stingy. 'My father had the opposite nature—he was very generous, loving, genuine and charming. My mother loved and appreciated him for his values very much.' After Zaki and Mira divorced, Zaki did not marry again. 'He told me that he could not live with anyone, that women had made a mess of his life,' says Zvi.

THE POLITICAL AND military forces in Palestine were also heading for divorce. As the war entered its final phase, the marriage of convenience between the Haganah and Irgun and the British began to fall apart. In February 1944 the new commander of the Irgun declared war against Britain. It was clear, the Irgun argued, that the Allies would win the war. But there was no guarantee that the British would give the Jews their own state. News of the horrors of the Nazi concentration and extermination camps was leaking out. The Royal Navy was still turning away refugee ships and detaining the Jews in camps, in line with the 1939 White Paper.

The Irgun's commander was a Polish Jew called Menachem Begin, a former leader of Betar and a friend of Vladimir Jabotinsky. Begin's communiqué announcing the Irgun's revolt was illustrated by a map of Palestine with borders reaching Iraq. The Irgun demanded that a provisional Hebrew government be established, with a Hebrew national army, and that negotiations be initiated to evacuate all Jews from Europe to the Holy Land. Begin ordered a campaign of terror against the British. Irgun members bombed, blew up and raided police stations and government buildings. Immigration offices in particular were targeted. Mandate officials granted only 1,500 entry certificates a month, and any Jews who immigrated illegally and were caught by the authorities were deducted from that figure. By mid-February all immigration offices in Tel Aviv, Haifa and Jerusalem had been destroyed. Tax offices were next, followed by the British intelligence headquarters in Jaffa. Lehi would not be outdone: its members twice tried to kill Harold MacMichael, the British high commissioner for Palestine, and succeeded in wounding him.

By now the Bulgarian Yaakov Yosefov was no more. He had Hebraised his family name to Aharoni and usually went by the Hebrew nickname of Yoram. In addition he used several aliases, for Yoram lived underground. Released from prison in 1942, he went to Tel Aviv and found a job in a clothing factory. He made contact with the Bulgarian Lehi member he had met in Mizra prison. 'They set up a meeting in a safe house in Tel Aviv. I went there at night, and it was completely dark,' Yoram recalls. A Lehi commander, possibly Yitzhak Shamir—later prime minister of Israel—sat waiting for Yoram, his face in the shadows. Yoram was closely questioned, for Lehi was organised on a strict cell structure and security was watertight. Once in, there was no going back, but Yoram felt he had come home. 'This was a war. If the British had let in one hundred thousand Jews, the Haganah and the Irgun would have stopped fighting. But we would not have. We wanted the British out and a Jewish state,' he explains. 'We considered all British administration, military and police as legitimate targets. But no civilians, women, families or children—only officials.'

The Irgun and Lehi stepped up their operations against the British

during the autumn of 1944. In November, two members of Lehi killed
Lord Moyne, the British minister responsible for the 1939 White
Paper, in Cairo. The two were caught and sentenced to death. They
told the court: 'We accuse Lord Moyne and the government he represents of murdering hundreds of thousands of our brethren.' The Jewish Agency reacted with fury, denouncing Lehi and the Irgun as
traitors, and the *Yishuv* split in two as Jew turned on Jew. The Jewish
Agency instructed any Jews who knew members of either Lehi or
Irgun to report them to the British police, either in writing or by telephone. Fathers were even told to denounce their rebellious offspring.
Special squads of Haganah fighters were despatched to track Irgun
and Lehi members in what became known as the 'Hunting Season'.
Almost one thousand Irgun and Lehi members were then handed
over to the British, some kidnapped and beaten by their fellow Jews.[3]
Even today the Hunting Season's legacy of bitterness still shapes
Israeli politics and the divide between left and right.

By the end of the war, *Falastin*'s journalists were also disillusioned
with their support for the Allies. Democracy had triumphed, but they
did not believe that the Allied victory would lead to a free and independent Palestine.[4] The British Labour and Conservative parties
were both imperialists, one writer concluded, and nothing really
changed, whoever was in power in London: 'One Englishman
comes, and another Englishman goes.' In April 1944 the Palestine
Arab Party had been formally relaunched. The following year the
Arab League was founded in Egypt. The Palestinians had delegate
status and were recognised as a nation. In November the Arab
Higher Committee, disbanded by the British, was re-established. It
was packed with placemen selected by Hajj Amin al-Husseini, the

mufti of Jerusalem, who had relocated to Cairo, from where he intrigued and plotted. Both Jews and Arabs knew that soon all the Englishmen would go. Then the conflict would be settled by military rather than political means.

In Jebaliyyeh, Ahmad Hammami's wife and children missed him intensely. He had not yet returned from his sheep drive, and Nafise was left alone with nine children to feed and clothe on tight rations, in the middle of a war, with no man in the house. Of course Ahmad's relatives, who lived next door, helped as much as they could. But it was not the same as having her husband there. Worst of all, there was no way to communicate with him. 'I think my father must have been gone for months, but at the time it felt like years,' says Hasan. Until one day there was a knock on the door. Leaner, browner, dustier and smelling distinctly of sheep, there was Ahmad, and the whole family rejoiced. 'When my father came back he was wind-burned and covered with the dust of the desert. His legs were covered with deep brown scars. He told us how bitterly cold the desert was during the night and that he could not keep warm, how they tended every sheep as if it were a human being; how they could not follow the old desert routes since they were too long and too slow, and closed because of military and border restrictions. And how they kept running out of water and firewood to keep warm or prepare food. He was a hero to us all.'

Nafise too was happy to see her husband, but her joy was tempered. 'She could not quite restrain herself from criticising my father for leaving her alone with the children for so long,' says Hasan. The sheep fetched a good sum, and the family, for now at least, had enough to live on. But by the following autumn, the funds began to run low. Ahmad suggested to his wife that he go on another sheep drive. After all, he argued, he was now an experienced hand. Nafise refused point blank, and Ahmad knew when he was beaten. Anyway, perhaps it was not such a good idea to push his luck. Instead Ahmad opened a wholesale shop for dried and perishable foods in Jaffa's market, by Clock Tower Square.

Hasan loved going to the shop to help his father. He spent most of his summers and weekends there. 'I sat behind the oversized dark wood roller desk, using the heavy scales, moving bags of potatoes, onions, beans or whatever there was. The sacks were frequently piled up to the ceiling. The store would smell bad if the onions had not sold fast enough, so they had to be moved quickly. The busiest days in that market were Thursday and Friday, when the merchants from the villages and the retailers would come in to buy their supplies.' Hasan often looked out for an elderly east European Jewish lady, desperately poor, judging by her ragged clothes. She did the rounds of the merchants, and most had a bag of surplus vegetables for her. The Muslim obligation to provide for the poor is called *zakat* and *sadaqah* in Arabic, while for Jews it is the Hebrew *tsedakah*. The words are almost identical. 'By the end of the day, the market was deserted of people, but it looked like there had been a hurricane, with all the abandoned empty bags, the loose vegetables and other goods that had been spilled or left behind after being picked over,' says Hasan.

Ahmad Hammami, like many other Palestinian merchants, also had Jewish business associates. Commerce cut across national and ideological divisions. But Tel Aviv's open democratic spirit did not quite extend to Jaffa's Arabs. They were not barred or openly discouraged from the cafés and shops. But when Hasan and his friends went for a walk in the city or to the cinema, they were uneasy. They did not speak Hebrew, and it was instantly apparent that they were not Jews. 'Tel Aviv was crowded and noisy and buzzed like a beehive. But we Jaffa boys did not feel comfortable there, or welcome,' says Hasan. The Peel and Woodhead Commissions' plans to divide Palestine had faded away, but in a sense, partition had already begun.

8

Jaffa Prepares for War

Mid- to Late 1940s

I asked Palestinians about love. They said Palestine has no
love.... I asked them about their jokes. They said Palestine
has no jokes. I cracked some jokes but they did not laugh.
Why, Palestine? Laugh and smile. Or at least, return my smile
and my laugh to me. I lost them between Jerusalem and Jaffa.

Egyptian journalist on his visit to Palestine
in 1945, published in Falastin[1]

Hasan Hammami stood in front of the microphone and
looked out nervously at the crowd in front of him. His
father, Ahmad, liked to spring surprises on him, it
seemed. Once he had tipped him into the sea, to ensure that he could
swim. Now, without warning, he had appointed Hasan master of ceremonies for the Hammami municipal election campaign meeting.
The Second World War was over and Hasan was thirteen years old.
The Hammami house and gardens were full of people, and hundreds
more spilled out onto the surrounding streets. A large open-sided
tent was set up with a modern public announcement system, and several lambs were slaughtered and cooked. The audience looked back at
Hasan expectantly. 'That was my first political experience. Father
asked me to give the welcome speech, and I took up the challenge,' he
recalls. 'I took a deep breath and said: "I welcome you in the name of

the Hammami family, to this meeting for the election of my uncle Adel Hammami to the City Council. Thank you." When I finished speaking, the applause seemed deafening.'

Palestine's economy was finally recovering. Imports from Europe were once again appearing in the shops. Ahmad bought a Dutch Phillips bicycle for Hasan and an Italian racing bicycle for his brother Hussein. 'The bicycle opened up a whole new world of discovery for me. I cycled to school, along the beach, and I found the secret of cycling along the sand. You had to be close enough to the water for the sand to be firm, but not too close or you went into the water and slowed down. And not too far back or you would get stuck in the dry sand.' Sometimes Hasan headed south to the Jewish town of Bat Yam, past the edge of Jebaliyyeh. 'Bat Yam was heavily reinforced. It had a brewery that looked like a fort with gun slits. There were small white houses, simple but clean, but the people seemed like they came from another planet. They did not want to talk, even to each other— they were very quiet. It all seemed out of place, there on the sand dunes. The bus from Bat Yam ran through the street next to ours, but it never stopped. The windows were always closed, even in the summer. I was a young boy, but I still felt that there must be a sinister reason for these colonies being built, encircling Jaffa. Later on, I found out that I was right.'

Ahmad was back in the citrus business and had signed contracts with several growers, including Jewish ones such as Pardes, the Zionist agricultural co-operative movement. He leased citrus groves from Pardes for the export season, or he might exchange the lease on a Jewish-owned grove for an Arab one, if that was more convenient. The question now was how to travel to the remote farms. Ahmad's fine pre-war Mercedes, requisitioned for the war effort, was still in the hands of the British. He knew it would be a long time, if ever, before he sat behind its wheel again. But Ahmad was a problem solver. If he could drive to Iraq in the middle of the war and bring back thousands of sheep, then he could certainly sort out a car. 'My father arranged with a friend of his who owned a garage to buy a military surplus jeep. He mounted the frame and seats of an Austin 12 onto the jeep's chassis. This was cheap, creative and available immediately. And because it was four-wheel drive, Father could drive on remote, unpaved roads to the distant groves.' Before Ahmad would sign any contract, the leased citrus groves had to be checked and measured. Hasan now accompanied his father on his trips. 'As I approached adolescence, I remember a gradual change in my relationship with Mother and Father. Mother stopped treating me like a kid and paid more attention to the younger ones. She asked me to do chores, tidy my desk, care for my younger brothers and sisters, and to "behave more like a man than a child". Father started gradually involving me in his work.' Once Ahmad and Hasan arrived at the leased grove, Hasan counted the number of horizontal lines of trees while Ahmad counted vertically. Father and son then met in the middle.

All the while Ahmad was checking the health and size of the trees, so he could estimate each grove's potential yield and then make the best bid for the lease. Hasan was glad to help. He was a diligent boy, not as playful as his younger brother Hussein, who was the family joker and storyteller, or young Mustafa, who was always getting into trouble, skipping off from school to go fishing by the Jami'a al-Bahr, the mosque by the sea where Hasan and his father prayed, especially on Fridays during school summer holidays. Sometimes Mustafa brought home his catch, the long thin fish dubbed 'Bolsheviks' because they started to appear in 1917. As his relationship with Hasan evolved, Ahmad began to treat his son as a protégé, or trainee partner. Just as Yaakov Chelouche had taken his son Shlomo on his rounds, Ahmad took Hasan along to business meetings. He met Mr Beiruti, who was in the shipping business; the clerks of the Ottoman Bank, by Clock Tower Square, where Ahmad arranged his financial affairs, and Mr Abdel Rahim, who printed Ahmad's letterheads and business forms. Hasan was very proud.

THE THREE ZIONIST militias, the Labour-Zionist Haganah, the Revisionist-Zionist Irgun and the extremist Stern Group (Lehi), were also drawing closer. Across the *Yishuv* there was a sense that the end of the war with Nazi Germany and worldwide horror about the extent of the Holocaust were building support for the idea of a Jewish state. It was time for even the fractious Zionist leaders to try to unite. Winston Churchill was swept from power in the summer of 1945, and the Labour Party had promised to rescind the 1939 White Paper that restricted Jewish immigration to 75,000. But Ernest Bevin, the foreign secretary, announced that immigration would remain fixed at 1,500 permits a month. Bevin was strongly anti-Zionist and widely condemned across the *Yishuv* as an anti-Semite. The British blockade of refugee ships continued. The ragged survivors of Nazi camps were once again held behind barbed wire, this time in British-run detention camps. Anti-British feeling surged, not just in Palestine but across the world.

Pressure grew in the United States to open the gates, and President Truman eventually called for 100,000 Jewish refugees to be let into Palestine. In 1945 the Anglo-American Committee of Enquiry was established. Albert Einstein appeared before it, arguing in favour of a Jewish state. The Zionists echoed Truman's call for the immigrants to be allowed in and demanded that control over Jewish immigration be handed to them. Meanwhile the Palestinian leadership called for an independent Palestine and for Jewish immigration to cease. The two sides were as far apart as ever. The committee's recommendations, that 100,000 Jews be allowed to immigrate at once, were rejected by the British government, and the 1939 White Paper stayed in force.

In response Ben-Gurion and the Haganah leadership changed strategy. The new enemy was Britain. In October 1945, Ben-Gurion cabled instructions from London: 'We must not confine our reaction in Palestine to immigration and settlement. It is essential to adopt tactics of S. [sabotage] and reprisal. Not individual terror, but retaliation for each and every Jew murdered by the White Paper. The S. action must carry weight and be impressive, and care should be taken, insofar as possible, to avoid casualties. . . .'[2]

The Haganah's 'Hunting Season' against the Irgun and Lehi was closed, and the United Resistance (UR) was founded. Its leadership was composed of two representatives from the Haganah and one each from the Irgun and Lehi. This was a triumph for Lehi, which had at most a few hundred members, compared to the thousands in the Irgun and Haganah. On 1 November 1945, the UR sabotaged railway tracks in more than 150 places, blew up patrol boats in Jaffa and Haifa and attacked Lydda railway station. The following month British intelligence headquarters in Jerusalem and Jaffa were destroyed, the latter by Lehi.

Yoram Aharoni had already been at war with Britain for several years. He was now a specialist in explosives and demolition, and he supplied the weapons for Lehi's attack on the British intelligence headquarters in Jaffa. 'I did not participate but I brought the grenades and explosives. I handed them to a girl and they blew up the building. When the operation was over everyone returned their weapons, and she gave the unused grenades back to me. I didn't think anything more of it.' On the wet, cold night of 25 February 1946, Yoram took a more active role. He was crawling along the ground in the dark towards the perimeter fence of a Royal Air Force base at Kfar Syrkin, in central Palestine. His squad of nine Lehi fighters was part of a team of thirty. 'At this time the groups were all working together. The Haganah attacked the railway tracks, the Irgun the airport at Lydda, and we targeted the aircraft at Kfar Syrkin. We cut through the fence, and crawled along the ground until we got to the planes. There was only one guard with a torch and one British armoured vehicle. We waited in the dark until the vehicle went by and ran to the planes. We each had three kilos of explosives with a two-minute fuse.' Yoram and his comrades jammed the explosives into the space where the under-carriage struts joined the wing. This was one of the most vulnerable spots on the plane, and the explosion would destroy both the landing gear and the wing, almost certainly rendering it irreparable. 'We lit the fuses and ran back to the fence. We made it out.' The rapid thumps of the explosions lit up the night sky. 'We destroyed nine Spitfires. It was a very successful mission.'

Yoram often came to Jaffa to buy weapons and explosives that his Arab contacts had stolen from British army stores. Some Arabs were sympathetic to Lehi, seeing them as useful allies in the battle to get Britain out of Palestine. British soldiers also sold munitions—a kilo of explosives, for example, cost two pounds. Some time after the Kfar Syrkin attack, Yoram met the young woman in Lehi who had returned the unused grenades. Her name was Rina Bloomshtein and she lived on Allenby Street, in central Tel Aviv. The Bloomshtein home was occasionally hit by bullets fired by Arab snipers in Jaffa. Rina was an only child, and her father was a member of the Haganah who, like most of his comrades, detested Lehi. Rina's father knew nothing of her secret life until he discovered her pasting up Lehi posters on a nearby street. He chased her down the street with a broom, and after a furious row, Rina left home.

Now a new relationship was beginning. Before Yoram had left Bulgaria, his father had given him a ring, and he wore it all the time. Rina was interested in the ring and asked to see it, so Yoram took it off and put it on her finger. If there were three witnesses, he joked, they would be married. Rina smiled and handed the ring back. 'When I met her in Tel Aviv, I would say, "Hallo, my wife", and she always replied, "Hallo, my husband". I didn't want to marry her then, it was a joke,' says Yoram. The Lehi leadership sent Yoram to a Jewish town called Raanana, on the coast north of Jaffa. Yoram had just completed a two-week course in guerrilla warfare, taught by Jewish soldiers who had fought in the British army, some of whom were also Haganah veterans. They taught the use of weapons, combat tactics, mines and explosives, training on deserted sections of the coastline. Yoram was now the Lehi commander for a large region, and as a wanted man, he travelled everywhere under cover. But it was harder to live a clandestine life in sleepy Raanana than in Tel Aviv, for newcomers were noticed in the small town. So Rina was sent to join him, and they posed as a married couple.

Yoram's cover was that he was a flower seller. It was an inspired legend, as it gave him a reason to travel across Palestine legitimately. 'I had all the equipment and the seeds but I never sold any flowers. I dressed in simple clothes, like a man from a village, and when I was stopped and questioned, I could show that I really was a flower seller.

I would go from place to place, organise actions or command actions myself and undertake all the training in weapons and arms.' Like every clandestine military organisation, Lehi had a hard core of active members and a wider ring of supporters that provided safe houses, shops and warehouses to store weapons and ammunition. One of these owned a real flower shop in Tel Aviv and supplied Yoram with enough seeds, bills of sales and other necessities to verify his cover. Rina was a runner, bringing orders from Lehi's high command. Cooped up together, living in constant danger of discovery, the inevitable eventually happened. 'After a while we realised that we really did want to get married. Usually there were no marriages, because a man with family ties is trouble for a group like Lehi,' explains Yoram. His previous girlfriend had been a member of the Haganah. She had not known he was in Lehi and he certainly could not tell her. Yoram asked his commander for permission to marry Rina. It was decided there would be no objection. After all, Yoram and Rina were already pretending to be married. But first, Yoram was ordered to carry out a new mission, a 'confiscation', otherwise known as a bank robbery.

THAT SAME YEAR, 1946, in Jebaliyyeh, the Hammami children were counting the days until the festival of Nabi Rubeen. Nabi Rubeen took place every summer at a village of the same name, just south of Jaffa. It was built around a shrine where, according to tradition, Rubeen, the firstborn son of Jacob, was buried. Nabi Rubeen was one of the highlights of the year, a cross between a holiday camp and a spiritual and religious folk festival. Cloistered in their homes, Arab women especially counted the days until it began and they would have at least a week of freedom. 'Either you take me to Nabi Rubeen or you divorce me,' they threatened their husbands, only half joking. Musicians played, singers crooned popular love songs, poets declaimed their works, Sufi dervishes whirled and magicians entranced their audiences with tricks.

Fadwa Hammami looked forward to Nabi Rubeen even more than her brothers. Born in 1937, Fadwa was a studious little girl, nine years old, quieter and more introspective perhaps than her twin sister, Leila. 'Usually I could only go out with my mother and her sisters. I could not just go to a shop on my own. We visited other families for the religious feasts. So I was always exicited to go to Nabi Rubeen,' explains Fadwa, who now lives in East Jerusalem, the only one of Ahmad Hammami's children still living in Israel/Palestine. But her conviviality is underscored by sadness, for the idyllic Jaffa of her childhood and the richness of Palestinian culture before 1948 have vanished for ever. 'This was our family holiday, and we enjoyed it very much. If you ask anyone in Palestine about Nabi Rubeen, they would love to have it again—it was so nice. That was the first time I went to the cinema and I saw an Egyptian film. There was a mosque, and temporary shops in small tents. You could buy special things, trinkets, glass bracelets and necklaces.'

A whole holiday complex appeared on the sands: there were streets lined with kebab stalls, cafés and soft drink and ice-cream parlours. The Hammamis stayed in roomy tents, large, white, double-walled canvas constructs, decorated inside with embroidered verses from the Quran. Ahmad had a fence put up so that the family could have some privacy. Inside they slept on camp beds, while the floor was covered with rugs and straw mats. There were electric lights, a shower and a toilet. Everybody changed out of their city clothes, which anyway were too hot for the summer, and wore traditional Arab robes. Friends and relatives came to visit from all over Palestine. The whole week was a kind of *istiqbal*, a chance to forget about politics and the conflict with the Jews. The Israeli writer S. Yizhar sneaked into Nabi Rubeen as a child and was entranced: 'Ho, not to return, to be and to be in this colourful spinning, which tempts and leads astray and sings, and which is within the distant night, surrounded by white sands and millions of stars.'[3]

Hasan took a ride on a white Arabian stallion, trotting down to the beach. It was a more successful trip than his last ride, when he had jumped onto the gardener's horse. Fadwa and her brothers and sisters hiked along the banks of the Al-Auja River, down to the sea. Each time she went the route was slightly different, as the wind blew the sand dunes back and forth. Some days whole hills vanished from one place and reappeared somewhere else. 'Our food always tasted of sand, and that was the taste, the memory of Nabi Rubeen.'

YORAM AHARONI'S 'CONFISCATION' was set for 25 September 1947. 'We had someone on the inside who gave us the information that on a specific day a car was moving cash from Barclay's Bank in central Tel Aviv to Jerusalem. The police organised the transport, in a big armoured car with a machine gun on the top. We knew how the loading worked, that there were two lots of banknotes. The bank workers brought the first one out and loaded it into the van, while the police stood guard. Then they went back into the bank with them for the second bundle. We wanted both.'

Yoram and two others were to grab the money, while about twenty more armed Lehi members were positioned in the square, in case things went wrong. Yoram and his comrades dressed in suits on the day of the robbery, like businessmen who had legitimate affairs to attend to at the bank, and hid their weapons beneath their clothes. They took up their positions not far away. They had already had several practice runs, working out the best place to wait before going into action. They chatted amiably, as if they were going to a business meeting. All the time they were watching the bank's doors. 'There were three of us: one to take care of the sergeant who went back into the bank, one for the policeman on the roof, and one for the driver. When the bank workers went back inside for the second package we started walking forward. The problem was the timing, to get both packages. We got to the bank and were standing right by the sergeant, but we were too quick, and they had not brought the other package of notes out yet. So we stopped walking and stood there talking. When they brought the second bundle out we ran forward and opened fire on the car. I shot the man on the roof, the sergeant was shot, and I ran towards the driver.'

As Yoram sprinted ahead he felt a hammer blow to his back. One of his comrades had shot him accidentally in the shoulder. He wobbled, righted himself and tried to ignore the pain. 'We got the first package of money to our vehicle. As we went to grab the second one, a British armoured vehicle drove into the street and opened fire on us. There was shooting everywhere. Our driver drove off with the first package. We threw the second one into a nearby garden, and ran off.' Once out of the square, he stopped running and strolled down into nearby Shenkin Street, past the rows of pavement cafés. 1940s fashion helped to save Yoram as he fled the half-bungled robbery; his suit had thick padded shoulders, which absorbed the blood seeping from his shoulder wound. A few blocks down he got into a waiting taxi. The fleet owner was a Lehi sympathizer, and the taxi driver took Yoram back to the Lehi safe house, where his wound was treated. The package of notes that had been thrown away, Yoram found out later, contained £105,000. The one that the Lehi men had escaped with contained £45,000, all in ten-shilling notes.

Two days later Yoram married Rina Bloomshtein, and his family came to the wedding. Yoram's father, Shabat, his mother, Leah, and his brothers had arrived in 1946. Unlike most eastern European Jews, they were at least alive—and able to celebrate Yoram's marriage. 'There were fifteen people at the wedding, but I didn't tell my father that I had been shot. I said I had hurt my shoulder. Only my brother knew that I was in Lehi. These kind of actions against the British were not new to me. This was a war, and we were fighting for a Jewish state.' Soon Lehi would no longer exist, and Yoram would fight in the first Hebrew army for almost two millennia.

9

Al-Nakba—The Catastrophe

April–May 1948

The conquest of Jaffa, however, stands out as
an event of first-rate importance in the
struggle for Hebrew independence.
Menachem Begin, The Revolt[1]

Jaffa's Arab sentries were suspicious of the truck loaded with
oranges coming from Tel Aviv. The driver was dressed in Arab
clothes, but something felt wrong. As the vehicle approached
their checkpoint, they opened fire and the truck turned back. But the
driver and his companion returned on 4 January 1948, and this time
they had better luck. The driver parked his truck, again piled high
with oranges, in an alley off Clock Tower Square, alongside the New
Seray, Sultan Abdul Hamid's imposing government building. It
housed Jaffa's municipal offices, welfare workers and a kitchen for
needy children. The two men walked to a nearby café for coffee. They
departed soon after, and left the vehicle behind.

By now Britain wanted to leave Palestine, and London had handed
over the Mandate to the United Nations in February 1947. British
public opinion, the press, Parliament, all were clamouring for their

soldiers to come home. It was increasingly clear that the days of empire were over. Even India had become independent in August 1947, and compared to the Indian elephant, Palestine was little more than an annoying mouse. In addition, the deaths of British soldiers at the hands of the Zionists were fomenting widespread anti-Semitism and threatening social unrest. The United Nations set up a special committee for Palestine. UNSCOP, like the Peel and Woodhead Commissions before it, concluded that Palestine should be partitioned. In November 1947 the United Nations General Assembly voted to divide Palestine into two states, one Arab and one Jewish, with Jerusalem remaining under international control. The Arab state would have 42 per cent of Palestine, and the Jewish state 56 per cent (much of its allocated territory was in the Negev desert), while an international zone would be created around Jerusalem. Jaffa would be a tiny Arab island, surrounded by Jewish territory.

The Jewish Agency, the government of the state-in-waiting, accepted the plan and celebrated. The 'yes' vote in favour of UN Resolution 181 was a defining moment in the history of the Israeli-Palestinian conflict. Ben-Gurion himself said it was the greatest moment in Jewish history. Thirty-three states voted yes, thirteen no, and ten abstained. Both the United States and the Soviet Union, who had already expressed their support for partition, voted yes, together with western Europe, the Soviet bloc, the British Commonwealth and Latin America. The Muslim and Arab states voted no. The agreement between Washington and Moscow was a rare instance of superpower co-operation across the divisions of the Cold War, which the Zionists deftly exploited over the next few crucial months. The principle of Jewish statehood was now established—only the borders remained to be defined.

Western guilt over the failure to prevent or halt the Holocaust was an important factor, but the Palestinians were furious that they had to pay the price for the Nazi genocide, in which they had taken no part. The Palestinian leadership unequivocally rejected the plan and called a three-day general strike. Fighting erupted within a few hours of the vote. Jewish and Arab snipers traded shots across Jaffa's border areas, shooting into homes and cafés and onto the streets. On 8 December 1947, after several days of skirmishes between Arab fighters and the Haganah, hundreds of Arab fighters attacked the Tel Aviv quarter of Hatikvah in a major frontal assault. The attack was repulsed, with sixty Arabs and two Jews killed.[2] The Arab exodus from Jaffa began. Much of the middle class and the *a'yan*, who could have provided leadership in the testing days ahead, relocated to relatives or to their summer homes in Cairo and Beirut, believing they would return once the situation calmed down. Flight, like panic, is infectious. When Jaffa's artisans and workers saw that their bosses were leaving, they too began to desert their homes. The Haganah's intelligence service reported that inhabitants of Manshiyyeh and Abu Kabir, to the south, were moving out of the city, pushing handcarts full of their possessions. Many of the middle-class employers also closed their shops and businesses, leaving Arab males jobless. Most Jewish businessmen had already sacked their Arab workers. Unemployment, poverty and food shortages all fuelled the rising tension.

Palestine burned throughout the winter of 1947–48. It was a brutal conflict, with neither side observing the rules of war. The Irgun set off bombs in the Arab quarters of Haifa, Jaffa and Jerusalem. On 30 December an Irgun squad threw bombs at a bus stop near the Haifa oil refinery. Six people were killed and dozens more wounded. Arab workers immediately attacked their Jewish colleagues with chisels, hammers and stones. Thirty-nine were killed and fifty wounded. A week later, a Haganah unit blew up the Semiramis Hotel in Jerusalem, believing it to be a command post for Arab irregulars, killing twenty-six people. Arab gunmen ambushed Jewish vehicle convoys, especially in isolated areas or en route to Jerusalem, killing everyone they could before melting away back to their villages. Seeing the terror wrought by the Irgun attacks, the mufti of Jerusalem's forces began bombing the cities. His chief bomb-maker, Fawzi al-Kutub, had trained on an SS course in Nazi Germany.[3] On 22 February 1948, aided by deserters from the British army, al-Kutub set off three truck bombs in Jewish Jerusalem, killing fifty-eight. In response Irgun and Lehi fighters shot dead sixteen British soldiers and policemen. It was less a war than anarchy. But in Tel Aviv and Jaffa, some groups on both sides were still talking. Jewish and Arab orange-grove owners had signed a non-aggression pact, so that the plantations around the city at least would not be targeted and the crop could be safely gathered and exported.

But Jaffa's heart received no such quarter. Soon after the truck driver and his companion left that morning in January 1948, a thunderous explosion shook the city. Broken glass and shattered masonry blew out across Clock Tower Square. The New Seray's centre and side walls collapsed in a pile of rubble and twisted beams. Only the neo-classical façade survived. Windows shattered for yards around, and a thick choking cloud of dust billowed out. After a moment of silence, the screams and moans began. Twenty-six were killed, and hundreds injured. Most were civilians, including many children who had been eating at the charity kitchen. The bomb missed its target completely, as the Arab Higher Committee, which was organising Jaffa's resistance, had moved from the New Seray to Ajami.

Ismail Abou-Shehade was working in a nearby garage when he heard the explosion. He sprinted to the square and helped dig out the casualties from beneath the rubble. Ismail was twenty-four years old. He had once hoped to study Islamic law at the prestigious Al-Azhar University in Cairo, to become a *qadi*, an Islamic judge. The family home was filled with shelves of books on Islamic law. The Second World War rendered that dream impossible, so he went instead to technical school. Ismail still lives in Jaffa. He is an articulate man who speaks a vivid, poetic Arabic. But his voice chokes as he recalls the darkest months of his life. 'They claimed that the Seray was a centre for terrorists, but it was nothing but an orphanage. Lots of children were killed. I personally was one of those who helped get the dead bodies out from under the wreckage. When the journalists came to ask me what I saw, I told them everything.'

The bomb was terrorism in its classic form: it terrorised Jaffa and destroyed Arab morale and leadership. Municipal services all but collapsed. The exodus of the middle class further accelerated, angry accusations of abandoning Jaffa following in their wake. 'Whoever could leave [Jaffa] has left, there is fear everywhere, and there is no safety,' an Arab informant told Elias Sasson, head of the Jewish Agency's Arab Affairs department, in January 1948.[4] Those who stayed prepared for the worst: in Jebaliyyeh, Hasan Hammami and his friends were training in first aid.

UNLIKE THE PREVIOUS conflicts of 1929 and 1936, this was war, the start of the struggle for command of territory and the future frontiers of a Jewish or Arab state once Palestine was partitioned. The intricate borders drawn up by UN bureaucrats were one thing, but the 'facts on the ground', the control of land, quite another. Militarily and politically, the Zionists were far more prepared than the Arabs. Jewish fighters outnumbered the Arab militias. They had been trained by the British, and many had military experience fighting the Nazis. The Jews were better armed, disciplined, highly motivated and fighting for a country that was all but ready to be born. The Haganah had about 35,000 members, including more than 3,000 troops in its elite strike force, the Palmach; the Irgun had about 3,000 and Lehi several hundred. The Haganah boasted a general staff with a coordinated command structure, and a highly efficient intelligence service, largely dependent on Arab informers. The split between the Haganah's policy of restraint and the Irgun and Lehi's use of pre-emptive strikes was over. Attack was now the best form of defence. Auschwitz had been liberated just three years before; Jews would never again follow orders to walk to their deaths.

Jaffa was the centre of the Palestinian *Najjada* (auxiliary corps), with 2,000–3,000 members, some of whom had also fought in the British army, but they lacked arms and proper leadership. Several thousand troops of the Arab Liberation Army crossed the border into Palestine, but most were poorly trained and badly armed. There was no effective national command structure, and many Arab villages formed their own militias, a rather grandiose term for a group of local men with rifles and no military training. Some villages even allied themselves with the Jews, adding to the complicated feuds that bedevilled Arab society. Bands of paramilitaries and irregulars roamed the countryside, answering to no one but themselves. The lack of clear-sighted Arab leadership and the low calibre of many Arab fighters would prove to be among the Zionists' best assets. The Arab irregulars robbed and intimidated their own people, behaving like conquerors, as Nimr al-Khatib, a member of the Arab National Committee, noted: 'They confiscated their weapons and sold them, imposed fines and stole, and confiscated cars and sold them. . . . The inhabitants were more afraid of their defenders/saviours than of the Jews, their enemies.'[5] Jaffa's disparate defence guards were not even properly fed. The Irgun's intelligence service recorded a conversation between a militia commander and an Arab political leader in Jaffa. The fighters in Manshiyyeh and Jebaliyyeh were complaining that they did not have enough to eat. The commander reported that they were fed pitta bread, cheese, oranges and olives. The political leader said they should be given meat when possible. There was no meat, the militia commander replied.[6]

Even as the Palestinians began to flee, rival Arab leaders continued their feuding and vendettas. Blinded by his hatred of the Jews, Hajj Amin al-Husseini, the mufti of Jerusalem, now exiled in Cairo, led his people to disaster. The Palestinians rejected one partition plan after another and demanded independence. But they made little, if any, serious preparation for statehood. There was no Palestinian equivalent of the Jewish Agency or the Haganah. There was no strategic plan for capturing and holding Palestine, or even a united military leadership. In Damascus the Arab League intrigued against the Palestinians' Arab Higher Committee, and vice versa. The Palestinian leadership was still divided by the feud between the mufti of Jerusalem and Ragheb al-Nashashibi, the city's mayor. The former was a Nazi enthusiast, and the latter was on the Zionists' payroll.

Jaffa was left leaderless. 'Even before the battle,' writes Benny Morris, 'Jaffa, far more than the other Arab cities in Palestine, was characterised by disunity of command.' There were seven distinct and overlapping power centres in the city, including autonomous militia commanders, the *Najjada*, the municipality itself and the representative of the mufti.[7] The irregulars, many of whom were not from Jaffa, refused to follow orders from the national leadership. Jaffa's mayor, Yousef Heikal, understood that the city could never withstand a full-blown assault. He favoured a truce or agreement with the Haganah, but was opposed by the commander of Jaffa's paramilitaries, who was not from Jaffa. In addition the mufti's men were provoking the Haganah in and around Jaffa, and sabotaging, probably intentionally, Heikal's attempts to reach some kind of agreement with the Haganah.

'There was a belief that the Jews were generally cowards. Thus the people of Jaffa, as well as the members of the National Committee, believed that if they made ready a bit, and the British did not interfere on the side of the Jews, they would emerge victorious,' wrote the Palestinian political scientist Ibrahim Abu-Lughod, who left Jaffa in May 1948. 'They believed this, despite the fact that the National Committee had not succeeded in mobilising people or in finding a substantial number who were willing to engage in military action, and despite the fact that the results of the first encounters between the Arabs and the Jews had not been promising.'[8] Rather, noted Abu-Lughod, 'The "military confrontation" pitted a largely disarmed, pitifully led, and tightly controlled Palestinian community against a much enlarged, modern, tightly organised, brilliantly led, and internationally anchored and connected Palestinian Jewish community that was determined to fulfil its goal of establishing a Jewish state.'[9]

AS WINTER TURNED to spring in 1948, darkness descended. There was a growing sense of anarchy. Ahmad Hammami joined Jebaliyyeh's defence guard. 'Every day there was a funeral near us, because our house was by the cemetery,' says Fadwa. 'We heard the bombing and the shootings. Of course we were frightened. It started on a lower level, and there was no television then, to tell you everything that is happening. Then it got worse. They started to tell us that there was no school that day, because there had been fighting the night before, and the Jews were coming to attack Jaffa.' Manshiyyeh was Jaffa's northern front line, Jebaliyyeh its southern. Hasan Hammami's premonitions about Bat Yam, to the south—that it was a Zionist fortress-town—came true. 'Every night they shot from Bat Yam to Jaffa, and the Arabs shot back.'

Ahmad was often out all night at the security post. A few neighbouring families packed up and left, but Ahmad and Nafise were determined to stay, says Fadwa. 'My parents started to prepare the house for war. They put sandbags against the wall, outside and inside. Of course they were nervous, but I was sure that they did not want to leave. They laid down enough stocks to last for a year. All the food that we normally ate, but in massive quantities. Olives, olive oil, goat's cheese salted in water, dry goods like wheat and rice, butter, honey, and my mother made jams and marmalade.'

Jaffa's long porous border with Tel Aviv made it difficult to defend and easy to infiltrate. Arab men met in cafés at certain times of the day to hear the daily news broadcasts. The Irgun, aware of this, would drive into the city and roll barrels filled with explosives into the coffee houses at those times.[10] In response, Arab snipers shot into Tel Aviv, killing civilians. Still Ahmad Hammami would not leave. 'He said that this is our country and we will die here,' says Fadwa. 'He had many Jewish friends, and they told him that he should take his family and go. They told him that there were going to be "vicious days". They knew he had children—girls—and the Arabs are always afraid for their women.'

Then came news of Deir Yassin. This small Arab village not far from Jerusalem was captured by a joint force of Irgun and Lehi troops, supported by the Haganah, on 9 April 1948. A bloodbath ensued. Whole families, including women and children, were shot as they came out of their homes; others were killed and their houses demolished on top of them. At least 100, and possibly more than 250, people were killed. The survivors were rounded up, their money and jewellery were stolen and they were loaded onto trucks to be driven around Jewish West Jerusalem in a macabre 'victory parade', where they were abused, cursed and spat at. The Jewish Agency and the Haganah condemned the killings, but the Arab response was quick. On 13 April, fighters attacked a convoy of ten vehicles carrying unarmed medical staff and two Irgun fighters wounded at Deir Yassin to the Hebrew University in Jerusalem. The convoy was captured after a six-hour battle, while the British looked on. Seventy Jews were killed in the fighting, and the buses were drenched in petrol and set on fire. Deir Yassin was a little over an hour's drive from Jaffa, and the news of the massacre there spread quickly across Palestine. The Arab media's repeated claims that the Zionists had raped women would have a crucial effect in the coming days. 'Everybody was panicking,' says Fadwa. 'My mother and father started telling the stories that they had heard, that people were massacred. They were especially afraid for their girls, because some of the women had been raped.'

North of Jaffa, the Haganah captured Haifa in late April, and most of its Arab population evacuated the city, despite the pleas of the Jewish mayor that they should stay. At this time the Haganah was still opposed to attacking Jaffa, which it felt posed no real strategic threat. Instead it planned to blockade the city, and capture it after the British withdrew on 14 May, when the Mandate formally came to an end and the Jewish state would be declared. The Haganah wanted to take only Manshiyyeh, the southern suburbs of Abu Kabir and Tel Arish. But the Irgun vehemently disagreed. Menachem Begin's men wanted to take Jaffa, seeing it as a dangerous Arab enclave in the heart of the Jewish state. 'The UN plan was issued on 29 November 1947. We Jews accepted it, but the Arabs said no, and that when the British leave they will invade and throw us into the sea,' recalls Yoseph Nachmias, an Irgun veteran who fought in the battle for Jaffa. 'Within less than twenty-four hours, the Arabs started shooting into Tel Aviv. They put snipers on every tall building. Within five months we had more than one thousand inhabitants of Tel Aviv, men, women and children, killed or wounded. The Irgun decided to crush this arm sending death into Tel Aviv. And we were worried that the Egyptians would land in Jaffa, and the war would start there.'

Born in Jerusalem in 1926, Yoseph joined the British Royal Engineers in 1940 at the age of fourteen by forging his birth certificate. He fought across north Africa, and at the same time was a member of the Irgun. After six and a half years, he went underground. Expert in explosives and fluent in English, Yoseph could pass for British. He led raids into army camps for ammunition and weapons. 'The British didn't know what they were preparing me for. They made me a good warrior, and then I had to turn it on them, but I had no choice.' In early April 1948, Yoseph took part in a raid on a munitions train. It yielded many tons of arms and ammunition, including 20,000 mortar shells. These munitions decided Jaffa's fate, wrote Menachem Begin in his memoir, *The Revolt*: 'Our plan was to attack Jaffa at the narrow bottleneck linking the main town with its Manshiyyeh quarter which thrust northwards, like a peninsula, into Jewish Tel Aviv. The tactical aim was to break the "neck of the bottle" and reach the sea, in order to cut off the bulk of Manshiyyeh from Tel Aviv. The strategic aim was to subjugate Jaffa and free Tel Aviv once and for all from the loaded pistol pointed at its heart.'[11]

On Saturday 24 April 1948, at the start of the Jewish festival of Passover, Menachem Begin addressed the troops at the Irgun's headquarters in Tel Aviv: 'We are going to conquer Jaffa. This will be one of the most decisive battles in the war for Israel's independence. Know who is before you, remember those you have left behind. You face a ruthless enemy who intends to wipe us out. Behind you are your parents, our brothers and our children. Snipe the enemy. Aim well, conserve ammunition. Show no mercy in battle, just as the enemy has no pity for our people. Be compassionate with women and children. Whoever lifts his hand in surrender, spare him.'[12] Amichai Paglin, known as Gidi, commanded the attack. Paglin had masterminded the bombing of the British military headquarters in Jerusalem's King David Hotel, when ninety-one people were killed, including fifteen Jews. His instructions to his troops were unequivocal—they were 'to prevent constant military traffic in the city, to break the spirit of the enemy troops, to cause chaos among the civilian population in order to create a mass flight.'[13] The Irgun onslaught would eventually succeed far beyond their dreams. Several years earlier Irgun fighters had captured two three-inch mortars from an RAF camp. The mortars were known as 'orphans', as there were no shells for them. But the orphans would soon have parents: the tons of shells that the Irgun had taken from the British munitions train.

The battle for Jaffa began in the early hours of Sunday 25 April. Irgun gunners directed a steady rain of mortar fire onto the city. In theory the gunners were not supposed to target hospitals, religious sites or consulates. In practice the shells fell indiscriminately across

Clock Tower Square, smashing into the markets, and south into the heart of Ajami, killing and wounding large numbers of civilians. Panic and hysteria swept through the city. 'There were six hundred Irgun fighters. I was a company commander,' says Yoseph Nachmias. 'We opened the barrage, started firing and began to advance.' Two Irgun companies were deployed, one heading towards the railway tracks, and Yoseph's, trying to break through to the sea. Jaffa's defenders were reinforced by Bosnian Muslims, Syrian and Iraqi volunteers and Palestinian Germans from the old Templar colonies of Sarona and Walhalla, which dated back to the late nineteenth century. The narrow lanes and cramped alleys of Manshiyyeh gave them good cover. The Irgun had Bren light machine guns, but the Arab fighters had heavy Spandau guns.

The Irgun quickly discovered that a frontal urban attack demanded different military skills, and weapons, from guerrilla warfare. They had no tanks or artillery. Their mortars bounced off the houses where the Arabs were dug in. The Spandau machine guns laid down heavy fire. 'In the bottleneck of Manshiyyeh we learnt what all the armies had learnt in the Second World War: there are few better defensive positions than a row of ruined buildings. . . . Jaffa's defence line was thick and very deep. The Arabs were working under trained and skilful advisers,' wrote Begin.[14] Behind the Arab fighters stood the British army, with tanks and heavy artillery, ready to repulse any attempt by the Jews to capture Jaffa, territory that was not granted to them under the UN partition plan. Yoseph Nachmias and his fighters pulled back. 'They had such firepower and we had strict orders to conserve ammunition. That afternoon we withdrew, to lick our wounds and bury our dead. We had lost about six soldiers.'

· · ·

AHMAD HAMMAMI WAS downtown by Clock Tower Square when the mortars began falling. He never told his children what he saw as they exploded around him, but it was enough to change his mind about staying in Jaffa. Fadwa remembers: 'In one day my parents decided to leave. But not for good, because we left everything in the house. They said we are going on holiday, to Lebanon, for a month, and then we will come home. We were just escaping the bombardment. We took what was in the house, some bread, special holiday cakes my mother had just baked with dates inside, and some boiled eggs. We did not have anything with us, except the clothes on our back. My mother and her sisters brought their jewellery, my father had some money and some Persian rugs. He rolled up some of our belongings in them, including some blankets. The road of Jerusalem was closed, and the airport was shut, so we took a taxi to the port. The strangest thing was that my mother took her iron, I don't know why.'

Fadwa, then eleven years old, understood the reality of what was happening better than her younger siblings. Mustafa Hammami was nine that fateful day. At first it all seemed like a great adventure, especially when his parents told him the family would be travelling on an Italian cruise ship, the SS *Argentina*. 'The taxi came and I pleaded with my mother to take our cat, Ferooze, with us, but to no avail. We all sat in the back of the taxi in front of our house. Our cleaning lady was sitting nearby, weeping and waving to my mother,' recalls Mustafa, who now lives in Toronto. 'I looked at my mother and I noticed that she too was weeping and waving back. My father was sitting in the front passenger seat. He looked grim and tense, staring straight out at nothing. I still did not understand. Then suddenly the car moved.' Mustafa's days of skipping school to go fishing and bringing home a catch of skinny 'Bolshevik' fish were over for ever.

The journey to the port took just a few minutes. There the Hammamis were swept up in the chaos. Thousands of refugees were pouring down to the waterfront, trying to find a place on the armada of
boats bobbing in the water, jammed with passengers, as they went
back and forth from the harbour to the larger ships moored out at sea.
The Hammami children are grown now, with children and grandchildren of their own. But they all remember the scene at Jaffa's port
clearly. 'The port looked so different from my idyllic visits in the summer, watching the boats go in and out and staring at the big cargo
ships lined up out in the distance,' says Hasan. 'People were crammed
into boats of every size and shape. Feluccas with their sails, launches,
tugs and lighters were all full and all heading out to the open sea. We
boarded a long boat that took us out to a sailing ship.'

Mustafa and his younger siblings were still excited, swept up in
the drama. 'It all seemed very romantic and adventurous that we were
boarding a sailing ship. When our boat came to the side of the ship
there was a narrow rope ladder dangling and swinging in the breeze.
With some pushing and heaving we all managed to get on board. The
ship was already loaded with cargo and we sat on a crate of timber
boards. The decks were packed.' Fadwa, however, understood that this
journey was not an adventure but something far more profound.
'When we got on it was full of people, but they kept letting more on
board. Wherever you looked on the boat there were people. We knew
many of them. One of my teachers sat next to me—some of my
mother's friends and father's colleagues were nearby. There were no
chairs, no shelter, nothing. We just sat on the stacks of wood. I will
never forget that day. Never.'

Eventually the ship began to move. The Hammamis stared at Jaffa's
harbour, its familiar yellow sandstone buildings now wreathed in

smoke. 'We slowly sailed out to sea in the late afternoon. As we passed by Tel Aviv the water kept spouting and popping to our side. The Jews were firing shells at us, to ensure that we really left, and to wish us "bon voyage",' says Mustafa.

For Ismail Abou-Shehade, too, the memories of the exodus are unforgettable. 'If you ask me about this time, I can tell you about it, like it happened an hour ago. I can still see the people leaving, the women and children shouting, "To the sea, to the sea!" I carried my friends on my back and I buried them. The ones who saw don't like to remember, and those who cannot forget are suffering all the time.'

The Irgun was satisfied with the results of the mortar bombardment. Jaffa had not fallen, but the attack had cut communications and electricity, flooded the water mains and pinned down the enemy, wrote Menachem Begin. 'Confusion and terror, deepened by the noise of the battle raging at no great distance from the central streets, reigned in the town. Thus the morale of the enemy was broken and the great flight began, by sea and by land, on wheels and on foot.... Jaffa was in utter confusion. The streets were flooded, the houses gaping and tottering, looting and murder were rife.'[15] Jaffa's inhabitants were fleeing, but its defenders had not. They were holding their ground, while the Irgun were taking increasing numbers of casualties. Irgun commanders decided on a new tactic: groups of sappers would advance to an enemy position, blow it up and hold the new ground while reinforcements arrived. The Arab gunners picked them off one by one. 'We tried to reach the Arab positions but we were not successful. Sometimes three or four of our fighters were killed on the way,' says the Irgun veteran Yoseph Nachmias.

On Monday 26 April, the Irgun and the Haganah temporarily settled their differences over whether or not to take Jaffa. The disagreement was symbolic of a greater split, over who would govern the Jewish state once it came into being. The Irgun, the right-wing Zionists, were maximalists, who sought control of all of Mandate Palestine, even across the River Jordan into the Kingdom of Transjordan. The Haganah drew their support from the socialists, who were more ready to reach an accommodation with the Arabs—inside and outside Palestine—albeit on their terms. There was bad blood, too, over the Haganah's 'Hunting Season', when in 1944 the Haganah had handed over Irgun members to the British. The two militias signed an agreement under which the Irgun would operate only under Haganah command, and the battle for Jaffa continued. However, each time the Irgun fighters began to advance into Manshiyyeh, they could not hold the ground they captured and fell back. At the end of the second day of fighting Begin called for a halt and ordered a retreat, but his officers wanted to fight on. Yoseph Nachmias recalls: 'Begin wrote in his book that it was a mutiny, but we did not want to revolt. We said we cannot move back, and we know we can overcome the enemy.' Amichai Paglin, the commander of the attack, pleaded for more time and explained his new tactic. Eventually Begin was persuaded and the attack continued. Yoseph explains: 'Gidi asked us for our most courageous men. He demanded twenty-seven of my guys. When I decided who was going now to the fighting and who would remain in reserve, the ones staying behind started crying like babies, calling me names, saying that they had stood behind me in fire and water and now I was betraying them.'

Gidi's innovation was to advance *through* the buildings. The Irgun had no tanks, but it did have hammers and chisels. 'The houses were linked together like wagons in a train. We broke through, making holes in one room after another, like a hidden tunnel. We started on

Tuesday morning. What we could not achieve in two days, we did in two hours. We got under the Arabs' positions and put the explosives in. The explosives blew up, there was a cloud of dust and smoke and we stormed in and took their positions.' The Irgun fighters also built tunnels of sandbags to give them cover as they crawled towards the front line, passing down each sack by hand as they inched forward. 'It was the work of ants,' says Yoseph. The Arab gunners rained down fire on the sandbags. The dead and injured Irgun fighters were dragged clear, and others immediately took their place. Eventually the tunnels were long enough for the sappers to place their charges. The Arab fighters began to fall back. When Manshiyyeh police station was taken, the battle was almost over. By 7 a.m. on Wednesday the Irgun fighters had broken through the Arab lines and could see the sea in front of them. 'There were thirty of us, and as soon as we saw the sea we started running towards it, shouting *"ha-yam, ha-yam"* [the sea, the sea]. The Arabs ran away. We captured two of them—they said they thought hundreds of Jews were coming,' says Yoseph. The last pocket of resistance at Hasan Bey mosque was mopped up and the blue and white Zionist flag hoisted from the minaret.

In London, Foreign Secretary Ernest Bevin was furious. British prestige, already diminished by the fall of Haifa and the Arab exodus, was being further battered by the hated Irgun's advance. Britain would take full responsibility for the defence of Jaffa. Reinforcements arrived from Cyprus and Malta. Bevin ordered the British General Staff to 'see to it that the Jews did not manage to occupy Jaffa, or if they did, were immediately turned out'. The high commissioner for Palestine, General Sir Alan Cunningham, ordered the Irgun to withdraw from Manshiyyeh. Israel Rokach, the mayor of Tel Aviv, was warned that if the Irgun did not stop fighting, Tel Aviv would be shelled by tanks, bombed by the Royal Air Force and bombarded by the Royal Navy. Spitfire planes buzzed Tel Aviv and Manshiyyeh. Royal Navy ships moored offshore, guns pointed at the Irgun positions. Begin ignored the British ultimatum, British forces shelled the area around the Irgun headquarters, and tanks opened fire on the new Irgun positions in Manshiyyeh. Irgun sappers blew up more buildings, spreading the rubble across the road to block any British advance.

'The British gave us hell. We lost forty-one in the fighting for Jaffa, and eighty per cent of those were killed by the British. They shelled us and shelled us, and when they thought we were exhausted they advanced in tanks,' says Yoseph. 'We had four rounds of anti-tank ammunition. When we saw the first tank we fired, but it missed. The second one hit, and they pulled back, and left the tank there. I talked to them through a loud-hailer. I told them, I said, "Why should you die, this is not your war. In two weeks you are going back to Old Blighty. We would like to see you walking back to Old Blighty and not in coffins." It helped—they pulled back the tanks—but they kept shelling us.'

Meanwhile, the Irgun's high command informed the British that if their attack did not cease, it would launch a mortar barrage at the British headquarters in Jaffa's Templar colony, and at other British camps across Palestine. The Palestine Mandate would end on 14 May. British officials were torn between destroying their most hated enemy and sacrificing further troops in a cause they all knew was now hopeless. Britain blinked first. It no longer insisted on a complete evacuation of Manshiyyeh. The new terms were that the Irgun evacuate the police station and hand it over to the British, and that the other Irgun positions be handed over to the Haganah. The Irgun responded by blowing up the police station and more houses. Only then did it surrender its positions to the Haganah.

Apart from Manshiyyeh, Jaffa stayed in Arab hands, protected by British troops. By now, 30 April, perhaps 20,000 people remained, less than a quarter of the population. Among them was Hussein Abou-Shehade, father of Ismail, who had helped pull out the bodies from the rubble of the New Seray. 'My father refused to leave because he knew how difficult it is to move to a foreign country. He had already emigrated once, so we stayed.' Tragically for Jaffa, its mayor, Yousef Heikal, had shown less fortitude. 'At first he told us not to leave. He said that he was leaving the country only for three days in order to get some news about what was going on,' recalls Ismail. Heikal returned on 28 April. 'Then he gathered us again. He said that Jaffa was going to be occupied by the Jews soon, since there was no defence—no weapons— and nothing could stop them from taking our dear Jaffa. He then gave people permission to leave the country if they wished. He said that he himself was leaving with his family. People then started to leave by ships and trains. All the routes to the Arab countries were opened, and people could leave for free. The Arab countries were responsible. After a week there was nothing left but cats and dogs. We few families who stayed went to live in the orange groves.'

Too scared to remain in Jaffa once the British departed, thousands more left at the beginning of May, either by sea or with the help of the British as they crossed the Haganah lines. The Arab Liberation Army contingent finally arrived at the end of April, and behaved in characteristic fashion: looting, terrorising and molesting women, records Nimr al-Khatib.[16] By early May the city had collapsed. Mayor Heikal and the rest of the municipal leaders had fled. The Irgun and Haganah finally entered Jaffa proper on 14 May, after the British troops had left. Between four and five thousand Arabs remained. 'Jaffa had surrendered,' says Yoseph Nachmias. 'We field commanders wanted to put those few thousand on buses as well and send them away. That is what they would have done to us. But our leader, Menachem Begin, said not to touch those who remained, and to let them be. He said if they did not leave with their brothers, then let them live in peace with us.'

But most of Jaffa's inhabitants did not believe they could live in peace with the victorious Jews. Those who fled recall days of terror: a seemingly endless rain of mortars, a city starving and sealed off from its surroundings, civilians killed and injured by bombings and sniping. Flight from violence and anarchy is a natural human instinct, especially for parents desperate to protect their children. Yet some of the few thousand who did stay argue that their compatriots should have shown more fortitude. Even today the bitter debate continues among Palestinians—both within Jaffa and in the diaspora—over whether the city was unnecessarily abandoned. On 18 May Ben-Gurion visited Jaffa. 'I couldn't understand,' he wrote in his diary. 'Why did the inhabitants leave?'[17] Haganah intelligence reports from 1948 describe the Palestinians as being possessed by a 'psychosis of flight'. The Haganah's Operation Chametz, which had captured several villages near Jaffa at the end of April, was a factor, as Jaffa was cut off, with no food supply. So was the massacre at Deir Yassin. The Irgun's terrifying mortar bombardment of Jaffa was the first stage of ethnic cleansing and triggered the mass panic and exodus. But the bombardment stopped after the British intervened, and most of the close-quarter urban warfare was confined to Manshiyyeh. Jaffa was not bombarded for weeks by tanks, bombed by aeroplanes or shelled to rubble by heavy artillery. The mortars did damage buildings, killing and wounding civilians, but mortar fire alone cannot destroy a city and did not destroy Jaffa. The Irgun did not advance street by street into Clock Tower Square, or Ajami, or Jebaliyyeh, setting houses on fire and killing civilians. They were held back by the British. When the British left and the Irgun and Haganah did take over the city, they met no resistance, because Jaffa was empty. The Arab exodus had begun in the winter of 1947–48, six months before the Irgun attacked Manshiyyeh. Most of those who left, it seems, thought they would soon return. But they were wrong.

BY THE SECOND day at sea, Mustafa Hammami no longer thought that the journey was a great adventure. There was barely any food and little water, and most of what he ate came straight back up again. 'We were seasick. We vomited into a drainage pipe. I had never before smelled that acrid stench of vomit and urine, and I still remember it now.' That night the boat ran into a storm. It was dangerously overloaded and began to list to one side. Several millennia before, the prophet Jonah had fled from Jaffa on a cargo ship. Jonah was trying to escape God's command to go and preach at Nineveh. Jonah's boat hit bad weather. 'Then the Lord sent a great wind on the sea, and such a violent storm arose that the ship threatened to break up. All the sailors were afraid and each cried out to his own god. And they threw the cargo into the sea to lighten the ship' (Jonah 1:4–5).

The Hammamis' captain also ordered the passengers to throw all heavy belongings overboard. 'We were all frightened. The next morning one woman could not find her newborn baby. In the darkness and confusion she must have accidentally thrown it overboard. Her wailing broke our hearts. That night an old man passed away, and a woman delivered a baby. We were very shocked, and a sombre mood fell on us. We sat quietly for the rest of the voyage,' says Mustafa. A Royal Navy vessel passed by and a sailor barked into his loud-hailer:

who were they, and what were they doing? 'We are Arabs, leaving Jaffa and heading for Beirut,' someone shouted. The ship sailed closer. The crew swept the spotlight up and down the rows of shivering, frightened refugees before pulling away. 'I often wonder what went through that captain's mind when he saw us, packed like sardines, and then steamed away without offering us any help,' says Hasan Hammami.

On the last morning a Lebanese fighter flew overhead, so low Mustafa could see its markings. The journey by boat from Jaffa to Beirut normally took twelve hours. After three days at sea, the Hammamis disembarked at the southern Lebanese port of Tyre. Ahmad Hammami never saw Jaffa, or his house, again. His wife, Nafise, and several of their children would return, decades later. By then Ahmad's house would have new owners, and Jaffa new rulers.

10

Jaffa Has New Masters

Summer 1948

Jaffa the Great, clamorous with sounds of the Orient—
silence reigns there, and the silence frightens me.

*Joseph Weitz, member of the committee responsible
for renaming abandoned Arab villages after the Nakba[1]*

I n May 1948 Amin Andraus' house was a fortress. There were
sandbags around the walls and sandbags on the roof. Amin was
a widower, living with his mother, Haya, and these were the most
difficult days of his life. His family was in exile, his business ruined, his
hometown abandoned and his country no longer in existence. Amin's
wife, Hanneh, had died in 1945, leaving him with four children to raise.
As the fighting worsened, Amin sent his son, Salim, and daughters,
Wedad, Suad and Leila, to Jordan with his sister Fahima. Amin's car
showroom had been demolished by the British after a policeman went
up to the roof for a cigarette and was shot dead by a sniper. Amin had
had nothing to do with the incident. But despite his vociferous
protests, he had just half an hour to get out what he could before the
explosives were detonated and the building came crashing down on
his stock of cars, crushing them beneath the rubble.

Amin was a member of Jaffa's Emergency Committee, and by now also the Arab mayor in all but name. Yousef Heikal, the actual mayor, had left the keys to the New Seray (or what was left of it) with Amin when he left, saying, 'You look after the city until I get back.' Heikal did not return. Despite Amin's entreaties, most of his friends had fled. From Clock Tower Square, through the markets, down into Ajami and Jebaliyyeh, Jaffa was eerily empty. For Amin it was a tragedy. 'My father believed in staying and tried to convince people to stay. But they left, because they thought it was only for a few days. It was very sad. Jaffa was let down by its population,' says Amin's son, Salim. Amin tried to persuade his mother, Haya, to leave with his children, but she refused. 'I will not leave my house, and I will not leave my son,' she said. 'I want to die in my country.'

Amin understood that further military resistance was pointless. On 9 May the Emergency Committee wrote to the British district commissioner, declaring that Jaffa was no longer defensible. It would be an 'open city' once the Mandate ended, and would not 'be used for military purposes'. On 13 May 1948 Jaffa capitulated. Amin Andraus and three others, including Abdel Rahim, a cousin of Ahmad Hammami, signed the surrender agreement. 'My father explained that Jaffa was a peaceful town, there was nobody there to fight, just old people and foreign workers who did not have money to leave. He wanted Jaffa to be an "open city", with no looting or destruction,' says his daughter Suad. 'There has been criticism of this, but they had to do it. It was heartbreaking but it was the best option they had at the time. There was no way to fight, and he wanted to save Jaffa from being destroyed.'

The agreement stipulated that all arms and ammunition must be surrendered, on pain of severe punishment; that any information about mines or booby traps must be submitted to the Haganah; that anyone considered dangerous to peace and security would be interrogated and possibly interned and that all municipal records and documents must be left intact.[2] Arab males, even if they had fought against the Haganah, would not be detained unless they were criminals or a threat to peace and security. However, they would be gathered in Ajami until they were properly identified. Tel Aviv municipality would assist in the restoration of normal life. Clause Eight seemed to leave the door open for some to return: 'Any male Arab who has left Jaffa and who wishes to return to Jaffa may apply for a permit to do so. Permits will be granted after their bona fides have been proved, provided that the Commander of the Haganah is convinced that applicants will not, at any time, constitute a threat to peace and security'.[3] The Haganah commander may have been sincere, but his political masters had other plans.

ON 14 MAY 1948, David Ben-Gurion declared the establishment of the State of Israel and took office as prime minister. Israel was recognised immediately by the United States, and three days later by the Soviet Union. After the first Zionist Congress in 1897, Theodor Herzl had written: 'At Basel I founded the Jewish state. If I were to say this today, I would be greeted by universal laughter. In five years' time, and certainly in fifty, everyone will see it.'[4] Herzl was off by one year. There were rapturous, if brief, celebrations across the new state, which was still at war. The Israeli Defence Forces (IDF) were formed, eventually absorbing most of the fighters of the Haganah, Irgun and Lehi, except in Jerusalem, where some Irgun and Lehi fighters continued to operate independently. Old enmities between the different factions did not fade quickly. The Lehi fighter Yoram Aharoni was happy to serve in a Hebrew army, but his wife, Rina, was more ambivalent. The IDF took its orders from the new Israeli government, the same people who launched the 'Hunting Season' in 1944 and handed over Irgun and Lehi members to the British. 'Lehi did not take part in the celebrations. We were an underground [movement], used to working in very small groups, and now we were in an army,' says Rina. 'The others in the IDF who knew I was in Lehi were afraid to talk to me at first. It was hard for them and hard for me.'

There were more pressing threats than intra-Zionist rivalry. Four Arab armies invaded the new state: Egypt from the south and Jordan, Iraq and Syria from the north and west. Other Arab states sent reinforcements, and the 1948 war entered its second phase. These were not the rag-tag Palestinian militias but well-armed national armies, with tanks, artillery and planes. Arab leaders loudly proclaimed that they would annihilate the Jewish state. 'This will be a war of extermination and a momentous massacre, which will be spoken of like the Mongolian massacres and the Crusades,' announced Abd al-Rahman Azzam Pasha, secretary general of the Arab League. He confidently predicted that 'it does not matter how many Jews there are. We will sweep them into the sea'.[5]

Which was why, on 17 May 1948, when Israel was three days old, Shlomo Chelouche was steadily tracking an Egyptian fighter plane in the sights of his machine gun. Shlomo was a Haganah commander for north Tel Aviv, based at Sde Dov airport. The airport had already been bombed that morning, shortly after dawn. A tent holding arms and ammunition was hit. Shlomo had helped pull the wounded from the wreckage. He was later decorated for his bravery. 'Who goes in to pull out the wounded when ammunition is exploding everywhere? Only a fool,' he says, laughing. 'The second plane came towards us an hour later, from the direction of Jaffa. He was not flying very high. I positioned the gun and waited for him for a few minutes. He was coming and I was waiting. I was calm, I aimed. I gave him everything I had and the plane flew out to sea.'

Shlomo shot well. Aharon Remez, commander of the Israeli Air Force, told Shlomo that the plane had gone down near Herzliya and he was going to look for the pilot. 'After an hour Remez came back to Sde Dov with the pilot. I spoke to him in Arabic. He was shivering. I asked him if he wanted to drink something. He said, "No, no, no." He was afraid. Remez wanted to take him to the big chief, Ben-Gurion, to question him. I told him that you don't take an officer to Ben-Gurion. I said he was a prisoner of war and Remez should leave him with me. He laughed, and agreed. I gave the Arab a comb, for his hair. He took the comb and started combing—he was so nervous, he couldn't hold it.' The pilot was then held as a prisoner of war.

Down the coast in Jaffa, the Haganah command did not keep its promise to guarantee safety and security. Jewish troops ran wild, looting and robbing at will. Houses were broken into, cars towed away, silverware and valuables plundered. Even cows were stolen. On 20 May the Emergency Committee wrote a letter of protest to the Israeli authorities, complaining that properties belonging to absentee owners were being broken into and robbed. Movable items were taken away in broad daylight, while heavier furniture was 'smashed into pieces due to nothing but destructive motives only'. People were being openly robbed on the street, a girl of twelve was raped, and the outrages were even happening at night, when the population was under curfew. But if any Jewish soldiers were caught plundering, the letter continued, they were immediately released and carried on where they had left off.[6]

It seems Amin Andraus had a reasonable working relationship with Yitzhak Chisik, the military governor. But Chisik lacked the authority to bring law and order. By 10 June, Amin had had enough. He wrote to Chisik, resigning from the Emergency Committee, and asked for a permit to leave Jaffa, 'as I cannot see any benefit from my staying here'.[7] In the end, though, Amin stayed. Six days later the Israeli cabinet met to discuss the question of the Arab refugees. Mapam, the left-wing party in the coalition, was pushing for some to be allowed home. Ben-Gurion refused: no refugees would be permitted to return, at least not as long as hostilities continued. 'I believe we should prevent their return. . . . We must settle Jaffa, Jaffa will become a Jewish city,' he proclaimed.[8] The issue would be considered once Israel was at peace. This was enough for Mapam to stay in the coalition. But by the time the fighting had ended, opposition to any return was so widespread that the doors stayed closed, and remain so to this day.

Amin Andraus and the Jaffa Emergency Committee knew nothing of this. On 26 June they wrote to Yitzhak Chisik, asking for permission for the relatives of Arabs still in Jaffa to return. Chisik, a decent man, forwarded the appeal on to Bechor Shitrit, the Minority Affairs minister. He enclosed a copy of the 13 May surrender agreement, and pointed out the wording of the crucial Clause Eight. Similar appeals were arriving from the remaining Arabs of Haifa. Shitrit in turn wrote to Ben-Gurion. His answer was still no, 'so long as the war continues and the enemy stands at the gates'. The appeals of Amin Andraus and the Jaffa Emergency Committee were brushed aside.

Other pressures were less easy to ignore. At the end of July 1948 Count Folke Bernadotte, the United Nations mediator, demanded that Israel allow the return of a limited number of displaced Palestinians, especially those from Jaffa and Haifa. The port cities had a special resonance and symbolic value. Israel again refused. In August Count Bernadotte met with Moshe Shertok, Israel's foreign minister. He pointed out the anomaly of Israel demanding the immediate immigration of Jewish refugees while 'they refused to recognise the existence of the Arab refugees which they had created'. On 17 September Count Bernadotte, who had helped save thousands of Jews from the Nazi camps, was killed in his car in Jerusalem by members of Lehi.

Amin's robust defence of Jaffa's Arab population made him many enemies, especially in the Israeli military administration that controlled Jaffa. For Amin, experienced in dealing with the British, there was room to manoeuvre in the cracks and crevices of the Israeli state, much of which, especially the legal system, had been inherited from the Mandate. 'My father immediately learnt Hebrew, even when everything was happening around him, says Suad. 'He said you have to know your enemy and their language. They didn't know he spoke fluent German, and the Israeli officials spoke Yiddish, which was very similar. He managed to keep a poker face for a long time, listening to everything, until one day he was in an office where someone who knew he spoke German began speaking to him in German.' Amin began to sense that he was in danger. On the afternoon of 1 July, Amin and other Jaffa notables were meeting newspaper correspondents. Someone interrupted the discussion and told him that his house was being looted. He rushed home to find his mother, Haya, furious. The robbers, she explained, had jumped over the garden fence while she had been on the other side of the house talking to a neighbour. When Haya and the neighbour heard noises they rushed over and surprised the burglars, who were trying to steal two carpets. They escaped with one, some rolls of cloth and Amin's Kodak camera.

Robbery was a hazard for every Jaffa resident in those lawless days. But Amin had more sinister adversaries. Two days later, on the night of 2 July, two shots hit the western side of his house. On 5 July he wrote to the military governor, explaining that 'a group of Jewish soldiers and civilians came in bus no. M 4233 to the garage in my house and wanted to break in and take its contents away.' The looters were prevented from doing so by Abraham Cohen, of the Special Police, who was in charge of the checkpoint at Jebaliyyeh. 'These incidents, having taken place immediately after each other in the course of three days, made me suspect that I have been earmarked for injury,' Amin continued, before asking for measures to be taken to ensure his safety, and for police officer Cohen to be properly rewarded and promoted for his diligence.[9]

ACROSS PALESTINE THE Arab exodus continued through the summer of 1948. No systematic plan was drawn up for the nation-wide expulsion of the Palestinians, nor did Ben-Gurion issue written orders to that effect. But he did not need to, as it was understood that population displacement was inevitable, and in some places necessary. Plan Dalet, which outlined the IDF's military strategy, ordered that the Arab villages, where the irregulars were based, be 'pacified', meaning they would either surrender or be depopulated. Hostile villages were to be levelled. In military terms this was standard strategy. Israel, at war on several fronts, was fighting for its very survival, and its territory needed to be secured and contiguous. The Palestinians were a potential, or actual, fifth column. In the 1948 war, as in countless other conflicts where an army fights an enemy supported by the local population, the distinction between military and civilian was at best blurred, and often non-existent. Plan Dalet was a military blueprint, not an order to expel the Palestinians, as Benny Morris notes, but by providing for the destruction of communities that resisted the IDF, it gave a 'strategic-ideological anchor and basis for expulsions'.[10]

More than 700,000 Palestinians left, and about 120,000 stayed. Precisely how many were intentionally expelled and how many fled—perhaps unnecessarily—will never be known.[11] The causes of the Palestinian exodus varied at different stages of the war, and in different areas. Few conflicts have been examined in as much detail as the events in Israel/Palestine in spring and summer 1948. Almost sixty years later, the question as to whether the Palestinians fled voluntarily or were expelled has crucial contemporary relevance to solving the conflict. Israelis argue that if the Palestinians left voluntarily, they have no right to return. But Palestinians claim that they were indeed forced out and do have the right to go home. Several peace plans in recent years have foundered on this central issue.

In Haifa, 70,000 departed despite the pleas of the Jewish mayor for them to stay. Ninety-five thousand fled from Jaffa, but many perhaps could have stayed had they, as Amin Andraus asked, shown greater endurance. It is important to note that thousands had left from both ports months before serious fighting began in the spring of 1948. Israeli historians such as Benny Morris and Tom Segev have done valuable work to disentangle the myths that have grown up around 1948. Arab archives still remain closed, but the underlying reasons for the Palestinian exodus are universal. Conflicts produce refugees. As the Palestinian political scientist Ibrahim Abu-Lughod noted: 'That bicommunal wars inevitably produce victims is obvious. . . . As in all such wars, some people were dislocated as a result.'[12]

The key question was, would they be allowed home? The Israeli response was: not to Israel, and especially not to Jaffa. The Israeli government formed a Transfer Committee to prevent the return of the refugees, and to settle new Jewish *olim* (immigrants) in their abandoned houses, starting in Haifa and Jaffa. The few Arabs who remained were to be relocated from their homes, to make room for the Jews. Yitzhak Chisik, the military governor of Jaffa, resigned on 25 July, no longer able to protect Jaffa's remaining Arabs and their property from looters and vandals.[13] Under the new relocation plan, Jaffa was to be divided into Zones A, B and C. All Arab inhabitants of Jaffa were to be relocated to Zone A, and/or Zone B if hostilities resumed. Both were surrounded by a wire fence, and the Arab population would not be allowed to enter or leave without a special permit. Zone C was to be evacuated immediately. On 20 August, Amin Andraus and the Emergency Committee submitted a detailed memorandum of protest to Meir Laniado, Chisik's successor. The relocating plan repeatedly violated the 13 May surrender agreement. It violated Clause Eight, that Arab refugees would be allowed home after security checks; Clause Five, that remaining Arab inhabitants would be allowed to return home, and Clause Six, which stated that Jaffa's male population would not be interned. The plan violated the Geneva Conventions, which the Haganah commander had pledged to observe; breached international law, and split Jaffa into two parts, one Jewish and one Arab, to be divided by a wire fence.

The Arab quarter was a ghetto in all but name. 'They surrounded us with barbed wire. There were three gates in the wire and we were only allowed to go out if we wanted to work in the orange groves, and we had to get a permit from those people we were working for,' recalls Ismail Abou-Shehade. For Ismail and his father, Hussein, the Arab leaders like Amin Andraus, who negotiated with the Israelis, were turncoats. 'Those people, whose names I don't even want to remem-

ber, were betrayers who gave Jaffa up to the Jews.' Ismail left soon
after, for Tiberias. The Emergency Committee's protest memorandum
was ignored. When the time came, Israeli soldiers simply threw the
Arabs and their furniture out of their homes—even the Emergency
Committee was expelled from its offices.

Still Amin continued on his rounds, like a doctor checking his
patients, and Jaffa then needed much attention. 'My father looked
after the water supply, all the things to keep the city going, even the
flour for the bakeries,' says Suad. Amin's idea of how Jaffa should be
run often clashed with the plans of its new masters. His formative
years at the tough Schneller School in Jerusalem, where he learnt to
be independent and self-reliant, soon proved useful. 'When he
became too troublesome for the Israelis, and was really interfering
with the way they wanted to do things, they put him under house
arrest, with a guard. He could only go into the garden. But he was
absolutely independent. He had chickens and pigeons. He built an
oven where my grandmother baked bread.'

Eventually the Israelis realised what Amin already knew. They
needed him to keep Jaffa functioning. 'After a while nothing worked
in Jaffa without him. The Israelis started asking him questions about
how to sort things out. He said he could not do anything if he was
under house arrest,' explains Suad. 'So they allowed him out, but
with a guard, who enjoyed my grandmother's cooking.' One day Amin
paid a call at a tiny fishermen's café. 'He sat with them while they
explained their problems. He sat and sat, and the guard was getting
annoyed, saying, "Mr Andraus, it is already lunchtime." My father
said he just wanted to sit a while longer. The guard said he did not
know what interest he had talking to these simple people, but my
father said, no, they were his friends. Out of devilment he stretched it

out a bit, and in the end the guard could not take it any more. He said, "Mr Andraus, I want you to tell me one thing, who is the prisoner, you or me?"'

Amin's doughty defence of Jaffa brought him more trouble. On 25 October 1948 he wrote to the Jaffa Security Office to say that seven armed men dressed in khaki had broken into his yard and towed away his maroon Humber Sedan on a truck (registration number 2351), accompanied by a motorcycle (registration number 161N). 'My Jewish neighbours intervened and asked them in Hebrew if they had any written order to take the car. They refused to show such an order, and threatened them with their arms.'[14]

THE WAR MAROONED the pharmacy student Fakhri Geday in Lebanon, unable to return home or to communicate with his family. He spent many days at Beirut's port in late April and early May 1948, watching the boats disgorge thousands of Palestinian refugees, looking for his family. The poorer refugees had gone to Gaza, but the middle classes preferred Beirut. Fakhri was twenty-one years old. He did not know if his family was alive or dead. 'Before the war started I had a letter from my father asking me to find a house for them in Beirut until the fighting was over. Then I got another one that my mother and my sister refused to leave, and the whole family planned to hide in the French hospital if there were massacres. That was the last I heard. It was very stressful to know nothing, a very difficult time. I looked for my family, and I asked the people coming in if they knew about them.'

One man told Fakhri that his father had left Jaffa. Then the Damianis, who owned the soap factory in Old Jaffa, arrived. 'Your father is still in Jaffa, because your mother refused to leave,' Mrs Damiani told

Fakhri. 'She urged me not to leave. But my husband insisted.' Only a year later, in the summer of 1949, did Fakhri receive a letter from his father, Youssef, via the International Red Cross. He and the rest of the family were alive. The pharmacy on the Gaza Road, now renamed Yefet Street, still stood. The house was still theirs. Fakhri finished his studies and applied for a permit to return to Jaffa, under Israel's family reunification law, which allowed a few Palestinians to go home.

II

Sofia-by-the-Sea

Autumn 1948

Bulgarian became the language of the streets, and shop signs
appeared in Bulgarian almost overnight. Bulgarian branches
of the major political parties were set up, and a newspaper,
Far (lighthouse), was published daily in Bulgarian.

Ethnologist Guy Haskell on the Bulgarian immigration to Jaffa[1]

One morning in the autumn of 1948, Julia Chelouche
awoke feeling disturbed. She dreamt that her husband,
David, got up from his bed, kissed her and then died.
David was not well. He was fifty-eight, suffered from severe diabetes
and had recently had a heart attack. Julia's dreams were powerful por-
tents. Decades earlier she had dreamt that Yaakov Chelouche had
placed a necklace of jewels around her neck, and soon after she had
married his nephew, David. 'I was seized by panic. I went into David's
room, and he was sleeping. The nurse sat in an armchair, covered with
a blanket, dozing,' Julia wrote in her memoir. 'The symbol of my
dream was: when I kiss my husband, he will die.'

Julia and her husband still lived in Haifa. The family had all survived the 1948 war. Haifa, like Jaffa and Tel Aviv, saw heavy fighting in
the border neighbourhoods between Arab and Jewish quarters. Julia's

neighbours' son, Moshe, had been killed by a sniper on his way to work. 'That day, fifteen boys were buried. The crying could be heard from afar,' wrote Julia of his funeral.

During the war Julia's own son, Aharon, had been a student in New York. Her daughter Edith had returned from school in Beirut and was now a communications officer in the army. Unknown to Edith, her brother had showed her picture to an American friend called Ben Krygier, who was heading for Israel. Ben and Edith met, and quickly fell in love and married soon after. Some time after her dream Julia did kiss her husband, and shortly before dawn on 16 October, David Chelouche, grandson of the great patriarch Aharon, died. Hundreds attended his funeral. The family sat *shiva*, the Jewish mourning ritual, for a week, and all of Haifa, it seemed, came to pay their respects.

A month later, Julia travelled to Tel Aviv for the synagogue service to mark the thirty days since David's death. Her beloved grandmother Mazal, now ninety-one, had promised to meet her there and return with her to Haifa for several months. Julia and Mazal were very close, as Julia's mother had died young. The night before Julia left for Tel Aviv, she dreamt of Mazal. In her dream, Julia asked her why she had come now, a day early. 'My daughter, I came to see you,' said Mazal. When Julia arrived in Tel Aviv, her brothers-in-law, Marco and Zaki, sat down with her and gently broke the news: Mazal had died the day before. 'I burst out crying. My grandmother, whom I loved like a mother,' wrote Julia. 'That's when I understood my dream: her soul came to me and she was already in her grave.' And so the cycle of the generations continued, for Edith soon gave birth to a daughter, Irit, whom Julia adored. She felt like 'half a person' without David, she wrote, but still 'took pleasure from my granddaughter. . . . She was a good girl and very pretty.'

. . .

AROUND THIS TIME, Shabat Aharoni, father of Yoram, opened his shop Tiv (quality) at 6 Nagib Bustros Street. The street had once been the commercial heartland of Jaffa. After 1948, it was a dead zone. The shops were silent and shuttered, their owners and customers now eking out a living in the refugee camps of Gaza and Lebanon or building new lives in Cairo and Amman. Shabat had obtained the shop through the state company that processed abandoned Arab property. Of this there was plenty, and Bustros Street soon echoed to two new languages: the sing-song medieval Spanish of Ladino (the old dialect spoken by Sephardic Jews) and the Slavic consonants of Bulgarian.

Tiv sold spices and coffee, although initially Shabat knew little about either. 'My father knew about paprika, but that was all. He bought a coffee machine and two hundred kilos of coffee a month, and started to sell it,' says Yoram. By now Yoram and his wife, Rina, had renounced their explosives and were raising their family. They lived in a small flat in the centre of Tel Aviv. Their first son, Dov, was born in 1949, and their second, Ofer, three years later. Yoram worked with his father. They built up the business steadily, without a great fuss, for that was the Bulgarian way. At first they sold mainly coffee, paprika and black pepper, the spices used in Bulgarian dishes, a synthesis of Spanish, Balkan and Turkish cooking. Shabat taught Yoram about coffee, and how to blend it. The Bulgarians took theirs with roasted ground chicory, the Arabs with fragrant cardamom. Each wave of new immigrants sought new spices and coffees.

Tiv soon became renowned across the coastal plain, a Jaffa institution. 'We searched for the best-quality coffee, the highest grade of spices. There are ways to tell the quality of pepper—you have to see the way it is cleaned. Spices can be adulterated, cut with something else. Black pepper is cut with burnt bread crumbs. Cumin can be padded out with other powders. I knew all the tricks. We only sold the best,' says Yoram. 'We developed the shop slowly. Each time a customer came and asked for a certain kind of spice or coffee, we would find a supplier and would buy it. Every group of Jews had their own preferences. Jews from Tripoli, for example, roasted their coffee at home, then brought it in to us to grind finely.'

Shabat was a kind-hearted man. Many of his Jewish customers were homesick and disoriented. They didn't speak Hebrew properly. Arrogant Ashkenazi officials bossed them about. They had no family contacts among the bureaucracy. Shabat always had time for a chat and a few kind words. He was a fine role model. Shabat had arrived in Jaffa with his family and two shoeshine brushes, and was now running a successful shop. With its familiar smells of spices and coffee, Tiv was almost a home from home for the new arrivals, says Yoram. 'When my father passed away, people told me that when they first came to Israel and they had nothing, he would give them spices to cook with for the holidays. He told them to pay him when they had some money. They could cook the food that they were used to and drink their own type of coffee. My father helped people start their new lives in Israel, and that was very important for him.'

Life was hard in Israel's early years. The economy barely functioned and food was rationed. The ruling socialist Mapai Party (also known as the Workers' Party and the Labour Party) was slow, bureaucratic and inefficient. The heavy hand of state control, the need for endless permits demanding the necessary contacts, known as 'proteksia' or 'Vitamin P', stifled initiative and bred nepotism and corruption. In effect, Mapai ran a one-party state, which was not surprising as its leaders were eastern European socialists. Israelis, especially on the kibbutzim, addressed each other as *haver*, meaning 'friend' or 'comrade'. They wore egalitarian open-neck shirts and sandals; ties were disapproved of as a bourgeois affectation, even anti-Zionist. Rightwing Jews and the remaining Palestinians did have members of the Knesset—the parliament—to represent their interests. But there was little they could achieve. Mapai, together with the Histadrut, the state trade union organisation, controlled the health services, the economy, the state administration and much of the media.

Businessmen and capitalists were frowned on, especially those with ambitious ideas, as Ben Krygier, husband of Edith Chelouche, soon discovered. Ben wanted to develop Israel's tourist business. 'My husband was a real promoter,' says Edith. 'He thought that all the Jews in America would want to visit Israel, but there was no infrastructure, no hotels or proper transport then.' Ben travelled across the country, trying to make contacts and set up a network for tourists and visitors. 'But at the time Israel was not ready for private enterprise, so we left Israel in 1951 for New York,' says Edith. Julia Chelouche, Edith's mother, soon followed, and stayed for seventeen years, before the whole family returned to Israel.

ISRAEL THEN HAD other priorities. It had signed armistice agreements with the Arab states, but these merely afforded a pause in the conflict. Israel was ringed by implacably hostile neighbours who remained committed to its destruction. The country was a strategic nightmare to defend: at one point the border with the West Bank was barely ten miles from the coast. Major cities such as Tel Aviv were well within enemy artillery range. Hostilities could erupt again at any moment. Israel was nervous and insecure, with much of its population traumatised. About one in three were Holocaust survivors. Many had seen their families killed. Six thousand Israelis, one per cent of the population, had been killed in the 1948 war, and many of them were young.

Israel needed people. From Krakow to Casablanca, Berlin to Benghazi, wave after wave of immigrants poured in. Between May 1948 and the end of 1951, Israel absorbed 684,000 newcomers. Their receptions varied dramatically: Jews from Arab countries were put in tents, while those from Europe were given hotel rooms. The Jews of Bulgaria arrived en masse. They came from all over the country: the capital, Sofia, the port of Varna and the hometown of Yoram Aharoni, Pazardjik. By 1949, 45,000 of the 50,000-strong community had relocated to Israel. Many thousands started their new lives in Jaffa and other coastal towns, filling up the abandoned Arab villas. Socially cohesive, with a strong work ethic and an entrepreneurial spirit, they were a welcome addition. 'The Bulgarians are very modest and not afraid of working,' says Yoram Aharoni. 'They did not make exaggerated demands. They had initiative. They opened small shops, garages, grocery stores, the everyday things that are needed. They worked, and they kept together. Many of them had known each other in Bulgaria.' The Bulgarian Jews were Sephardim. But their European origins meant that the Ashkenazi elite regarded them as 'honorary' Ashkenazim. They formed the Tsadikov Bulgarian choir, and established a library. Jaffa was a little Sofia, crowded with Bulgarian cafés, restaurants and social clubs. For many years Communist-inclined Bulgarians held a lecture or poetry reading at the Jaffa library in order to celebrate 9 September, the day the Red Army entered Bulgaria in 1944. Yet there was only one small Bulgarian synagogue. Like many Zionist Jews, the Bulgarians felt that once they were in Israel, there was little need for religious observance.

Jaffa, like the ports of Haifa and Acre, was unusual in the new Jewish state. Although only a tiny fraction of its Arab population remained, Jews and Arabs still encountered each other on a daily basis, whereas across much of the country, the Arabs had vanished completely. There were no Arab traders selling fruits and vegetables, no Arab workers tilling the fields, no Arab children scampering home from school. The Palestinian exodus left an unsettling vacuum; many Israelis were astonished at its speed and extent. The aftermath of the *Nakba* made some Jews uneasy, as they themselves were refugees from Nazi persecution. One soldier wrote: 'It is amazing, hard to believe. Houses full of possessions, and no life: Shops full, and no buyers. Valuable properties abandoned. Our soldiers roam the alleyways and can't believe their eyes. Despite the victory, there is a feeling of emptiness.'[2]

In theory, Israel granted full civil rights to its remaining Arab citizens. They, like all Israelis, could vote, attend university and become members of the Knesset, where they could even represent non-Zionist parties, such as the Communists.[3] Arabic was declared an official language, together with Hebrew and English. There were no separate park benches or washrooms, such as in apartheid South Africa. The Israeli declaration of independence promised to ensure social and political equality for all its citizens, regardless of their religion, race or sex. The reality was very different, however. The daily lives of the Palestinians within Israel—and, to a lesser extent, of the north African and Arab-Jewish immigrants—were testimony to the institutionalised discrimination of Labour Party rule.

The 'Israeli Arabs', as remaining Palestinians were known, were regarded by state security agencies as little better than a potential fifth column, and were treated as such. And with reason, for few, if any, felt loyalty to the Jewish state; Israel's very *raison d'être* demanded the negation of Palestinian nationhood. It was a democracy, but one with a built-in Jewish majority, and Israel described itself as a Jewish state. Arabs were citizens, but without all the freedoms enjoyed by the Jews. Jaffa, like all areas with a substantial Palestinian minority, was brought under military rule. Most Palestinians could not travel without permission and were subjected to serious restrictions. When the Jaffa mechanic Ismail Abou-Shehade left for Tiberias, he lived and worked there illegally. Each time he was caught, he was arrested and fined.[4]

Israeli promises of full civil rights for its Arab minority did not prevent several expulsions even after the cessation of hostilities. Senior politicians discussed 'transferring' the Palestinians. Many Palestinians who might have proved loyal citizens of the new state were never given the option.[5] Once they had left, hundreds of villages were demolished or absorbed by the Jewish settlements, the kibbutzim often proving particularly rapacious devourers of Arab land. A new Israeli national map was drawn up with Biblical Hebrew place names replacing Arabic ones. This was more than a question of cartography or nomenclature—it was a political act, with two main purposes: to establish a link between the toponomy of the new Israel and the Hebrew states of the Biblical era, and to erase the very idea of a Palestinian community with its own history and roots in the land.

Ironically, Jaffa's citrus groves survived the war but not the peace. Israeli farmers had little interest in the crop. Citrus trees demanded large quantities of water and the proper maintenance of irrigation machinery, all of which was very labour intensive. The citrus groves were also a permanent reminder of the Palestinian society that had been destroyed. Many trees were pulled up, and the land was handed over for housing developments. Israel had no monopoly on destroying the homes of the vanquished in the 1948 war, however. After the

Old City of Jerusalem fell that year to the Jordanian army, its Jewish inhabitants were evacuated, much of the historic Jewish quarter was demolished and dozens of ancient synagogues were destroyed.

RENAMING IS ITSELF an act of conquest. Jaffa was merely renamed Yafo in Hebrew, a minor difference of pronunciation from the Arabic Yafa. But the Arab names of its streets and lanes were replaced by numbers, before being named after Jewish heroes and rabbis. Nagib Bustros Street, site of Tiv, Shabat Aharoni's shop, became Raziel Street, in honour of David Raziel, the Irgun commander killed in Iraq during the Second World War. King George Boulevard was renamed Jerusalem Boulevard. Ajami's name survived, but Jebaliyyeh, where Amin Andraus and Ahmad Hammami had built their houses, was renamed Givat Aliyah, 'Hill of Aliyah' (immigration to Israel). Israel was not unique in this process. Throughout history conquerors have erased their predecessors' heritage and culture. Under Ottoman rule Salonica was a dazzling mosaic of Greeks and Turks, Sephardic Jews, Slavs and Albanians, renowned for its mosques, synagogues and dervish tombs. Even the shoeshine boys spoke half a dozen languages, from Greek to Ladino. After Salonica passed to Greek control, its Muslim population was expelled in 1923, in exchange for the return of Greeks living in Turkey. The population exchange was swift and brutal, the Hellenisation of the city no less so. The Greek authorities demolished Salonica's mosques and all but eradicated its centuries-old Islamic heritage. Twenty years later 45,000 of Salonica's Jews were deported to Auschwitz. The Jewish quarter, which dated back centuries, no longer exists, and in the post-war years a university campus was constructed on the old Jewish cemetery. Salonica is now a pleasant, unremarkable modern Greek metropolis, whose Islamic and Jewish heritage lives on only in the memory of elderly survivors.[6]

During the Yugoslav wars of the early 1990s the Bosnian Serbs erased not just Muslim communities but any physical presence of Islamic culture. In the Ottoman-era city of Banja Luka, for instance, the Muslim population was killed or driven out, and its sixteen ancient mosques were systematically destroyed. Their stones were trucked out to the outskirts of the city and used to build car parks. The mosque sites were bulldozed flat, for it was not only the reality of Islamic Bosnia that had to be eradicated but its very memory. But renaming is also a symptom of insecurity. People can flee or be expelled, their homes demolished or appropriated, but still something of their presence lingers—the spirit, perhaps, of the original inhabitants, who carry and pass on their memories to their children, whether in refugee camps or new homes in a far-flung suburbia. An unease underpins modern Israel, just as the ruins of abandoned Arab villages underpin many Israeli settlements. The Israeli writer S. Yizhar, who once sneaked into Nabi Rubeen, wrote: 'Old tales, so well known we're sick of them. Abandoned villages? And where aren't they? What was the name of this place? A few years ago there was a place and it had a name. The place was lost and the name was lost. What was left? At first, a name stripped of a place. Soon enough, that too was erased. No place and no name. May G-d have mercy.'[7]

The fate of Salama, five kilometres east of Jaffa, is indicative. Before 1948, Salama was a thriving agricultural and commercial centre, home to 6,670 Muslims and 60 Christians, built around the tomb of a companion of the prophet Muhammad, Salama Abu Hashim. It had two elementary schools, a soccer team, a bus company and five coffee shops, records the Palestinian historian Walid Khalidi.[8] Nearby Jewish settlements bought its cereals and citrus fruits, which were also sold in Jaffa. Its inhabitants lived in houses clustered around a courtyard, with a common entrance. Children played in the yard, women did their chores and families gathered for feasts and celebrations. In December 1947 fighting erupted there. Haganah units attacked, but were beaten back. The villagers dug defensive ditches and set up checkpoints. *Falastin* newspaper reported ten attacks on Salama in January 1948. Reinforced by twenty fighters from the Arab Liberation Army, they held out until mid-April, when they ran out of ammunition. Salama fell at the end of the month during Operation Chametz, the Haganah's drive to encircle Jaffa and capture the surrounding villages. When David Ben-Gurion visited Salama he found a single Palestinian, 'one old blind woman'. Salama no longer exists, and its lands have been absorbed by Tel Aviv. One cemetery is now a park; the other, like the tomb of Salama Abu Hashim, is abandoned and no longer visited.

The new cartography led to unsettling lacunae, both on the map and in reality. As the Israeli geographer Meron Benvenisti notes, four hundred villages were physically 'disappeared', but the roads leading to them, and the green fields around them, remained. At first the destroyed Palestinian villages with visible ruins were classified as *iyim*, meaning 'heaps'. By 1959 most of the 'heaps' were also erased from the map. The irony was, as Benvenisti points out, that many of the Arabic place names were themselves rooted in Aramaic, the everyday language of the Biblical era that is cognate with both Hebrew and Arabic. So it was the Palestinians who had inadvertently helped to preserve the link between the toponymies of Biblical and modern Israel.

IN 1950, JAFFA ceased to exist. Not physically, but administratively. Jaffa was no longer an independent conurbation. The Bride of

Palestine was forced into an arranged marriage with Tel Aviv, a union officially known as Tel Aviv–Yafo. The Tel Aviv municipality had little or no interest in Jaffa. Manshiyyeh was a pile of rubble, never rebuilt after the fighting in April 1948. The medieval lanes and alleys of Old Jaffa rapidly deteriorated and the city's heart became a slum, home to prostitutes, junkies and drug dealers. 'There was no municipal order here then. There were floods in the winter, and a lot of crime,' says Yoram Aharoni. Jaffa's absorption into Tel Aviv symbolised the final destruction of Palestinian nationhood within Israel's borders. Despite this—or perhaps because of it—the city was chaotic. The pre-1948 Arab municipal administration no longer existed and the New Seray had been destroyed. Almost all of Jaffa's middle class and elite had fled and were unable to return. Many of the Palestinians inside Israel were poor and ill-educated, frightened of their precarious position in the new Jewish state. Apart from a handful of community leaders such as Amin Andraus, few had the skills to negotiate with their new Israeli masters. A good number were not even from Jaffa but were internally displaced, having fled the fighting in the nearby villages or Galilee.

Despite everything, day-to-day relations and commercial dealings between Jews and Arabs were often cordial. Not only Jews shopped at Tiv; Arabs also bought their coffee and spices there. 'We delivered coffee all over Jaffa, to all the factories and workshops. I had many connections with Arabs,' says Yoram. 'I was often invited to lunch at their home.' Such friendships, while often genuine, could not be a relationship of equals. The state exercised complete control—physical, political and economic—over its Arab minority. And over all this lay the shadow of the dreaded Shin Bet, the Israeli internal security service. Arabs could be called in for interrogation at any moment, and some were broken men when they were finally released. The guarantee of human rights enshrined in Israeli law did not always apply in Shin Bet's interrogation rooms. Ismail Abou-Shehade's illegal sojourn in Tiberias soon came to the attention of the Shin Bet. He was arrested and questioned before being eventually released. 'They accused me of being a spy for Nasser, and of planting a bomb in Haifa. I never did any of this.' Yet despite the restrictions and the shadow of Shin Bet, he was still in Israel. Unlike Fakhri Geday and the Hammami family, both stranded in Lebanon, Ismail did not have to wonder if he would ever see Jaffa again.

PART TWO

12

Coming Home to Jaffa

1949–50

Your time has gone.

Israeli official at the Ministry of Commerce,
a former customer of Amin Andraus, explaining why
Amin's car import permit was so restrictive

For a long time after the 1948 war Amin Andraus would find
bodies washed up on Jaffa's beaches or floating in the water
by Ajami and Givat Aliyah. They were the bodies of watchmen, employed by the Arab families who had fled in 1948 to look after
their villas. Some said the watchmen were killed by burglars who simply wanted to break into the villas. Others saw darker forces at work.
Amin had kept his home and re-established his car import business,
but life was a perpetual struggle in the new state. Civil servants were
often petty tyrants, imposing restrictions and making difficulties at
will. Worse, the Israeli state was steadily appropriating Arab holdings
and land.

One Saturday Amin decided to go to check his orange grove, which
was south of Jaffa on the way to Ramle. He drove to the site together

with one of his workmen. Somehow he no longer had free access to his holdings. 'Suddenly, out of nowhere, all these people wearing black hats appeared, shouting "Shabbes, Shabbes",' recalls Amin's daughter Suad. 'Shabbes' is the Yiddish word for the Sabbath, when it is forbidden for Jews to do any work or drive a car. 'My father asked them what was going on, and told them this was his orange grove. They said that it was not his any more. They kept shouting "Shabbes", and would not let him go nearer.' The situation soon began to turn nasty. The Jews started rocking Amin's car from side to side. The workman with him grabbed a piece of wood. Amin tried to calm the situation, for the police, he knew, would not be sympathetic if things turned violent.

Suad continues: 'My father told them that he was not a Jew, and that he did not know that he was not supposed to drive on a Saturday. But this did not pacify them, and they told him they would burn his car. My father looked around and saw an older, white-bearded man in the crowd, and turned to him. He told him that if they burnt his car, they would be desecrating the Sabbath, and before Moses came down with the ten commandments, they too did not know the laws. So they should have a sign put up at the entrance to their village saying that it is not allowed to drive there on the Sabbath. The older man turned to the others and said, "He is right, he is right." The atmosphere calmed down and the crowd backed off.'

In the end the discussion was irrelevant. The state expropriated the land, and now the town of Kfar Chabad stands there. After a legal battle lasting many years, Amin eventually received compensation for his holdings, but only enough to buy a small car, a fraction of what his land had been worth. The episode revealed much about the new state and its relations with its Arab minority. Israeli citizens, both Jews and

Arabs, had the right to fight legal battles with the state, and Amin was not harassed or intimidated. The expropriations were all conducted strictly legally as the Knesset simply passed the necessary laws. 'The judge told my father he was in the right, but not to fight any more,' recalls Amin's son, Salim. 'He says he was wasting his money because he was fighting against a government.'

All the lands formerly owned by the Palestinian refugees who had fled Israel were taken into state ownership. In addition, between 1948 and 1990 Israel's Arab citizens lost almost one million acres.¹ Much was given to the Jewish National Fund (JNF), to be held in the name of 'the Jewish People'. The distinction between the Jewish People and the Israeli state is crucial—Israel's Arab minority are citizens, but they are not Jewish. Nor are any Palestinians who might return after a future peace deal and ask for the restitution of their former family holdings. In 1955, Moshe Keren, the Arab affairs editor for *Haaretz* newspaper, described the seizures as 'wholesale robbery in legal guise'.² The law evolved according to the needs of the state, whose ultimate triumph was always assured.

Youssef Geday, the pharmacist, had resisted the attempts of the Christian Rock family to persuade him to sell his land before 1948. Youssef owned 1,830 dunams south of Jaffa. But perhaps he should have sold, for the Geday holdings, like those of Amin Andraus, were expropriated in the early 1950s. Like Amin, Youssef fought the case in the Israeli courts. 'The judge ruled against us,' recalls Youssef's son Fakhri. 'My father jumped up in the court and said, "I don't want the land. Abu-Khaled will come here and give it back to me." The judge asked our lawyer who Abu-Khaled was. My father told him, "Gamal Abdel Nasser!"' Not surprisingly, this did not help Youssef's case; Nasser, the president of Egypt, was one of Israel's most strident enemies. Youssef's land is now the site of several apartment blocks in the town of Bat Yam, just south of Jaffa. 'My father always said, "When the Arabs return one day, we will get our land back." I think, unfortunately, he believed that until the day he died,' says Fakhri.

Amin Andraus had more pressing concerns than his orange grove. His son, Salim, and daughters Leila, Wedad and Suad were still in Jordan, together with his sister Fahima. Active hostilities were over, but Jordan was still technically at war with Israel. The borders were closed, and Israeli policy was to prevent the return of Palestinians. Communication was extremely difficult. There were no telephone or postal services, although occasionally smugglers and infiltrators carried letters across. These were empty and lonely days, for both Amin and his children. 'Christmas, birthdays and school holidays were the worst when we were in Jordan. Somehow my father had correspondence with my aunt Fahima,' recalls Suad. 'Once he was meeting Jaffa's military governor, and someone brought him a letter from my aunt. He realised who it was from, that it had been smuggled in. The governor asked why he didn't open and read it. He said he would later.'

During the summer of 1948 Fahima and the children had lived in the Jordanian town of Salt. They shared one room, together with the Bawarshi family, friends of Amin who had also left Jaffa. 'We missed the comforts of home,' says Suad. 'There was no running water. In the evenings we put the mattresses down, and in the mornings picked them up. We had a makeshift table, made from our suitcases. We could only have a bath in the coal house, standing in the basin. You had to be careful not to touch anything, or you were black again.' The children left Salt in the autumn of 1948 and went to school in the Jordanian capital, Amman, where Salim's fellow pupils included the future King Hussein. 'We worried all the time about our father, as there were rumours that he had been killed. But you know how children are—in time you start to forget. We got on with our school, and with our new lives. Later on we had some news through the Red Cross.'

Using intermediaries and smuggled communications, Amin made plans to sneak his children across the border. It was a nerve-wracking undertaking. Infiltrators, as illegal crossers were called, were often shot, and many areas were mined. On the appointed day, Salim and his sisters travelled from Amman to the town of Tulkarm. Tulkarm is now in the Israeli-occupied West Bank but was then still part of Jordan, beside the 1948 armistice line. The nearest town on the other side was the Arab town of Tayibe, one of several which had been ceded by Jordan to Israel after the cessation of hostilities. The border between the two states did not follow any topography or natural barriers—it was drawn up arbitrarily according to the front lines held by both armies when the fighting stopped. For all four children it was a day they would never forget. 'The mayor of Tayibe had a brother, and he was a good friend of my father,' recalls Wedad. 'They arranged for us to cross the border illegally. When we got to Tulkarm we gave away all our belongings. The plan was to walk across with our aunt Fahima and a peasant woman, who would show us the way.'

The mayor of Tulkarm informed the Jordanian border police that a family of four children was crossing into Israel, together with two women. Salim had a letter informing the Jordanians who they were. The Jordanians had no objection, but the Israelis were a different matter. The children would not be allowed to stay if they were caught. Wedad continues: 'We followed the peasant woman, walking until we got into Israel. I was very young, but I could feel we were doing something illegal. Once we arrived in Tayibe we went straight to my father's

friend's house. But Tayibe was a small village and we were immediately spotted as strangers—and there were informers everywhere.'

Tayibe was a sensitive border area, under strict military rule. Palestinian fighters often crossed into Israel to carry out sabotage missions.
Palestinian farmers and refugees also regularly crossed into Israel, as
there were several dozen villages in Jordanian territory whose fields
were now part of Israel. Farmers crossed back and forth when they
could, to tend and even harvest their crops, and refugees made repeated
attempts to return home if their village was still standing, or to salvage
what they could if it had been demolished. The new borders made little
sense to those whose families had lived there for many decades.

The peasant woman who had led Fahima and the children to Tayibe disappeared immediately. The Israeli police, doubtless alerted by
an informer, arrived quickly. They found Wedad playing outside the
mayor's house. They asked her where her aunt was and soon found
Fahima. The whole family was taken to the police station, says
Wedad, where Fahima tried to bluff her way out of the situation. 'She
played the fool. She pretended she did not know we had crossed into
Israel, as Tayibe had once been in Jordan. The police did not believe
her. They told her that she did not seem to be uneducated and that she
knew exactly what she had done.'

While the police were interrogating Fahima, Amin Andraus was
racing across the country to get to Tayibe. Word had come through
that his children would be crossing over that day, so he had set off as
fast as he could, bumping along the roads in an Austin 8. He travelled with Yitzhak Chisik, the former governor of Jaffa. The two men
were now friends, and Amin needed his help to talk their way
through the military checkpoints. He ignored Chisik's protests that
he was 'being kidnapped'.

Fahima's claims that she did not understand the difference between Tulkarm in Jordan and Tayibe in Israel were rejected. The police officers returned her and the four children to the border and ordered them to walk back the way they had come. Fahima and the children were in serious danger; the Jordanian border guards had known the family was crossing over into Israel, but they did not know that they were coming back. Dusk was falling, and Fahima and the children now faced a perilous trip across a military frontier without any kind of protection or assistance, even on paper. The Jordanians could easily open fire on them. 'I was terrified. I did not know what was happening,' recalls Suad. 'I remember how dark it was. Even today I am afraid of the dark. Coming into Israel, everything had been arranged. Going back to Jordan, nothing was. Fahima told Salim to run up the hill and tell the border guards that it had not worked, that we were coming back. It was quite a distance and they could have shot him. I was only seven. I remember that there was a dead body at the side of the road. My aunt told the others not to let me look.'

Amin arrived in Tayibe just fifteen minutes after his family had been dumped at the border with Jordan. He could not follow them, and he had no way of knowing if they would make it across—or what would happen to them if they did. Had he arrived just a few minutes earlier, he might have been able to keep them in Israel. He was a lawyer who spoke fluent Hebrew, and he was used to negotiating with Israeli officials. 'The people who saw him said they thought he was going to die on the spot,' recalls Wedad. 'He was so worried because we had no protection whatsoever on the way back. He thought he had lost us.'

But Fahima and the children made it across unharmed. First they moved to Tulkarm, then to Bir Zeit, a village not far from Ramallah,

says Suad. 'We had given away all our possessions and we had nothing left but the clothes we stood in.' In Bir Zeit the children went to a
school run by the Nasser family. 'We rented a room from Kamal
Nasser, who later became a PLO spokesman in Beirut.' In 1950, the
Andraus family was finally reunited by the Red Cross. Fahima and the
children crossed from Jordan into Israel at the Mandlebaum Gate in
the Old City of Jerusalem. The children's memories of their father had
grown hazy. 'When we came through the gate, my father rushed over
and kissed me,' says Suad. 'I asked Wedad, "Who is this man?"'

IN JAFFA, AHARON Chelouche, great-grandson of his name-
sake, was now a military governor, in charge of the city's remaining
Arabs. The old ties of friendship and commerce between the Chelouche family and the Arab notables of Jaffa had been severed for ever
by the 1948 war. There were no more cups of coffee with the Arab
traders in the port or around Clock Tower Square, and no more invitations to lunch. The Arabs whom Aharon knew from before 1948
now came to him as supplicants. He had the power to turn their lives
upside down, if he so chose, or ease their paths through the maze of
bureaucracy and security services.

Born in 1921, Aharon Chelouche lived in Tel Aviv until his death in
2004. Tall and well dressed, with a head of thick white hair, he exuded
the legendary Chelouche charisma. Like many of his generation, he
spoke an almost quaint English, learnt during the Mandate, which
was peppered with expressions such as 'a certain fellow'. In the
autumn of his years, Aharon looked back on his life. Some episodes,
it seems, troubled him. 'In those years between 1948 and 1950, I
could give out—not only in Jaffa, but in the whole country—licences
and permissions, and even decide the nomination of teachers. I had

to provide accommodation and give the Arabs permission to move, as Jaffa was a military zone. I gave out visas, or permission for someone to return to Jaffa from outside Israel. They had many troubles, many problems to solve, and I was at their service.'

The needs of the new state came before old ties of friendship. Before 1948 the Mustakim family, part of Jaffa's Arab elite, were close friends with the Chelouches. They were rich landowners who owned large parts of Jaffa around Bustros Street. 'Ali Mustakim fled as soon as he could to Lebanon, before the war started. He took a boat and a girl with him,' said Aharon. 'After a few months, he wanted to come back. He was a good friend of the family. But we did not give him permission, because he was not in the country when we entered Jaffa. According to the law, he would be an infiltrator. It was very difficult for me, as I knew the man. I will tell you a story I don't like to tell. Ali Mustakim came back two or three times and each time we refused him permission. He took a boat to Haifa and we did not let him in. He took a plane to Haifa airport and we did not let him in. Then he came through from Jordan. He wanted his houses back. We didn't give him permission, because all these houses now belonged to the state.' Still Ali Mustakim did not give up. He returned bearing gifts, things he thought would touch the hearts of the Israelis. 'He crossed over again, carrying two Sefer Torahs.' They had been captured by the Arab Legion in 1948. Ali Mustakim had bought them from Arabs in Bethlehem. Still we did not let him in, and he went back. Three months later he had a heart attack and died.'

Some time after, Aharon was sent to the area around Tayibe. Jordan had ceded this area to Israel under the 1949 agreement that fixed the armistice line between the two countries. But were the Arabs living in the 'Triangle', as the area was known, to be citizens of Jordan or

Israel? The Triangle's fate was extremely sensitive. Britain, the United States and Jordan all feared that Israel would expel the Arabs of the Triangle once it took possession in June 1949. Certainly the Israeli army would have preferred this. President Truman conveyed his concerns to Israel. Emptying the Triangle would put paid to any hope of a settlement in the tortuous negotiations between Israel and the Arab states that had continued without success since 1948. The agreement between Israel and Jordan stated that those Arabs in the Triangle who could prove residency would be allowed to stay, but those who could not would be expelled to Jordan. Many of those told to leave did not want to, as they had no means of earning a living or finding a home for their family in Jordan.

Aharon recalled: 'I was given an army platoon and we gave out identity cards to those who were allowed to stay. Within a few years they were given Israeli citizenship. We came to the town of Tirah, and I heard a lot of shouting and crying. I asked a fellow from the army what was going on.' The officer told Aharon that one man was proving particularly stubborn, an Arab who was a resident not of the Triangle but of Jordan. Aharon told the officer that he had to deal with hundreds of people like this and went into his office. The Arab man burst into Aharon's office. He begged, pleaded and began to kiss Aharon's leg. Aharon recalled: 'He asked if I could please let him stay in Israel. He said he could not go to Jordan, he had nothing to eat there, he was responsible for six people, and that he would die if he had to go back.'

Aharon picked up the man's file and opened it. His eyes widened. The man's name was Samarra, from the region of Tulkarm, where the Chelouche family had found sanctuary at the end of the First World War. It was the home of Ibrahim Samarra. Now Aharon did have some further questions. 'I asked him if he knew any Jews, and who his grandfather was. He said he did not know any Jews, but his grandfather, who was called Hajj Ibrahim Samarra, did know a family of Jews who lived in Tel Aviv and Jaffa.' The wheel of history had turned full circle. 'I called Ben-Gurion's office. I told them that I could not leave this man to his fate. I asked them for permission to let him stay. They were not bothered what I did. They said I was the decision maker, and I could decide myself.' Over a thousand Arabs were expelled to Jordan from the Triangle but Aharon Chelouche granted the grandson of Hajj Ibrahim Samarra, together with his family and relatives, permission to stay in Israel. 'I never told him why. I didn't want to.'

On 15 October 1950, the pharmacy student Fakhri Geday returned home to Jaffa from Beirut, under a family reunion scheme that allowed Israeli officials to exercise compassionate discretion. The scheme was a response to the severe diplomatic pressure from the United Nations and the United States to allow a substantial number of Palestinian refugees to return home. Israel and the Arab states had been negotiating for months in Lausanne, but the talks were deadlocked. Israel's public position was that any such return would be conditional on the Arab states' signing a full peace agreement. The Arab states refused; the refugees were of more use in keeping up political and diplomatic pressure on Israel.

Tel Aviv had to concede something. Israeli officials announced the family reunion programme, 'a broad measure easing the lot of Arab families disrupted as a result of the war'.[4] In fact it was extremely narrow. Israel issued 3,113 permits, and by September 1951 just 1,965 refugees had returned.[5] Those few suffered severe culture shock. 'It felt as if I had been dropped in a strange country. The people, their behaviour, the language, everything was totally different. I had no friends here any more. I could not find a single one of my friends.' Jaffa was turned into a giant transit camp, says Fakhri. 'We had Jews here from all over the world. The Arab houses are big, and each has four rooms, a hall and a salon. Each room had a family living in it. The city was totally full. To know Jaffa how it was, and to see it like that, it was a terrible shock. Everything was lost. The glory days were gone, the people, the aristocracy of old Palestine, all gone.'

13

New Lives

1948–early 1950s

In some way, all of us are still travelling.

Frank Meisler, who left Danzig in 1939
and settled in Tel Aviv in the early 1950s

Exhausted, filthy and disorientated, the Hammami family disembarked at the Lebanese port of Tyre at the end of April
1948. The children headed straight for the jugs of fresh
orange juice laid out at a nearby café. 'To this day I am not sure
whether our father paid for the juice or whether it was an act of kindness and hospitality on the part of our Lebanese hosts. I like to think
it was the latter,' says Mustafa Hammami. 'Either way, the juice was
delicious. It not only quenched our thirst but calmed us somehow
into a strange but still sombre mood. We felt strangely quiet after the
shock of leaving Jaffa, mixed with our expectations of experiencing a
new and different land.'

In Jaffa the Hammamis had lived a comfortable, middle-class life.
Now they were refugees, to be processed by the Lebanese authorities,
and partly dependent on the charity of others. Fadwa explains: 'They

wanted to take us to a refugee camp. But we could not live in a tent. My father said that we had family in Lebanon. My mother did, because she was a Shattila, a family who are well known in Lebanon.' After a few days in Beirut, the Hammamis moved to Faluga, a village in the mountains, where they spent their first year. For Fadwa and her family it was a harsh awakening to the reality of life in exile. 'In Jaffa we had a lovely life, we were well-to-do. My mother was pampered, with people to serve her. We lived comfortably. Then my parents had to leave with all their children and give them a new life in a new country. Suddenly we had nothing. I was a child and felt deprived, of my friends, my school and the beautiful surroundings of Jaffa.'

Ahmad's funds steadily dwindled. He was not allowed to work, and everything had to be paid for. He hired a private tutor to teach the children, selling off the carpets and Nafise's jewellery to keep the family warm and fed. After a year, Ahmad and Nafise decided to move to the Syrian capital, Damascus. They had family there. But the city offered little sanctuary. The winter of 1949 was particularly cold. The political situation was very unstable. At the end of March, Colonel Husni Za'im, the army chief of staff, took power in a coup. During his brief period in command Colonel Za'im made several overtures to Israel, offering to absorb 250,000 refugees in exchange for peace and Israeli concessions over land and water. These were rejected by Ben-Gurion, and Za'im was soon toppled in another coup. The Hammamis could not settle in Damascus. The severe winters were unpleasant and the political situation disturbing. Ahmad wanted a stable environment for his wife and children, where they could make a home and enrol in a proper school. He decided that the family should move to Beirut. Perhaps there the Hammamis could find, if not peace, at least some stability to try and rebuild their lives.

Once the family had found a house, the priority was the nine children's education. But finding decent schools was expensive and prob-
lematic. Fadwa says: 'Steadily our standard of living became lower
and lower. We were not accepted in the Lebanese state-school system.
The government said that we would have to go to school in the
refugee camps if we wanted to study in Lebanon. We would not do
that.' Nafise went to see her relatives in the Shattila family. 'She asked
them for help. She told them that her sons and daughters needed to
go to school, and that we could not live in a refugee camp.' Eventually
some of the Hammami children were allowed to enrol in a state
school, while others went to a private one. 'For Leila and me it was a
disaster, as the school taught in French and in Jaffa we had studied in
Arabic and English. It was very difficult for us to start all over again.'

Ahmad's funds were finally released from the bank in Palestine,
which eased the family's financial situation. But he still could not work.
Lebanon, like most Arab countries, was unwilling to naturalise the
Palestinian refugees. Its leaders feared that a large influx of Palestinians
would tip the delicate balance between Sunni and Shiite Muslims and
Maronite Christians. Most Palestinians mixed only with other refugees
in Lebanon, says Fadwa. 'We went to each other's houses. We didn't
know Lebanese people. But the Palestinians in Beirut kept up their
social life: they visited each other, and invited each other to their homes,
going to weddings and so on. The Lebanese were friendly, but we didn't
even have enough money to live properly, so we could not make a social
life.' Some new pleasures were free. In Beirut, more liberal and cosmopolitan than Jaffa, Fadwa swam in the sea for the first time.

FRANK MEISLER, THE young Jewish student who had left
Danzig for London on a *Kindertransport* in 1939, had a warmer wel-

come than many young refugees. His grandmother and two aunts were waiting for him in London. He moved in with his mother's older sister, Ruth, and her husband, Kurt, in Putney. Frank's English was soon good enough for him to attend a private school in north London, and after the initial adjustment—pupils could address teachers by name instead of as 'Herr Professor', and even stay seated—he thrived. He learnt the British arts of understatement and diffidence. There were occasional postcards from his parents in Warsaw: 'We are well—write,' instructed his father, the brevity of the communication concealing his fear. Frank had his photograph taken in school uniform and sent it to his parents. He studied hard, but however well he seemed to be doing, he was still a teenage boy, alone in a foreign country. When homesickness overwhelmed him, Frank found comfort in art, mining his memories of Danzig to create the impression, at least, of somewhere familiar. 'I drew the Dutch gables, the stone stairs and the gargoyles that spouted water in the rain. I often dreamt of walking familiar streets, looking through familiar windows,' he wrote in his memoir, *On the Vistula, Facing East*. Meanwhile, rumours steadily drifted across Nazi-occupied Europe to Putney about the fate of the Jews and the strange camps the Germans were building.

In 1945, at the age of eighteen, Frank joined the Polish armed forces, serving more than two years as a meteorological observer in the air force. At the boarding house where he was billeted, he met a courier for the Polish underground who travelled back and forth between Poland and the Polish government-in-exile in London. From a distance, the courier had seen the extermination of Jews at a death camp. There was still no word from Frank's parents. When the courier described what he had seen—the smell, the smoke and the piles of corpses—Frank realised they could not have survived.

When he was released from the army, Frank studied architecture at Manchester University. There he realised that he was an exile, displaced from a city and a homeland that no longer existed. He was neither a Pole, nor a German, nor British. Once he graduated he was unwilling to stay in England and unable to go home to Danzig. He decided on Israel. He was not a devout Zionist, but he was a young man ready for adventure. In 1952, Frank went to the Jewish Agency in London to offer his services. 'I was not so much committed to the Jewish state as I was at a loose end. I had read in a magazine that if you were an architect, they would get you a job in an architect's office, and so on,' he recalls. Frank travelled by ship from Venice to Israel and duly started work at an architect's office in Tel Aviv. Tel Aviv in the early 1950s was certainly much sunnier than Manchester, and life was pleasant. He found a flat on Rothschild Boulevard, where the Chelouches lived. 'I was fairly well paid and it was very easy to meet people. There were cafés, and the girls were nice looking. I had a very busy social life, and I liked the Mediterranean climate and ambiance.'

Still there was something strange, even unsettling, about Tel Aviv. The modern Hebrew city was now capital of the Hebrew state. But underneath the apparent normality, disturbing currents swirled. The Holocaust cast a long and dark shadow. The threat of extermination was still real. The Arab armies could return at any moment, to restart the 1948 war. 'Tel Aviv was a bit crude, rough and ready. I thought Israel was a peculiar country. Very unbalanced, even primitive, with a lot of post-war neurotic and displaced people. I could not speak Hebrew, so I used English. You could go into a shop and speak English because the owners did, and then somebody would shout, "Speak Hebrew!" Sometimes I spoke German. There would often be someone who had been in the camps, screaming, "Don't speak German!"

The country was traumatised by the Kasztner affair. It all felt unstable." When Frank saw Menachem Begin, leader of the right-wing Herut Party, addressing his followers in downtown Tel Aviv, it reminded him of Danzig and the young Revisionist Zionists who modelled themselves on Italy's fascist movement. 'There was a demonstration with Begin on a soapbox, screaming at the crowd, with a lot of Herut thugs. To me they were fascists. They made a clever alliance with the disenfranchised Sephardim, small shopkeepers and petty bourgeoisie.'

THE WORLD'S HORROR at the Nazi genocide hastened diplomatic recognition of Israel. But it took many years for the Holocaust to be internalised as part of Israel's national identity. In Israel's early years Holocaust survivors did not feel particularly welcome. There was little interest in hearing their stories. Many Israelis who had spent the Second World War in the comparative safety of Palestine felt guilty when confronted with camp survivors. They did not know how to deal with these new immigrants, most of whom, not surprisingly, were suffering severe psychological problems. One unspoken— and sometimes even spoken—question was: 'How did *you* manage to survive when so many died?' Other Israelis, sure that they would have fought, asked, 'Why did so many go like lambs to the slaughter?' Some, especially among the anti-Zionist ultra-Orthodox Jews, accused the Zionists, in Palestine and Europe, of 'abandoning' the Jews, although it was hard to see what the *Yishuv*—in international terms a weak and powerless community—could have done to stop the Nazi extermination.

Many survivors' accounts of the horrors they had endured were simply not believed, which only added to their trauma. They had the tattoos of their camp numbers surgically removed from their arms, or kept them hidden under long sleeves. One man told his son that it was his telephone number at work. Yet as Tom Segev notes, there were miracles too. Parents met children they had believed were dead, in chance encounters in shops or cafés. A radio programme called *Who Knows* broadcast survivors' details in the hope that a relative would still be alive and they would be brought together.[2]

The answer was to rebuild the Holocaust survivors as Israeli New Men and Women. The first step was to change their names, a symbolic rejection of the diaspora and its values. Frank was soon pressured to Hebraise Meisler. For those in public life or who held a senior position in the state, this was virtually compulsory. Golda Myerson became Golda Meir. David Gruen became David Ben-Gurion. Changing names was an integral part of Jewish history. Most of the German-sounding names of central Europe's Jews had no Jewish roots. They had been adopted in the late eighteenth century, as part of the Habsburg Empire's process of emancipation. Those who could not bribe the official Austro-Hungarian name-changer were usually given the choice of Gross, Klein, Schwartz or Weiss—Big, Small, Black or White. Those who could were allowed more mellifluous choices, such as Rosenfeld—'field of roses', Silberberg—'silver mountain' or Goldberg—'golden hill'. The new Hebrew names served the same purpose as the Habsburg ones they often replaced, as did those given at Ellis Island to new immigrants to the United States: they were symbols of a new identity and statements of loyalty to the host society. Jews from Arab countries had Arabic names, which were easier to Hebraise or were often sufficiently Semitic to pass as 'genuine' Israeli ones.

Soon after he arrived in Tel Aviv, Frank Meisler met David Ben-Gurion and his wife, Paula. She told Frank he should change Meisler

to Mazaar. 'In those days if you came to Israel and your name was
Grunberg, you changed it to Harari, which means mountain. Some
relatives of mine had changed their name to Mazaar. Paula Ben-
Gurion was a busybody.' Frank remained, and remains, Meisler,
proud of his Ashkenazi Jewish name and the hint of an accent from
Mittel Europa. 'I was brought up in a fragmented environment and I
took that to be a natural part of my existence. I was not, let's say, an
uprooted German Jew who is immediately looking for new soil in
which to put down roots. I came from a town which had no roots.
Danzig was a free city. The people around me were Poles, White Russians, Nazis, Jewish Poles, Polish Poles, Kashubians, and God knows
what.[3] There you were everything, or you were nothing.'

And Israel in the 1950s was a place where Jews, especially the
young and the talented, could be everything and anything. Like the
United States or Australia, it was a place where people went to re-
invent themselves, and few questions were asked if the job got done.
Frank recalls: 'I had a friend from Australia who told me he was an
architect there, a sheep-shearer, a baker and had planted eucalyptus
trees. There was no structure—you did what you wanted. Israel was
like that. If you wanted to be an architect, then you'd study to be one
and not expect great honours. Wherever you went, people would ask
you where you came from, what you did and how much you were
paid. If I told the man selling me a bagel how much I earned, he would
drop it, and say, 'What am I doing here, selling bagels—I should be
an architect!''

Israel was a young and vibrant country in a state of flux, with
tremendous opportunities, not least for party apparatchiks. Frank
had two jobs, the first in private practice, and the second in a government office. There he shared space with an 'employee' whose sole

function was to report back to his party bosses. 'He did nothing
except keep people in line and make sure they followed the correct
political thinking. He was a stooge. Both Mapam and Mapai were
corrupt. The ruling elite thought the country was a kind of grocery
shop, and you just helped yourself to sugar or rice or whatever you
wanted.'

On the weekends Frank often travelled to Jaffa. A century earlier
the British artist David Roberts had also visited Jaffa on his tour
through the Levant and the Holy Land. The Arabs he had painted
were gone, as were their descendants. But the azure sea still lapped at
the beach, and Jaffa's translucent light always entranced. Frank loved
to sketch the port and its surroundings. Like most Israelis in the early
1950s, he did not think much about the Palestinians. 'They were
innocent days. The legend was that the Arabs had left, abandoned
their buildings, and the Jews came and took them over. There were
Arabs in Ajami, but I was not aware of them. The Arabs did not seem
to exist. People did not see them, except as a nuisance. Golda Meir
said there was no such people as the Palestinians. Where was she, did
she need new glasses? But I was shallow then, and I did not know the
background.'

IN CAIRO, THE young Mary Hayon had a clearer understanding
of the new politics of the Middle East. Mary was twenty years old in
1948, when Israel was established. The Hayons were an old Sephardic
family who had lived in Jerusalem for generations but had moved to
Cairo after 1918. Mary, who now lives in Tel Aviv, is a trim and
sprightly lady, fluent in Arabic, French and English as well as Hebrew.
Like Fadwa Hammami and Frank Meisler, she grew up in a world now
vanished: in her case cosmopolitan pre-war Egypt. The country's

great cities such as Cairo and Alexandria were melting pots, home to Greek and Italian traders, Sephardic and Ashkenazi Jews, White Russians, Armenians and Circassians, Coptic Christians and Muslims. Jews had lived in Egypt for millennia. Most of Egypt's 80,000 Jews were Sephardim, but there was an Ashkenazi minority. Many had arrived in the nineteenth century, when Muhammad Pasha, Egypt's ruler, invited them to settle, to help modernise the country. They were industrialists and politicians, bankers and businessmen. Prominent heads of families were called 'Bey' or 'Pasha' in recognition of their contribution.

Mary's family were not part of the elite, but they had a comfortable life. Her father owned a pharmacy on Ibrahim Street, in the middle-class suburb of Heliopolis. 'There were Sephardic ministers and members of Parliament, literary salons, a real intellectual life. I went to a Jewish school, and then one run by Irish nuns.' Among Mary's classmates was a young woman called Dina Abdel Hamid, who later married King Hussein of Jordan. 'She was a beautiful girl, very sweet. But you couldn't really be normal friends with her. She was never let out alone. She came to school with a servant and he would sit waiting for her outside the class. He brought her to school and took her home. We would say to her, "Princess, you go first, your slave is waiting for you."'

Before 1948 Mary could travel with ease from Cairo to Palestine and back. An overnight train ran from Cairo to Ramle. There was no border, as both Egypt and Palestine were under British rule. Egypt's Jews were seen as an integral part of society, but the war with Israel changed everything. Mary was working for the newspaper *Le Progrès Egyptien*, many of whose staff were Jewish. 'I did not feel anti-Semitism when I was growing up. It started after 1948, once Egypt and the Arab countries were beaten by little Israel. But even when I lived in Egypt I did not feel that it was my country. We knew that we would eventually come back to Israel. When you know that, you don't feel at home somewhere else. Even though I was born there, my roots were not there. My parents were not born there. They had no stories to tell me about Egypt.'

In the second half of 1948, a series of bombs in Cairo's Jewish quarter killed more than seventy Jews and injured over two hundred. The exodus of one of the world's oldest Jewish communities began.[4] Mary Hayon decided to emigrate to Israel in 1951, and the following year a group of army officers, including Anwar Sadat and Gamal Abdel Nasser, overthrew King Farouk in a bloodless coup. Egypt's transformation into a socialist state began with the destruction of the old multi-ethnic society; the Jews and other minorities were easy scapegoats. Nasser appeared to take Israel's continued existence personally. He had fought in the 1948 war, and his battalion had been trapped for weeks by Israeli forces. The Jews, Greeks and Italians, who ran much of the economy, packed their bags. Businesses closed, capital flowed out of the country, poverty and unemployment soared. Nasser's policies quickly transformed Egypt's ethnic mosaic into a near-homogenous nation-state. Xenophobia and anti-Semitism flourished. Mary recalls 'It changed after Nasser took power, and became much nastier. If you mentioned Israel you had to say "the so-called state of Israel". My parents were frightened. We could not communicate directly. We wrote to each other through a third party in France.'

Mary was drafted into the Israeli army when she arrived in Jerusalem. One day, soon after she was demobilised, she met a relation while out walking. He was a distant cousin of her grandfather, handsome, vigorous and good-humoured, with thick black hair and a ready smile. 'I was not happy in the army—my parents were still in

Cairo. He asked me out to dinner. I thought, Why not? He came from a very good family. That's how it started—it went very fast.' Soon afterwards, Mary's boyfriend proposed. She accepted, and became Mrs Shlomo Chelouche. But the young newlyweds would not stay long in Jerusalem. A little over a century earlier, Shlomo's great-grandfather Avraham Chelouche had travelled from Oran, in Algeria, to Palestine. Soon it would be Shlomo's turn to travel back to north Africa. There he and Mary would run a perilous clandestine operation, bringing the Jews of north Africa to Israel.

14

Repopulating Jaffa

1950s

I looked for Jews who wanted a change.
Shlomo Chelouche, on his mission in north Africa in
the 1950s to aid Jewish emigration to Israel

B y the summer of 1951, Ahmad Hammami had sold his last
Persian carpet, while Nafise and her daughters had no more
jewellery left. Ahmad had tried everything he could to restart
both his citrus and his dry-goods business in Lebanon, but it was an
impossible venture for a refugee without funds, proper papers or permits, the citizen of a country that no longer existed. With the
resilience of youth, Hasan Hammami adapted more easily to life in
exile. He enrolled at the American University in Beirut, and quickly
found his feet in a very different world from that of pre-1948 Palestine. 'Coming from a conservative Islamic background in Jaffa, where
I went to an all-boys Catholic school, I was suddenly surrounded by
the most gorgeous girls in the world,' says Hasan. He studied hard,
learnt to tango and to rumba and to ski. But Hasan was also the eldest
boy, and as the family's funds drained away he knew what had to be

done. 'With no hint from anyone, I understood that my responsibility was to get a job to support my parents and siblings.'

He turned down job offers in Libya and Kuwait and moved to Dhahran, Saudi Arabia, to work as a translator for Aramco on a salary of $110 a month. He sent $100 to his parents and kept $10 for himself. Like Beirut, Dhahran was also a culture shock, but one a good deal less pleasant. 'I lived in a shoddy work camp, and experienced real racism for the first time in my life. Everything—facilities, services and salaries—was divided into three classes, and we were the lowest. Even the water fountain was reserved for Americans, although I drank from it.' But there were weekends at the beach with his new friends, and Hasan earned extra money teaching French. The strict masters at St Joseph's in Jaffa had taught Hasan well. Better still, he was eventually granted Saudi citizenship, with a proper passport, and this would open up new possibilities for work and study.

MARY CHELOUCHE COULD not understand why the young man she had just greeted had completely ignored her. How many Israeli Jews could there be walking the streets of Casablanca? They had met socially, but now he had walked straight past her without even a smile. By the early 1950s, Mary and Shlomo had relocated to the Moroccan port city, travelling on French passports. The kibbutz movement, Israeli political parties, government departments, the Jewish Agency and American Jewish organisations had all opened offices there, planning the emigration of Morocco's 265,000 Jews.' Mary worked for the Hebrew Immigrant Aid Society, while Shlomo was working undercover for the Israeli government, setting up a complicated series of fund transfers so that Moroccan Jews could move their assets out of the country when they finally left for Israel. Mary's friend did not acknowledge her because he was an agent of Mossad, the Israeli intelligence service, which arranged the details of the clandestine emigration.

Morocco, like the rest of the Arab world, did not recognise Israel. There were no official relations between the two countries, but there were covert links. The Moroccan royal family did not share the visceral anti-Semitism of many Arab leaders. Moroccan Islam was more tolerant, influenced by its close ties to Spain, where the Jews had enjoyed a golden age under Islamic rule before the Catholic *reconquista* and their expulsion in 1492. Many Jews then emigrated to Morocco, although they were forced to live in special quarters of the city, known as the *mellah*. During the Second World War, King Muhammad V had resisted the demands of Vichy France to deport Morocco's Jews, replying, 'We have no Jews in Morocco, only Moroccan citizens.' The fortunes of the Jews had waxed and waned under Islam, but Moroccan Jews were integrated into society and enjoyed considerable religious and legal autonomy. Most did not want to leave.

It is one of the darker ironies of Jewish history that political Zionism, the European movement which aimed to ensure the Jews' peace and security, greatly imperilled the ancient Jewish communities of the Middle East. The establishment of Israel destroyed the fine balance between Jews and Muslims in the Arab states. Islamic tolerance of Jews did not extend to them founding their own country. Across the Arab world many Jews feared for their future in the new independent post-colonial regimes. The upsurge in nationalism bred anti-Semitism and xenophobia. The ancient and prosperous Iraqi Jewish community was viciously persecuted: Jews were sacked from their jobs, large numbers were arrested, tortured and jailed and their properties were confiscated. Zionism was declared a criminal offence, and a Jewish businessman was hanged in public for selling trucks to Israel. In 1950 and 1951 Israel organised operations Ezra and Nehemiah to airlift out 120,000 Jews, 95 per cent of the community. The Jews were permitted to leave Iraq with little more than the clothes in which they travelled.

In Morocco anti-Jewish riots erupted in the summer of 1948, and forty-four Jews were killed. The Moroccan Jews also needed 'rescuing', Israel decided, although this was debatable. In fact Israel itself was in greater need. The state existed, the Palestinians had gone, their land and houses had been appropriated, but the Jews were not coming. The substantial and prosperous communities of the United States, France and Britain, apart from a minority of idealists, stayed at home. The Jews of the Soviet Union were not able to depart. The answer, Ben-Gurion and the other Israeli leaders believed, was to bring over the Jews of the Arab states. There were rumours—never wholly proven—that the Israelis themselves fomented anti-Semitism to persuade the Jews in Arab countries to leave, launching whispering campaigns and rumours like those that had so unsettled the Palestinians in 1948. There were even claims that the Mossad had bombed synagogues in Baghdad.[2] True or not, the Moroccan Jews began to leave in their thousands. Much of the educated, multilingual elite went to France or Canada. The rest went to Israel.

As a fluent Arabic speaker, Shlomo was a natural choice for Israel's operations in Morocco. He and Mary were well established in Casablanca before organisations such as the Jewish Agency arrived. 'I had to organise a bank, all sorts of things. The aim was to make it easier once the Jewish Agency arrived. I travelled across north Africa, to Algeria, Tunis and Morocco. It was all secret.' Until 1956, when Morocco became independent, Jews were allowed to emigrate from

Morocco. The difficulty was moving their funds out of the country; international funds transfers in the 1950s were complicated and slow. Money could not be sent directly to Israel, so Shlomo set up a system of promissory notes. The immigrant deposited his money with Shlomo, and it was then transferred to a bank in Paris, less a commission of 2 per cent. From there the money was sent to a bank in Switzerland, and then on to Israel.

Shlomo explains: 'It demands a lot of trust for somebody to give you everything he has. I had to be a nice fellow, very pleasant, with no enemies.' Inevitably, things sometimes went wrong in this complicated chain of transactions that relied so heavily on honesty. 'Sometimes there were cases where Jews took money. I had to come and investigate what had happened. There were others who had money and could not get it out at all.' Shlomo's work was not without risk. Officially he was a businessman involved in property and banking. But he was breaking the law, and he was an agent of a foreign power. If a Moroccan government official suspected anything, he received a 'present' in exchange for his silence. The weakest links in the chain were the intermediaries, who handled vast sums of cash. Mary recalls: 'One morning Shlomo called the middleman and there was no answer. He got worried. He went to the man's office, and the building was surrounded by policemen. He came straight home and took all the money that we had in cash—enough to make us very rich—and hid it in a cupboard. He said he would go to France to find another way to move the money. But we were young then. I never worried about what would happen if we were caught.'

In the mid-1950s, as Morocco prepared for independence, Shlomo was given a more hazardous mission. Jews who wanted to leave were finding it increasingly difficult. Ever more obscure bureaucratic obstacles would spring up in their path. Shlomo set up a complicated underground operation to print thousands of fake travel documents, in case Morocco closed its gates completely. He travelled to Gibraltar to set up a transit camp, in preparation for a sudden mass exodus. In 1956, Morocco declared independence and emigration to Israel was banned. It was no longer possible for the Zionist and Israeli organisations to continue their work. Shlomo and Mary relocated to Paris, where he masterminded the distribution of forged passports, which the Jewish emigrants used to get to Gibraltar. In Paris, Mary worked on the Egyptian desk at the Hebrew Immigrant Aid Society. She soon saw a stream of familiar faces from her days in Cairo.

THE 1956 SUEZ crisis and subsequent war triggered the final exodus of Egypt's Jews. In July of that year Nasser nationalised the company that owned the Suez Canal, threatening British and French trade routes to Africa and Asia. Nasser then closed the canal completely to Israeli shipping and blockaded the Gulf of Aqaba, which controlled access to Israel's southernmost port of Eilat. Combined with Egyptian sponsorship of repeated raids by *fedayeen* (Arab guerrillas) into Israeli territory, the blockade was seen by Ben-Gurion as an adequate *casus belli*. Nasser's growing links with the Soviet bloc and Communist China were causing alarm in western capitals, enough to prompt a secret agreement between Britain, France and Israel to take military control of the canal. Any lingering ideological sympathy the Ashkenazi socialist elite had for the Soviet experiment had by now been replaced by the demands of realpolitik, aligning the young state with the West.

Israel invaded Sinai at the end of October, quickly capturing Gaza, Rafah and El-Arish. Britain and France deployed aircraft carriers and began bombing to force Egypt to reopen the canal, while paratroops fought house to house with Egyptian forces. Enraged and humiliated by both the West and his most hated enemy, Nasser took out his fury on Egypt's Jews. A state-sponsored pogrom was unleashed. Community leaders were arrested; Jews were sacked from their workplaces and forbidden to practise their professions; communal properties were expropriated by the state; schools and synagogues were closed down and businesses and bank accounts taken over. A proclamation was read out in mosques across the country that 'all Jews are Zionists and enemies of the state' and would soon be expelled.[3] Most Jews living in Egypt were stateless, as Egypt had refused to naturalise them after independence in 1922. Traumatised and impoverished, they relied on the assistance of the Red Cross and other refugee aid agencies. Mary Chelouche's parents returned to Jerusalem; others left for Canada, Britain, the United States and the Hebrew Immigrant Aid Society in Paris. 'I knew many people that came through our office,' recalls Mary. 'They arrived and they saw me, and they said, "Oh, Mary, it's you!" Of course it was very difficult for my parents when they came back to Israel. But they had their family and their friends, and they knew Hebrew. It was easier for them than for the Moroccan Jews, who came with nothing.'

The Anglo-French-Israeli attack on Egypt was a military success but a political disaster. Nasser was saved by both the Soviet Union and the United States. The Soviet leader Khrushchev threatened to intervene on Egypt's side and even attack the West, with an implied threat of nuclear weapons, if the three countries did not withdraw. The United States was distracted by the Soviet crushing of the 1956 Hungarian revolution, and found it hard to justify its allies' attack on Egypt while condemning the Soviet onslaught on Budapest. Under pressure from the United States and the United Nations, Britain, France and Israel withdrew and Nasser emerged triumphant. United Nations troops were deployed to keep the peace, one of many missions to be launched over the next decades to clean up after the latest round of the Arab-Israeli conflict.[4]

THE EGYPTIAN AND north African Jews were demographically useful to build up Israel's numbers, but they were not made welcome once they arrived. The prejudice against them was institutionalised, and it came from the very top. They were described as 'backward' and 'primitive', and it was assumed that they would not need basic comforts such as hot or even running water, unlike their Ashkenazi coreligionists. Apparently ignorant of the twelfth-century philosopher Moses Maimonides, Judaism's greatest thinker, who wrote in Arabic, Ben-Gurion wrote that European Jews had 'shaped the image of the Jewish people throughout the world', while Arabic-speaking Jews had played a 'passive' role in Jewish history.[5] One Israeli journalist opined: 'The primitiveness of these people is insurmountable. They have almost no education at all, and what is worse is their inability to comprehend anything intellectual. As a rule, they are only slightly more advanced than the Arabs, Negroes or Berbers in their countries. It is certainly even lower than the former Palestinian Arabs.'[6]

In Jaffa, the Moroccans were given rooms in the abandoned villas of Ajami. Others were less fortunate and were dumped in the ruins of deserted Arab villages, or in wooden huts in the middle of nowhere, and told to start building a settlement. Rabbis were forced to work as labourers, Talmudic scholars became gravediggers, bankers and businessmen worked as cleaners and porters. 'There were no rules then— people made it up as they went along,' says Frank Meisler. 'If you were European and you had a cousin who came over, you found him a good flat. But an Iraqi would be put in a tent. Nobody said, "Wait a minute."' Yet from the Zionists' perspective, it was a miracle that the Arab Jews had been ingathered at all. Looking back, perhaps some mistakes were made, believes Mary Chelouche, but the country needed manpower. Israel had already fought one war, food was rationed, its economy was in a state of near collapse and it was surrounded by enemies pledged to its destruction. 'You have to realise Israel's situation then. There were cities, and there were kibbutzim. But you cannot have a country with only these. You could not look after everyone who is complaining that they were mistreated. You had to say to them, "Look, this is it." The country was very socialist then.'

At number 6 Raziel Street, the Moroccan influx was good for business. Tiv's spice range expanded rapidly from black pepper and paprika. The north African Jews used pepper so hot it would make you sweat, says Yoram. 'The immigrants from Morocco, Tripoli and Tunis used a lot of red pepper. If I used a hundred grams of chili powder in a year, they would use that in a few days. Most people bought sweet paprika and sweet chili in quantities of a hundred grams. They bought them in kilo or half-kilo bags.' Yoram soon became an expert in the different types of north African cuisine. 'Each community had their own spice mix for different dishes, and also for their tea, with cinnamon, or with rose petals. The Jews from Tripoli and Morocco cook a lot of meatballs, and their spice mix was called baharat. It was based on cumin, with plenty of black pepper, ginger and garlic. Some of them also used caraway seeds. The fish spices were the hottest. The Jews from Tripoli made a sauce with cumin, caraway and garlic, and they would buy half a kilo of red pepper at a time.'

A brisk twenty minutes' walk from number 6 Raziel, at his pharmacy on Yefet Street, Fakhri Geday had adjusted to the new reality. In 1957, Fakhri was thirty years old. He was now an Israeli, a law-abiding citizen of a state to whose existence he was utterly opposed. 'I had no special feelings when they gave me my Israeli identity card. I am a person who can accept new facts. I don't revolt against them. I was dropped in a land with new facts, and I had to accommodate myself to the situation.' After Fakhri returned in 1950 he wanted to leave Jaffa, to study for his doctorate in France. But his father, Youssef, wanted him to stay. Fakhri's mother was sick, and Youssef wanted to retire, so Fakhri took over his father's shop.

Fakhri was an ardent Nasserite. The Egyptian leader's rise to power galvanised Arabs across the Middle East, including many of Israel's Arab minority. The swashbuckling colonel, they believed, would finally make up for the humiliations the Arabs had suffered at the hands of the West, and would erase the alien, imperialist implant of Israel from the map. They cheered when he nationalised the Suez Canal. Fakhri recalls: 'We were against Ben-Gurion because he was an occupier. We were all with Nasser. We are still with Nasser. The nationalist Palestinians here consider him a hero. I am a one-hundred-per-cent Nasserite. He represents the ideals of Palestinian decency, Palestinian nationalism, freeing the Arab lands from foreign occupiers and uniting the Arab world from ocean to ocean.'

THAT SAME YEAR in Istanbul the Albo family were preparing to leave for Israel. Sarah Albo was overjoyed, but her husband, Yaakov, had severe doubts. Like the Aharonis, the Albo family were Sephardim. They spoke Ladino at home, and lived a comfortable, bourgeois life. Five-year-old Sami and his sister, Jenni, were taken to school each day by a driver. The family lived in a spacious apartment with a concierge. Yaakov owned two shoe shops together with an Armenian business partner, but when a Muslim mob burnt down one of the shops, Yaakov finally accepted it was time to go. The Albos spent a year at a *ma'abara* (reception camp) near Haifa when they arrived in 1957. It was a very different world from Istanbul. 'My father did not want to come to Israel. My mother was the Zionist in the family, and she did everything so we could come here. They left everything in Turkey and came here,' says Sami.

Now in his early fifties, Sami lives with his wife, Rachel, daughter, Adi, and son, Aviv, in a flat just behind Jerusalem Boulevard. He is a determined and articulate man, active in Jaffa's community politics as a moderate right-winger. Sami is named after his grandfather Shmuel. Shmuel Albo, like many Turkish Jews, also took a Turkish name, Kemal. Unlike Jews in Arab countries, those in Turkey were not subjected to persecution and restrictions after 1948. Kemal Attaturk, the founder of modern Turkey, declared it a secular state, where all would be equal. Under Ottoman rule, Jews had often prospered, rising to high government positions. But during the Second World War Turkey turned on its Jewish community. Although Turkey remained neutral—finally declaring war on the Axis in February 1945—the Turkish press launched an anti-Semitic campaign, and an extremely punitive capital tax was levied on Jewish businesses. Jews and Christians were rounded up and deported to harsh labour camps. The persecutions were a severe shock, and helped trigger the exodus after 1948.

For Sarah Albo, Israel was the only insurance against a fresh round of persecutions, but Yaakov was profoundly unhappy there, explains Sami. 'At the reception camp we lived in a wooden hut. The toilets were a long walk away. It was not like the situation now for immigrants, who are helped with language classes, buying a house and so on. They were difficult times, and it was a massive shock for him. He found it hard to manage. My mother was a Zionist, she knew that this is our place, so she could better manage the difficulties.' Conditions at the camp exacerbated the tensions in an already difficult marriage. The two were cousins, as their mothers were sisters, and Sarah was ten years older than Yaakov. She was better educated than Yaakov, and had finished the Alliance Française school in Istanbul. She spoke French, Spanish, Turkish, some English and Ladino. Yaakov had worked from an early age and knew Greek and Armenian.

Yaakov also brought his mother, Sinyora, to Israel. 'She was like her son. My father had a lot of money in Istanbul, and it was a severe shock for him to live in a hut. My grandmother hardly spoke at all,' recalls Sami. 'I did not have a good relationship with her. She used to sit quietly in her corner. She was very strict. I think it was because she did not want to be here. They did not talk about that in front of us, but I can imagine that was the reason.' After a year, the Albos moved to an Arab house in Jaffa. Sami, his sister, his parents and his grand-mother lived in the one and half rooms in the roof that had once been the laundry space. Sarah took in sewing to help make ends meet. Yaakov struggled, both to earn money and to reconcile himself with his new life. He could not settle, and decided to return to Turkey to assess the situation there. 'His plan was to see if things were better now, and to convince my mother to go back,' says Sami. In 1959, Yaakov left Jaffa on his reconnaissance mission to Istanbul. Turkey, he thought hopefully, would have something better to offer than living in a laundry room.

15

Saving Old Jaffa

1960s

*In Jaffa the most ardent tourist need not worry about
remains of the past, but can simply relax and enjoy the
cosmopolitan human scenery of the present.*

Extract from a 1962 Israeli guidebook to Jaffa
by Joan Comay, with a foreword by Ben-Gurion[1]

In May 1960, Jaffa's old Turkish *kishle* (prison) received a high-security inmate. The *kishle's* usual clients were petty criminals, drug dealers and the prostitutes working Old Jaffa. The new arrival, an Austrian man in late middle age with a narrow face and thinning hair, did not look very dangerous, but he was locked in a small cell and held under armed guard. Adolf Eichmann, the former head of the Gestapo's Department for Jewish Affairs, had been kidnapped on the streets of Buenos Aires by Mossad. Nine days later he was dressed as an airline steward, drugged and put on board an El Al jet. His arrest electrified the world. Few in Jaffa knew of his brief sojourn, but the customers at Tiv, just a few minutes' walk away, applauded Mossad's success. 'Everyone was talking about it. Eichmann's capture was a very important event for Israel. I was happy that he was caught,' says Yoram Aharoni.

Eichmann's trial began on 11 April 1961. It lasted fourteen weeks, and more than a hundred survivors gave evidence. The transcript of the trial is 6,000 pages long. In a sense, Eichmann was not the only person on trial. There were traumatic scenes when Holocaust survivors screamed abuse at Jewish leaders giving evidence, accusing them of helping the Nazis to save themselves and their families. Hannah Arendt covered the trial for the *New Yorker* magazine, turning her articles into the seminal work *Eichmann in Jerusalem: A Report on the Banality of Evil*. Frank Meisler agreed with her summing-up of Eichmann's legacy. 'I thought she expressed the terrible lesson of the Eichmann trial well. He was a little clerk with charts and blackboards, engaging the prosecutors in discussions on railways trucks and train schedules.' But the verdict was never in doubt. On the evening of 31 May 1961, Eichmann was hanged in Ramle prison.

For Ben-Gurion the trial also served a political purpose. Israel had not until then shown much enthusiasm for finding Nazi war criminals. The government was under attack for its rapprochement with Germany and its acceptance of restitution payments. Social tensions soared as Jews from Arab countries protested over their often dismal living conditions. They had little consciousness of the Holocaust. Despite their fiery rhetoric in 1948, the Arabs had never attempted to exterminate the world's Jews. At Eichmann's trial, writes Tom Segev, Ben-Gurion 'had two goals: one was to remind the countries of the world that the Holocaust obligated them to support the only Jewish state on earth. The second was to impress the lessons of the Holocaust on the people of Israel, especially the young generation'.[2] It did. The Holocaust and the threat—real or perceived—of a successful Arab/Islamic onslaught shape the Israeli psyche, and Israeli politics, to this day.

.   .   .

IN THE SUMMER of 1962, Hasan Hammami moved to Baghdad, where his father, Ahmad, had been living since 1953. Hasan was now a married man. He had returned to school in the mid-1950s, enrolling at Nottingham University to study engineering. In the university coffee bar he met a pretty and vivacious young woman called Barbara Paulson. Hasan and Barbara fell in love, and after a year together they decided to get married. Both families were opposed to this, recalls Hasan. 'They said it would not work, no matter how much we loved each other, because we came from such different backgrounds, cultures, religions and societies.' Hasan's brother Hussein even wrote to Barbara in the name of his parents, a letter known as 'Dear Barbara' in the family folklore, outlining their fears over the couple's compatibility. The 'Dear Barbara' letter did not work, but fifty years on, the marriage is still a success. After graduating in 1959, Hasan returned to his old employers, Aramco, and he, Barbara and their young daughter, Fawzia, moved to Dhahran in Saudi Arabia. A second daughter, Rema, was born in 1960. But Aramco had not changed its employment practices, and Hasan's salary was a mere 20 per cent of that of his American colleagues. Hasan left Aramco for a position with Procter & Gamble, managing a detergent factory. He was posted to Baghdad for his training. 'There I could renew my relationship with Father. The evenings he spent with us were precious, and he formed a special attachment with his granddaughter Fawzia.'

Iraq in the early 1960s was an unstable and dangerous place. In 1963, the country's leader, General Abdul Karim Qassim, was overthrown in a military coup. The new government included members of the revolutionary Baath Party. Four years earlier a young Baath Party member called Saddam Hussein had tried to assassinate General

Qassim, but failed and fled to Egypt, where he then studied law. Saddam returned to Baghdad after the coup, and the days of fear began. 'The Baath Party began the process of taking over the country. They started to purge anyone opposed to them, especially Communists, anyone who had been to Russia, or even anyone who was suspected of being anti-Baathist,' recalls Hasan. Baath Party thugs came to the factory, threatened Hasan and posted signs on the walls: 'The land belongs to the farmer and the factory to the worker'. Hasan threw them out, but they returned. For several nights Hasan received threatening telephone calls, before discovering that the thugs were concerned that some of the workers might be sacked. Hasan reassured them that nobody would lose their jobs. Special customs permits were quickly issued, impounded goods were released and the factory was soon up and running again.

New problems soon arose. Hasan and Barbara's passports were confiscated. Barbara was accused of being a spy for Britain, Hasan for Saudi Arabia. The accusations were not serious, but rather primitive attempts at extortion. Still, it was with relief that the family boarded their flight for Amman once the year-long posting was at an end. After a well-deserved holiday of several weeks with Hasan's sister Faizeh, they moved to Jeddah in Saudi Arabia. Then came dreadful news. That year, 1964, Ahmad Hammami died in Baghdad, where he was then buried. For Hasan this was a hammer blow, dislodging the pain of exile that he had buried deep inside. Hasan had lost his father, and somehow part of his past, his childhood in Jaffa, had passed away with him. He flew to Beirut to console his mother, Nafise, and his siblings. 'I was overwhelmed with sorrow about not being there to help my father in his last days, or attend his funeral. The pressure built up inside me so much I thought I would burst, but I could not cry, no matter how sad I was. I cannot ever forget this. It was a milestone in my life in the diaspora.'

IN JAFFA, LIFE continued as though the Palestinians had never existed. The Hammami family villa, with its gardens, terrace and fruit trees, was confiscated by the Israeli state and used as a residential care institution. Like Trotsky after Stalin's triumph, Jaffa's Arabs were airbrushed out of history. Joan Comay's 1962 guidebook gushed:

> An extraordinary medley of languages bubbles up from the pavements, or is scrawled on the stores, and just as extraordinary a variety of national dishes can be sampled in the little neon-lighted cafés and eating places.
>
> In a single swift leap, the young children have become Israelis. To their parents, they talk the tongue of the country from which the family came, whether it is Yiddish, French, Bulgarian, Arabic or what you will; but in their street games, they scream at each other in Hebrew.[3]

Despite such delights, most of the Jewish immigrants from the Balkans left as soon as they could, heading further south down the coast for Bat Yam, or north to Tel Aviv proper. Some complained that the stone villas were too cold in the winter; others said there were ghosts in the Arab houses.

But the Palestine Liberation Organisation (PLO), formed in East Jerusalem in 1964, was real enough. Its covenant pledged to destroy Israel, and asserted that 'armed struggle is the only way to liberate Palestine'. It denied all Jewish historical or religious ties to Palestine/Israel and described Zionism as racist, fanatic, colonialist and expansionist. Israel would, in theory, be replaced by a secular democratic state where Jews, Muslims and Christians would live together in peace. The PLO included various Marxist and quasi-Marxist factions, such as the Popular Front for the Liberation of Palestine, but the largest and most important grouping was Fatah (Victory). Fatah was led by a former Egyptian army officer and engineering graduate called Muhammad al-Husseini, better known as Yasser Arafat. Arafat claimed to have been born in Jerusalem in 1929, although others said his birthplace was Cairo. Safe in their offices in Arab capitals or refugee camps, the PLO commanders sent a stream of poorly-trained boys to die on suicide missions in Israel, attacking pipelines and grain silos. These cynical acts of theatre were of no military value, but they provided worldwide publicity for the PLO and increased tension inside Israel. Others hijacked aeroplanes and attacked Jewish targets across the world. But behind the fiery rhetoric about eliminating the 'Zionist entity' the organisation was already fracturing. Many PLO leaders, including Arafat, understood that the real struggle for Palestinian statehood would be won or lost through political and diplomatic means.

Palestinians inside Israel were also finding their voice. The pharmacist Fakhri Geday was a founder member of the Al-Ard (The Land) nationalist movement. Fakhri's acceptance of Israel's existence did not mean that he felt any loyalty or attachment to the state. He explains: 'They don't have any feelings of attachment to us, so why would I feel attached to Israel? I live in my country, I obey the laws, and I have nothing against them. This is a fact of life and I admit it. But my feelings, my aspirations, my soul is with my people.' Israel's Arab minority certainly had more rights than the citizens of the neighbouring Arab states. Most were despotic monarchies or dictatorships, where torture was routine and where the secret police ruled by fear. Israel was a functioning democracy. Arab politicians were elected to the Knesset, where they could freely, if impotently, oppose government policies—for example, on the demolition of the abandoned villages. Amin Andraus was approached several times by Israeli politicians and encouraged to stand for election on the Labour Party list. Understandably, he preferred to concentrate on raising his children and running his business, rather than join a political system that had appropriated his family's lands.

But it was one thing for an Arab politician to work within the accepted Zionist/non-Zionist framework, and quite another to openly espouse the Palestinian nationalist cause. Al-Ard was, or aimed to be, a legal political party. The choice of name was powerfully symbolic, a protest against Israel's continuing seizures of Arab land. Fakhri wrote to politicians and prominent people abroad such as Bertrand Russell and Arnold Toynbee. Russell wrote back to Fakhri, extolling Al-Ard as the most noble political movement on Palestinian soil for over a century. 'Al-Ard renewed the idea of nationalism among our people. All the Arabs of Israel were with us—only the Communist Party was opposed,' says Fakhri. Al-Ard also defined the limits of Israeli democracy. The party was banned from fielding candidates in the 1965 elections to the Knesset. The High Court ruled that Al-Ard was a subversive party, aiming to 'damage the existence of the state and its territorial integrity'. Fakhri and his colleagues challenged the ruling, without success. But as Fakhri once wrote to a US senator, quoting a Bedouin proverb, 'Let the dogs bark, and the caravans will continue'. The banning of Al-Ard was a setback, but the struggle for Palestinian rights within Israel was only just beginning.

There were some victories. In the following year, 1966, the military administration that governed Israel's Arab minority was abolished. This did not mean that Israeli Arabs enjoyed full legal and political equality. They did not serve in the army and could not work in sectors related to defence, which ruled out much of the economy, and it was almost impossible for an Arab to buy land. Petty day-to-day discrimination was widespread. Israel's Arabs were still non-Jews in a Jewish state. But under Mapai those who played the system could flourish. Ismail Abou-Shehade, the mechanic who had once hoped to be an Islamic judge, opened a repair shop in Jaffa's port and employed two workers to repair boat engines. State subsidies gave Ismail a steady flow of work. The government paid boat owners 50 per cent of the cost of any repairs that were needed. A boat owner would come to Ismail, who had the power to certify if a boat needed repairing. It usually did. The boat owner then collected his subsidy and spent it at Ismail's repair shop. It was a cosy arrangement, and Ismail prospered.

His business expanded: he bought several fishing boats and hired new workers. 'In those days the sea was rich, and the fishermen made a lot of money. The fishermen did not get paid by me, but took part of the catch, around seven or eight per cent. The wholesaler then bought the fish and we divided the money.' Ismail loved to go fishing himself, and was also on call if a ship ran into trouble. 'If ships at sea had problems, we went out to help them. There were no cellular phones then,' he explains. 'You stopped the boat and fired a red flare if it was during the night, or a smoke bomb during the day. We were called out a lot, once or twice a month. Once they saw the red flare go off, they came to get us. Once a boat did not return. They did not have any flares with them. After twelve hours a spotter plane was sent out, but they did not see anything. So we called the government and they sent out a fighter plane, which found the ship. It had just got lost.'

The seas around Jaffa were powerful and dangerous. Then, as now, the water could be deadly, recalls Ismail. One friend of his had a leg bitten off by a shark. 'Once we were sailing between Netanya and Herzliya. They said the sea was fine, and we headed north. The wind came up, very strong. We fired out flares, but nobody saw them. We had problems, but luckily we were near the shore. The boat capsized, but we managed to swim to land.' But the sea never recovered from attempts to discover oil, says Ismail. 'The companies looking for oil bombed the sea with tons of dynamite, from ten to two hundred metres down. We, the fishermen, demonstrated and wrote to the government, but nothing happened. They gave us compensation—sixty lire, enough for ten kilos of meat. They said the sea would recover after ten years, and now it is thirty years later and the sea is still not living. You should not play with nature. God made nature and you should not alter these things. If they put me on the television, I would tell them, "You burnt the sea."'

BY NOW, THE mid-1960s, Jaffa had fallen into decay. State funds were being directed towards new towns for immigrants, not old cities that were mainly home to Arabs. Old Jaffa was especially dilapidated, home to brothels, drug dealers and prostitutes working the narrow, dark alleys. Few of the buildings damaged in 1948 had been repaired. Stray dogs scampered across the rubble, picking through the piles of rotting rubbish. Manshiyyeh, the front-line border area between Tel Aviv and Jaffa, was a wasteland. The novelist Max Brod compared its ruins to Pompeii. It was 'a vast expanse of rubble, reaching almost to the horizon', he wrote in *Unambo: A Novel of the Jewish Arab War*:

The difference is that in Pompeii the mounds of debris have been carefully stacked and tidied, while here in Manshiyyeh, the no-man's-land between Tel Aviv and Jaffa, where battles had raged for weeks on end, no one had yet got round to clearing up. Of some houses half a wall remained, behind which heavy iron beams had collapsed. Other buildings had been razed to the ground, so that an area where this happened to a number of houses looked more like a ground-plan or sketch of a plan than the town itself.[4]

Not everyone mourned Manshiyyeh's destruction. Evelyn Sert, the heroine of Linda Grant's novel set in 1940s Tel Aviv, *When I Lived in Modern Times*, is taken to a safe house in Manshiyyeh by Irgun fighters before the 1948 war.

There are slums in every city but why should there be slums in the newest, most modern city in the world? The car pushed through the peddlers and hawkers and pimps and prostitutes and people with the scars of diseases I did not want to think about. It was raining again and the air smelled of rotting vegetables and shit. . . . What *was* that place? It was chaos. It was dirt and disorder, squalid and stinking. The white city [Tel Aviv] didn't touch it. Perhaps it had its own charms but I couldn't see them.

Evelyn Sert's opinions were widely shared. The last houses, still wrecked from the fighting of 1948, were finally demolished in the late 1960s, and Manshiyyeh, former home to Jewish Communists, Arab businessmen, refugees and immigrants, was no more. The rubble was bulldozed towards the sea, covered with grass and turned into a park, named for Sir Charles Clore, the British Jewish businessman and philanthropist.[5] It is ironic that the only house still standing in Manshiyyeh's former seafront is now the Irgun museum—commemorating those who first destroyed the quarter in the 1948 fighting—overlooked by the nearby Hasan Bey mosque, which also survived.

Next on the list for demolition was Old Jaffa itself, the heart of the ancient city. Old Jaffa had survived almost three millennia of invasion and capture, from the pharaohs to the British Mandate. But now it seemed it would be Israeli bureaucrats who would deliver the *coup de grâce*. Israel had already launched a new campaign of demolition in 1966, named 'Levelling Villages', to flatten abandoned settlements. Nabi Rubeen, the site of the annual festival where the Hammamis had spent their summer holidays before 1948, was one of the first to be destroyed. Bulldozers demolished every building except for the mosque and adjacent shrine. When an Arab member of the Knesset protested, Prime Minister Levi Eshkol replied: 'Not destroying the abandoned villages would be contrary to the policy of development and revitalisation of wasteland, which every state is obliged to implement.'[6]

Luckily for Jaffa, the mayor of Jerusalem, Teddy Kollek, had other ideas. Kollek knew the architect Frank Meisler, and planned to recruit him to save the Old City. Frank's days of carousing in cafés were over. He was living in Tel Aviv, married to Batya, a distant American relation. 'Kollek told us that there was a plan to renovate Jaffa, to make it into an artists' colony. He said he wanted to show us around,' recalls Frank. Saving Old Jaffa would need a lot of work, and a strong political will. Renovating old Arab houses ran contrary to the political thinking of the day, says Frank. 'Jaffa then was a tumble-down slum.

The city fathers wanted to bulldoze the whole thing. That was the mentality then: everything Arab was horrible and should be demolished and high-rise buildings put up in its place. There were kibbutzim that moved into Arab villages, that destroyed the Arab houses and built corrugated iron shacks. The idea was to get rid of Jaffa, which was seen as an Arab dump, and build high-rise, cheap workers' housing, like Bat Yam. But then a few people with some aesthetic sense stood up against that and said it would be a desecration to demolish Old Jaffa.'

Kollek won. The Tel Aviv municipality agreed that Old Jaffa was to be saved, or rather converted into an artists' and tourists' quarter, and a committee was set up to vet potential applicants. Frank Meisler and Batya were accepted. They sold their flat in Tel Aviv and bought two derelict piles in the middle of Old Jaffa, one to live in and one to convert into a workshop. In 1966 this was considered a daring if not foolhardy move. Few Jews voluntarily moved to the heart of an Arab quarter, especially one as ramshackle as Old Jaffa, but Frank's motives, like most life-changing decisions, were mixed. While he knew the city and liked it, economics also played a role. 'I had seen villages in southern France where the local people had left for the cities, and artists had moved in and renovated them. So from a property point of view, I thought it wouldn't be a bad deal. People bought cheaply and renovated, an artists' colony appeared, the buses started arriving and the tourists came.'

Israel's first artists' colony was sited in the village of Ein Hod, near Haifa. Before 1948, Ein Hod was a Palestinian settlement called Ein Hawd. Its farmers grew olives, carobs and sesame and produced honey. After 1948 most fled, but a dozen or so stayed on a nearby hill, living in shacks. Tenaciously loyal to their land, they rebuffed Israel's attempts to disperse them and were eventually granted Israeli citizenship. They were, however, not allowed to return to their houses. Like many Israeli Arabs they were classified as 'present absentees', an Orwellian phrase applied to Palestinians whose property was confiscated under the 1950 Absentee Property Law but who were present within Israel's borders and granted Israeli citizenship. Ein Hawd was Hebraised to Ein Hod. A Romanian artist called Marcel Yanko launched a campaign to 'save' Ein Hod. The village mosque was converted into a restaurant and bar modelled after the Café Voltaire in Zurich, birthplace of the Dada movement.

The abandoned Arab family homes soon had new owners—writers and sculptors who converted them to art galleries and summer homes. Some of the sons of the original Arab owners, who lived in the adjacent shacks, even worked on the restoration of the houses or as day labourers in their former fields, which had been appropriated by Kibbutz Nir Etzion. Many of the artists and writers were leftists, although not quite 'leftist' enough to give back the Arab houses to their owners. When a parking lot was built on top of part of Ein Hawd's cemetery, the surviving villagers asked the artists for permission to fence off the remainder of the cemetery and preserve the graves. It was refused. One of the artists told the Israeli author David Grossman: 'If you give them a toehold here you are immediately acknowledging thereby that some sort of—I don't know—injustice took place, and turning them into unfortunates who were uprooted from their land. . . . Their having a hold here would undermine our right to the place and our possession.'[7]

The makeshift shacks eventually evolved into the nearby village of

Ein Hawd al-Jadida, one of many 'unrecognised' Arab villages, all of which lack proper water and electricity supplies, access roads, sewage systems and any legal recognition. Much of the tangled connection between Ein Hawd and Ein Hod—displacement, appropriation, denial and renaming—would be mirrored in the relationship between the renovated artists' quarter of Old Jaffa and its Arab surrounds.

16

Six Days That Shook the World

1967

There were also the grim preparations that had to be kept secret:
the parks in each city that had been consecrated for possible
use as mass cemeteries; the hotels cleared of guests so they
could be turned into huge emergency first-aid stations.

Golda Meir, on the days before
the start of the Six Day War[1]

They came for Fakhri Geday at 8 a.m. on Monday 5 June 1967. He opened the door of his pharmacy to find two policemen in uniform and a plainclothes officer from Shin Bet standing on the step. The Six Day War was fifteen minutes old and Fakhri was under arrest. As a leading member of Al-Ard, the banned Arab nationalist party, he was considered a security risk and was one of many Arab activists to be interned. But Fakhri was not worried. 'They told me I would be held in detention until the end of the war. I knew one of them very well. We always spoke in French together. He told me that he was very sorry, but he had orders to take me. My sister was here, together with a girl who worked for me. They both began to cry. I told them, "Don't cry, don't cry, it is only for two or three days. Then Nasser will be here in Jaffa,"' he recalls, laughing out loud at the memory.

The policemen and the Shin Bet officer were shocked. Dr Geday was a well-respected figure, popular in Jaffa. Both Jews and Arabs turned to him for medical advice, which he dispensed with courtesy and professionalism. But Fakhri's mordant humour did not seem so funny to the rest of Israel: Nasser, the Egyptian leader, was Israel's sworn enemy. Numerous high-ranking Nazis had found refuge in Egypt, including rocket scientists and former SS and Gestapo officers, many given senior government positions or posts in the secret police.[2] Most Israelis believed that together with their Nazi advisers, the massed Arab armies would slaughter every Jew they could.

Fakhri thought otherwise, and believed that Nasser's army would be liberators of Palestine, not killers of civilians. 'The policeman asked me how I could say such a thing in front of him. I told him that this was the truth. I asked him what he wanted me to say—this was what I believed.' More practically, Fakhri gave his sister the telephone number of his Jewish lawyer in Tel Aviv, Abraham Suchovolsky, and told her to call him to explain what had happened. Fakhri's lawyer was a friend of Moshe Dayan, the charismatic one-eyed general who had just been appointed Israel's minister of defence. 'I told my sister to call him, only Suchovolsky, and tell him what had happened.' Fakhri's lawyer finally got through to Dayan after midnight. Not surprisingly, with Israel fighting for its survival against the Egyptian, Syrian and Jordanian armies, Moshe Dayan was not overjoyed to hear from his friend. 'Dayan asked why he was calling him at that hour. My lawyer told him because the man whose detention he had ordered was like his own brother. Dayan replied that I was dangerous, that I planned to make demonstrations. But I had never even thought about it.' Fakhri Geday was not a threat to Israel's security, but his detention highlighted the ever ambiguous position of Israel's Arab minority.

. . .

THROUGHOUT THE 1960S the Arab states had refused to make peace with or recognise Israel, although there was clandestine communication between Israel and Jordan. For the radical regimes in Cairo and Damascus especially, Israel's very existence was a national humiliation: proof that Arab lands could be parcelled out and an alien implant imposed, by the same powers that had always coveted Arab resources and betrayed their peoples, right back to the Sykes-Picot agreement of 1916, which had secretly carved up the Ottoman Empire and denied Arab national aspirations. By invading Egypt with Britain and France in the 1956 Suez crisis, Israel had firmly placed itself in the western camp. The Arab-Israeli conflict seemed to be a proxy Cold War, with Israel allied to the United States on one side and the Arab states supported by the Soviet Union on the other.

Yet Cold War politics, while important, were not the only factor. The lines of superpower allegiance were not as clearly drawn in 1967 as in 2007: Israel maintained diplomatic relations with the Soviet Union and the Communist countries of eastern Europe. France, not the United States, had been Israel's principal arms supplier in the state's early years, and the two countries traded intelligence on the Arab world, some of it gleaned by Israel from the immigrants pouring into Jaffa during the 1950s. France helped Israel build its nuclear reactor at Dimona, in the Negev, as a payoff for Israel's participation in the Suez campaign. In addition, Egypt was aiding the rebels in Algeria, and France hoped that a nuclear Israel would be a strategic counterweight to Cairo's ambitions.[3]

Into this complex geo-political mix was added another factor, less concrete but also important in deciding Israeli policy: the Jew-hatred that the Arab state-controlled media daily pumped out across the

Middle East. Jews had once prospered under Islam, but that tolerance had vanished, replaced by a mix of shrill nationalism and atavistic loathing. Nasser and the other Arab leaders spoke openly of the need for a 'third round', in which Israel—referred to not by name but as the 'Zionist entity'—would be wiped off the map. As Benny Morris notes, Nasser himself wrote of Israel: 'We believe that the evil introduced into the heart of the Arab world must be uprooted.'[4] Barely twenty years after the liberation of Auschwitz, such proclamations had an effect, feeding Israel's Holocaust complex and reinforcing the views of those who believed attack, possibly pre-emptive, was still the best form of defence.

Tension rose steadily during the mid-1960s, especially between Israel and Syria, with armed clashes over water resources in and around the Sea of Galilee. Fighting continued in early 1967 as Syrian troops shot at nearby farmers and kibbutzim. In early April of that year more than two hundred shells were fired onto Kibbutz Gadot. The incident rapidly escalated into an artillery and tank duel. Israeli fighters swooped over the Syrian positions, shooting down six MiG-21s in as many minutes, the aerial dogfight extending as far as the skies over Damascus. Humiliated, the Syrians despatched an agent to Jerusalem to set off bombs; he was quickly discovered by Israeli intelligence. In mid-May Nasser demanded that the UN pull its 3,400 troops out of the Sinai peninsula. The UN soldiers were charged with monitoring the ceasefire between Israel and Egypt after the 1956 Suez crisis. U Thant, the UN secretary general, did not even call a meeting of the Security Council, but immediately acquiesced. It became increasingly clear that war was inevitable, and that Israel would stand alone. At Tiv, there was talk of little else, says Yoram Aharoni. 'Those weeks before the war started were full of tension. Everywhere there was an atmosphere that we were facing a great danger. It was a very difficult situation and people were very afraid of what was going to happen. We thought that any war—which we did not want to start—would be a fight for survival. The Egyptians had a big army in the Sinai. In a way, the feeling was similar to that of 1948.'

Nasser appeared cool and determined in his new role as de facto leader of the Arab world. On 22 May, he announced that Egypt was blockading the Straits of Tiran, which closed off Israel's access to the Red Sea and isolated its southern port of Eilat. This was an act of war. Nasser poured Egyptian troops into the Sinai and Gaza Strip; Israel mobilised, and Yoram was called up. He handed over the keys to Tiv to his wife, Rina, and went off to war. He would be away for two months.

Israel in 1967 was very different from the military power it is now. The state was less than twenty years old, with a population of just two and a half million. It had already fought two wars, and then the West Bank and East Jerusalem were part of Jordan. Tel Aviv was well within artillery range. A swift, coordinated tank attack from Jordan could cut Israel in half in less than an hour. Few Israelis believed that the Geneva Conventions would be observed if the Egyptians took Jaffa and Tel Aviv, or the Syrians Haifa, nor did they expect that the West would come to their rescue. In Cairo, Baghdad and Amman, Arab crowds called for death to Israel and death to the Jews. For the corrupt monarchs and dictators of the Middle East, anti-Israel fury was a useful safety valve for populations deliberately kept mired in poverty and fear. But that was no reason not to believe the crowds' sincerity.

'The battle will be a general one and our basic objective will be to destroy Israel. I probably could not have said such things five or even three years ago. Today I say such things because I am confident,' Nasser proclaimed on 26 May.[5] That same day Egyptian fighters flew over Israel's Dimona nuclear reactor on a reconnaissance mission, triggering fears that Cairo was about to attack the site. Ahmed Shukeiry, the first leader of the PLO, promised that all Israelis born outside the country would be 'repatriated'. As for those who had been born in pre-1948 Palestine or Israel, he explained, 'Those who survive will remain in Palestine, but I estimate that none of them will survive.'[6] Prime Minister Eshkol, who also held the defence portfolio, made a conciliatory radio broadcast on 28 May, saying that Israel did not seek war. His delivery was stumbling, and he had problems reading his script. It made a poor impression, says Yoram. 'It was a bad speech. I was very concerned, especially for my family. The government did not seem to have a proper policy.' Energised by the apparent prospect of finally wiping Israel off the map, the Arabs discovered a new-found unity. Egypt signed mutual defence pacts with Jordan and Iraq, and Egyptian commandos and Iraqi troops were despatched to Jordan.[7]

IN RESPONSE, ON 1 June Eshkol formed Israel's first National-Unity government, drafting Menachem Begin, leader of the right-wing Herut opposition party, to the cabinet. On the home front, families stockpiled food and water and taped over windows to prevent flying glass. Ordinary life, wrote Golda Meir, soon to be Israel's first woman prime minister, had come to an end. 'And, of course, there were the military preparations, because even though we had by now absorbed the fact that we were entirely on our own, there wasn't a single person in Israel, as far as I know, who had any illusions about the fact that there was no alternative whatsoever to winning the war that was being thrust on us.'[8]

Israel bordered four hostile Arab countries: Lebanon, Syria, Jordan and Egypt. The combined Arab armed forces totalled 207,000 soldiers, 1,600 tanks and 700 combat aircraft, writes Martin Gilbert.[9] Other Arab nations such as Sudan and Algeria also began to mobilise. With full deployment of its reserves, Israel could muster 264,000 soldiers, 800 tanks and 300 combat aircraft. Should Israel lose what was now being hailed in the Arab world as 'the final battle', the Jewish state would be wiped off the map. The 'Voice of the Arabs' radio station proclaimed: 'The sole method we shall apply against Israel is total war, which will result in the extermination of Zionist existence.' Syrian defence minister (and later president) Hafez Assad announced: 'I, as a military man, believe the time has come to enter into a battle of annihilation.'[10] Yet at the height of the tension, Tel Aviv's beaches and the seafront by Manshiyyeh were crowded with soldiers and officers on leave from the front. Was war *really* inevitable? In fact, the strolling soldiers were a trick to mislead the Egyptians, Israel's greatest enemy, about the extent of the mobilisation.

YORAM AHARONI WAS himself surrounded by sand, but he was not at the beach. Yoram was deputy commander of armoured vehicles Battalion 141, stationed in the Negev desert in the south of Israel, near the city of Beersheba. Battalion 141 was composed of four platoons— two combat, one auxiliary and one logistics, a total of seven hundred soldiers and more than forty armoured vehicles. The hours and days of waiting passed very slowly at their desert camp. Each morning Yoram and the troops were up at 4 a.m., with the vehicles armed and ready to go. They trained and prepared for an order that could come through at any moment, he recalls. Sometimes it seemed it never would. 'The tension was very high while we were waiting. At the start of every day we thought we were going to war. When the order did not come through, we went back to our routine.'

On Sunday 4 June, Defence Minister Moshe Dayan presented his war plan to the Israeli cabinet. Based on an audacious pre-emptive strike, it was accepted. At 7.45 the next morning, Israel launched its attacks against the Egyptian, Syrian and Jordanian air forces. In essence, the Six Day War was won on the first day. The Israeli air-strikes destroyed over four hundred enemy aircraft, many on the ground, including one third of the Egyptian air force, together with its communications network. The land battles would continue for another five days on several fronts, but Israel's air superiority had turned the tide. The swift destruction of the Arab air forces was a humiliating blow, further proof for the Arab masses of the incompetence of their leaders. The bitter defeat was later summed up in a sour joke: Soviet leader Leonid Brezhnev telephones Egyptian President Nasser after the war is over. 'We have your next batch of fighter planes here. Shall we bother delivering them to you, or just blow them up ourselves on the ground?'

The destruction of the Egyptian air force was welcome news for Yoram Aharoni and Battalion 141. Without air cover, the Egyptians were almost defenceless. When the order finally came through, the battalion was so practised that it was mobile in ten minutes. Battalion 141 pushed through the Sinai desert, until at the end of the first day the tanks halted. They had run out of fuel. The Israeli military planners had not accounted for the depth of the sand, which slowed progress and used up fuel faster. The battalion was resupplied by air and pushed on towards El-Arish, in northern Sinai. Yoram's troops engaged a new Russian T-54 tank which had hit an Israeli truck, killing an army cook who had been sitting on the roof. Yoram and his comrades knocked out and captured the T-54, killing the lone Egyptian soldier inside—a valuable prize, as it was the first to fall into

Israeli hands. The battalion then helped take control of the strategically important Bir Gafgafa junction, but the Egyptians made a
counter-attack during the night, unleashing a barrage of gunfire on
the Israeli forces and trying to punch through the lines.

It was one of the longest nights of Yoram's life. Yoram was forty-
three years old. He was a seasoned soldier who had killed for his
country and would do so again when necessary. He was ready, too, to
lay down his own life for Israel. He had fought as a guerrilla for Lehi,
against the British, and in the 1948 and 1956 wars against the Arabs.
Like most Israeli men of military age, he served two months every
year in the reserves, to keep his training and skills up to date. But the
battle to hold Bir Gafgafa was one of the toughest and bloodiest of
his long military career. Jammed inside the Israeli tank as shells
crashed around him, the air rent by the sound of gunfire and men's
screams, to Yoram, Raziel Street in Jaffa and the sacks of spices and
coffee at Tiv seemed like another universe. 'Anyone who says they are
not scared during battle is lying. Fighting a war is a terrible thing,'
recalls Yoram. 'There was smoke everywhere, and the air was filled
with the smell of gunpowder and fuel. You hear the sounds of the
shells exploding around you, mixed with the noise of the engines, and
the orders blaring out of the radio. But when you are in the middle of
it, you concentrate so hard that nothing else is on your mind. The tension is at its peak. But somehow you feel quite protected inside the
tank. Everyone inside knows his job, but if the vehicle is hit by a shell
the results are terrible. Some soldiers went into battle shock when
they saw that.'

Eventually most of the Egyptian forces attempted to retreat back
to the Suez Canal, but the Israelis cut off their path. The armoured
columns were trapped in the mountain passes. The Egyptians were

easy prey for the Israeli air force, which bombed and strafed them at will. The tanks were reduced to piles of charred, twisted metal, and the men died in their hundreds; the desert was littered with corpses, recalls Yoram. 'The smell and the sight of the dead bodies was horrifying, something unimaginable. Sometimes we found whole units which had been hit by the air force. The dead soldiers just lay there, full of flies.' About 15,000 Egyptian troops were killed in the Sinai. 'It was a sight that even the victors did not savour,' wrote Yitzhak Rabin, then Israeli chief of staff. Once a ceasefire was signed, Rabin issued orders that Egyptian POWs should be allowed to go back to Egypt, although officers were to be detained. Yoram and his troops helped them return home. 'We caught many Egyptian prisoners after the fighting was finished. They were hiding or they gave themselves up. We took them to the Suez Canal and blew a whistle. An Egyptian boat crossed over and took them back.'

The Six Day War ended on 11 June. It was a stunning victory. Israel had fought a three-front war, defeating Egypt, Jordan and Syria. It had captured the Sinai desert and the Gaza Strip from Egypt, the Golan Heights from Syria and, from Jordan, the West Bank of the River Jordan and East Jerusalem, including the Western Wall of Solomon's Temple, thus returning the whole of the city to Jewish rule for the first time in two millennia. King Hussein had paid a heavy price for ignoring Israel's repeated requests not to join the hostilities. Not just Israelis but Jews across the world rejoiced. The Israeli army seemed unstoppable. There was even talk of rescuing the last 15,000 Jews of Damascus if Israel pushed into the capital. Including the Sinai desert, Israel's territory had increased by four times. The country had lost 777 soldiers, a fraction of the casualties in 1948, when 6,000 were killed. A million Arabs, most of whom were Palestinians—some refugees from 1948, including a good number from Jaffa living in Ramallah and Jerusalem—were now under Israeli control.

Yoram eventually went home in late July, after two months away. The Tiv spice and coffee shop had stayed open, run by his wife, Rina, and other relatives. The Aharoni family, like every Israeli, were proud and triumphant. Yoram recalls: 'We felt we were the strongest country in the world in 1967. And it was those feelings that helped lead to what happened in the Yom Kippur War in 1973.'

ON THE OTHER side of the front lines, in newly-captured East Jerusalem, Fadwa Hammami, now Fadwa Hasna, was neither proud nor triumphant. Fadwa had moved to Jerusalem from Beirut in 1958, after marrying Suleiman Hasna. Suleiman was the scion of an old Jerusalem family and could trace his ancestry back to the time of the prophet Muhammad. Suleiman was thirty-seven, seventeen years older than Fadwa, when they married. He was a well-established figure in the city, a senior manager at the electricity company. Fadwa and Suleiman lived in a spacious Arab stone house in the suburb of Shuafat, on the road going north towards Ramallah. 'I was very happy to move to Jerusalem, because it meant I was going back to Palestine. Everyone in the family was excited. Jerusalem then was better than now, cleaner and more prosperous. We had a very active life. Tourism was flourishing. Everyone came here from all over the Arab world to pray in the Al-Aqsa mosque.'"

Before 1967, Jerusalem, like Berlin, was a divided city. The eastern half, including the Old City and the holy sites, was in Jordan. The western half was in Israel. Tourists and pilgrims were allowed to cross from one side to the other, but the border was closed to Israelis and most Arabs. 'At Christmas time we saw the Christian Palestinian pilgrims who were allowed to visit the holy places as they came across from West Jerusalem. They told us how miserable it was in Israel, that it was not flourishing, and it was very difficult for Arabs to live in Israel,' says Fadwa. In some ways Jerusalem seemed rather provincial compared to life in Beirut. The Lebanese capital was known as the Paris of the Middle East, a vibrant and cosmopolitan city, filled with foreigners from all over the world. But Suleiman and his friends worked hard to build up Jerusalem. They founded the Ambassador Hotel, a shopping centre and a cinema.

Fadwa also had her nieces nearby. Hasan and Barbara Hammami sent Fawzia and Rema to school in Jerusalem, to the Schmidt Girls' College, the best girls' boarding school in the Middle East. Rema was a lively, wilful child and frequently got into trouble with the nuns. Shortly before the war began, Fadwa telephoned the school to check on her nieces. 'Rema told me there were plans to take them to Amman. They asked me about the road and I told them it was not safe.' One of the teachers said Fadwa could come and shelter in the school basement, but she wanted to stay at home with her family. When the war broke out, it all seemed horribly familiar to Fadwa. 'The same story as 1948 repeated itself, but this time with children and my husband. The signs are always the same, even now. They told the foreigners to leave, and then we knew that it was a serious business. We didn't have guns to defend ourselves. The Israelis started bombarding on Monday. My husband was at work and I was at home. Two of my children came home from school and told me the war had started. I didn't know. So I turned on the radio and there it was, we were at war.'

Fadwa telephoned Suleiman at the electricity company. He tried to reassure her that nothing would happen. He was wrong. The Jordanians and Israelis fought artillery duels along the front line, in some

The port of Old Jaffa and the house of Simon the Tanner in 1921, where, according to the Christian scriptures, the apostle Peter stayed.

Founded in 1909 as a suburb of Jaffa, the new Jewish city of Tel Aviv was laid out on modern European lines with detached homes and gardens.

The Aharoni family in Pazardjik, Bulgaria, c. 1930. Yoram is centre right, sitting on the floor in front of his mother, Lea, who is holding his brother Haim. His father, Shabat, is standing behind, next to his brother Josef and the Bulgarian maid. On the left are Yoram's aunt, uncle and cousins.

Yoram Aharoni as a member of the Jewish youth group Maccabi.

Hanneh Andraus, wife of Amin. Hanneh died tragically young, in 1945, at the age of thirty-seven. Amin never remarried.

The Andraus family socialising: Amin (third from right), together with his wife, Hanneh, and a group of friends. Jaffa boasted a rich social, sporting and intellectual life.

Frank Meisler with his mother, Meta. The Meisler family enjoyed a comfortable middle-class lifestyle in the free port of Danzig.

Frank Meisler and his father, Misha, who came from Warsaw.

The Hammami family in 1947. From left to right, back row: Fatmeh, Hasan, Faizeh and her husband, Mamdouh, Nahida, Nafise, wife of Ahmad, the head of the family (not pictured), and Hussein. Front row: the twins, Laila and Fadwa, and Mustafa.

Two of the Hammami brothers with friends. The family was very active in Jaffa's municipal politics. Adel (far left) was a fruit and vegetable merchant and a member of the city council. Next to Adel is Ahmad Hammami, father of Hasan and Fadwa.

Aharon Chelouche, the great family patriarch, and his wife, Sarah. Aharon Chelouche came to Palestine with his father, Avraham, from Oran in Algeria in 1838.

Julia Chelouche (*née* Bohbout), wife of David Chelouche.

Zaki Chelouche. Zaki was an architect who built several landmark Bauhaus-style buildings in Tel Aviv.

Avraham Haim Chelouche, his wife, Sarina, and their family, including sons Marco, Zaki and David and daughter Simha.

Yosef Pomrock and his wife, Simha, daughter of Avraham Haim Chelouche.

THE MANDATE BEGINS TO CRACK

Arab demonstrators in Jaffa's Central Square, October 1933. The year Hitler came to power saw a fresh wave of Jewish emigration from Nazi Germany to Palestine.

British military engineers blow up a large swath of Old Jaffa during the Arab Revolt in 1936. Supposedly carried out in the name of 'urban improvements', the real motive was to blast a path for armoured vehicles.

Amin Andraus leaning against a pillar of his former car showroom, the morning after the British blew it up in retaliation when a sniper shot and killed a policeman who was smoking a cigarette on the roof. Neither had any connection to Amin.

Yaakov Chelouche sitting at his desk in the Anglo-Palestine Company bank, in Jaffa c. 1900. He was always preceded on his rounds by a *kawas*, a ceremonial bearer.

Yefet Street, today: the door of the first branch of the Anglo-Palestine Company, which funded the early Zionist settlements.

Amin Andraus (second from right) and several of his friends on a shooting party in the 1930s. Amin was a keen outdoorsman who loved to hike through Palestine's countryside.

Dr Fakhri Geday at the counter of his pharmacy at 65 Yefet Street. Stranded in Beirut when war broke out in 1948, Fakhri was later allowed to return home.

Yoram Aharoni in Tiv, his spice and coffee shop on Raziel Street, in Jaffa's commercial district. Each new wave of Jewish immigrants demanded different coffees and spices for their food, and Yoram soon became an expert blender.

The Abulafia bakery, by Clock Tower Square. The bakery is a Jaffa landmark, popular with both Arabs and Jews. Its Arab owners close the shop on Jewish holidays as a show of respect.

The wreckage of Jaffa's New Seray administrative building after it was blown up by the Stern Group in January 1948. Dozens of civilians were killed or wounded.

Hasan Hammami (top, far right) with his classmates on a course in first aid. Fighting erupted in Jaffa between Jews and Arabs after the United Nations voted in November 1947 to partition Palestine.

Two members of the Haganah, the main Jewish militia, in action on the border between Jaffa and Tel Aviv. Mixed Jewish-Arab areas were the scene of heavy fighting.

Palestinian refugees fleeing from Jaffa in May 1948. Of Jaffa's population of 100,000, just a few thousand remained. Many left months before the fighting began.

Yoram and Rina Aharoni in 1947. Both were underground fighters and members of Lehi, also known as the Stern Group, and known to the British as the 'Stern Gang'.

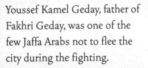

Youssef Kamel Geday, father of Fakhri Geday, was one of the few Jaffa Arabs not to flee the city during the fighting.

David Ben-Gurion, the first prime minister of Israel, proclaiming the birth of the new Jewish state of Israel at the Tel Aviv Museum on May 14, 1948.

Cheering citizens gather in Tel Aviv as the State of Israel is declared. The new state was immediately invaded by four Arab armies, who pledged to sweep the Jews into the sea.

Suad Andraus (centre) standing next to Kamal Nasser, a Palestinian poet, in the village of Bir Zeit. The Andraus children spent two years in exile in Jordan before being reunited with their father in Jaffa by the Red Cross in 1950.

Hasan Hammami on his wedding day in England, September 1956. Soon after arriving at Nottingham University he met Barbara Paulson in the university coffee bar. They were married a year later.

Tank crews in southern Israel wait for the order to go into action during the Six Day War. Yoram Aharoni spent days in the Negev desert before the battle began.

Ofer Aharoni as a young conscript at the Suez Canal, c. 1970. Ofer joined the paratroops, one of the toughest regiments in the army. Three years later he would be fighting in the Yom Kippur War.

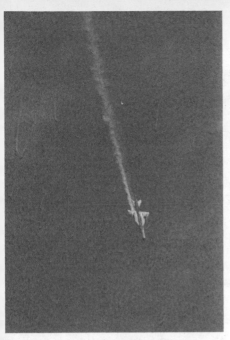

Israeli units moving into battle to counter-attack Syrian troops on the Golan Heights during the Yom Kippur War, 1973.

An Egyptian Mig shot down during the Yom Kippur War, 1973. The war ended in a stalemate which later helped start the Arab-Israeli peace process.

Palestinian youths hurl rocks and stones at Israeli troops during the Al-Aqsa Intifada, which erupted in September 2000. The violence spread into Israel proper, including Jaffa.

JAFFA TODAY

The Clock Tower, one of more than a hundred commissioned across the Ottoman Empire by Sultan Abdul Hamid II as a symbol of modernisation.

The Old Seray, once a Turkish government building, is built over Crusader ruins in the heart of Old Jaffa. It was used as a soap factory by the Damiani family and now houses the municipal museum.

The façade of the New Seray being rebuilt in the summer of 2003. The Tel Aviv municipality is renovating and restoring many Jaffa landmarks.

A row of shops and houses on Raziel Street, formerly Nagib Bustros Street, named for the Lebanese businessman who financed its construction in the nineteenth century.

Neve Tsedek as seen from the roof of Beit Chelouche. The settlement founded by Aharon Chelouche is now a bohemian and artistic quarter of Tel Aviv.

The alley known in the nineteenth century as Sharia Serafeen, street of the money-changers. The site of Aharon Chelouche's jeweller's shop (front, right) still has rows of holes above the entrance to let fumes escape.

THE FAMILIES TODAY

The Andraus family. Clockwise from left: Leila, Wedad, Salim and Suad in the house by the sea built by their father, Amin. His gong, with which he announced lunch, is on the table in front of them.

Frank Meisler, with his sculpture of King David and Bathsheba. Frank is now one of Israel's most successful and best-known artists.

Born in 1899, Julia Chelouche lived to be one hundred. She lived through the British Mandate, the Arab Revolt, the birth of Israel and several wars.

Hasan Hammami, his sister Fadwa and daughter Rema on the beach at Jaffa in 1993, near where he swam as a boy. It was the first time that he had returned home since the family fled in 1948.

Yoram and Rina Aharoni. The former members of the notorious Stern Group now live in quiet and comfortable retirement north of Tel Aviv.

Sami Abou-Shehade and his grandfather Ismail. Sami is compiling the history of his grandfather's generation in Jaffa before 1948.

Shlomo Chelouche at home in Tel Aviv. The plaque on his shirt is taken from the cockpit of the Egyptian fighter plane he shot down in May 1948 and gives instructions for an emergency bail-out.

The hotels and urban sprawl of Tel Aviv, looking north from Jaffa. The two cities are now one, known as Tel Aviv–Jaffa.

The view of Jaffa from the promenade above Tel Aviv's beach. The minaret is part of the Jami'a al-bahr, the mosque of the sea, where Hasan Hammami prayed as a young boy with his father, Ahmad.

places just a few yards apart. The shelling was intense. At dawn on Tuesday Jordanian tanks took up position outside Fadwa's house and opened fire on the Israeli positions. That day Suleiman stayed at home. The house was crowded with friends whose own homes were too near the front line. 'The Jordanians did not last long. I know from relatives who lived near Herod's Gate in the Old City that the Israelis had captured the post office by dawn on Tuesday,' says Fadwa. 'The shelling was incredibly loud. All the windows were broken, but luckily we were not injured. I put mattresses against the windows, the three children under the bed, and we lay flat on the ground. I was afraid because the Jordanian tanks were on our doorstep. Because if a plane hits the tanks, the tanks explode. And if they miss the tanks, they hit the houses.'

Fadwa went outside to see what could be done. 'I asked the man who was on the tank, "Are you going to stay here for a long time?" and he said he was. I asked him why, and he said, "We are fighting for Jordan and you are considered Jordanian." I told him if he was staying, I was leaving. I would leave him the house, because I did not want to die. I thought we should go to Ramallah, where it might be safer and where I have family.' When the tank commander radioed for instructions and somebody answered him in Hebrew, it was clear that the battle was over.

Fadwa went back inside. The Israeli tanks trundled up soon after. 'I didn't see them but I heard them talking. My husband and I were sitting on the floor, and the children were under the bed. He knew Hebrew, he could read and write Hebrew. He said, "These are Jews—*khalas* [it's over], we are finished." He thought they would kill him, that they would take the men and leave the women and children. He told me to take care of the children. We hid our money and our jewellery—

I told the children to hide it in their pockets. I thought they would not search them. This was a good idea, because some of our friends who were wearing jewellery when the Israelis came had it taken.'

The Israelis did not kill Suleiman Hasna. They told him to go back to work and get the electricity supply running again. Meanwhile, in Jeddah, Hasan and Barbara were distraught with worry over Fawzia and Rema. Their youngest daughter, Haifa, had been sent to her grandmother in Nottingham after an outbreak of meningitis in Saudi Arabia; these were frantic and desperate days. Like Amin Andraus, who more than twenty years earlier had arrived at the border village of Tayibe too late to find his children, Hasan had no idea if his daughters were still alive and no way of finding out. 'We tried the International Red Cross, the British Embassy, family, friends, the airlines, business colleagues, Procter & Gamble and everything else we could think of, all to no avail,' says Hasan. Barbara flew to Geneva on the first flight out to see if the Red Cross could help, while Hasan stayed in Jeddah in case Fawzia and Rema could be brought out through Jordan. This was Hasan's most wretched time since leaving Jaffa. Once again war threatened his family's survival. First in Jaffa in 1948, and now in Jeddah and Jerusalem in 1967—it seemed there would never be peace for the Hammamis.

As soon as the curfew in Jerusalem was lifted, Fadwa set out to look for Rema and Fawzia. The Schmidt College was on the edge of the Old City, which had been captured by the Israelis in fierce hand-to-hand fighting. The girls were alive and healthy. Rema ran up to Fadwa as soon as she saw her, wide-eyed with excitement. 'Auntie,' she proclaimed, 'there was a war here!' After three weeks of agonising waiting, Hasan got a telephone call to say that Fadwa had put Rema and Fawzia in a taxi to the Jordanian border, where they were sent to their aunt Faizeh in Amman, who then put them on a plane to Jeddah. Hasan and Barbara's relief was indescribable. The traumatic episode forced them both to reconsider the family's future. Saudi Arabia had given Hasan citizenship and a new start, but the restrictions of life under Islamic rule, especially for women, led them to imagine their family's future elsewhere. Until now, the demands of Hasan's career and the children's schooling had scattered them in different countries, but now Hasan and Barbara decided to return to England, where they could live together in a stable, peaceful environment and rebuild their family.

Fadwa, too, would soon be travelling, although hers was only a short trip. It was a strange twist of history that with all of Palestine conquered, Jaffa's exiles on the West Bank—indeed, all Palestinians living in Israel's newly conquered territories—could now freely cross into Israel proper. Defence Minister Moshe Dayan's 'open door' policy even allowed Palestinians to cross into Jordan to visit relatives and to trade. For the first time since 1948, one of Ahmad Hammami's children could go home to Jaffa.

17

The Ghosts of Old Jaffa

Late 1960s

> The Arabs have a case. It's a very difficult thing. Just as
> I didn't understand the gravity of what was happening
> when I said goodbye to my parents in 1939, I didn't
> understand the implications when I arrived in Jaffa.
>
> *Frank Meisler*

After decades of neglect the two Arab houses that Frank Meisler bought in Old Jaffa were in a parlous state, if not completely ruined. Their ancient walls were crumbling, the roofs sagged dangerously and they had barely any floors. But the views from the window and the terrace were breathtaking. The sea stretched away to the horizon, fleets of fishing boats bobbing on the azure waters. The waves broke over the rocky shore, bleached white in the sun. The sky was a lighter shade of blue, dotted with pale streaks of cloud. Frank's houses were falling to bits, but they breathed history. Old Jaffa was where generations of medieval pilgrims had stumbled ashore on the Holy Land after weeks on board ship, and where the first Jewish immigrants in the nineteenth century had stood, dazzled by the sun and disorientated by the clamour and smells of the Levant.

The port was just a short walk away. The Mamlukes and the

Ottomans had built up Old Jaffa, while its most recent foreign rulers, the British, had destroyed part of it. Israel had done nothing to repair the damage done by the 1936 demolitions, when the British army had blasted a T-shaped path through the quarter. 'It was destroyed ground. The British had cleared a path so they could drive their armoured cars up and down the middle,' says Frank. But now, after the victories of 1967, was a time for rebuilding. One morning Frank was overseeing the Arab workers as they began to renovate the living room. In each corner there was a niche. Frank ordered the workers to remove the old plaster. As they chipped away and the room filled with dust, they began to shout. In one corner behind the old walls were several skeletons, probably of former inhabitants. Frank recalls: 'The builders became hysterical. They ran away and we did not see them for a week.' The skeletons were disposed of, and the authorities were decidedly *not* informed; once Israel's bureaucracy lumbered into action, work could be stopped for months. 'The one thing you don't ever want to do is tell the antiquities department that you have found something. I am sure that many beautiful mosaics have been ploughed over. If you find one in a field, the department comes in, everything is fenced off and your home is gone.'

Frank had had an easier war than Yoram Aharoni, although he too saw combat. He was first sent to the port of Ashdod, south of Jaffa, where he worked to prepare landing barges for a planned D-Day style invasion of the Gaza Strip, which never happened. From Ashdod he was redeployed to central Israel, where he fought with the Golani Brigade in Latrun, about thirty kilometres west of Jaffa. The village took its name from the nearby Crusader castle, Le Toron des Chevaliers. In 1948 Latrun, which overlooks the old road between Tel Aviv and Jerusalem, had been the scene of very heavy fighting. Ariel Sharon had commanded a platoon there and was wounded in battle. When the Israelis captured the area in 1967, Latrun's fort and monastery were left standing, but not much else. The neighbouring villages of Imwas, Yalu and Beit Nuba were also demolished, and their inhabitants fled to the West Bank.' 'Latrun's fate was decided by politics,' says Frank. 'Within twenty minutes the bulldozers came, and a day later you would not have guessed there had been a village there.'

Old Jaffa fared better. Frank had a degree in architecture from Manchester University and a good knowledge of house construction, but Ottoman building techniques were a revelation. 'I had a very preconceived idea about how to restore a Turkish house, based on my ideas of the Thousand and One Nights. There was a lot to learn. There is no timber here to make the beams for roofs. You have a dome instead. Once the four walls are built, a potter makes small wedge-shaped vases. You put the vases on top of the wall and fill up the whole row. Then you put down the next row on top of the first, slightly further in. You keep adding more rows until you hit the centre. Then you plaster the whole thing, and you've got a dome.' Understanding the principles of building a dome triggered an epiphany. Suddenly Frank grasped the connection that ran through history, through his new house, back through the millennia. 'I suddenly realised what my house was made of: it was a Byzantine concept, maybe even Roman. A dome gives you a roof with ventilation, because the vases are hollow. There is good insulation against heat, and it is very light. The technology has not changed since then. The Turks took what the Byzantines did and worked with it. As long as the walls stand, the dome cannot collapse. Until then I knew what I was doing technically. But I didn't have a sense of its roots, in what it was grounded.'

The floors and the roofs of Old Jaffa were also a revelation. In the jumble of houses down by the seafront, each built on top of the next, some surfaces served as both. The restoration of the houses was a kind of time travel, as Frank's builders peeled away the walls and floors constructed centuries earlier. 'I also restored a house for a rich South African, and we pulled up the floors to put in the heating and lay down Italian tiles. Under the floorboards were rows and rows of ceramic pots. The floor had been built on top of them. The ceramic pots filled all the spaces between the domes of the houses underneath, and were covered with wood. People had walked over those boards, with the pots underneath, for two or three hundred years.' Frank and the builders often found coins as they worked. Ottoman builders would mix them in with the mortar when they constructed a house, for good luck. The coins were usually engraved with Arabic phrases, praising Allah and his blessings. One afternoon Frank saw a ghost while he was dozing off, a bearded Arab man dressed in baggy Turkish trousers flying out of the corridor and into the bedroom.

Old Jaffa was also haunted by those of its former residents who were still alive. With the border between the newly occupied West Bank and Israel proper now open, they sometimes came back to see their former homes. One visit to the South African's house lingers in Frank's mind. 'A man came in and asked me whether he could look around. He was an Arab man, from Ramallah, I think. I brought him in and showed him what we were doing to the house. He cried.' But few Israelis were bothered about the fate of Old Jaffa's previous inhabitants. Many of the Jews from Arab countries had themselves been expelled, their homes and businesses confiscated, and many Ashkenazim were Holocaust survivors who had lost their families. In Israel, like everywhere else, suffering did not ennoble. It often made people hard, suspicious and cynical. One of Frank's neighbours did check that the property in which he was interested had not been owned by Arab refugees. His conscience was satisfied—the house belonged to the Armenian Church and was leased to the Jaffa Development Corporation. But such cases were the exception, Frank explains. 'There was no consciousness then of what had happened to the Palestinians, or of their lives in exile. Israel was a new country, an "empty" place. People just accepted it. Maybe because it was a convenient concept—that the Arabs ran away, so it serves them right, and so why bother about them?'

The visitor from Ramallah and the scruples of Frank's neighbour began to change Frank's way of thinking. 'I began to realise that, actually, there was a consideration here. The Arabs have a case. Now when I see the pictures by David Roberts, who painted here in the nineteenth century, of the Arabs who lived in Jaffa then, the men in their baggy trousers and the women in their costumes, I wonder, Where are they? Today we are far more conscious of these things. I would like to see the situation from the point of view of an intelligent Arab, which I am sure is a totally different picture from the one I have.'

SOON AFTER THE fighting stopped in Jerusalem, Israeli soldiers came into Fadwa Hammami's house in Shuafat, East Jerusalem. It was Fadwa's great good fortune that she and her family had not left Jerusalem during the war. Those Palestinians who had fled the fighting or were away on holiday or business, even elsewhere in the West Bank, when the war broke out lost the right to reside in Jerusalem. 'The Israelis counted us and gave us identity cards with a number. Nobody should experience the feelings I had, the first time the Israelis came into our home, of humiliation and defeat,' she says. The identity cards were not passports and gave no right of travel abroad, nor was Fadwa given Israeli citizenship, which anyway she did not want. But the identity card did allow her to travel freely within Israel. Unlike today, when the West Bank and areas now under Palestinian control are sealed off by a security fence and a maze of army checkpoints controls access in and out of Israel proper, in 1967 the roads were open. She wasted little time in returning to Jaffa. She recalls: 'I was really happy because I had always wanted to see Jaffa again. I was the first one to see our house again. They always told me that I was the lucky one.'

But the reality of her homecoming was bitter. Fadwa and Suleiman found an East Jerusalem tour company that was taking back other Jaffa exiles who had not seen the city since 1948. The journey stirred powerful and very mixed emotions. Fadwa was going home for the first time in nineteen years to the city of her birth, where she had gone to school and enjoyed an idyllic childhood in the Hammami villa, always surrounded by her siblings and cousins. The last time she had seen Jaffa was from a boat, as she and her family sailed away into exile, shells exploding in the water around them, their home town wreathed in smoke. Jaffa still stood, but Palestine no longer existed except in her memory. Even the villages that once marked Jaffa's outskirts had gone, replaced by modern Israeli tower blocks.

Fadwa's heart thumped and her stomach twisted as the tour bus drove down the dusty, bumpy lane into Jebaliyyeh, now renamed Givat Aliyah. Their house still stood. But it was now a state-run children's home. Rooms had been added and divided, walls moved and rebuilt, the gardens truncated. The stone corridors now echoed to the sound of Hebrew. Israeli children lined up for meals, and played in what was left of the garden, *her* family's garden, where she had once tended her own pink rosebush. Fadwa went inside. An Israeli official, seeing the bus outside, at first believed that she was a tourist and asked her to make a donation to the home. 'I did not tell him at first that it was my house. And then when he knew, he told me that I was not allowed there. I told him that he was not allowed there but he had taken my house. It was awful to see this. They took our house from us, they buried it, and I was forced to let them use it.'

Fadwa returned to Jaffa again in 1970, together with her mother, Nafise, and sisters Faizeh and Nahida. It was too traumatic. Nafise's husband, Ahmad, had died in Baghdad in 1964. In a way, they were returning for him, making the journey home he never could. But the reality of seeing the family villa for the first time since 1948 was more than Nafise could bear, recalls Fadwa. 'It was very difficult, very emotional for her. She would not get out of the taxi. She just said she did not want to see it.' Nafise, who passed away in 1988, never returned to Jaffa again. Since that first visit in the summer of 1967, Fadwa and her relatives have made regular visits to the Hammami villa. 'After so many years of occupation, most of my family has come here, and their sons and daughters. Three generations have come to see our house. The last time I was there the manager asked me how many of us there were. "You come and you come, and you never finish," he said to me. I told him, "Yes, we never finish."'

ONCE THE SIX Day War was over, the pharmacist Fakhri Geday was released from detention. Fakhri had been treated reasonably. He was held in Abu Kabir, on the southern edge of Jaffa. He was not beaten or abused and, apart from the deprivation of his liberty, he had no complaints. Despite his friendship with Moshe Dayan, Abraham Suchovolsky, Fakhri's lawyer, had not managed to get him released. But he visited his client every day to check up on him and take him meals, Fakhri recalls. 'I didn't like the food there. There was no other reason why I didn't eat it. I was treated with total respect.' Fakhri was now forty years old. Like most of the Palestinians living in Israel, he was frustrated at the ease with which Israel had swept through the West Bank and the Sinai desert. Contrary to his predictions, his hero, the Egyptian leader Nasser, had not arrived in three days. He had not arrived at all. Shamed and humiliated by the destruction of the Egyptian air force and the capture of Gaza and Sinai, Nasser tried to resign. But when Egyptians took to the streets in massive demonstrations to show their support and the parliament (which his party controlled) passed a vote of confidence in his leadership, he decided to stay in power.

Nasser enjoyed the greatest popular support of any modern Arab leader, buttressed by a police state. His charisma stretched from Cairo, over the Sinai desert, along Israel's coastline, to Jaffa and the pharmacy at number 65 Yefet Street. Even after 1967, Fakhri's faith in Nasser was unshaken. Fakhri's belief that one day he and the Palestinians would be liberated by the Arab armies lived on: 'As long as Nasser was still living, there was still hope, although there was also frustration, because everything that happens in the Arab world has an impact here in Israel.' A good number of Palestinians living inside Israel left after the Six Day War, many of them Christians with family in the West. 'They had lost hope. Many people left for Canada. I myself believed that now there was no hope for the Arab countries as long as they were governed by tyrants, those rulers who are imposed on the people. This is the first and foremost aspect of the problem.' In the meantime, Fakhri reopened his green-painted shop and went back to work, dispensing pills and ointments, salves and bandages to his customers, whether they were Christians, Muslims or Jews.

NOT FAR FROM Yefet Street, at the Albo household, the atmosphere was very different. Like all Jewish Israelis, the Albos were celebrating. Yaakov Albo, the former shoe-shop owner from Istanbul who had not wanted to come to Israel, had returned to Jaffa after his reconnaissance mission to Turkey. He stayed in Israel and established himself as a fruit seller, setting off every morning at dawn to the market to load up his tricycle and then riding north to Tel Aviv. With its expansion to the south blocked by Jaffa, Tel Aviv had spread up the coast. The emergence of an Israeli middle class had generated new quarters such as Ramat Aviv and Ramat Hasharon, made up of houses with gardens rather than Bauhaus-era apartment blocks. Jaffa's residents disparagingly referred to their neighbours in Tel Aviv as *sfonim*, or northerners. The word carried the suggestion of being rich and spoilt, of living in a bourgeois bubble, compared to the gritty reality of Jaffa with its mixed Jewish and Arab populations.

But the *sfonim* had money, and what they paid for Yaakov Albo's fruit kept the family warm and fed. In the mid-1960s, Yaakov had bought a small van and set himself up in the removals business. It was an ill-timed move, for soon afterwards Israel was hit by an economic depression. Once again Yaakov planned to leave, explains his son, Sami. 'He had another idea then, to go to Canada. Many people were emigrating at that time. I was fourteen and at school in 1966. But I didn't bother studying any more because I knew I was going to Canada.' Then everything changed after the victories of 1967. Finally, after twenty years of equivocation, Yaakov felt he really had come home. There was no more talk of Canada. 'My father became a real Zionist. He was very proud to be an Israeli.'

Jaffa then was a good place to grow up. Socially and economically, the relationship between Arabs and Jews in Jaffa during the 1950s and 1960s was in some ways reminiscent of the era before 1948. The two communities lived side by side, but separately. Their lives intersected in commerce and business, but deep friendships were rare. Jews took their prescriptions to Fakhri Geday's pharmacy, Arabs bought their coffee and spices at Yoram Aharoni's shop, Tiv. But there was a profound political difference between the Jaffa of the 1940s and that of the 1960s. Jaffa's Arabs were now a minority in a Jewish state. Apart from activists such as Fakhri Geday, Jaffa's Arab population was usually peaceful and quiescent. For most, politics was too trouble-some, and would attract the attention of Shin Bet. Sami recalls: 'At first, in the 1950s, Jews and Arabs physically lived together, in the same Arab houses. The children played in the same backyards. They were separate but correct with each other, and nobody did anything to harm the other. The Arabs were weak and quiet. They were frightened to say they had families outside the country and they also wanted to come back. In those days, when I was a child, the Jews lived here, on this side of Yefet Street, and the Arabs lived there, in Ajami. We some-times went to Ajami, but there was nothing for us to do there.'

By the 1960s most of the post-1948 Jewish immigrants had left Jaffa for Bat Yam and other modern towns further down the coast, or for Tel Aviv itself. The old villas of Ajami had new tenants once more: Arab families who moved to Jaffa from Galilee or nearby Arab villages. Sami Albo recalls: 'The first Jews to leave Jaffa were the ones who had lived in Ajami. They understood that they could not raise their chil-dren there. I myself did not have any Arab friends. Arab neighbours, yes, with a very good relationship. But friends, never. A friend means you play together, you hang out together. This kind of friendship I did not have.' Sami watched some of the Palestinians who returned to Jaffa after 1967 as they retraced their family history. He was not concerned: 'I looked on it as a fact. They lived here before and now they wanted to see their houses. Some people I know were a bit frightened in the beginning, but the Arab people just wanted to see how the place was arranged now. They were treated as guests and invited in. There was nothing to worry about. I knew that nobody could kick us out.'

Opening the road from the West Bank to Jaffa would have more far-reaching consequences than mere nostalgic visits to former family homes. Both Palestinian communities had been isolated from each other, and had been differently moulded by two decades under Israeli and Jordanian rule. The encounters between the two were sometimes painful. Many Israeli Arabs were angry at the Palestinians who had fled in 1948. They believed that by staying in Palestine—even though it was now called Israel—and by fighting for their rights, they were the real guardians of the Palestinian cause. In turn, those from the West Bank sometimes regarded the Israeli Arabs as near traitors for taking Israeli citizenship and learning Hebrew. After 1967 a complex and symbiotic relationship began, shaped by a rising nationalist consciousness and the steady growth of radical Islam on both sides of the border. Eventually, the two communities would entwine to the point that the violence of the Intifada—the uprising against Israeli rule on the West Bank—would trigger a similar outbreak across the streets of Jaffa.

18

War, Once More

Early 1970s

You are twenty years old and you see so many people
get killed, and so many bodies from the other side as well.
You see terrible things. Some people lost their minds.

Ofer Aharoni, on his experience in
the 1973 Yom Kippur War

I n January 1972, Amin Andraus died of lung cancer. He was
seventy-four years old, a heavy smoker all his life. In his later
years there was little Amin enjoyed more than sitting in his garden, cigarette in hand, discussing politics and world events with his
many friends, both Arabs and Jews. His 1930s home, perched at the
end of Kedem Street, was a frontier post in both place and time. It
was one of the last houses in Jaffa before the ever-expanding Bat
Yam to the south. It was also a kind of time capsule, a micro-
universe where the lost world of pre-1948 Jaffa lived on—a place of
grace, courtesy and intelligent conversation. Amin's visitors ranged
from poor Arab fishermen, seeking his help and advice, to senior
Israeli officials who wanted to talk politics and sought Amin's opinions on Arab issues.

Even after 1948—perhaps especially after 1948, when almost every

Arab notable had fled—the Andraus name still had a powerful resonance. 'Our home was very much a meeting place for all sorts of people from many walks of life,' says his daughter Suad. 'He was very
charismatic and knew how to tell a good story. At home there were
discussions from history to politics to different cultures.' In the first
years of Israel's independence, General Yitzhak Sadeh was a frequent
visitor. Sadeh seemed an unlikely friend. A former champion wrestler,
he was the founder of the Palmach, the elite strike force of the
Haganah, and had initiated the concept of pre-emptive strikes that
shaped much of Israeli military doctrine. Sadeh left military service in
1949 and became a writer. Like all writers, he loved to talk about
books, says Amin's son, Salim. 'Politically they had completely opposite views, but intellectually they had a lot in common. Sadeh wrote
books, and my father loved to read.'

Amin never remarried, although he would not have found it difficult to find a new bride, says Suad. 'Life would have been much easier for him if he had remarried. He was good looking, and he was a
great personality. I am sure he would have been able to find someone
if he had wanted. But people lived differently then, with a different
philosophy. He married once, and then he stayed a widower.' Amin's
philosophy was to live ethically and help when he could. Amin had a
complex, ambiguous relationship with Israel. He was a law-abiding
citizen of a state he had not wanted to see born. Yet he was a realist
and he accepted the reality of Israel's existence. Its legal system had
not served him well, but when Israeli officials asked him to mediate
in complex disputes involving Israeli Arabs, to help settle them out of
court, he agreed. When Salim was accepted at an American university
in the 1950s, Israel's exchange control laws prevented Amin from
exporting enough money out of the country to support him. Other

Israelis simply sent the funds out illegally, but Amin would never countenance lawbreaking.

Punctuality, too, was crucial, recalls Salim: 'My father was very strict about keeping appointments. If I told him I would come back at nine in the evening and I came back at five past nine, that was a bad mistake. He kept his appointments to the minute, and he kept his word. He was very upset when people did not keep their word, especially the agreement that Jaffa would be an "open city".' Sunday lunches were always announced by the sounding of a small gong, which always caused much merriment among visitors. Amin is still remembered with affection and gratitude in Jaffa. Suad says: 'He inspired confidence in people. The Jaffa folk came to ask his advice, help to find jobs or settle disputes, and he never let them down. He spent his later years very much at home. He read, and worked in the garden. Whenever he went to town people would stop him for a chat. The older people love to tell us that they remember him. The young ones also say that they have heard of him, and how he helped their parents sort out a problem or wrote a letter to some authority on their behalf. My father always lived by his principles, even when they caused him problems.'

AMIN'S FRIEND YITZHAK Sadeh once published a collection of articles under the pen name 'The Wanderer'. For centuries the themes of exile, dispersal and a longing for a lost homeland had shaped Jewish literature and liturgy. But after 1948 the Palestinians, not the Jews, were wanderers, and the same themes shaped the Palestinian literary renaissance. In works by authors such as Ghassan Kanafani, Jaffa often served as a metaphor for Palestine. Kanafani was born in 1936 and was a pupil at St Joseph's College in Jaffa, where

Fakhri Geday and Hasan Hammami had studied. Even at an early age, Kanafani showed a talent for imagination and flights of fancy, and he would construct elaborate games of make-believe. But in 1948 there was no flight from tragic reality. Kanafani and his family left Jaffa for Lebanon. He eventually studied in Syria and worked as a teacher in Kuwait before moving to Beirut. The monks at St Joseph's had taught Kanafani well. He was a skilled and prolific writer, whose oeuvre ranged from historical studies to a detective novel. Most of Kanafani's work examined the Palestinian experience and the trauma of the *Nakba* and its aftermath. In 'The Land of the Sad Oranges', Jaffa's oranges serve as a metaphor for the loss of Palestine as the family arrives at the Lebanese border:

> The women emerged from amid the luggage, stepped down and went over to an orange vendor sitting by the wayside. As the women walked back with the oranges, the sound of their sobs reached us. Only then did oranges seem to me something dear, that each of these big, clean fruits was something to be cherished. Your father alighted from beside the driver, took an orange, gazed at it silently, then began to weep like a helpless child....[1]

Kanafani's work is reminiscent of that of Joseph Roth, the early twentieth-century Jewish writer: it too is an elegy for a lost world. For Roth, it was the vanished Austro-Hungarian Empire; for Kanafani, Palestine before the *Nakba*. But whether in Palestine in 1948 or in Germany after the First World War, the end of empire spawns the same misery and chaos. Roth's description of refugees in 1920s Europe could just as well represent the Palestinian refugee camps: 'I can picture the women arguing among themselves, over a child or a cooking pot, say. Poor people come to blows over such things. The children are fair-haired and slightly dirty. They don't have any nice toys. Their world consists of a courtyard, a dozen bits of gravel, and one another. The one another is the best bit.'[2]

Kanafani's first novel, *Men in the Sun*, published in 1963, was the story of three Palestinians, each representing a different generation, who perish trying to escape to Kuwait in a water truck. 'We are here, we are dying, let us out, let us be free,' the refugees proclaim. Kanafani's seminal work, *Return to Haifa*, published in 1970, recounts the return of a Palestinian family to their home in Haifa after 1967 and their encounter with the Jewish family now living there. It was a ground-breaking work that portrayed the Israelis as refugees themselves, and humanised them. Kanafani's journalism and wide-ranging literary oeuvre soon placed him in the limelight. He edited *al-Hadaf*, the magazine of the Popular Front for the Liberation of Palestine (PFLP), and was appointed its spokesman. Later the PFLP would carry out some of the most murderous and spectacular terrorist attacks of the early 1970s.

THE END OF the Six Day War had brought no peace. Shamed and humiliated by their defeat, the Arab states announced the policies known as the 'Three Nos' at a conference in Khartoum in August 1967: no peace, no negotiations, no recognition. 'No recognition' at least, was reciprocated. Prime Minister Golda Meir said: 'It was not as though there was a Palestinian people in Palestine considering itself as a Palestinian people and we came and threw them out and took their country away from them. They did not exist.'[3]

In 1969 fighting erupted again between Israel and Egypt, along the

Suez Canal. The War of Attrition, as it was known, lasted until August 1970, when a truce was signed. It was a temporary respite. Israel and Egypt, indeed all the Arab states, had unfinished business. The following month Nasser died and was succeeded by his vice-president, Anwar Sadat. The stage was set for the next full-scale conflict. But the fighting by the Suez Canal was not the only military threat to Israel. By 1970 the Palestine Liberation Organisation was dominated by Fatah, and its leader, Yasser Arafat, had been appointed PLO chairman. The military struggle continued in the world's airport lounges, along their runways and in the aeroplanes themselves. The Palestinians launched a wave of terror attacks, with hijackings, bombings and shootings. In May 1972, PFLP-trained Japanese terrorists killed twenty-seven and wounded seventy-one when they opened fire at Lydda airport in Israel. Six weeks later, Ghassan Kanafani was killed, together with his seventeen-year-old niece, when a bomb blew up his car in Beirut.

KANAFANI WAS NOT the only Palestinian writer to pay with his life. Back in 1949, after their failed attempt to cross the border illegally at Tayibe, the Andraus children and their aunt Fahima had moved to Bir Zeit, just north of Ramallah. There they lived with the Nasser family. Kamal Nasser was a journalist and poet, author of verses such as 'Palestine the Proud', 'British Injustice' and 'Jewish Flood'. Kamal gave his room to the Andraus children. Like Vladimir Mayakovsky, the poet of the Russian Revolution, he scrawled his verses on the walls, and the Andraus children enjoyed deciphering them. After 1967, Kamal Nasser was expelled by the Israelis from the West Bank. He moved to Beirut, where he edited the PLO journal *Falastin at-Thawra*. Like Ghassan Kanafani, he was an articulate and fluent writer, and was a natural choice to be PLO spokesman. In April 1973 a team of Israeli commandos landed in Beirut led by Lt. Col. Ehud Barak, who was disguised as a woman. Barak had three targets, and one of them was Kamal Nasser. All three were shot dead with silenced pistols. Back in Tel Aviv at the debriefing, the raid was judged a resounding success. In Jaffa, at the Andraus household, there were no celebrations. The news of Nasser's death caused great sadness. Suad says, 'He was a very gentle man, an intellectual, not a terrorist.'

OFER AHARONI, SON of Yoram, decided there was only one way to conquer his fear of heights, and that was to join the paratroopers. Born in 1952, Ofer spent a happy youth in Tel Aviv going to school, studying, working, partying and chasing girls. 'I also spent a lot of time in Jaffa, helping my father deliver coffee to the coffee houses. It was amazing—there were so many different people from all over the world, and all their languages. Bustros Street, or Raziel, was one of the best and most beautiful in Jaffa,' explains Ofer. In the long term, Ofer was not sure he wanted to take over his father's shop. But he had three years in the army to think about it. The military was the glue holding Israeli society together. Military service was compulsory, three years for boys and two years for girls. Arabs did not serve, apart from the Druse, Circassians and some Bedouin. They missed more than military service—it was in the army that life-long friendships were forged, easing the path through civilian life. 'The army gives Israeli society a cohesion and a shared set of values,' says Ofer. 'I grew up in north Tel Aviv, a middle-class area. In the army I met people from kibbutzim, from small towns, completely different types. Some of them couldn't even speak Hebrew properly, but we became great friends. I met Yemenis and

Moroccans, and they all had something to contribute. It taught me that homogeneity is not good for society.'

When the call came, Ofer was ready. He had spent many hours with his father and his friends, listening to their exploits in the Stern Group. Ofer's brother, Dov, had joined the air force as a pilot, the most prestigious of all the armed forces. The pilots were the elite of the elite, and their uniform was a guaranteed magnet for the girls. In February 1971, Ofer was accepted as a paratrooper. The training lasted eighteen months and was tough and dangerous. Most days began at 4.30 a.m. and ended at 11 p.m. Ofer and his comrades were taught close-quarter fighting in urban areas and in open spaces, and how to jump from aeroplanes. The first jump was the worst. 'I was very anxious. You see your friends disappear into the air, and in a second you will be there with them. But you jump. You do what you have to do. You fall for about fifteen seconds and then the parachute opens automatically. Once it happens it is incredible.'

After eighteen months Ofer was promoted to corporal. The ceremony took place at Masada, a two-millennia-old mountaintop fortress near the Dead Sea. Masada had a powerful resonance: in the year 66 the Zealots, a fanatical Jewish sect, captured it from the Romans. The Zealots, barely 1,000 men strong, held out against 15,000 Roman troops for almost two years. When the Romans eventually breached the walls, the Zealots committed suicide en masse. The ceremony's message was clear: Israel will never surrender. It had been a very difficult eighteen months for Ofer—some of the soldiers had dropped out in the middle, or were wounded or killed accidentally in training. Barely a year later, Ofer would see his comrades die around him in a real-life battle. He would need all his military skills, courage and plenty of luck to survive.

. . .

THE WAR OF ATTRITION had ended in 1970 with Israel feeling more powerful than ever, a pride rooted in 1967. The speed and extent of Israel's conquests in the Six Day War—of Sinai, the Golan Heights, the West Bank and East Jerusalem—had fostered a sense of invincibility. A complacent military and political leadership claimed that the Egyptians would never be able to cross the Bar-Lev line of forts and ramparts on the eastern, Israeli-held side of the Suez Canal; Israel's intelligence establishments ignored several warnings that a new war was likely. The political situation, too, had developed. Anwar Sadat, more pragmatic than Nasser, was prepared to consider making peace with Israel if it withdrew to the pre-1967 lines. But Israel's refusal only hardened his determination to recapture Sinai.[4]

In April 1973, Sadat gave an interview to *Newsweek* magazine in which he again threatened a new war. Words were one thing, deeds another. That summer, Egypt and Syria conducted several large-scale military exercises, including an Egyptian training operation along the banks of the Suez Canal. Each exercise put the Israeli military on alert, but any sense of urgency faded when the attacks failed to materialise. Worried that a new conflict might entail further territorial losses for Jordan, King Hussein flew to Tel Aviv on 25 September—his ninth secret visit to Israel—to warn Prime Minister Golda Meir that Syria was positioned to attack. Golda Meir seemed unconcerned, and travelled to Strasbourg the next day. Even the expulsion in early October of the last Soviet advisers in Egypt failed to sound the alarm. It was the pride that comes before a fall.

'I didn't like the atmosphere in 1973. It felt as though the government was incompetent,' recalls Ofer Aharoni. 'But it was more than that. The other part was the legacy of 1967, that it was such a victory, so in 1973 people thought they could do everything and anything and it would be successful. It was too much.' The fall began at 2 p.m. on 6 October, when Egyptian guns opened fire over the Suez Canal and the Syrians bombarded the Golan Heights. Egypt and Syria hoped that by launching the war on Yom Kippur, the Day of Atonement and the holiest day in the Jewish calendar, they would catch the country by surprise—and they did. Israel was outnumbered five to one in tanks and twenty to one in guns. This time it was the Arab armies that launched a lightning strike. Over 150 Egyptian planes attacked Israeli bases inside Sinai, while tens of thousands of artillery shells and mortar rounds rained down on the Bar-Lev line.[5]

Despite the ferocity of the bombardment, this war was not an attempt to annihilate Israel, as it had been in 1967. Rather, Egypt and Syria aimed to recapture enough of the territory lost in the Sinai and on the Golan Heights both to salvage Arab honour and to deliver a bloody nose to Israel. Initially, at least, it seemed they would triumph. The Bar-Lev line, in which the Israelis had placed so much faith, proved as effective as the French Maginot line in 1940. The Egyptians used high-power hoses to wash away the mud that made up the foundations of Israeli fortresses. They advanced across the Suez Canal, broke through the Israeli defences and moved fifteen kilometres into the Sinai. An air umbrella of SAM missiles protected the troops from the Israeli air force. By 4.15 p.m., just over two hours into the war, ten brigades had crossed, a total of 25,000 soldiers. By 11.00 p.m. six heavy bridges spanned the canal, and Egyptian tanks, artillery and armoured vehicles rolled into the Sinai. By the evening of 7 October, 100,000 troops and over 1,000 tanks had crossed the canal. As Benny Morris notes, the Egyptian troops of 1973 'proved to be of radically different stuff from those encountered in 1948, 1956 and 1967'.[6]

Israel counter-attacked on the morning of 8 October, aiming to destroy the Egyptian bridgeheads in the Sinai and even cross over to the west bank of the canal. But the Israeli generals ignored intelligence about the heavy concentration of anti-tank weapons, and the attack was repulsed, with both sides losing eighty tanks. At both command headquarters and on the front lines, Israeli officers and troops were in shock at their failure to beat back the Egyptians. A stalemate settled for the next few days as both sides considered their options. On 14 October the Egyptians advanced again, along the 160-kilometre-long front. This time Israel regained momentum and counter-attacked with speed and dexterity. The Egyptian tanks, Soviet T-55s and T-62s, were far inferior armour to Israel's Centurions and Pattons. By now the Egyptian armour was outside the SAM umbrella and was easy prey for the Israeli fighters.

The following day a division led by General Ariel Sharon managed to punch through the Egyptian lines and build a bridgehead on the east bank. By dawn on 16 October, over 700 Israeli paratroopers had crossed the waterway and were dug in on the west bank, backed up by tanks and other armour, which had been transported on amphibious vehicles.[7] But the Israeli forward position was dangerously exposed. There was still no bridge across the canal, and no secure road to bring up more armour. An Israeli tank attack to secure one approach to the road was beaten back. The second option was to clear out the Egyptian troops at a site known as the 'Chinese Farm', a large agricultural project. Ofer Aharoni's battalion was sent into action there. Nothing in his training could have prepared him for the hell in which he soon found himself: 'There was one road to our bridgehead. Our commander ordered us to advance during the night to clear out the Egyptian commandos holding the road. We were infantry with light weapons. But they weren't just commandos, they had a whole division, one thousand strong, with tanks and machine guns, dug into the sand. They saw us coming. They waited until we were between fifty and one hundred metres away, and then they opened fire.'

Ofer and his comrades were trapped beneath a rain of bullets, rockets and artillery. They could not move forward or back, and they only had light weapons: bazookas, Uzi submachine guns and semi-automatic rifles. Ofer saw his friends killed and wounded all around him. The air hissed with shrapnel and bullets; the shells lit up the night with staccato flashes; everywhere was the smell of blood and cordite. The screams and moans of the wounded carried clearly through lulls in battle. 'The Egyptians did not know how many of us there were. If they had moved out from their positions, they could have walked over us,' says Ofer. It was the longest night of his life. By the next morning, of the 200 soldiers in Ofer's unit, 40 had been killed and 60 wounded. A tank force, commanded by Col. Ehud Barak, broke through and rescued the survivors.

On the northern front, the war against Syria initially went just as badly for the Israelis. The Syrians captured Mount Hermon and pushed south towards the Sea of Galilee. But after three days of ferocious fighting the Israelis rallied and repulsed the Syrians. By 14 October the Israelis had advanced far enough to shell the outskirts of the capital, Damascus. Once again there was even talk of rescuing the last Syrian Jews. The United States' resupply mission to Israel, launched in mid-October, helped turn the course of the war. Over the following four weeks Operation Nickel Grass flew more than 800 sorties, bringing Israel more than 20,000 tons of supplies, including combat aircraft, tanks, artillery and munitions, reinforcing the Israeli military on all fronts. The Israeli offensive in Sinai continued, and by

19 October the situation had reversed. Israel had 350 tanks massed on the east bank of the canal, while Israeli troops on the west bank were pushing forward into Egypt. Now Cairo, not Tel Aviv, was panicking. Sadat soon pressed for a ceasefire, and US Secretary of State Henry Kissinger flew to Moscow to discuss how the United States and the Soviet Union could end the war. Both superpowers were fearful that the war could trigger a regional conflagration. On 22 October the UN Security Council passed Resolution 338, which called for a ceasefire, but this was swiftly violated by both sides, and Israel launched a futile attempt to capture Suez City on 24 October. By 25 October, however, the Yom Kippur War was over. By the time the fighting had stopped, Israeli troops had captured 1,600 square kilometres on the west bank of the canal, and they were 97 kilometres from Cairo and only 40 from Damascus.[8]

Ofer Aharoni eventually met his brother, Dov, on the west bank of the canal. Dov was a helicopter pilot and had brought souvenirs for the Israeli soldiers in the field hospital: captured Egyptian pistols. By the end of the war Ofer was twenty-two years old. His hopes and dreams were those of any young man: to make a successful career, marry and have a family. But the latter had nearly been denied him; the magazine of his Uzi sub-machine gun had saved him from a shrapnel wound in the groin. Ofer survived the battle for the Chinese Farm, but it changed his life for ever. 'The middle of a war is not like a training operation—it is a big mess, so much so that you cannot understand how it continues. When so many people are killed around you, and you go on to fight again, it has a dramatic effect. It changes your life and your values completely. It's very tough to experience. You come from a group of guys who listened to rock and roll and used to smoke pot and were quite happy. After the war you are not the same.

You were in hell, and you are lucky because you are alive, but you are changed. I went to a concert with my friends. The audience was sitting, all really into the music, clapping their hands and shouting. I looked at them and I thought, What's the matter with them? They have no idea what is really happening out there.'

Both the international situation and Israeli politics had also drastically altered. The Yom Kippur War was a stalemate—the Arabs had not won, but, for the first time, neither had they lost. After months of negotiations and shuttle diplomacy by Henry Kissinger, in the spring of 1974 Israel pulled back more or less to its 1967 lines, surrendering strips of territory in Sinai and on the Syrian border, where UN troops would henceforth be based. Strategically the concessions, just a few miles wide, made little difference, but they were psychologically significant. The Yom Kippur War was a profound shock to Israel. Sadat had destroyed the myth of Israeli military invincibility, a necessary precursor, many believed, for any longer-term peace agreement between Israel and its neighbours. On the home front, the acrimonious fallout from the Yom Kippur War would eventually end twenty-five years of Mapai rule.

19

Talking and Fighting

1973–early 1980s

It is no small thing for a people who have been wronged as
we have to take the first step towards reconciliation for the
sake of a just peace that should satisfy all parties.

Said Hammami, writing in The Times of London, *16 November 1973*

Less than a month after the Yom Kippur War, Said Hammami,
the PLO ambassador in London and a cousin of Fadwa and
Hasan, published a lengthy article in *The Times*. It called for 'a
just peace' and a Palestinian state on the West Bank and Gaza Strip,
implicitly rejecting the PLO's demand for a 'secular democratic state'
in all of pre-1948 Palestine. Such arguments are now theoretically
accepted by all sides, but then they were revolutionary. Said and his
family had also fled Jaffa in 1948, when he was seven years old, and
travelled east to Amman. He studied English at Damascus University
and worked as a journalist and teacher. Said's foresight and willingness to compromise with Israel would eventually cost him his life.

His article represented the shift in thinking of one wing of the
PLO. It was described as his 'personal view', but as the editor's intro-
duction explained: 'Since he is known to be very close to the PLO

chairman, Mr Yasser Arafat, his decision to make his views public is of considerable significance.' Headlined 'The Palestinian Way to Middle East Peace', the article argued, 'Such a Palestinian state would lead to the emptying and closing down of the refugee camps, thereby drawing out the poison at the heart of Arab-Israeli enmity.' It did not guarantee that the PLO would fully recognise Israel and sign a peace treaty—the ultimate diplomatic card—but that was certainly implied. Hammami also referred twice to Israel by name, instead of using the usual term 'Zionist entity', which was preferred by most Arab commentators. Said's article reflected the new geo-political reality in the Middle East. The situation after the 1973 war, in which neither side could claim absolute victory, upset the old order. Israel had paid a high price: more than two and a half thousand servicemen had been killed, more than five thousand were wounded and more than one hundred combat aircraft had been shot down. Public confidence in the government and the military was severely shaken by the speed and severity of the two-front Egyptian-Syrian attack and the slow pace of Israeli counter-attacks. Despite this, Labour won the elections in December 1973. But Prime Minister Golda Meir and her government resigned in April 1974 after the Agranat Commission, formed to investigate the conduct of the war, was strongly critical of Israeli military intelligence. Labour remained in power under a new government, headed by Yitzhak Rabin, a former chief of staff for Israel's armed forces and ambassador to the United States.

Behind the scenes, secret negotiations and contacts between moderate Israelis and Palestinians were under way. Like every national liberation movement, the PLO began to split between the realists, ready to sacrifice principles for compromise, and the ideologues. These wings were embodied in two refugees from Jaffa: Said Hammami and

Sabri al-Banna, better known as Abu Nidal. Said Hammami and his family lived in Berkeley Court in London's West End, a luxury block of flats not far from Marble Arch. Curiously, the Hammamis' flat shared a kitchen wall and a long balcony with the next-door residence of an Israeli diplomat. It was impossible to tell if there was contact between them, recalls one neighbour, but the layout of the flats would have facilitated clandestine meetings: the back doors to both opened onto the balcony.[1] The neighbour recalls: 'Said Hammami was always very friendly and dapper, dressed in a western style. I once met his children in the lift and when I asked them where they came from, they told me that they were homeless, as their country had been taken from them.'

For Sabri al-Banna, Said's overtures, supported by the PLO leadership, were treachery. He split from Fatah and formed the Fatah Revolutionary Council, better known as the Abu Nidal group. Some believed his extremism and violence were rooted in a fractured childhood. Al-Banna's elderly father, Khalil, owned substantial orange groves on the coastal plain south of Jaffa. Khalil had eleven children by his first wife and then took a second, a sixteen-year-old girl who bore him Sabri in 1937. Sabri was never accepted by his siblings, and in 1945, when his father died, his mother was thrown out, further fuelling his anger at the world.[2] The family lost everything in the *Nakba*. After scraping by in refugee camps, al-Banna moved up the ranks of Fatah. He was appointed its representative in Sudan and Iraq, where he developed strong links with Iraqi intelligence. The Abu Nidal group was the most extreme of the 'rejectionists'. Its targets were almost exclusively moderate Palestinians and other Arab politicians. Some claimed it was connected to Mossad. In the 1970s Abu Nidal worked for Saddam Hussein, launching terrorist attacks inside

Syria. In the 1980s he moved to Damascus and attacked Jordanian targets. When Abu Nidal met the British journalist Christopher Hitchens, he told Hitchens to warn Said Hammami about the consequences of 'treason to the revolution'.[3] Hitchens duly passed on the threat.

On 5 January 1978, Said was shot dead in his London office by a gunman working for Abu Nidal. He had paid the ultimate price for his belief in co-existence. Said's family, exiled around the world, mourned his death. 'Said was a rarity among his siblings, the only one to go to university, while the others worked in their father's food business or married early,' says Hasan Hammami. 'He was one of the earliest Palestinian leaders to conduct serious peace negotiations with the Israelis, inside and outside the government. To this day, I believe his assassination was jointly organised by the Israelis and a PLO faction. Extremists on both sides will stop at nothing to prevent a peace agreement between our people. Said's life was important because it showed two things: that there were peace activists among Palestinians and Israelis with both a presence and a vision, and that somehow, their blood had to be shed in the path of peace.' The Israeli diplomat quickly moved out of Berkeley Court after Said's murder, and the flat was sold. The new purchaser discovered that the long balcony that extended around both flats had been extensively bugged.

WITH EGYPT'S HONOUR sufficiently satisfied by the outcome of the 1973 war, President Sadat took a drastic step for peace. In November 1977 he flew to Israel and made an historic speech at the Knesset in Jerusalem, calling for Israel to withdraw from the West Bank, and proclaiming: 'It is no use to refrain from recognising the Palestinian people and their right to statehood.' There were—and are—those in Israel who argue that only right-wing governments can make peace, but Sadat's appeal for the recognition of Palestinian rights received a chilly reception from Israel's new leader, Menachem Begin. The former Irgun commander who had directed the attack on Jaffa in April 1948 was elected prime minister in May 1977. Begin had served in the cabinet before, but during the National-Unity government that brought Labour and Likud together between 1967 and 1970. Now the right had triumphed, toppling the leftist establishment that had ruled Israel since 1948.

Unlike in most countries, in Israel the difference between right and left was not primarily to do with economic policies, the role of the market or welfare provision. It was rooted in a schism that dated back to the very first years of political Zionism, and in essence it was about the borders of the future Jewish state and its policies towards the Arabs. Broadly speaking, the early socialist Zionists believed that large-scale Jewish immigration to Palestine would help build a classless society, where Jews would be liberated from the oppression of both capitalism and anti-Semitism. The precise nature of the new state's relationship with the indigenous Palestinians was never clearly defined, but until 1948 there was a general sense, or hope, that somehow, with goodwill and moderation, an accommodation would be reached, albeit on the Zionists' terms. The biggest grouping was Mapai (the Workers' Party), led by David Ben-Gurion. After 1948 Mapai governed in left-wing coalitions, until it merged with two other parties to form the Labour Party in 1968.

Begin's Likud Party was rooted in Revisionist Zionism, which called for a Jewish state on both banks of the Jordan. The Revisionists were interested not in an accommodation with the Palestinians, but in appropriating their lands (indeed, just as the leftist Israeli governments had done after 1948). Begin formed the Herut Party in 1948, when it won just fourteen seats in the 120-member Knesset. In 1965 Herut merged with the Liberals to form Gahal, which in 1973 merged with several other right-wing groups to form Likud. Whatever the name of the grouping he led, Menachem Begin was the unrivalled leader of the Israeli right. Short, belligerent, his world view profoundly shaped by the Holocaust, Begin understood best the new Zeitgeist and the reasons why Labour had lost power. There were the legacies of both 1967 and 1973: the capture of the West Bank and Sinai naturally boosted the maximalist Zionists, who called for the annexation of the new territories, while the initial debacle of the 1973 war was proof of the incompetence of the old guard, who had simply been in power too long. Just as important was Likud's ability to exploit the deep grievances of the Jews from Arab countries, who had been treated with such patronising indifference on their arrival in Israel. When the Sephardim finally found their voice, they turned to Likud, the natural opposition to the paternalistic Labour Party.

Begin and Likud regarded the West Bank as an inalienable part of the land of Israel, as Jewish as Tel Aviv or Haifa, despite its overwhelmingly Arab population. But while Begin had no interest in giving the Palestinians a homeland, he did want peace with Egypt. Begin travelled to Romania and met with President Ceauçescu, asking him to set up a meeting with President Sadat. (Romania was the only member of the Soviet bloc which had not broken off diplomatic relations with Israel after 1967.) Moshe Dayan, architect of Israel's victory in 1967, flew to Morocco, disguised as a hippy, to ask King Hassan, who had long maintained clandestine relations with Israel, to do the same.[4] Despite their disagreements over the Palestinians, Israel and Egypt continued negotiating through 1978 and 1979. Economics were a major factor: Egypt simply could not afford another war. In

1979, following the Camp David Accord of 1978, the two countries signed a full peace agreement, the first between Israel and an Arab country. The treaty was greeted with fury in the Arab world—Sadat was denounced as a traitor, and Egypt was expelled from the Arab League. But the borders were open, and buses were soon running from Tel Aviv to Cairo.

The peace with Egypt was greeted with joy across Israel. But not at 65 Yefet Street, where the pharmacist Fakhri Geday took a very different view. Sadat was a traitor to the Arab cause, says Fakhri. 'We thought that the Arabs might win the 1973 war. But Sadat made a real mess of it. It was a disgraceful gesture for him to come to Jerusalem. Sadat was an agent of the CIA. I always call him the donkey, the ass. I said so to an Egyptian diplomat, that Sadat is a *hamar* [donkey], and he will always be a *hamar*.' Fakhri often talked politics with a French diplomat. 'When Sadat was on television he [the diplomat] said he knew I was very sad. He took my hand and told me not to worry, that Sadat will not last long. I told him that it would be a most graceful, glorious day when Sadat is killed. There was another customer in the shop, an Arab man. He said the Israelis were like squatters who have taken the land, and now Sadat has given them permission. I said to the diplomat, "Look, this man is illiterate, and this is what he thinks." The diplomat agreed.'

Fakhri's grim wish was granted. In October 1981, Sadat was assassinated by Muslim extremists. When Fakhri visited Cairo he went to the cemetery where Sadat was buried. 'There was an Egyptian army officer nearby who asked me if I wanted to see Sadat's tomb. I told him I will go there when I take a laxative, and then I will visit Sadat.'

Mary Chelouche also travelled to Egypt, with her husband, Shlomo. The Alexandria and Cairo of her youth no longer existed.

The Jews and Greeks, White Russians and Italians had all gone. Everything seemed sad and empty, run down, dilapidated. There was no more babel of languages—only Arabic was spoken. Mary and Shlomo made a trip to Heliopolis, in Cairo. Mary's father's Anglo-American Pharmacy still stood on Ibrahim Street. The owner was very friendly and welcoming. 'Shlomo was very excited about it, but I am not as sentimental as he is,' says Mary. 'We bought something and I asked to go into the laboratory. I looked around and it was exactly the same, forty years after my parents had left. Nothing had changed. The owner was very nice. Maybe he thought I wanted to buy it.' While Mary was looking around the shop she suddenly heard a familiar voice, one she had not heard in four decades. 'Someone asked, "*Mary*, what are *you* doing here?" It was a neighbour of ours. She was very happy to see us. She rang her maid and told her to prepare four coffees. She told me, "Ever since you left life is miserable here, because there are no Jews."'

ON 3 JUNE 1982, four years after the murder of Said Hammami, Abu Nidal struck again in London. Shlomo Argov, the Israeli ambassador, was critically wounded after being shot in the head outside the Dorchester Hotel.[5] For Prime Minister Begin this was reason enough to invade Lebanon, in order to 'stabilise' the country. Lebanon had been wracked by civil war since 1975. It was a brutal and vicious conflict, marked by massacres, cruelty and hatred, most of all between the Lebanese Maronite Christians—who were intermittently supported by Israel—and the Palestinians. Sunni and Shiite Muslims, Druse and Maronite Christians, all had their own militias which controlled patchworks of territories. The PLO ran a state-within-a-state in the south and around southern Beirut, with its own army, schools, hospitals and tax and education systems. For years PLO fighters launched raids against Israel and fought artillery duels with the Israeli army. Israel bombed and strafed the refugee camps after each terrorist attack.

Despite a ceasefire between the two sides, Begin and his defence minister, Ariel Sharon, aimed to destroy the PLO and expel it from Lebanon. And so, soon after Abu Nidal shot Shlomo Argov, Ofer Aharoni once again found himself at war. By 1982 Ofer was a family man, married to a Jewish woman from South Africa. They had one daughter, Ella, and lived in Tel Aviv. Ofer had been released from the army in 1974, although like all Israeli soldiers, he was called up for reserve duty for sometimes as much as four months a year. But going to war as a husband and father, at the age of thirty-one, was very different from fighting in 1973, when he was a young man in his early twenties. And this was a very different war: 'I had a family, and I had another point of view. This was not the same as 1973 because there was no danger to Israel's survival, but still Lebanon was a mess. If Sharon had said before it started, "We will go right to Beirut and we will save Lebanon from the Palestinians," I would have said that may be a good idea. But the war turned into chaos and divided Israel in two.'

Operation 'Peace for Galilee' began on 6 June. The Israelis reached the southern outskirts of Beirut within a week, pounding the city with artillery and bombing it from the air, causing high civilian casualties. Ariel Sharon pushed for a full-scale assault, and Begin agreed. But when the cabinet voted only nine to eight in favour, he dropped the idea. The war was exacting a high price. Television coverage of the siege of Beirut was eroding diplomatic support, especially in the United States. For the first time, Israel's domestic consensus on defence collapsed. The country split in two as the ever more outspoken peace camp voiced its opposition to the onslaught against Beirut.

The fissure was rooted in the days of the *Yishuv*, between socialist Zionists and the Haganah on one side, and the Revisionists and the Irgun (and Lehi) on the other. Now it was tearing Israel apart.

A group of army refuseniks formed the *Yesh Gvul* ('There is a limit') protest group and refused to cross into Lebanon. In 1967 or 1973 it would have been unimaginable for soldiers to refuse to serve. Military courts sentenced 168 soldiers to prison; many escaped punishment because of its damaging effect on morale. Begin press-ganged the Holocaust into service, further angering many Israelis. He compared Yasser Arafat to Hitler, describing them both as 'two-legged beasts', and told his cabinet that the alternative to invading Lebanon was 'Treblinka', one of the worst Nazi extermination camps. The writer Amos Oz responded: 'But Mr Begin, Adolf Hitler died thirty-seven years ago. Unfortunately or not, it is a fact: Hitler is not in hiding in Nabatea, in Sidon or in Beirut. He is dead and gone.'[6]

Together with his reserve paratroop battalion, Ofer Aharoni was sent to Ein el-Hilweh, the largest Palestinian refugee camp in Lebanon, home to over 50,000 refugees. By 1982, Ein el-Hilweh was a small city of narrow lanes, winding alleys and jerry-built houses. Like Manshiyyeh, Ein el-Hilweh should have been difficult territory for any invading army to conquer. But the PLO fighters fared poorly against the experienced and better-armed Israelis. Ofer saw combat, but it was nothing like the battle for the Chinese Farm in Sinai in 1973. Ein el-Hilweh was taken, the PLO fighters killed or disarmed. 'It was not a big battle. We did what we had to do there. In my experience the Palestinians did not fight that well, although people said they did in other places. There were small fire-fights all the time. They shot at us, we shot back at them, until we forced them to stop.'

In the thick of the fighting Ofer had no doubts about his mission to pacify Lebanon. It was only when he was demobilised and safely back at home in Tel Aviv that he mulled over what he had seen. 'When the war was finishing, we went back to Ein el-Hilweh. I watched all the children, how they were playing in the streets and already training themselves to be fighters. They were only five or ten years old but they came up to us and pretended to shoot us, like they were in a play. I said to the others that in ten or twenty years' time, they will be doing this for real.' In August 1982 the PLO finally left Beirut, and Yasser Arafat set up a new headquarters in Tunis. The prospect of peace seemed more distant than ever.

AHARON CHELOUCHE, THE former military governor of Jaffa, did not fight in Lebanon. At sixty-one he was long past military age, and after a distinguished career in the police, he had retired. Now it was time, he decided, to do something more uplifting. Aharon decided to become an educator, in the Chelouche tradition of public service. He recalled: 'I asked myself what was wrong with our education system, and why we had these problems between the Jews from north Africa and the Jews from Germany? We had to focus more on the disadvantaged, and help them improve themselves.' The answer, he decided, was that too much money was being spent on higher education and not enough on the formative pre-school years.

Aharon decided to open three kindergartens. 'I arranged the money, the places, the teachers, but I still wasn't sure. I asked a friend of mine at Tel Aviv University, in the School of Education, to send some of his people over to check how we were managing, and to suggest any changes that might be needed.' Aharon's friend had other ideas. 'He told me not to bother with kindergartens. He asked me to be the university's academic secretary. He told me I could take anyone

I wanted as a student. I told him that I didn't know how a university worked. But I read many books, and soon I was so busy with that that I abandoned the idea of opening the kindergartens.' Aharon accepted the post and bloomed in his new metier, so much so that he was soon promoted to dean of students.

The thousands of students at Tel Aviv University included many Israeli Arabs. Some sought dialogue, others confrontation. When the clashes between the Arab and Jewish students became too frequent and academic life was disrupted, one particular gang of four were sent to Aharon Chelouche to be disciplined. 'They were troublemakers, extreme nationalists. They were bad students, and always having arguments with the other students. Three men, and a woman with curly red hair. We decided that they would not be accepted into the second year. I told her she had to leave, and she began to curse me, cursing the Jews and the Zionists, saying that her family had been in Tirah since the time of Muhammad until today. I could not calm her.'

But at the mention of Tirah, Aharon's interest perked up. Tirah was a village in the area known as the Triangle. It was there, soon after Israel's establishment in 1948, that Aharon had bent the rules to allow some of the Samarra family to stay on. Aharon looked at the young woman's file. Her family name was indeed Samarra, and she was the granddaughter of the Samarra to whom Aharon had granted residence inside Israel. That made her the great-great-granddaughter of Hajj Ibrahim Samarra. Aharon bade her sit down. 'I told her that her story, that her family had been here since the time of Muhammad, was all lies. I told her the truth, that her family was not from Tirah and had only been there since after the establishment of Israel. She began to cry and begged me to let her stay at the university.'

Here then, in the century-long relationship between the Chelouche and Samarra families, was a metaphor for the Israeli-Palestinian conflict. It had begun a century earlier, with an act of kindness by the great patriarch Aharon Chelouche to a lost young Arab boy called Ibrahim Samarra. The state of Israel did not exist. Political Zionism and Arab nationalism had not yet been born. The Arab boy had grown to become a person of substance himself. The code of hospitality ensured that, when the Chelouches' world was turned upside down in 1917, Hajj Ibrahim Samarra came to their rescue. For almost twenty years thereafter, Hajj Ibrahim had sent an annual camel train to the Chelouche house. With mutual respect and understanding, perhaps Jews and Arabs could live together in Palestine. But after the Arab Revolt in 1936, the camel trains stopped. The families lost touch and the long-standing connection was broken—until one day in the late 1940s, when Aharon Chelouche was posted to the Triangle and the Samarras came as supplicants. Aharon had shown generosity then, and in his office at Tel Aviv University he did so again. 'I allowed her to remain for another year, but she was anyway a very bad student, so at the end of it she was out.'

The symbolism of the Chelouche-Samarra association was one part of the Israeli-Palestinian narrative. But new currents were swirling among Israel's Arab minority, especially the young and educated. This was not the *Nakba* generation, but its successor, increasingly confident and articulate. These were full Israeli citizens who spoke fluent Hebrew as well as Arabic, and they did not share their parents' fear of the authorities. Raised in an open society, they were taught to think critically. Israel's universities, and its liberal education policies, were the breeding ground for a new generation of Arab activists who used Israel's freedoms to articulate the Palestinian cause. The first step was no longer to be identified as 'Israeli Arabs' but as 'Palestinian citizens of Israel' or 'Palestinians within Israel'. The small semantic alteration had powerful implications, about their complex identity and loyalties and about their relationship with their brethren outside the border.

The ground-breaking research of the 'New Israeli Historians' such as Tom Segev and Benny Morris, which began to be published in the late 1980s, deconstructed many of the founding myths of Israel. It became clear that the Palestinians had not all fled voluntarily in 1948, but that a substantial number had been ethnically cleansed in military operations carefully recorded by the officers who commanded them. Zionist fighters, like their Arab foes, had also carried out atrocities. The patterns of warfare in Israel/Palestine in 1948—and its human cost— differed little from most conflicts fought to seize territory. It also became clear that the arrival of the Jews from Arab countries had not been a universally 'miraculous' ingathering, but had often caused the immigrants considerable distress. Ironically, it was Israel's own liberal policy—allowing researchers access to government and some military archives—that helped provide the intellectual underpinning for the new narrative on the reality of the *Nakba* in 1948 and the fate and future of the Palestinians and Israel. The students expelled by Aharon Chelouche were strident and aggressive, disrupting the running of the university. The new Palestinian-Israeli history, and the examination of Jaffa's own turbulent past, would, for some, be built on reasoned argument and provocative, intelligent debate.

20

Seaside Urban Sprawl

1960s–1980s

Within a few years a real new city will be erected in the area
that witnessed the events of the Independence War.

*Yehoshua Rabinowitz, vice-mayor of Tel Aviv in the 1960s,
on plans to redevelop the ruined quarter of Manshiyyeh*[1]

Frank Meisler eventually finished renovating his Arab house. The family loved living in the heart of the Old City, overlooking the sea. Just as Teddy Kollek, the mayor of Jerusalem, had planned, Old Jaffa had been saved from the wrecker's ball and transformed into an artists' quarter. The yellow sandstone buildings had been carefully restored, their bricks scraped and polished. The narrow alleys and crooked lanes were now home to painters, sculptors and jewellers, advertising their wares with ornate iron signs lit by pretty art deco lamps. Even the paving stones had been cleaned and shined. The prostitutes and drug dealers were gone, and the brothels had been turned into shops crowded with tourists buying knick-knacks and works of art before enjoying a leisurely lunch at one of the seafront restaurants.

Frank had given up architecture and was now a full-time sculptor,

producing stylish, intricate metal sculptures and statues in his neighbouring workshop. Frank's recollections of Danzig had helped to sustain him mentally as a refugee in wartime London, and inspired his
first attempts at draughtsmanship. In Jaffa, too, pre-war Danzig
would prove creatively fruitful. Frank's home town, his parents and
the whole world in which he grew up were gone. In a sense, his twin
metiers of sculpture and architecture, even restoring his Arab house,
were an attempt to fill that gap. The Hasidic rabbis and musicians of
eastern Europe had vanished in the Holocaust, but their *joie de vivre* at
least was immortalised in the burnished metal of Frank's art. 'I felt
that I was bringing things from my childhood into existence, recreat-
ing them in a new and sophisticated way, that I was getting the inspiration from somewhere,' says Frank. His art flourished, and he
received commissions from the Israeli government and Jewish organisations. Israeli diplomats took one of his sculptures to Camp David,
when Menachem Begin and Anwar Sadat made peace, and his rendi-
tion of Jerusalem was presented to Margaret Thatcher.

But Frank, like many of Old Jaffa's more perceptive inhabitants,
knew that something was missing there too, lost for ever in the renovation—lost, if the truth be told, in 1948. Like an elderly actress wearing too much make-up, Old Jaffa deceived only at a distance. 'We
called Old Jaffa "chocolate Jaffa", because only the rest of the city was
the real Jaffa,' recalls Michal Meisler, Frank's eldest daughter. Born in
1969, Michal was one of a handful of children to grow up in Old Jaffa.
It was an idyllic childhood, commuting between two worlds: the
bohemian mix of artists and Arab fishermen and nearby Tel Aviv.
Frank and his wife, Batya, toyed with the idea of sending Michal either
to Tabeetha, the Scottish mission school, or St Joseph's College. In the
end they chose a school in Tel Aviv. At the age of six Michal walked for

fifteen minutes to Clock Tower Square, where she took a bus to the capital. Now a mother herself, with striking features and short-cropped hair, Michal admits she would not allow her young children to travel alone on public transport. But those were more innocent days. 'Then it was safe, although people thought my parents were very brave for allowing me to do that. I had two lives, each very different. School in Tel Aviv and home here in Jaffa. It made me quite different from my friends. I was more independent and more self-confident.'

The port was Michal's playground. Jaffa no longer accepted ocean-going ships, which now docked at Ashdod or Ashkelon, down the coast. But the fishermen still set out every morning at dawn, returning a few hours later with their catch, which they would spread on the quayside, glistening silver in the mid-morning sun, or sell to Old Jaffa's fish restaurants. 'I learnt how to walk there, how to ride a bicycle and how to roller-skate. It was lovely and it was safe. Now a little girl could not walk back through the port at night. But Jaffa still had a bad reputation. If I wanted a school friend to come and stay the night, her parents often would not allow it. It took a whole operation to convince them. Everyone thought that "good people" did not go to Jaffa.' The Arab fishermen were wary of the independent Jewish girl, allowed to play on her own. 'I was friendly with the Jewish fishermen, but not with the Arabs. They would say hallo, but that was it. Probably I was a bit frightening for them. I was a young Jewish girl, and they may have worried that I would bring them to the attention of the police.'

In 1984, when Michal was fourteen, there was one Arab man who did not worry about striking up a friendship with her. Michal had often seen him driving his BMW through the port at top speed, as though he were on a race-track. Michal felt protective of the port, and was annoyed at his presumption. With all the confidence of a genuine *sabra* (a native-born Israeli), she decided to take a stand. One day she knocked on the car window to confront him. 'I asked him who he was, driving around like a maniac. He asked me who I was. I told him, I was Michal, and this was my port. He said his name was Yosi, which could be Hebrew or Arabic.[2] He spoke without an accent. I asked him for a ride and got in.' The two became friends. Yosi would cruise through Jaffa in his BMW, toot the horn and Michal would jump in. 'They were roller-coaster rides. He would drive through the narrow streets at high speed, taking turns like crazy. Every now and then we would stop and he would buy me an ice cream. There was no romantic side to this friendship: it was completely platonic. He never took advantage or tried to. I was a kind of jewel he enjoyed wearing around Jaffa, and he was the same for me. He was my rebellious side, and I was his dignified side.'

Yosi told Michal he bought and sold cucumbers. She did not quite believe him, but it didn't seem to matter. 'It was our joke. I asked him how the cucumber business was, and he would say it was going very well.' Yosi spoke Hebrew flawlessly, but his real name was Youssef. By the time Michal was sixteen she realised that Yosi was indeed a dealer, but not in cucumbers. Jaffa was the centre of Israel's drug trade. Much of the hashish smoked in Tel Aviv was—and still is—channelled through Jaffa, smuggled from Egypt through the Sinai desert by the Bedouin or brought south through the Lebanese border. 'Once I knew what Yosi really did I went and got my identity card, in case I was arrested while I was with him. When I began smoking cigarettes he would tell me off and say what a bad habit it was. I told him what he was doing was much worse. He just said, "What are you talking about?"' Eventually Michal left Jaffa, to do three years of army service and to study law at university. She wanted to become a criminal lawyer. 'Yosi could have been my entry ticket to that world. It was the kind of friendship that could have brought me clients. We often joked that I would be a criminal lawyer and would save him.' But when Yosi was finally arrested, he needed emergency medical care more than legal help.

WITH MANSHIYYEH GONE, the balance between Jaffa and Tel Aviv was out of kilter. There was nothing to stop the gargantuan plans of municipal bureaucrats, in thrall to the new wave of property developers. Tel Aviv municipality announced the Manshiyyeh development competition. More than a hundred and fifty architects entered, from thirty-three countries. Like the early years of Bolshevik Russia, Tel Aviv in the 1960s was a *tabula rasa* on which architects could draw radical modernist fantasies. Great plans were laid to reclaim the sea, and to build islands connected by walkways. International architecture journals portrayed Israel as a major centre of development, open to radical design ideas. Critics' protests went unheeded.

While Manshiyyeh was being radically 'developed', precisely the opposite process—of quaint conservation—was taking place in Old Jaffa. The Manshiyyeh–Old Jaffa nexus highlighted one of Zionism's inherent paradoxes: the creation of a modern Jewish state peopled by brash, confident, Hebrew-speaking Israelis—a state sometimes scornful of the history of diaspora Jewry, but which simultaneously sought its legitimacy in that same history, which it carefully preserved. The competition to develop Manshiyyeh was won by an Israeli firm. When a symposium was held on the development plan, the quarter's rich past was barely discussed; the divide between Jaffa and Tel Aviv grew even wider. As the critic Zvi Elhyani noted: 'The worn-out disciplinary rhetoric declaring that the plan would "bridge the gap between Tel Aviv and Jaffa" in actual fact perpetuated the alienating barrier and derelict site between the two cities.'³

Historic Jewish buildings were also destroyed in the drive to modernise Tel Aviv. The Herzliya Gymnasium, where Shlomo Chelouche had gone to school, was the city's first public building, constructed in 1909, and the first modern Hebrew school. The Gymnasium and neighbouring houses were the heart of old Tel Aviv. They were flattened, replaced by the Shalom Mayer Tower, a thirty-four-storey rectangular office building that mars the skyline for kilometres. The Bauhaus quarters and Zaki Chelouche's masterpieces were spared the developers. But the Manshiyyeh development plan spawned an aesthetic wasteland. The beachfront was ruined by an uneven row of high-rise hotels, drab glass towers better suited to Detroit or Düsseldorf than the Mediterranean. A four-lane road filled with traffic ran just yards from the sand, choking the air with exhaust fumes. The land behind the beach was dotted with gaping parking lots and decrepit shacks. In short it was, and is, a *balagan*, the Hebrew word for 'mess'.

Perhaps Ashkenazi Jews and the sea simply did not go together, says Frank Meisler. 'Tel Aviv is a wasted opportunity. To build properly by the sea, to utilise public spaces properly, you need a tradition of living in that kind of environment. It works best when people know how to live outdoors, like in Seville. Jaffa has a much more organic relationship with its environment. Seville, like Jaffa, was originally Roman, and then Arab. Andalusia mixed two different heritages—Roman and Arab. They both understood how to use light and shade, and the luxury of water and how to exploit it, the purpose of decorating a public space with a fountain. None of that reached Poland and Russia, or anywhere else the Ashkenazi Jews came from to build Tel Aviv. They were business people, entrepreneurs from eastern Europe, and that shaped the city.'

The contrast was starkest in Ajami. Ajami was unique in Israel—it fused Arab and Ottoman styles with the modernist influences that spilled over from neighbouring Tel Aviv. Its villas were palatial and ornate, many incorporating the architectural ornaments manufactured by the Chelouche factory: iron balustrades, patterned floor tiles and window frames. The houses were built of sandstone, then covered with plaster to protect them from the salty air and painted a light pastel colour, often blue or pink. But Ajami had not fared well. After the Balkan and north African Jews left in the 1960s for more modern homes elsewhere in Israel, Israeli Arab economic migrants moved in. Many were poor and could not afford to maintain the villas, which then crumbled and decayed.

Ajami bordered Old Jaffa, but there was no improvement overspill. On the contrary, the renovation of Old Jaffa only highlighted Ajami's ramshackle state. By 1983 it was the most run-down neighbourhood in Tel Aviv–Jaffa. Most of the city received about 57 points out of 100 on the town planners' scale for amenities. Ajami had 4 points. The municipality's response was to demolish the old villas and rehouse their inhabitants in new modern blocks. Ajami's residents certainly wanted new roads, a better sewerage system, public transport and street lights. But they also wanted their houses to be restored. Hundreds of beautiful Ottoman houses were demolished, and the rubble was simply dumped on the beach. The municipality then trumpeted a new reconstruction plan for Ajami's coastline. There would be new hotels, gardens and a promenade, and Ajami would finally rise from the ruins. But it never happened—the hotels were never built. Ajami was doubly scarred: by gaping holes in the streets, and by the piles of smashed bricks and rubble, sarcastically dubbed 'Tel Jaffa' ('Hill of Jaffa'), that littered the seafront.

The clash between developers and conservationists was not unique to Jaffa. Cities all over the world have to find a balance between preserving their heritage and modernising their infrastructure. Doubtless some of the demolished villas were beyond repair and no longer safe to live in, but others could have been restored. And why had they been allowed to fall into such a state of decay? Jaffa's tangled history, its central place in the Israeli-Palestinian conflict and the sour relations between Ajami's Arab inhabitants and Israeli officialdom added extra layers of acrimony. The pharmacist Fakhri Geday watched, angry and powerless, as Ajami's villas were flattened. 'This policy was intentional. They had an idea in their minds, that the Arabs of Jaffa should go and live in Lydda or other Arab towns. They said this openly, that the Arabs should leave Jaffa. Nobody can deny this, this intentional discrimination against the Arabs.'

NOBODY EXCEPT PERHAPS Shlomo Lahat, mayor of Tel Aviv between 1974 and 1993. Born in Berlin in 1927, Shlomo is now retired, and lives in north Tel Aviv. Lahat, nicknamed 'Cheech', was a national institution, and still has the brisk no-nonsense manner of the archetypal *yekke*, the German Jewish immigrants who poured into Tel Aviv during the 1930s. The Lindner family, as they were then called, arrived from Berlin in November 1933. Shlomo's father, Max, had owned a textile factory with thirty-two employees, and the family lived in an eight-room apartment with a maid. Soon after Hitler came to power, a group of Nazis came to take Max to 'register at the police station'. He escaped out the back door. When his wife, Rosa, discovered he was to be sent to Dachau, she decided that the family had to leave

Germany as soon as possible. They re-settled in Rehovot, near Tel Aviv, in a small apartment. There was no maid; Max Lindner drove trucks, and Rosa worked as a cleaner. 'My parents were not proud—they did not complain, they did not cry and think everybody owed them something. They said we saved our lives, and that's it.' The contrast between Shlomo's memories of his parents and his perception of Jaffa's Arab population is stark. 'They are never thankful, they never appreciate anything and they always claim they are neglected. Whenever you do something for them, they never appreciate it, only what was not done. It is a matter of culture, of having an inferiority complex.'

Ajami was not the only quarter that needed renovating during his office as mayor, he argues: 'There were many Jewish neighbourhoods in Tel Aviv with problems with their infrastructure, housing and culture. They were my first priority, then I turned to Jaffa. But I was always very concerned with Jaffa. The city's name is Tel Aviv–Jaffa, and when I became mayor I said, Jaffa is an equal name. It is one city, but there is a great difference between Tel Aviv and Jaffa. The Arab population of Jaffa does not try and do things for itself. The state should do more for Jaffa, but the Arab population needs good will, leaders to speak for the population. When you come and ask them something, they answer, but on their own initiative, they do nothing.' Cheech also launched a drive to save the city's famed Bauhaus architecture from the corroding effect of decades of sea spray and salty air. 'These buildings are very important. They are beautiful, modern and not obsolete. I believe that Israel should have a western culture, and Bauhaus is part of that.'

In 1987, the municipality changed its policy towards Ajami. The new emphasis was on restoring and renovating the quarter, in consultation with the local inhabitants. The Ajami Project was launched, part of a nationwide urban renewal campaign funded by private and public money. Planning committees were set up to improve child and youth care, community welfare and housing. Ajami was twinned with the Jewish community of Los Angeles, whose donation of $750,000— together with government funds—helped pay for a new Arab-Jewish community centre, day clubs for the elderly and job seekers and a centre for rehabilitating drug users. New education initiatives were launched; at the time only 12 per cent of Ajami's youth finished secondary school. The physical improvements were less impressive, and just fifty buildings—three hundred flats—were renovated. Much of the budget was not spent, and the funds were diverted to the rundown Jewish neighbourhood of Hatikvah in Tel Aviv. Some Israeli politicians opposed spending any money at all on Arab areas, but Shlomo Lahat argued that the Arab community of Ajami were also Israeli citizens.

OLD JAFFA WAS reserved for artists, but there were no restrictions on buying property in Ajami, so a second wave of Israelis moved in. Economics and geography played a role: the dilapidated Arab villas were cheap and plentiful, as most Israeli Jews wanted to live in modern apartments. Jaffa was adjacent to Tel Aviv, and it overlooked the sea. But more than this, the newcomers were idealistic and wanted to live in a mixed community.

Behira Buchbinder was born in Palestine in 1930 and moved to Jaffa in the early 1970s, together with her husband, Benjamin. After living in a kibbutz in the Negev desert and the southern city of Beersheba, Jaffa was a treat. Unusually for that time, Behira bought her house from its original Arab owners rather than the custodian of state property. 'When I came to Jaffa I did not think of the Arabs here as a political problem. I just thought, They lost, we won, but we are living together. We were very happy to have this house. We had nothing when we arrived, just a table and some old beds the Jewish Agency gave us.' She and Benjamin still live in the spacious Ajami villa with arched windows, high ceilings and stone floors. 'I looked around when we arrived and thought, who would be my friend? We never thought then that someone is an Arab, another is a Jew, he is from Morocco or she is from Poland—we just lived together. Our relationships were good. The children played together in the street—there were no cars. It was natural. My son's best friend was an Arab, and most people thought like me.' Many of Jaffa's Jews still do, and Behira is active in community politics, supporting joint Jewish-Arab projects and trying to preserve Jaffa's Ottoman and Arab architecture.

Ali Goughti also grew up in Ajami and is headmaster of Jaffa's Hassan Araffe School. Born in 1959, Ali almost became a professional footballer before reluctantly choosing education. He is a perceptive observer, and now defines himself as an Arab Palestinian who is an Israeli citizen, but the nuances of identity did not seem so critical during his Jaffa childhood, which he looks back on with nostalgia. 'We did not have the anxieties and the conflicts that children feel now. People were nicer—the doors were always open. I could go into any family house, to eat or play, whether they were Christians, Muslims or Jews. Now everyone asks why things have changed. It is to do with education, the environment in the street, trust between people, respect for elders, traditions and the many good things we had here in our city. Today people trust each other much less, the families are apart, and the father has less authority over his family and his children.' Yet even in the 1960s and 1970s there were unspoken limits to co-existence. Romantic relationships between young Arabs and Jews were rare and frowned upon. There was a sense, even among those who lived side by side in Jaffa, that it was too soon for intermarriage, which would cross boundaries—religious as well as ethnic—that should not yet be breached.

By the late 1980s Michal Meisler was growing into a vivacious and attractive young woman. A few minutes' walk away, in Old Jaffa, she stayed friends with Yosi. 'Sometimes we went to pubs, I got a bit drunk and he brought me home and put me on the doorstep. He was a good person, a kind-hearted drug dealer. My parents knew all about it. They thought I was having a great adventure.' Michal and Yosi's friendship was unique. Yosi did not even kiss her hallo on her cheek when they met. 'He did not take me into his world. Our friendship stayed in his car, or the cafés we went to. He never did business while I was with him.'

At the end of the decade, when Michal left home, she lost touch with Yosi, until one day she picked up a newspaper. 'I read that an Arab man had been stabbed in Jaffa. I recognised his name. The paper said he was in hospital. I went to visit him and he was connected up to lots of tubes with two bodyguards watching him. He was very embarrassed that I should see him like that.' Yosi recovered, and went to prison. Although they parted on good terms, he and Michal did not meet again for many years. But just as with the Chelouche and Samarra families, the turbulent politics of the Middle East would eventually intrude on their friendship.

21

Going Home to the Sea

Early 1990s

*For so many of the exiles, their lives stopped in 1948.
Their sense of whatever could be beautiful ended
once they left Jaffa.*

Rema Hammami, daughter of Hasan Hammami

The Labour Party never regained the almost continual hege-
mony it had enjoyed between 1948 and Likud's victory in
1977. Menachem Begin had triumphed again in the 1981
elections, forming a Likud-led coalition government with the
National Religious Party, with a slim majority of seven seats in the
Knesset. Israel remained split in two, between the leftists, prepared
to reach an accommodation with the Palestinians, and the right-
wingers, who believed the West Bank was an inalienable part of the
Jewish state. The bitter domestic fallout from the 1982 invasion of
Lebanon only accentuated the division. Ironically, the inconclusive
results of the September 1984 elections, when Labour won forty-four
seats and Likud forty-one, produced a National-Unity government
that shared power. The veteran Labour politician Shimon Peres
served first as prime minister, followed in 1986 by Yitzhak Shamir,

the former Stern Group commander. The two certainly agreed on one thing: the National-Unity government, like its predecessors, refused point-blank to deal with Yasser Arafat, or to countenance an independent Palestinian state.

At the end of 1987 the Palestinians seized the initiative and launched the Intifada. The Intifada—the word means 'shaking off'— was not an armed rebellion or a series of terrorist attacks. It was an organised campaign of civil disobedience, strikes and shut-downs within the occupied West Bank. It was an early example of the 'asymmetrical' political warfare that over a decade later would be employed in Serbia, Georgia and Ukraine: a kind of political ju-jitsu that turns the enemy's might against him. Palestinians threw stones and occasionally Molotov cocktails, blocked roads and slashed tyres of army vehicles, but generally they did not use guns. Israel's tanks and artillery were useless in the kasbahs of Hebron and Nablus. It was the Biblical story of David and Goliath, except this time David was a Palestinian, standing proud and unarmed against the might of the Israeli army.

The Intifada's roots lay in the century-long struggle between Arab and Jew for Palestine. But it was also ignited by more specific circumstances. After the Israeli invasion of Lebanon in 1982 the PLO was a marginalised force, expelled to Tunis, far across the Mediterranean. Mikhail Gorbachev, the Kremlin reformer, had abandoned the Arab cause and was allowing Soviet Jews to leave, often to Israel. Across the West Bank the Israeli state and the settlers appropriated many thousands of acres of Arab land at will, claiming a divine mandate. Once over the Green Line—the 1967 border—the *sabras'* self-confidence curdled into a sour arrogance. The settlers, many of whom were not even Israelis but fanatical American Zionists, enjoyed a culture of near-complete impunity and often used violence against the Palestinians. Ancient olive groves were bulldozed, trees uprooted and crops destroyed to build air-conditioned villas for Israelis and Jewish immigrants.

There was one set of rules for Israeli Jews and another for the indigenous Arabs. When Palestinians were forbidden from using or even gaining access to their land, they had no meaningful recourse to the law. Special roads were built for the use of settlers alone, supposedly to protect them from being stoned or shot at. The old idea of 'transferring' the Palestinians was once again discussed in cabinet. Yosef Shapira, of the National Religious Party, proposed offering $20,000 to any Palestinian willing to emigrate.¹ But like France in Algeria and Britain in Northern Ireland, Israel discovered that large-scale urban guerrilla warfare is impossible to win. As the Israeli army resorted to increasingly brutal tactics to suppress the riots and demonstrations, breaking bones and sometimes using live ammunition, the Palestinians banked more moral capital around the world. The Intifada changed the international perception of the Palestinians for ever, from cold-blooded terrorists and aeroplane hijackers to oppressed underdogs.

United against the occupation and riding the wave of international sympathy, Palestinian society gained a new degree of cohesion and a sense of self-empowerment during the late 1980s and early 1990s. Some Palestinian leaders understood that the PLO had to make the transition from being a national liberation movement to preparing for statehood and genuine democracy—although Yasser Arafat did not seem to be among them. Israel had allowed a nascent Palestinian civic society to take root on the West Bank and in Gaza: seven universities were founded (there were none before 1967), and the Palestinians set up local civic committees, trade unions, women's and youth groups, newspapers and professional associations. In some ways Palestinian society mirrored the organisations of the pre-1948 *Yishuv*. Despite the sporadic brutality of the occupation and the oppressive military administration, Israeli rule was not a reign of terror. Israeli hospitals often treated those unable to receive the right treatment in the West Bank. Much of the time Palestinians still studied, went to work, ran businesses, had parties and love affairs, got married and wrote poetry and novels. Every achievement was a kind of victory against the occupiers.[2]

But with the PLO exiled in Tunisia, the Palestinians were left leaderless. A new political force stepped into the power vacuum: the Islamists of Hamas and Islamic Jihad. Hamas—'courage' in Arabic—grew out of the Muslim Brotherhood, whose members had once thrown acid at women shopping in Jaffa's market during the 1930s. The spiritual heir of the pre-1948 mufti of Jerusalem, Hamas was fervently anti-Israel, stridently anti-Semitic and utterly opposed to any negotiated settlement. Calling for jihad, an Islamic war to liberate Palestine, Hamas cited the notorious tsarist forgery, *The Protocols of the Elders of Zion*, as its ideological inspiration. Its handbills described Jews as 'brothers of apes, the murderers of prophets' and 'the dirtiest and meanest of all races'.[3]

A darker triumph of the occupation was the brutalisation of Israeli society. The army and the domestic security service, Shin Bet, utilised techniques honed in southern Lebanon: curfews, beatings, assassinations, mass round-ups and detentions and violent interrogations that often resulted in injury, sometimes even in death. When two Palestinians who had hijacked a bus in 1984 were turned over to Shin Bet, they were beaten to death. And in 1987 an Israeli judicial commission ruled that, while torture was not permitted, Shin Bet could use 'moderate psychological and physical force' to extract confessions. In practice such 'moderate' techniques included violent shaking from behind, known as *tiltul*, tying up suspects under freezing air-conditioners, depriving them of sleep, forcing them to crouch in a frog position, bending them backwards over a chair with their hands and legs shackled and placing a stinking hood over their heads.[4] As Benny Morris notes, the commission's accompanying appendix, detailing the precise nature of what abuses were permitted, was 'a document unique in the annals of modern Western judicial history'.[5] Officials said such techniques were only used in 'ticking-bomb' situations, for example when faced with a terrorist threat, but this claim was contested by Israeli human rights groups. It was not until September 1999 that the Supreme Court finally banned the use of torture in interrogations. In the meantime the soldiers had returned home, stressed and traumatised by the violence and hatred they had encountered during their service in the West Bank and Gaza. Some turned to drugs, or left the country on long trips to India and Asia, to come to terms with what they had seen or done.

The Intifada helped catalyse a complicated set of intra-Arab emotions: Palestinians in Jaffa and across Israel felt a combination of guilt and pride—guilt that they were living fairly comfortable lives in comparison to their brethren languishing under Israeli military rule, and pride that they were fighting for the Palestinian cause inside Israel itself. After all, they had stayed in 1948. Yet despite their increasing 'Palestinianisation', the Intifada did not cross the Green Line, apart from occasional incidents when stones or Molotov cocktails were thrown at Israeli vehicles. There was no widespread civil disobedience in Jaffa. Taxes were paid and the buses still ran up and down Yefet

Street. The Abulafia bakery and the Geday pharmacy stayed open. The failure—as the Palestinians in the territories saw it—of Israel's Arabs to rise up in solidarity caused anger across Gaza and the West Bank. Across the Green Line, many Palestinians still viewed Israel's Arabs as Zionist lackeys.

Encounters between the two groups were often strained. The schoolteacher Ali Goughti received a guarded welcome on his visits to the occupied territories. 'For them we were very Israeli. They saw we are organised, we have done well economically. Their situation also influenced us and woke up the Palestinian identity among Arabs in Israel. But we, and Israeli society, also affected them. They learnt a lot from the Israelis, in building and construction, in culture, trading— everything. In the West Bank and Gaza they were dreaming about democracy from the beginning, which is different from any other Arab state. Israel played a big role in that. And they know, they even say, that the Jewish people made a very strong country in fifty years. They learnt the Jewish way of thinking and how to organise.' As the Intifada intensified, violence eventually spread to Jaffa, where Hamas terrorists killed several Israelis in a series of stabbing attacks.

IN JANUARY 1991, four years into the Intifada, Khamis Abulafia watched in dismay as his television screen filled with Palestinians on the West Bank joyously dancing on their roofs, cheering on Saddam's Scud missiles as they flew overhead towards Tel Aviv. The Gulf War was well under way as the US-led coalition stormed into Kuwait. Yasser Arafat was one of Saddam Hussein's strongest supporters, and this support was reciprocated. Saddam sent money to the families of Palestinian suicide bombers, and gave Palestinian refugees in Iraq spacious flats at nominal rents or sinecures in the state bureaucracy.

In return Arafat and the Palestinians were vocal in their solidarity with Saddam.

It seemed a line ran from the desert missile launchers in Iraq, across the Middle East, through the West Bank, to the Abulafia bakery on Yefet Street, by Clock Tower Square. The Gulf War was a testing time for Jaffa's Arabs. The conflict highlighted and exacerbated the contradictions of their lives—as part of the Arab and Palestinian nation, but also as law-abiding citizens in the Jewish state. It was a trial made more difficult by their cousins' support for the Scud missiles landing a kilometre or two away. Khamis Abulafia prided himself on his skills as a peacemaker, whether in reconciling rival Arab factions or in calming down angry Israelis who saw all Arabs as potential terrorists. The Abulafia bakery, with its non-stop supply of Arab breads and delicacies, was itself a symbol of co-existence in Jaffa, popular with everyone from Ajami street kids to the yuppies of northern Tel Aviv. When the radical youth took to the streets to demonstrate against Israel, they often demanded that Khamis and his brothers join them. They declined.

'When there is a demonstration we try not to be involved. We prefer to try and make a reconciliation. We help our people by supporting social and welfare projects. That is more important than confronting the police. I believe in peace, that we should live beside each other. And anyway, it would not be clever to say you hate and you oppose the others, when most of your customers are Jewish,' says Khamis. Instead he put pen to paper and wrote an article for the popular newspaper *Maariv*. 'When I saw the Palestinians applauding Saddam, shouting, "Hit, hit Tel Aviv with missiles", I wrote that this is a mistake. I said that Saddam is an illusion. Saddam destroyed Iraq. I said, let us deal with reality, and leave emotions behind. Because if you show the Israeli people that you are supporting Saddam, it means you are supporting the man who is declaring morning, noon and night that he wants to destroy the Israeli state. How can you convince these people that you really want peace? At first lots of people criticised me, then afterwards they said I was right.'

For a while events seemed to be moving Khamis' way. The end of the Gulf War in 1991, the collapse of Communism, the end of the Cold War and the continuing violence on the West Bank accelerated diplomatic drives to solve the Israeli-Palestinian conflict. Behind the fog of tear gas and the rain of stones and bullets, a nascent Palestinian state—or rather, national entity—was beginning to take shape. Consciousness of this slowly seeped into the Israeli political mainstream. The Israeli left believed the Palestinians should have some kind of viable, sovereign state. But the right would support no more than a Palestinian Bantustan, utterly dominated by Israel, with at most quasi-autonomy on municipal matters. Nevertheless, the new dynamic was diplomatic, not military. In October 1991 the United States and the Soviet Union sponsored a peace conference in Madrid, attended by Israel, Syria, Lebanon, Jordan and the Palestinians. The Madrid conference did not bring a final settlement, but the parties were at least talking instead of fighting.

The move towards peace boosted the Israeli left, and Labour returned to power after the June 1992 elections, with a government led by Yitzhak Rabin. Rabin, a former chief of staff in the Israeli military, had served before as prime minister, in 1974, after Golda Meir and her government had resigned following the 1973 war. During the Intifada, Rabin had ordered the highly controversial 'beatings policy' that authorised Israeli soldiers to break the limbs of Palestinians with riot sticks. But Rabin's views, like those of many warriors, had mellowed with age. His new government was a coalition of Labour and the more left-wing Meretz, and was supported by the Arab parties and Shas, the Sephardic religious party. It was as close to a mandate for peace as any Israeli leader had ever been granted. Secret negotiations continued behind the scenes between Israel and the PLO, and the process begun at Madrid laid the ground for the more radical Oslo Accords.

On 13 September 1993 the world watched in hope as Prime Minister Yitzhak Rabin shook hands with Yasser Arafat on the White House lawn, a scene previously unimaginable. Despite Rabin's obvious lack of enthusiasm for grasping the hand of Israel's former greatest enemy, at least it seemed the log jam had been unblocked. Israel recognised the PLO, while the PLO renounced violence and recognised Israel. Under the terms of the Oslo Agreement, the West Bank and Gaza Strip were divided into three zones: A, under full Palestinian control, B, under Palestinian civil and Israeli military control, and C, under full Israeli control. The map became a complicated patchwork of zones and checkpoints. The Oslo Accords were an interim measure, and did not yet provide resolutions for most complex and controversial issues, such as the status of Jerusalem, the return of refugees and the fate of the Israeli settlements in the occupied territories. The Israeli left rejoiced, as did much of the Palestinian diaspora, who planned to return home, or at least to the West Bank. But hardliners on both sides rejected Oslo. The Israeli right denounced Rabin as a quisling and compared his government to the Jewish Councils in the Second World War that had implemented Nazi orders. Palestinian radicals and Islamists said Arafat had sold out his people in a worthless surrender that let Israel keep control of borders and security.

Some time after Oslo, Shlomo Lahat, the former mayor of Tel

Aviv–Jaffa, met with Rabin, his former commander in the army, to discuss the peace process. By then Shlomo, like many of Israel's old warriors, wanted peace with the Palestinians. He was president of the Council for Peace and Security. Its 1,200 members were all high-ranking army officers, from lt. colonel to lt. general, who campaigned for a Palestinian state and Israeli withdrawal from much of the West Bank—subject to Israel maintaining strategic superiority. The Council, together with the rest of the Israeli peace movement, was planning a rally to shore up support for the Rabin government and Oslo. Shlomo recalls: 'Rabin asked me if I had met Yasser Arafat. I told him that I hadn't. Rabin told me to take some Council members and organise a meeting with him. Rabin said, "When I tell Arafat that we have twelve hundred retired army officers campaigning for peace—and normally army officers are more extreme—I look in his eyes and I see he does not believe me. He thinks it is propaganda."'

Shlomo Lahat and his fellow officers did eventually meet Yasser Arafat. But by then what Arafat thought of the peacenik army officers did not matter so much. On 4 November 1995, Yitzhak Rabin was shot dead by Yigal Amir, an Orthodox Israeli Jew, at a peace rally in Tel Aviv. Amir's express aim was to derail the peace process and prevent the emergence of a Palestinian state, and he succeeded. Shlomo continues: 'I organised the rally, this tragedy where Rabin was assassinated. He was a person with real authority. Arafat respected him. He would not do to Rabin what he did to Shimon Peres and Benjamin Netanyahu. Later we went to Arafat's home in Gaza. We talked about how the terror should stop, and how to make the arrangements for a Palestinian state. I believed that Arafat could be a partner for peace. We shook hands. We trusted him, and we supported the Oslo Agreement. But Arafat was not a partner. He established the Palestinian

nation, but he did not care about his people, only about how he will
be remembered in the history books.'

BACK IN 1980, Arafat had declared in Beirut: 'When we speak of
the Palestinians' return, we want to say: Acre before Gaza, Beersheba
before Hebron. We recognise one thing, namely that the Palestinian flag
will fly over Jaffa.'⁶ The Oslo Accords did not bring that prospect nearer.
In fact, they were recognition that Israel's existence and Israeli rule over
Jaffa were now permanent. But Oslo, and its brief interregnum of optimism, did open the door to Jaffa for a new generation of Palestinian
returnees. Thousands of exiles and their children moved to the West
Bank, and especially to Ramallah, the town just north of Jerusalem that
became the de facto capital of the nascent Palestinian state.

In the summer of 1993, Hasan Hammami returned home to Jaffa
for the first time since 1948, together with his sister Fadwa, his wife,
Barbara, and their thirty-three-year-old daughter, Rema. Rema had
first visited Jaffa in 1987, after graduating from university in the
United States. As an American citizen she could travel freely in Israel.
She decided to settle in East Jerusalem and took a job teaching at Bir
Zeit University, in Ramallah. Although her mother, Barbara, was English, Rema fully identified as a Palestinian. With her dark eyes, olive
skin and thick black hair, she did not look very English. 'We all think
of ourselves as Palestinians. I had wanted to come back to Palestine
since I was in my teens. I was never treated as though I was British. I
was dark, I had a funny name, kids used to call me "Paki". I became a
born-again Palestinian.'

The wilful child who disobeyed the nuns at the Schmidt School in
Jerusalem back in 1967 was now an articulate spokeswoman for the
new generation of Palestinians. In the United States Rema and Hasan

had started a Jewish-Arab discussion group with rabbinical students. In Jerusalem she developed links with Israeli peace groups and activists. 'I was pro-Oslo. I initially thought we needed some opening or way forward. Oslo in the beginning created a possibility, also for Israelis to face the deep truths about their responsibilities to the Palestinians. But instead of doing the necessary historical accounting, Israel detoured around what happened in 1948. Even worse, the Israelis saw Oslo as the final opportunity for a land grab in the West Bank and Gaza, while burying Palestinian rights to historical redress.'

Hasan's family odyssey began in East Jerusalem, where he stayed with Fadwa and her husband, Suleiman. The old stone buildings were as beautiful as ever, but life under occupation was filled with petty difficulties, humiliation and harassment. 'We experienced the euphoria of Oslo, which seemed to herald a new beginning, and we saw the excitement of both resident and returning Palestinians as they built new homes and businesses. But the harsh reality belied this. New settlements were still being built. This was Israel's instinctive destiny, whatever any Israeli leader or peacemaker said in public. And the military checkpoints everywhere made life very difficult. When Fadwa needed to go to the butcher's shop, she had to drive three kilometres, wait at a checkpoint while the young Israeli soldiers checked her identity, drive another hundred metres and then go through the same humiliating experience again to get home.'

The road to Jaffa at least was open. Hasan had lived in Lebanon, Syria, Iraq, Saudi Arabia, Britain and Belgium and had eventually settled in the United States. Now, finally, he was going home. The reality of the dream was more affecting than he had anticipated: 'I was not prepared for either the emotional or the spiritual experience of seeing my Jaffa for the first time in forty-five years. I did not recognise the town's entrance when we drove in, because so many of the small family homes and orange groves had been replaced by modern apartment blocks.' It was Jaffa and yet not Jaffa, a strange hybrid of the town that lived on in Hasan's memory, from before the *Nakba*, and the concrete reality that he saw in front of him. The Hammamis drove past the jeweller's shop where his mother, Nafise, had had a ring made for him when he was ten, engraved with his initials—HAH—in English, copies of which Hasan and Barbara exchanged in later years. As Jaffa sped by, Hasan began to call out the names of the landmarks of his boyhood, whether or not they still existed. Here were the sites of the old Ottoman Bank, the Halaby pharmacy, Abou Laban's shop and Barclays Bank, all gone now. But despite the depredations of war, the damage done to Ajami and the destruction of Manshiyyeh, much of Hasan's Jaffa had survived, albeit in varying states of disrepair. Here were the remains of the New Seray, still not rebuilt, the *kishle*, the Ottoman prison, the kebab restaurants by the side of Abou Nabout's Great Mosque and of course the Clock Tower itself, symbol of the city.

The Hammamis did not stop, but headed south to Jebaliyyeh. Hasan looked around in joy and wonder still, proclaiming the scenes of his youth: the Souk el-Balabseh (textile market), site of his grandfather Ahmad Shaker Hammami's shop; Sabanegh's, the commercial artist and sign-writer's store; the *Ad-Difaa* newspaper building, where Hasan and his friends trained in first aid in 1947 as war approached; the French Hospital; the Tabeetha Mission School; Hasan's own alma mater, St Joseph's College, where he had studied English, French and Arabic and played an Abbasid prince in the school play; the homes of family friends, long gone; the former *Falastin* newspaper building; the English hospital, the Latin school and the Bawarshi pharmacy.

For Hasan, these proclamations were an act of affirmation. Yes,

Jaffa's Palestinians had fled under a rain of mortar bombs. Yes, Jaffa was now a run-down outer fringe of Tel Aviv, and yes, the complex, intricate society of pre-*Nakba* Jaffa was lost for good. But the Bride of Palestine, serene and beautiful, lived on, both in Hasan's memory and in the minds of legions of Jaffan exiles, and that too was a kind of reality, one that could never be taken away. 'The list of names and places flew by like a kaleidoscope in front of my eyes. Recognition and memory all blended into one. I was reciting the names of the places so quickly that Barbara, Rema and Fadwa were worried that I was getting too stressed. After so many years away, and so many denials by the Israelis that we had ever existed, this was a declaration—that these were my roots, deep in a city which once had three daily newspapers, cinemas, schools, sports and social clubs, hospitals, mosques and churches.'

Hasan's journey back in time continued as they drove through Ajami, past the tennis club, his great-uncle Mohammad Abdel Rahim's Bauhaus mansion, the beach where his father had taught him to swim and once upended his *hasakeh* (canoe), toppling Hasan into the sea, and then, finally, the Hammami house. This was the most difficult part of the journey. 'The house was still there, but it looked different, strange and eerie. The large trees had gone, as had the ornamental pool and the flowerbeds. Fadwa had already told me that the house looked buried. I now understood what she meant. It was painted dark grey, and a second floor had been cheaply built on top of the roof. We went inside. I pointed out the bedroom where I was born. Our house was now an old people's home. I felt no grudge— indeed, I felt sorry for many of them, some in advanced stages of dementia. There was an unhealthy smell in the air. I walked through the room that I had shared with my brothers, circled round and looked for the vines which had grown at the back. They were also all gone. I took scores of pictures, of every aspect of the house and garden, the Mediterranean window designs, and wondered at the foresight and clarity of design that my father had shown, back in the 1930s.'

Revisiting his family home was painful, but like the recitation of Jaffa's place names, it too was a vindication, perhaps not just of the Hammami family history but of all Palestinians. The trees may be ripped out, the ornamental pool filled in and the house painted grey, with new tenants who knew nothing of its history, but this was still the Hammami family home. From there Hasan and his family progressed to the Muslim cemetery, through the Greek Orthodox graveyard. To his surprise Hasan found the cemetery crowded with new graves, with headstones carved in Cyrillic. The recent waves of Russian Jewish immigrants were not that Jewish after all, it seemed. Angered by this—Israel refused to let the Palestinians come home, but found a place for Christian Russians—Hasan was further dismayed by the poor condition of the Muslim cemetery. Many of the graves were dilapidated and falling apart. But the family was happy to find a tomb of clean white marble marking the resting place of Shaker Hammami, the family patriarch, next to the tomb of his wife, Umm Shaker. 'We read a prayer for their souls and their memories. I was overcome by sadness. My father, Ahmad Shaker, was buried in Baghdad, and my mother, Nafise, in Amman. For a moment I hoped that I would be buried in Jaffa, next to my grandparents. This was not morbid, more about being reconnected with my family, roots and home.'

Hasan had travelled back in time, but he also needed a link to the present, says Rema. 'He was so thrilled that he was physically there, and that so much of Jaffa remained. But by the end of the day, what was really traumatic was that Jaffa remained, but none of the people

did, the Jaffans that he had known. His city was standing but the people in it were strangers. There was this massive gap. He was desperate
to meet someone who knew him from before 1948, he, Hasan Hammami from Jaffa. He would really only be back in the city if he could
be linked to people who were still there.'

The Hammamis drove down Kedem Street, along the seafront, to
the southernmost edge of the city. There was one family Hasan hoped
would be at home. They parked the car, and he walked up to the gate
of a beautiful 1930s-style villa and rang the doorbell. Rema, Fadwa
and Barbara were shaking their heads, hopeful but not optimistic.
'*Min?* Who is it?' asked a voice through the entryphone. 'Hasan Hammami,' replied Hasan. 'Hasan? Hasan from next door?' the voice
asked, as though nothing had changed in over forty years. In seconds
Suad, Leila and Wedad Andraus ran down the garden path, shouting
with delight, and ushered the Hammamis inside.

They talked for hours, over coffee and lemonade, of their different
exiles: the Hammamis of life outside the land, and the Andraus sisters of theirs within Jaffa. Salim, his wife, Hillana, and their two children, Amin and Robyn, came to join the reunion. Rema recalls: 'They
were thrilled to see my father. For him it was a profoundly redemptive
moment, one so needed when he came back to face this incredible
loss. He could only be saved by that human connection. Israel's and
the world's denial of what happened to them and what was lost, that
they never belonged in Jaffa anyway, or weren't even there, just made
the wound harder. If it is never recognised, if it is never dealt with, you
cannot heal.' Hasan's reunion with the Andraus sisters stirred powerful emotions, says Rema: 'I could see there were two kinds of pain. My
father had the pain of leaving, while they had the pain of staying.
Somewhere in his heart he had lost so many things when he was

forced out of Jaffa, and then talking to the Andraus sisters, it was exactly the opposite. They had lost so much by staying. They had both lost their community, a whole vibrant world of people and their shared future. My dad and the Andrauses rebuilt their lives, but they could never rebuild that lost world.'

Hasan would return several times to Israel and Palestine, and to Jaffa, as a consultant with the United Nations. But like many diaspora Palestinians, he found that his decades of managerial experience and skills, and the 'can-do ethos' of the American business world, would soon run into the sands of bureaucracy, indifference and intra-Palestinian power politics.

22

Gaza Comes to Jaffa

Late 1990s

*I want to believe that most of the Arabs want to live together
with us in peace. But there is a minority, which has a big
influence, and is backed by Arab leaders, which does not.*

Sami Albo, Jaffa community activist

With the Jordanian border open after the 1994 peace treaty, Palestinians living there could travel to Israel. Many Jaffan exiles had settled in Jordan, including Massoud Abulafia, great-uncle of Khamis Abulafia, of the bakery family. But Massoud's pilgrimage home reopened old wounds, sometimes triggering bitter exchanges, especially over Jaffa's *Nakba*. Hanging always in the air, sometimes spoken and at others silent, was the perennial accusation that Jaffa had been betrayed by its inhabitants, that they had abandoned her in her hour of need. Khamis found himself caught between two lives: his own as an Israeli Palestinian and Massoud's as an exile. 'We face two different narratives about 1948, the Arab version and the Israeli one,' he explains. 'The question is, which one do we want to live with? I have Israeli nationality, but it is difficult for me to say that I adopt the Israeli story. I am part of the

Palestinian people, and it is easier for me to take the Palestinian one, but whether that is really the whole truth or reality, I don't know.'

There was tension and resentment on both sides. 'When Massoud came to visit us, he told the story of 1948 from his point of view. He started to cry. He said, "Here is my apartment, here is the place where my father sat, here is his grave." I asked him, if he was so sorry, then why did he leave in 1948? He made excuses about a conspiracy among the Arab countries, that they did not do enough to help the Palestinians. My grandmother told him that he did not know what was going on here, that we live in a very difficult situation, that he could not come back five decades later—come back to judge us.'

MEANWHILE, IN FLORIDA, Hasan Hammami's visit to Jaffa had also stirred powerful emotions: of nostalgia and yearning for his childhood, but also of a need to contribute to his people's future. In 1994 Hasan was sixty-two. He had retired from Procter & Gamble two years earlier, after a successful international career. The company had tried to persuade him to stay, offering him the choice of several well-paid senior posts across the world, but Hasan's mind was made up. He wanted to spend more time with his family, and use his business and commercial expertise for a good cause. He signed a contract to become a consultant with the United Nations Development Programme. In the spring of 1994, Hasan returned to the Palestinian Territories and Israel, where he spent four weeks consulting with the management board and production team at the new Citrus Processing Company in Gaza. The company had just started up, and manufactured fruit concentrates and juices for export.

The $12 million plant had been donated by Italy in the heady post-Oslo era. But the dream and the reality of setting up a manufacturing and export venture in Gaza were very different, as Hasan soon discovered. Despite Oslo, Israel still controlled Gaza's borders. Export shipments were subject to a myriad of commercial and transport restrictions, and much of the fruit rotted before it ever passed the frontier. Another problem was the management of the company itself, which lacked experience. Many directors had been appointed because of their connections rather than their ability. Still, with his international business experience, Hasan believed he could get the company running profitably. But there was a third problem. Like many of those who came back in the 'awda (the return), Hasan was often regarded with suspicion by those who had grown up in Gaza and the West Bank. Despite the many hours spent in meetings with the board, Hasan made little headway. He decided to go straight to the top. Eventually he met with Yasser Arafat.

Arafat's achievement was to establish modern Palestinian nationhood, but his government was a disaster, riddled with patronage, cronyism and corruption. Hundreds of millions of dollars of international aid were siphoned off and diverted to accounts abroad. The administration was a shambles.[1] Despite the poverty of life in Gaza, where many survived on two dollars a day, the PLO leadership regarded the public purse as a private savings account for themselves and their families. When, in July 1995, Yasser Arafat's wife, Suha, gave birth to their daughter, Zahwa, she stayed at a $2,200-a-night private hospital in Paris. She told reporters: 'Our child was conceived in Gaza, but sanitary conditions there are terrible. I don't want to be a hero and risk my baby.'[2]

Hasan met Arafat at midnight in his office. Their discussions lasted almost three hours. Hasan had spent many hours preparing for the meeting: he had drawn up plans outlining how to create an independent corporation to run the Citrus Processing Company and how the Palestinian government could foster a healthy economic environment. He discussed the role of citizens in drawing up a constitution and legislation, the rule of law and how it would regulate public and private institutions and commerce. 'I explained how Chairman Arafat would carve a role for himself as the father of Palestine, as well as the father of Palestinian liberation. The meeting was lively, and later on people told me how often I had said to him, "Please listen to me." He was charming, knowledgeable and deferential. But he had not yet made the transition from leading a liberation movement to leading a new nation. I was impressed at the respect and adulation he received. But so much so that there was no room for any public critiques or accountability.' The charm and emollience were a front for doing nothing that might upset the comfortable status quo. Hasan's proposals were filed away and nothing more was heard of them; he eventually resigned his consultancy, sad and disillusioned at the missed opportunity. Hasan's disappointment was shared by many Palestinians who felt that the Arafat-era leadership, which had been based in Tunis since 1982 and only returned to Gaza in 1994, simply did not understand the Israeli mentality and the obstinacy with which Israelis negotiated. It would have been better, they said, to draw on the pool of Palestinians who had been living under Israeli rule since 1967 and knew the Israeli modus operandi and way of thinking.

THE MURDERED PRIME minister Yitzhak Rabin was succeeded by his old rival, Shimon Peres. As foreign minister in Rabin's government, Peres had negotiated the Oslo Accords, for which he was awarded the 1994 Nobel Peace Prize along with Yasser Arafat and Rabin himself. Peres was a veteran peacenik who wanted to reach an agreement with the Palestinians, and he was also an architect of the treaty Yitzhak Rabin signed with Jordan barely ten days before his murder. Despite—or more likely because of—the Oslo Accords, the Islamists continued their bombing campaigns inside Israel and the West Bank during the mid-1990s. With the new threat from the Islamic radicals who were determined to destroy any rapprochement, peace looked more remote than ever. The militants took the concept of asymmetric warfare to a new level: young men, and sometimes women, were wrapped in explosive belts and despatched to bus stops, crowded cafés and restaurants, where they blew themselves—and as many bystanders as possible—to bits.

Ironically, the Israeli security services themselves had initially encouraged the build-up of the Islamists as a counterweight to the PLO, on the old principle of divide and rule. But secular nationalists can be negotiated with, while those who claim a heavenly mandate are less willing to compromise. Shin Bet had helped create a Palestinian version of the Golem, the monster brought to life by a rabbi in the medieval Prague Ghetto to save the Jews—which eventually ran amok. After Mossad agents killed Fathi Shkaki, head of Islamic Jihad, in Malta in October 1995, and Yayha Ayash, Hamas's bombmaker, in Gaza in January 1996 with a booby-trapped mobile telephone, the Islamists swore revenge. Their planning and attacks were unimpeded by Yasser Arafat's security forces. On the morning of 25 February 1996, twenty-six Israelis were killed and more than eighty injured in two suicide bombings in Jerusalem. The next day an Islamic funda-mentalist drove into a bus stop in Jerusalem, killing a woman and injuring twenty-three others. On 3 March a suicide bomber killed eighteen on a bus by the main post office, and on the following day another set off his charges in downtown Tel Aviv, killing thirteen and wounding one hundred.³ The series of bombings could not have taken place without Arafat's authorisation, or at least without his knowledge of them.

The Islamists and Arafat were the Likud's greatest electoral assets. In the May 1996 elections Likud, together with its religious and right-wing allies, won sixty-six seats and formed a coalition government headed by Benjamin Netanyahu, a former ambassador to the United Nations. Netanyahu, educated in the United States, was the son of a distinguished history professor who was an expert on Spanish and Sephardic Jewry. His brother Jonathan had been the only Israeli casualty of the dramatic raid on Entebbe, Uganda, in 1976. Despite his western background, Netanyahu was a divisive ideologue whose government deliberately wrecked what was left of the Oslo Accords, accelerating the settlement programme and the land grab across the West Bank. Likud and the Islamists were locked in a *danse macabre*. Netanyahu did not want to withdraw from any part of the occupied territories, although he did authorise a half-hearted pull-out from Hebron. The continuing Hamas attacks through 1997 gave him the perfect excuse to dig in, which in turn fostered support for the Islamists, and so the cycle continued.

Netanyahu was dubbed 'Bibi the Bungler' for his general air of incompetence, and the low point of his premiership was the botched attempt by two Mossad agents to kill a Hamas official in Amman by injecting him with a nerve toxin. The agents were caught, confessed and were only released in exchange for the freedom of Sheikh Yassin, Hamas's spiritual leader. Meanwhile Arafat's rule over his patchwork of territories degenerated into further authoritarianism, as he ordered the closure of independent media and the arrest of political opponents. The Palestinian Authority had more than ten security services, each a petty fiefdom of corruption and intimidation. On both sides of the Green Line, the old sense of gloom and hopelessness returned.

In May 1999 Israel went to the polls again. By now the changing demographics of Israeli society had fractured the old left-right divide. Labour, renamed 'One Israel' in an attempt to broaden its appeal, won twenty-six seats, while Likud took nineteen. Sephardic Jews no longer voted for Likud but for their own religious party, Shas, which was the real winner, with seventeen seats. Although not on the left, Shas was prepared to cooperate with Labour in exchange for sufficient state funds for its welfare and education projects. Labour's left-wing ally Meretz took ten seats, and a party representing Russian immigrants took six, while the remainder were divided between various left-centre and religious groupings and the Arab parties. Eventually Labour's new leader, Ehud Barak, formed a coalition of seventy-five seats with Shas, Meretz and several smaller groupings. Again it seemed Israel had a leader who wanted peace and a mandate to make it, although at first glance Barak was an unlikely candidate. He had served in the Israeli army for over thirty years and had led the commando team that had assassinated the poet Kamal Nasser in Beirut in 1973. Nevertheless, Barak received the overwhelming endorsement not just of the Israeli left but also of Israel's Arab voters, who saw in him the chance for a Palestinian state. Barak quickly restarted negotiations with both the Palestinians and Syria, and oversaw the withdrawal of Israeli forces from south Lebanon.

In July 2000 President Clinton invited Barak and Arafat to Camp David. Clinton hoped to build on the remains of the Oslo Accords to reach a final, overall settlement. Barak's concluding offer to Arafat included about 90 per cent of the West Bank and almost all of the Gaza Strip. He broke several great taboos of Israeli politics: he offered to divide Jerusalem and hand over some of the city to Palestinian sovereignty, to allow several thousand refugees to return home and even to pay compensation for confiscated property. In Tel Aviv the left rejoiced, believing a final settlement was about to be agreed, while those on the right were enraged. Barak's own foreign minister, David Levy, resigned in disgust. Barak had gone further than any Israeli politician had ever dared. But the talks ultimately failed, and the bitterness and recriminations continue to this day.

For Arafat it was not enough. Viewed from Ramallah, Camp David 2000 did not offer a viable and contiguous state, and was certainly not enough for the Palestinians to forgo their demand for a right of return for all refugees—no matter that Israel would never grant it. Israel would have retained control of the borders with Egypt and Jordan, of customs and water and of the territory along the Jordanian border. Many settlements would be annexed by Israel, while the numerous security checkpoints that made Palestinians' everyday life such a misery would remain. It was not a mistake to reject Camp David, says Rema Hammami. 'This was neither a proper nor a workable deal. Barak was offering to return only something close to 85 per cent, in three truncated areas that were divided by Israeli settlements, and the sovereignty over Jerusalem only applied to its outer suburbs. And Israel rejected making even a verbal expression of responsibility for the refugee problem. This was the same way we were conned under Oslo. Camp David was asking for us to legitimise the settlement project.' In addition, the failure of Oslo had left a legacy of anger and disillusionment, explains Rema: 'You have to see this in the context of all the broken promises: the prisoner release that never happened, the stepped-up land confiscation, the doubling of settlements while we were supposedly in a peace process. Palestinians came to understand during Oslo that if you sign something with Israel, it is meaningless, because everything is about power, their power.'

But there were no more offers like Camp David, nor are there likely to be in the near future. To outside observers it seemed that the Palestinians had missed their best chance for potential statehood.

TWO MONTHS LATER, on Thursday 28 September 2000, Ariel Sharon went for a walk at the Temple Mount/Al-Aqsa Mosque complex in Jerusalem, which is holy to both Muslims and Jews.[4] Furious Palestinians attacked Israeli police guarding the site. The demonstrations erupted again on Friday, the day of prayer for Muslims. Arab rioters flung stones at Israeli police and nearby Jewish worshippers. The police entered the compound and opened fire, killing four Palestinians and injuring more than a hundred. On Saturday the riots spread across the West Bank. Unlike in the first Intifada, this time Palestinian security troops joined forces with the rioters, opening fire on Israeli positions. Arab leaders called for a general strike. On Sunday, Jaffa's Arabs hung up protest signs and placards along Yefet Street, protesting about Sharon's visit. A crowd soon gathered, and the mood turned ugly. The consequences of the Al-Aqsa Intifada—as this second uprising was known—would be disastrous for Arab-Jewish co-existence in Jaffa. It left a legacy of bitterness that poisons intercommunal relations to this day.

In 1960, over forty years earlier, the Nobel laureate Elias Canetti published his classic study of mob dynamics, *Crowds and Power*. His analysis of a 'reversal crowd', committed to 'overturning the established order', perfectly applied to those on Yefet Street: 'People who are habitually ordered about . . . can free themselves in two different ways. They can pass onto others the orders which they have received from above; but for them to be able to do this, there must be others below who are ready to accept their orders.' The only people 'below' an Israeli Arab were illegal workers from Gaza and the West Bank. But Jaffa's Arabs were gathering in solidarity with their cousins across the Green Line. 'Or they can try to pay back to their superiors themselves what they have suffered and stored up for them.'⁵ The mob pelted passing cars with stones. Windows and windscreens shattered, scattering glass across the road. The crowd's chants grew louder, and more young men poured out of the side streets of Ajami and Jebaliyyeh, high on anger and adrenalin.

The rioters blocked off Yefet Street and fought with the police, hurling stones and bricks. Plumes of black smoke curled from burning tyres. Thick clouds of tear gas drifted along the road. Jaffa was now Gaza—the Intifada had finally crossed the Green Line into Israel proper. Violence erupted across Israel's major Arab population centres. Israeli police used live ammunition to break up the crowds, often deploying snipers, who shot several demonstrators in the head or chest. Each death or injury further inflamed the Arabs on the street, as did the deliberate incitement and provocation by Palestinian politicians and the Palestinian media. Just as in 1921 and 1936, the Arab riots provoked Jewish counter-attacks, often in the same places, even around the same buildings, where both sides had fought decades earlier. Once again, the Hasan Bey mosque, Jaffa's northernmost outpost and the last remnant of Manshiyyeh, was attacked by Jews, who tried to set it on fire. Jewish rioters attacked Arab-owned shops and restaurants. Jaffa, like all of Israel and Palestine, was a prisoner of its history, condemned to experience endless cycles of retribution. When the smoke cleared and the rubble was removed, thirteen Palestinians were dead across Israel—though none in Jaffa—and hundreds injured, as well as dozens of Israeli policemen. One Israeli had been killed when his car was hit by a stone.

Standing on his terrace, the Jewish community activist Sami Albo could hear the fighting in the street. But the violence did not spread inland as far as Jerusalem Boulevard, or his home a couple of blocks behind it. The phone kept ringing as friends and relatives called from nearby Tel Aviv, concerned for the family's safety. The Albos were all fine, but as for many of Jaffa's Jews, the family's feelings towards their Arab neighbours had hardened, probably permanently. Sami explains: 'We felt that we were living in another country, not in Israel. The burning tyres and stones being thrown reminded me of what my father told me about the pogrom in Turkey. The same pictures came into my head. The Arabs only attacked the Jewish businesses. They said this exploded because they are treated badly. I asked them what the connection was, to make an Intifada in Jaffa? If you want to demonstrate, then go to the police, get permission, demonstrate against the government, against the municipality, against everyone. But why are you making a progrom against me as a Jew?' The first Intifada in 1987 helped fuel the October 2000 riots, Sami believes. 'Something happened then to the Arabs in Israel in general, and to the Arabs of Jaffa after that. They said they were Palestinians first, then Israeli Arabs. This is their country as well, but I ask them, Please don't call yourselves Palestinians. You are not Palestinians. All this time they have been Israeli Arabs—now they decided, because of the situation on the West Bank, that they are Palestinians.'

The October 2000 violence and Arafat's rejection of Camp David were more than Barak's increasingly shaky coalition could bear. The concessions he had offered the Palestinians were opposed by a substantial part of public opinion. Barak resigned in December and elections for the post of prime minister were set for February 2001. Once again Yasser Arafat was the Likud's best electoral ally. Arafat's rejection of Camp David first caused dismay and confusion on the Israeli left, then a nationwide fatalism: as it seemed impossible to make peace with the Palestinians, there was simply no point trying any more. Barak ran for office again but won barely a million votes, compared to almost 1.7 million for Ariel Sharon, a hardline Likud ideologue who as minister of defence in 1982 had overseen Israel's disastrous invasion of southern Lebanon. Barak left politics tired and profoundly disillusioned, and Sharon formed a National-Unity government with Labour. The short-sighted decision by Israel's Arab minority to boycott the elections helped return Likud to power. The Arabs had reason to be angry: Barak had received over 95 per cent of Arab votes in the 1999 elections, but he did not invite any Arab parties into his coalition, meet with Arab leaders or bother with even a symbolic gesture of inclusion. Only 18 per cent of Israeli Arabs voted in 2001, compared with over 70 per cent in 1999, and this helped to open the door for Sharon.

The riots of 2000 highlighted the fundamental contradictions of Israel's Arab Palestinian minority. They live in an open society with more rights and freedoms than anywhere else in the Middle East. They are citizens of a democracy with free speech, an aggressively critical media and an independent judiciary. Arab Knesset members may call for the dissolution of the Israeli state, even as it pays their salaries and the bodyguards that protect them from Jewish extremists. Arabic is an official language, used on public street signs. Women in particular have benefited from the abolition of polygamy and child marriage, and unlike in several Arab countries they may vote and be elected to parliament. But ultimately Israel's Arab citizens are non-

Jews in a Jewish state. Discrimination is systematic and institution-alised. Israel's Arab minority makes up just over 19 per cent of the population of 6.7 million. Unemployment and child mortality rates are higher among Israeli Arabs than among Jews. More than a hun-dred 'unrecognised' villages lack proper water and electricity, or road and sewerage systems. Despite an affirmative action campaign to employ more Arabs, most ministries have fewer than 5 per cent on their staff, and these are generally working in minor positions. The Ministry of Religious Affairs' budget for 2000 allocated just 2.9 per cent of its resources to non-Jews.[6] Zionist organisations such as the Jewish Agency and the Jewish National Fund have quasi-governmental status in Israel, enjoying privileged access to funds and tax breaks and even taking part in decision-making. All are exclu-sively Jewish in their concerns.

The warnings of Shin Bet, the domestic security service, that Israel's Arab minority was ready to explode were ignored, says Nachman Tal, former head of the Arab affairs division. 'The service consistently and constantly demanded from every government ministry: Don't ignore the problem. The service heads went to the prime ministers and gov-ernments time after time and asked them to set out guidelines for a strategic, long-term programme regarding Israel's Arabs,' he told *Haaretz* newspaper. 'Give them budgets, close the gaps—they deserve equal rights—and in return, demand civil loyalty.'[7]

The new generation of Arab Palestinian activists, such as Sami Abou-Shehade, the grandson of the Jaffa fisherman Ismail Abou-Shehade, are more concerned with changing the very nature of the Israeli state. Bespectacled, articulate and highly intelligent, Sami is a postgraduate student at Tel Aviv University, specialising in Middle East history. Higher education is one sector of Israeli society where the Arab minority has a solid presence: nationally, Arab students make up 8.1 per cent of university students and 28 per cent of students at teacher training colleges.[8] Arab students even study at the College of Judea and Samaria, in the Ariel settlement on the West Bank. Sami skilfully utilises the freedoms of Israel's democracy to espouse the Palestinian cause. In his spare time he conducts lengthy interviews with Jaffa's elderly Arabs, to capture their memories of the city before the *Nakba* and build a library of oral history, and he gives 'alternative' guided tours of Jaffa from the Palestinian perspective. 'In many ways Israeli society is not modern,' he says. 'Israel sees all of its Jewish citizens as a big family, and that is how it deals with them. For example, when there is a car accident, there are five minutes on the news about everyone who was killed. It is a tragedy when people die in car accidents, but in most states the television news does not list the names and ages of everyone who died and then film the funeral. Israeli Jews think of the state as some kind of family business.'

This paternal approach by its nature excludes Israeli Arabs. 'This is a problem. When you are not part of the family, and you are excluded, then you don't deserve to have all your rights. The state gives you part of your rights, but as though this is more than you deserve.' The same mix of paternalism and exclusion is also evident at university, says Sami. 'I am treated differently in two ways. They try to be nice to me, because I am the only Arab in class, and they want to feel good about themselves, so they try to help. In Israel everyone talks about politics all the time, but when the professors ask the students what they think, they ignore me. If I have something to say, it's not important. I am not allowed to be part of any serious political discourse. It makes me feel that I am living in a racist society, every day. Still, I am articulate enough to participate in the discussions whether they want me to or not. I have enough things to say, and I know how to say them. But most Arab students are afraid to say what they think, or act on their feelings in anything to do with politics at the university, because anyone official, a teacher, professor or doctor, could get them into trouble.'

For Sami's generation, like his grandfather Ismail's, Shin Bet still casts a long shadow. Arab students may study alongside Jews, but they are carefully monitored, says Sami.[9] 'We know that Shin Bet monitors everything that we do, everything we publish, everything we say, all the time. For example, we are not allowed to demonstrate inside the university, so we demonstrate at the entrance. Shin Bet comes and takes photographs of us all the time, and asks us questions. There are Shin Bet people living in the student houses, together with Arab students. The state makes it legitimate to deal with us as though we are enemies, no matter that we are one of the quietest minorities in the world. The state should stop dealing with its citizens as belonging to a religious or national community. The state's function is to give services to its citizens, that's all.'

THERE IS AT LEAST one episode of Jaffa's history which closed peacefully. As the millennium came to an end Yoram Aharoni, owner of the Tiv coffee and spice shop, made up his mind and sent out an invitation to a small gathering. Yoram was seventy-five in 1999, and already working half-days. His son, Ofer, had worked in the shop for four years, but now wanted to make his own way in the world. Yoram recalls: 'I decided on Rosh Hashana that I would close the shop. If you don't decide a date, you stay open until Passover the next year, and carry on and on. I put up a sign, so that everyone would know that this was the final decision. About twenty people came, neighbours.

Only Tiv and one other shop had been there so long—all the rest had changed. Tiv was an institution, not just a shop.'

The gathering marked the end of an era. Tiv had provided for waves of immigrants, from Bucharest to Benghazi, its wares giving the comforting smells and tastes of home. Even when the newcomers left Jaffa they still returned, says Yoram. 'When they moved to Bat Yam and Holon they did not buy less. They bought more, because they came back to stock up.' Yoram and his shop are still missed in Jaffa, and when he returns to visit the city, his former customers plead for him to reopen. 'Tiv was there for fifty years. The first customers came with small children, then the children grew up, and they came with their children. We were like a family. People still come up to me and ask me where they can buy spices now, the best spices like I used to sell.'

Tiv's closure also marked the end of a chapter in the history of both Israel and Jaffa: that of the Bulgarian Aliyah, and Yoram's generation, which had struggled to establish a Jewish state. Yoram and his wife, Rina, took up arms against the British during the Mandate era. He fought in 1948, 1956, 1967 and 1973. He even volunteered for active service during the 1982 invasion of Lebanon, but was politely turned down. Yoram now looks back on his life with calm satisfaction. Jaffa is no longer Sofia-by-the-sea. Bulgarian is rarely heard on Raziel Street now, and the cafés and social clubs have almost all vanished. But the absorption of the Bulgarians is testimony to their contribution in building Israel. 'I am an example of a Bulgarian. I do not push myself. Once I was close to people in the government, like the prime minister, Yitzhak Shamir, who was also in Lehi. I had contacts in the army and the government. I could have got a comfortable job in the foreign ministry. But I never asked for anything and I don't regret it.

In Lehi and in the army I did what I needed to do, and I did a lot. I gave my best years to Israel. You can say that I can be proud of this.' Yoram kept true to his principles, fought for his people and provided for his family, which is as much as any man can hope for. Neither Yoram nor his son, Ofer, would fight in any more wars, but as a pioneer of Jaffa's renovation, Ofer would encounter a different kind of struggle with his Arab neighbours.

23

Separation

We used to live together in Jaffa like brothers,
but now all that has vanished. Jewish and Arab children
almost don't mix, and they do not know each other any
more. It happened without anyone realising.

Behira Buchbinder, Jewish resident of Ajami and community activist

There were no more queues at the Abulafia bakery for its fresh breads flavoured with hyssop and olive oil, crispy cheese pies and trays of sticky baklava. The fish restaurants along Jaffa's coast, where once it seemed all of Tel Aviv would decamp for Saturday lunch, stood silent, that day's catch wilting on piles of melted ice. Even the Ajami humous and pitta bread cafés were empty. Tel Aviv's Jews had voted with their feet, and with their wallets. Like the violence of 1921, the October 2000 riots fed the deepest, secret fears of even many liberal-leftists, that underneath all the talk of co-existence, the Arabs hated them and wanted to drive them out. Tel Aviv's response was swift and coordinated: Jaffa was boycotted. It was not an official decision, but in a way it did not need to be. It was a reflex, visceral and automatic.

And for Jaffa's Arabs, that in turn confirmed that there was no place

for them in Israeli society, that the Jews wanted nothing more than for
them to leave. So the cycle continued, and those caught in the middle,
like Khamis Abulafia, wavered between frustration and despair. 'It
was the most difficult time in our lives. There was a break between the
Jews and the Arabs. We felt that they had gone behind our backs and
turned against us. We believe our bakery is a special model of co-
existence. We respect the Jewish festival of Passover and we close the
bakery here and in Tel Aviv, and our other businesses.[1] You can imagine how much business we could do if we stayed open in that week.
My family thought this could not happen to us, because we were out
of this game. We thought there was a consensus about the Abulafias,
that we were a model of co-existence between the two sides.'

The Abulafias were wrong. There were even mutterings among the
more radical Arabs that the Abulafias were too close to the Israeli
establishment, and some refused to buy from the bakery. But whatever had been the family's position in the shifting sands of local politics, it was of no help to them now. In good times the Abulafia
bakeries employed more than 120 people, including many Israeli
Jews, making up to 100,000 baked items a day. Production plum-
meted by 90 per cent. At the Abulafia restaurant in Old Jaffa, takings
also plunged by 90 per cent, from around one million shekels a
month ($240,000) to around 100,000 shekels ($24,000). If the
Jews of Tel Aviv intended to repay Jaffa for the riots, they were successful. Still the footsoldiers of co-existence marched on: Khamis
began to hold meetings at the Abulafia restaurant to rebuild bridges.
'We believe that when you talk, when you make conversation, even
small talk, you can overcome prejudice and hate.' It saddened both
Khamis and his friend, the schoolteacher Ali Goughti, that many Jews
in Tel Aviv had never met an Arab socially.[2] It was only through

human contact, they believed, that the wall of prejudice and indifference could be broken down. The school curriculum teaches very little about Arab society, says Ali, who lectures young conscripts before they begin their military service. 'When I talk to them, they tell me that I am not one of the Arabs they've heard about until now, or the ones they think they know about. They say it was easier before they met me, easier to hate us, and the Arab people.'

ONE FRIDAY NIGHT in October 2000, a few yards from the Abulafia restaurant, in the ground floor of the Ottoman Old Seray building in Old Jaffa, a procession of Jews and Arabs were taking the stage at the Arabic-Hebrew Theatre. Founded in 1997, the theatre consists of two separate companies, El-Saraya, directed by Adib Jahashan, a Christian Arab who lives in Jaffa, and its Hebrew equivalent, Local Theatre, directed by Igal Ezraty, who commutes from Tel Aviv. They share a single space but enjoy artistic autonomy. Some productions are in Arabic, others in Hebrew, and some are co-productions in both languages. That night the theatre was hosting an open-microphone night called 'In Jaffa We Talk',[3] while not far from the angry, passionate debate Jews and Arabs were killing each other. Two army reservists who took a wrong turn near Ramallah were arrested by Palestinian police. A mob broke into the station and beat the soldiers to death. The body of one was chained to a car and dragged through the streets, while the killers held up their bloody hands at a window to the cheering crowd outside. In a further twist, some Israeli Arabs were arrested for helping suicide bombers, while others were killed in the explosions, which did not discriminate.

There was perhaps less talking than shouting that night at the theatre, but that did not matter, for the darkened auditorium was a safety valve for the audience's frustration and anger. It quickly divided along familiar lines: when Igal Ezraty read aloud the names of Israeli soldiers who had been killed, Arabs protested; when he read the names of Palestinian and Israeli Arab fatalities, some Jews were angry. But the evening passed without violence or gunfire, and in those hate-filled days, that was an achievement in itself. 'We said to Arabs and Jews, you have the stage, and the freedom to say what you want,' recalls Adib Jahashan. 'You can say what you like, what you don't like, what you are for and what you are against. It was magnificent. People threw out all kind of things that were inside them. Afterwards it was like the air was let out of a balloon. Everything was released. We sat together, we drank tea and coffee and talked as friends. We showed that if you are against somebody, you don't have to kill him. You can talk to him.' Weekly coffee-house evenings followed, with music, comedy and other performances. Just as valuable were the discussions afterwards, as Jews and Arabs sat together.

An eloquent, hospitable man in his early sixties, Adib was born in Haifa, and now lives in Jaffa with his wife and three daughters. Adib was the first Arab to study theatre in Israel, and he graduated from the London Academy of Music and Dramatic Art in 1972. He first worked in Haifa, specialising in child psycho-drama—a form of therapy—before moving to Jaffa. Now he manages a children's hostel by day, and works for the Arab-Jewish theatre company as a volunteer. Both theatre companies are supported by Tel Aviv municipality and divide expenses such as electricity and local taxes equally. But it is a very limited kind of equality. The Hebrew company receives one million shekels a year, whereas Adib's group receives only 200,000 shekels ($48,000) a year, and that even after its budget was doubled in 2004. That same year the Tel Aviv municipality awarded both men a shared prize for their contribution to co-existence and artistic collaboration between Arabs and Jews.

'The theatre is also a symbol, a return to Jaffa's golden era, before 1948, when it was the cultural capital of Palestine,' says Adib. 'We start with the children, we invite schools to come with the pupils and teachers. We make all kinds of theatre festivals, for women, for Arabs and Jews. We give back something of what Jaffa used to be. We add something to people's lives here.' For Jaffa's Arab community, the theatre and its café is more than a place to watch drama. Israeli Arab society, although slowly changing, remains deeply conservative; Jaffa lacks places for the young to meet. There is only one European-style café where people can sit, drink coffee and chat. Young women, in particular, would not go to a traditional Arab coffee house, while the tourist traps of Old Jaffa are too expensive. The theatre is a comfortable meeting point for both men and women, Arabs and Jews.

Despite his budget problems, Adib readily agrees that he has far more artistic freedom in Israel than he would in an Arab country. On a visit to Amman he asked the large Jaffan exile community there to help him stage *Memory*, a one-man show by an Israeli Arab playwright about the Palestinians who remained in Israel after the *Nakba*. It was, needless to say, very critical of Israel. Adib was amazed to learn that the play would have to be submitted to the Jordanian censor. 'Even after I told them this play has been performed in Israel more than fifty times, in Jerusalem, in Haifa, in Jaffa and other places, they still insisted that it didn't matter. They told me that when the answer comes back from the censor, they would contact me. We still did not get an answer, which is itself the answer.' There are no such problems staging controversial works in Israel. In 2004 El-Saraya staged *The Masked*, by the Israeli playwright Ilan Hatzor. *The Masked* was the first

Arab production to confront some of the most sensitive issues among Israel's Arab minority: collaboration with the Israeli government, dual identity, betrayal and divided loyalty.

The very existence of Jaffa's Arabic-Hebrew Theatre is a political statement. Both at home in Jaffa and on tour abroad—in Germany and England, Egypt and Armenia—it is testimony to the existence of another Israel, one where Arabs and Jews can work and even create great art together. 'This is the only sane place in Israel,' says Igal Ezraty. 'I am not so naive as to think a theatre can change people's views, but it has an effect, like other aspects of culture. It is an island, where every morning Jews and Arabs come and work together. The fact that we are here has a strong effect, sometimes more than the plays or the shows themselves.' A wiry, intensely political man, Igal has long been active in the peace movement. In 1982 he was one of the first members of *Yesh Gvul* ('There is a limit'), the group of Israeli soldiers who refused to serve in Lebanon.[4] 'I saw that they lied to me when I went to Lebanon in 1982, that this was a political war, that the Syrians did not want to fight us. I told my commanding officer that I did not want to go back. He released me, because otherwise he would have to send me to trial. They told me that I was betraying my friends, but I could not return, for political and moral reasons.' Igal also stuck to his principles when he was called up for duty in the West Bank during the first Intifada in 1987. This time his new commanding officer was less sympathetic. Igal was twice sentenced to a month in military prison.

The answer, says Igal, is for Israel to be 'a state of all its citizens'. Among Israeli Arabs this is a commonplace, everyday argument. But it remains a minority position among Israeli Jews, albeit one slowly moving away from the fringe into the leftist mainstream. For the simple-sounding phrase 'a state of all its citizens' is in fact revolutionary. It means, essentially, the de-Zionisation of Israel, the removal of privileges given to Jews, such as the Law of Return, which guarantees automatic Israeli citizenship, and the restrictions that prevent Arabs from buying land owned or administered by the state. The theory posits that Israel would keep its strong links with diaspora Jewry, but would be a Hebrew rather than Jewish state. It would keep its current borders and would not merge with any future Palestinian state. Instead Israel would evolve into a 'normal' country in which all of its citizens—whether Jewish, Christian or Muslim—would enjoy full and equal rights. Israeli identity would be based not on being Jewish but on the bonds of shared contemporary and historical experience: living on the same territory, commercial, family and social connections, the use of modern Hebrew and—eventually—Arabic culture and language.

Once the Arab minority felt sufficiently connected to this Israel, with a real stake in society, the state and its future, they too would serve in the army. This is also known as the 'post-Zionist' position, which argues essentially that Zionism's mission is completed, as the Jewish state now exists and has done so for almost sixty years. The question is, now what? Igal explains: 'I feel I have more in common with the Arabs of Jaffa than with religious Jews. I believe there should be equality between Jews and Arabs. I am not a Zionist in the sense that I believe the work of Zionism is finished. The Jewish state was an answer for what Hitler did—they had to solve the problem of the Jews in Europe. They came here, and they are here, but we don't need a Jewish state any more. Israel should be a democratic secular state, like Switzerland, or any other country with more than one language and culture.'

There is no artistic censorship in Israel, and nobody tells Igal what kind of play to produce with the public money he receives. But sometimes there are political pressures. When an Israeli poet dedicated his reading to those who died in Jenin after the Israeli army incursion in April 2002, Igal was telephoned by an unhappy municipal official.[5] 'He said I was not allowed to hold political events, as the theatre belongs to the city. But I said we were having an artistic performance, but [also] a political one. It's all part of the argument. We can do this in our shows, because we do political theatre.' Theatre can also highlight the many parallels of Israeli and Palestinian history: of exile and return, displacement and yearning for a lost homeland, whether it is Jaffa before the *Nakba* or multicultural Cairo before Nasser's expulsions.

The play *Longing* incorporates a mix of both Israeli and Palestinian personal narratives. It aims to confront the greatest psychological taboo of both peoples: that any recognition of each other's losses is a kind of surrender in the endless battle for memory as well as territory. Igal explains: 'In *Longing*, each actor tells his or her story. The audience sees that you can talk about your memories and longing for your past. Because of the Holocaust mentality here, every time an Israeli sees a story about Palestinians who had to leave in 1948, they think it means all the Jews have to go back to Europe. Israel should declare that our independence is the Palestinians' catastrophe—then we can start to solve the problem. But it does not mean that three million Palestinians will come home and all the Jews have to leave.'

KHAMIS ABULAFIA SAYS that he feels as though he is trapped between two competing narratives, Palestinian and Israeli. Yet even among those Jews who live in Ajami for idealistic reasons, who are committed to co-existence with their Arab neighbours, such as the community activist Behira Buchbinder, there is a sense that there is often less of a dialogue between Jews and Arabs than two self-contained narratives of national and personal history, and that each passes the other by, without even meeting. Behira's experiences in the 1948 war, when she fought at the battle for Kibbutz Ramat Yochanan, near Haifa, still haunt her, yet she has never spoken of them with her Arab friends. The kibbutz's defenders had no radios or means of communicating between different units, so Behira was deployed as a runner. The previous year one of her teachers had told her that when Israel declared its independence, within a couple of months nobody would be left alive. When the fighting began she feared he would be right.

'The Arabs began to shoot at the kibbutz at dawn, trying to capture it. I was seventeen years old and I saw the battle with my own eyes. We were all very young. The runners were the only soldiers that the Arabs could see. We ran, they shot at us. We ran, they shot at us. A platoon of Jewish soldiers arrived and planned to attack the Arabs. We saw through our binoculars that some of them were heading straight into an Arab ambush, but we could not communicate with them. They were all killed.' Behira lost a brother and a step-brother in the 1948 war. Many years later she sat talking with her friend and neighbour Abou Nasser. He recounted what happened in his home village in 1948, how he was there with his uncle when the Israeli soldiers conquered it. In fact Behira had already heard this story, but from the other side. 'I already knew how the Palmach attacked the place from behind, and how the fighting went. Two of my friends were killed there. Abou Nasser was really a good friend of mine, but I never told him that—how it looked from my side. I don't really know why—I didn't know how he would feel. I never told Arab friends about the people in my family who were killed in 1948. Arabs hate to feel guilty. It would have made them uncomfortable and I did not want that. It was more important for me to have good personal relationships with my neighbours. We weren't at the stage where I could tell them my personal history.'

Behira's arguments are a reminder of those advanced by the Tel Aviv history student Sami Abou-Shehade. Despite all the dialogue, it sometimes seems nobody is listening. Behira says: 'We are anonymous to the Arabs. This even happens with my friends sometimes. They talk to me, and blame everybody for what has happened to them, but they never think about who they're talking to, about who I am, that I also went through these things. When the Arabs start to tell their stories and they get really emotional, sometimes it makes me angry. If it's something personal, it's all right, but they always tell the story from one side. Sometimes it evolves into this general idea of all the Arabs just sitting there and being slaughtered by the Jews. I would like to start living together in simple co-existence, everyone being themselves, without the politics attached. We have to understand the past, not ignore it, but we also have to let it go.'

BUT SOME PARTS OF history should never be let go, argues Jacob Chelouche. Born in 1958 in Paris, while his parents were working for the Jewish Agency, Jacob Chelouche is the son of Shlomo Chelouche and his wife, Mary. Thoughtful and quietly spoken, Jacob is intensely aware of his family's role in the creation of modern Israel and the powerful resonance of the Chelouche family name. But just as Yoram Aharoni, the former Stern Group member, refused to exploit his old contacts when Yitzhak Shamir came to power, Jacob preferred to make his own way in the world. 'I have lived most of my life in Tel Aviv, and my roots are in Tel Aviv and Jaffa,' he explains. 'I always feel very touched when people say to me, "Oh, you are a Chelouche." It makes me feel very connected, as a Zionist, to Israel and to Tel Aviv. But I don't like to emphasise my family name. My wife used to joke about it and say that I should tell people more, but I prefer not to.'

Jacob is the great-grandson of the family patriarch, Aharon Chelouche, and the family's history is inextricably entwined with that of Zionism, the building of Tel Aviv and Israel itself. Jacob's father, Shlomo, fought in the 1948 war and spent years in north Africa, organising the emigration of its Jews to Israel. His grandfather Yaakov established the Anglo-Palestine Bank, which funded the construction of the first houses in Tel Aviv. Jacob's great-grandfather Aharon persuaded his wife and daughters to leave Jaffa and move to Beit Chelouche, the house on the sand dunes that were to become the settlement of Neve Tsedek. Much of Neve Tsedek has been renovated, and it is now a fashionable artists' quarter. Beit Chelouche still stands, together with the trees planted by Aharon Chelouche in its courtyard, but he would find the view from the roof terrace unrecognisable. The sand dunes that once stretched in every direction are long gone, although the Chelouche Bridge—built by the *kaymakam* of Jaffa—still stands. The city founded by Aharon Chelouche and his fellow pioneers is now a crowded modern metropolis, home to more than 360,000 people. Tel Aviv stretches for miles along the coastline, its skyline studded with skyscrapers. It is the epicenter of modern Hebrew culture, home to museums, world-class musicians, an orchestra and choirs, journalists, artists, writers and two universities. Most Israeli banks and companies have their headquarters here, not far from the Stock Exchange. Tel Aviv's nightlife rivals that of many European capitals, while its 2,500 Bauhaus buildings, including Zaki Chelouche's masterpieces, have been declared a UNESCO World Heritage Site, hopefully saved for ever from rapacious developers.

Shlomo Chelouche happily said he could never live anywhere else. This is the state he fought for and to which he dedicated his life, and nowhere better encapsulates that pioneer spirit than the White City, built on the sands. 'My father was a real Zionist in the true sense of the word. He took part in building the state before, during and after its birth. He fought in the British army and in the Haganah,' says Jacob. 'He developed Israel and brought the Jews from north Africa. These are memorable deeds—he is very proud of them and I am proud of them as well.' But Israel's idealistic pioneering spirit has now faded, Jacob admits. 'When I grew up in Tel Aviv there was a garden in the street. We all played together—there was no traffic and no worries about bombings. I came home from school, ate, played outside and my parents did not worry at all. Kids did not need mobile telephones. Israel today is something between where it was fifty years ago and, for example, France today, in the role of the state. Young people still volunteer for the most dangerous army units. I don't agree with the settlers on the West Bank, but they give up comfortable lives to live in a dangerous area because of their beliefs. There is still a sense of community, which you would not see in the United States.'

As Israel becomes more Americanised, the traditional family ties around which Jacob's ancestor Aharon Chelouche built his family life have faded[6]—except among Israeli Arabs, says Jacob. 'I have Muslim friends, and I see that their customs are very much like ours a hundred years ago, in a positive way. Everyone is in contact with each other, and has a close relationship. There is a family structure—they visit each other, and they support each other in a crisis. For kids it is wonderful. They can stay with their uncle one day, their grandfather the next. Everything is near, everyone is warm. It's something we lack today. I think it helps my Arab friends to endure hardships much bet-

ter than in the modern society, where everyone is left on their own.'
Sadly, the atomisation of Israeli society is reflected in the Chelouche
family's recent history. As the twentieth century drew to a close, one
wing of the family decided to sell off Beit Chelouche. Jacob fought
hard to keep the house in family ownership, but he lost his battle. 'I
feel very attached to the house in Neve Tsedek. It was sold against my
wishes. I made a serious attempt to buy it, but I had limited means
and the price was around two million dollars. Unfortunately, I did not
get enough support from the family to let me buy it at a more feasible
price. I was very sad that we, with our name and our history, lost such
a beautiful part of our heritage. Because so many people shared the
inheritance, the return was minimal, just a few thousand dollars.'

The stone floors laid down by Aharon Chelouche have been polished smooth over the decades. Beit Chelouche is now a museum,
with a permanent exhibition on the history and heritage of the Chelouche family. It recently hosted a family reunion. Aharon's three
sons—Yaakov, Yosef Eliyahu and Avraham Haim—had founded a
great dynasty with many branches. The title of Julia Chelouche's
memoir, *The Tree and the Roots*, is most apt. Julia had returned to Israel
in 1969, and died there in 1999 at the age of one hundred. 'We did
everything because we have memories of the past kings of Israel, and
because of God's promise to his people. All of history is written in the
Torah. I was never afraid of the situation and the wars. I always had
hope and was secure in God in the heavens, that the end would be
good,' she wrote in the last pages of her memoir.

At the reunion there was even a scandal about the family history.
Or Aleksandrowicz, a descendant of Yosef Eliyahu Chelouche,
claimed that the patriarch Aharon had another brother, Yosef, who
died in 1865, and that the Chelouches came from Morocco, not Alge-

ria.[7] In the Middle East even family histories, it seems, can never be untangled. But perhaps it is here at Beit Chelouche, an Arab house built on a sand dune by a Sephardic Jew from Algeria, and now part of Tel Aviv, that the two competing narratives, Jewish and Arab, can finally intertwine.

24

Islam on the March

Early 2000s

*Blessings for whoever has saved a bullet
in order to stick it in a Jew's head.*
*Sheikh Ibrahim Madhi, speaking at the Gaza main mosque
on 3 August 2001, broadcast on Palestine Television*

Parallel with the process of 'Palestinianisation' of Jaffa's Arabs is one of increasing Islamisation. When once a few hundred worshippers would gather at Abou Nabout's Great Mosque for Friday prayers, now the figure is more like several thousand. The call to prayer is a timeless summons, a reminder for Muslims that empires rise and fall, that governments and states are temporary, but Allah is eternal. Islam comes from the word *salaam*, peace, almost identical with the Hebrew *shalom*. But there is little peace between the faiths, says Ofer Aharoni: 'After September 11 I think that Arabs here felt under attack and so they became more extreme. I see more and more young women in black. I don't like it. One day we were at a humous restaurant and there was an Arab couple next to us. They looked like a nice couple. I thought, Maybe they have a son like ours, perhaps we could communicate. The woman was covered in black.

They wrap themselves in this flag, saying, We are *Islamic*. I thought it was a pity.' Islam itself means 'submission' to the will of Allah. It carries a sense of surrender, almost of the dissolution of the self into an all-powerful spiritual force. Its power is never more evident than when watching Muslims at prayer, perhaps especially for Jews, who are used to more chaotic synagogue services. Ofer Aharoni's children study at a mixed school in Jaffa. When the teachers organised a trip to a mosque, he went as well, his first visit. 'When the Arab kids started to pray, they all immediately knelt down with their heads on the ground. It was completely quiet. It was something completely new for me. It was an amazing experience. I realised that these people are different.'

Jaffa's Muslim Arabs are Israeli citizens, but they are also part of the *ummah*, the worldwide community of Muslims. In Jaffa—as in Jenin and Gaza—poverty, unemployment, alienation and discrimination are the best recruiting agents for radical Islam. Satellite television and the Internet bring news from the Middle East straight to Jaffa, and very little of it is good. Khamis Abulafia explains: 'To have women with their head, their hair and their face covered is something new in Jaffa. But the people here are part of the Palestinian people. They watch the Al-Jazeera and Al-Arabiya satellite channels every day. They see what is happening in Iraq and in Palestine. Because the situation has got much worse, people are coming back to religion. They are angry and disappointed with what is happening, and so they return to their roots. They don't trust their leaders, but they trust God, and they believe he can change things.'

Based in Qatar, Al-Jazeera, which launched in 1996, is the Arab world's first free, uncensored, independent television station. Al-Arabiya, based in Dubai, launched in 2003. Both are serious news channels, viewed across the region, and their reporting of social and political issues, from women's rights to the role of Islam, is having a profound effect on Arab society, opening up debates previously considered taboo by the state-run media. The channel's outspoken journalism often angers the United States as much as it does the Arab regimes: Al-Jazeera's Baghdad bureau was closed by the Iraqi authorities.[1] But other Arab satellite television stations simply disseminate hate, not just against Israel but against all Jews. In October and November 2003 Al-Manar, the influential Hizbollah station based in Lebanon, broadcast *Al-Shatat* ('The Diaspora'), a twenty-nine-part Syrian television series. *Al-Shatat* was described in the Syrian press as 'recording the criminal history of Zionism', purporting to detail how the Jews have sought to control the world for centuries via a secret government led by the Rothschild family. Although Syrian state television did not broadcast the series, the credits gave thanks to numerous Syrian state bodies, including the ministries of defence and culture and the Damascus police. Bizarrely, the series' producers claimed *Al-Shatat* was based on 'two hundred and fifty sources by Jewish and Israeli authors', although it was the crudest kind of anti-Semitism, reminiscent of Nazi propaganda. Episode six shows a rabbi directing the punishment of a man who had married a non-Jewish woman: his mouth is forced open with tongs while molten lead is poured down his throat, his ears are cut off and he is repeatedly stabbed. Episode twenty shows a rabbi directing his congregants to kidnap a Christian boy and take him to the synagogue, where his throat is slit and his blood drained to make *matzoh*, unleavened bread, repeating the ancient blood libel.[2]

These kinds of depictions of Jews are routine in the mainstream and government Arab media. The forty-one-part Egyptian television series *Knight without a Horse* was shown across the Middle East in

2002, to almost unanimous applause. *Knight without a Horse* is based on the notorious tsarist forgery *The Protocols of the Elders of Zion*, which outlines a sinister international Jewish conspiracy to rule the world. The *Protocols* are published across the Arab world, and accepted by many as fact.[3] Other Arab television programmes promote the dark cult of the suicide bombers, showing the videos bombers record before their mission. Preachers eulogise suicide bombers as *shaheedeen*, martyrs for Islam, who will go straight to heaven, there to be welcomed by seventy-two virgins. Bombers' families are visited by local dignitaries after their death. Children wear mock explosives belts at demonstrations and are encouraged to consider a brief career as a *shaheed*.

Every Friday, Palestinian television broadcasts sermons from the main mosque in Gaza. This was the message delivered on 17 August 2001: 'The body parts of our sons, brothers and children are witnesses, that they will find refuge in heaven. There is no loss for a martyr whose body is torn to pieces and is spread all over, for he is about to meet Allah, Muhammad and the Prophet's friends.' Two weeks earlier Palestinian television broadcast Sheikh Ibrahim Madhi, speaking at the same mosque, who told worshippers: 'I was touched when I heard a lad tell me, "I am fourteen years old. I have four more years, then I will blow myself up among the enemies of Allah, the Jews." I told him, "My son, I ask Allah to grant you martyrdom and I ask it for me too, truly, out of obedience to Allah, rushing towards it and not running away." The Quran is very clear on this—the greatest enemies of the Islamic nation are the Jews, may Allah fight them. We must turn all spears towards the Jews, towards the enemies of Allah, the nation cursed in Allah's book.'

One of the most extraordinary programmes was broadcast on 26

September 2004 by Saudi Arabia's Iqra channel. It featured vox-pop interviews in which a presenter asks passers-by if they would be willing to 'shake hands with a Jew'. Their replies included: 'No. Because the Jews are eternal enemies. The murderous Jews violate all agreements. I can't shake hands with someone who I know is full of hatred towards me,' and 'No, the Jew is an enemy. How can I shake my enemy's hand?' In answer to the question 'Would you refuse to shake hands with a Jew?' one respondent said, 'Of course, so I would not have to consider amputating my hand afterwards.' The programme passed unreported by the world's media. The likely media reaction to an Israeli television station asking passers-by if they would shake hands with an Arab can only be imagined.[4]

This stream of hate has an effect. Jaffa's Arabs have become angrier and more confrontational, says Khamis Abulafia. 'Even the children are asking, Where is the Arab world, where are the supporters of peace? These questions were not asked two or three years ago. When the planes crashed into the twin towers, people here were shocked— they were very upset about Bin Laden. Now, they still don't support what happened, but they start to say they understand what Bin Laden did. They do not distinguish between Bush and the Israeli government—for them they are one body.' Suad Andraus has also noticed the growing Islamisation. 'I have never seen so many women and young girls, even schoolgirls, wearing the *hejab* [Muslim headscarf] as now. The Muslims and the Christians in Jaffa are friendly—there are no conflicts. But they don't mix much except in school or business, or when there are important social and political issues relating to the Arab community.'

For Jewish community leaders, the growing Islamisation is profoundly unsettling. Sami Albo claims the call to prayer in the nearby mosque is getting louder and louder, as a political statement. 'For over ten years we have been asking them to reduce the volume. In the evening we like to sit on our terrace. But you cannot rest, all you hear is *"Allah howa Akbar"* [God is the most great]. Every year we have the day of remembrance for the Holocaust, with a siren at 11 a.m., then two minutes' silence. This year they started to recite the Koran through the siren and afterwards, because a religious leader had died. They couldn't wait half an hour. We were shocked. Is this the kind of relationship of someone who wants peace? It is louder than in Ramallah. I am not saying don't do it, just please turn down the volume.'

THERE IS YET another ingredient in this simmering and volatile mix: the rise in violent crime across Jaffa, from petty robberies to shootouts between drug mafias. Half of Jaffa's Arab population is under eighteen years old. Few have jobs, and their problems begin at an early age. Jaffa's Arab kindergartens and schools are underfunded, with poor facilities in comparison with their Hebrew equivalents. Anxious Arab mothers send their children to Hebrew-language schools, but many youngsters drop out because they are not fluent in the language, further increasing their sense of alienation. Many Arab teenagers leave school without being able to read or write properly in either Arabic or Hebrew. With few options for work or further education, young males are easily drawn into the lucrative drug trade.

'Jaffa is a high-crime area, with many problems and poor socioeconomic conditions. There are many Jews who don't feel safe here. But they don't get robbed because they are Jews, but because they have more money,' says Yaron Kaldes, Jaffa's chief of detectives and criminal intelligence, in his office at the Ottoman *kishle*. Jaffa's location makes it a central node of Israel's drugs trade. Certain side streets in

Ajami are known as drug purchase sites. Groups of young Arab men drive up and down in dilapidated Subaru cars, blaring out Arabic music. The vehicle is dubbed the 'Subaru Crime' model by the police: the car is worth $1,000, the stereo several times more. When buyers slowly progress up the narrow alleys, heavy-set men in mirror sunglasses track their progress. The buyer then leaves the car and enters a house where the deal is done. Heroin, hashish, marijuana and cocaine are easy to obtain—as simple as ordering a pizza. Regular customers do not even need to leave home, explains Yaron. Like pizzas, the drugs can be ordered for home delivery. 'You call a dealer and he will deliver what you need by messenger.'

Jaffa is bedevilled by feuds and vendettas between three Arab criminal families, harking back to a dispute over a divorce and property which began in 1987. It has claimed the lives of between twenty-five and thirty people, and many shops are forced to pay protection money, as much as 15,000 to 20,000 shekels ($3,600 to $4,800) a month. When one owner came to the police for help, Yaron sent in an undercover officer for six months. Eventually the racket was broken up, but the owner had to have police protection for some time afterwards. Like police officers all over the world, Yaron says he is understaffed and underresourced. But he has an extra drain on his resources. 'If I get a call that two bombers are on their way to Tel Aviv, I have to send officers there. That leaves me without enough manpower for everyday operations.'

There is often a 'national aspect' to crime, says Yaron. 'When someone is killed in Gaza or Nablus, sometimes they have family in Jaffa. There are terrorist sympathisers here. Sometimes the Shin Bet takes them away. I see that many Arabs hate me if I arrest them. They look at me with real hatred. They say to me, "If I was not an Arab, you would not be doing this to me." It's not pleasant. But I have many friends among the Muslim Arabs, and they know that I treat them the same as Jews.' Respect and the principle of 'saving face' are crucial when arresting an Arab man, says Yaron. 'The criminal gangs here are concerned about money and respect. For the Arabs, respect is very important. They have special customs, and if you don't know them it is very difficult to deal with them. It is very important how you act with a suspect, especially if he is with his family, his wife and children, or his friends. You must be polite. If you need to search him you must take him outside. I tell young officers, if you need to search a drug dealer, show full respect to the family. But the criminals know this— sometimes they hide the drugs with their wives, because we are reluctant to search women.'

Jews in Jaffa fear that the police cannot control crime. When the Israeli artist Gili Mitchel told a local youth to leave his car alone, he was stabbed to death. Sami Albo's son was robbed at knife-point by two Arab youths, who stole his watch and his mobile telephone. 'People are frightened,' says Sami. 'If you find the courage to say something, you can get killed. One of my neighbours saw someone breaking into her car. She called the police. They just told her to come in and make a report. But she is frightened she will be attacked if she does.' In fact crime is probably the only area in Israeli society where the Arab-Israeli divide is no obstacle, says Yaron Kaldes. 'We are seeing increasing cooperation between Jewish and Arab criminals. If there were cooperation like that in the peace process, we would have peace by now.' Yet despite Jaffa's problems, after seventeen years Yaron still loves working there. Jaffa's edgy ethnic mix, the beauty of its surrounds and its perpetual challenge are a seductive combination. 'We have plenty of action, all kinds of crime, the best restaurants and the sea. I like the Arabs and their way of life. It's not north Tel Aviv, but it's not the Bronx either.'

NIGHTLIFE IN TEL AVIV starts late and goes on until dawn. At 1 a.m. on 30 April 2003, Mike's Place was crowded with revellers, spilling out onto the beach promenade, enjoying the sea breeze. Overlooking the Charles Clore Memorial Park, which covers the remains of Manshiyyeh, Mike's Place was a fixture of Tel Aviv nightlife. That night a British Muslim called Asif Mohammed Hanif detonated his nail bomb by the entrance, killing himself and three others and wounding dozens more. The death toll would have been far higher but the courageous security guard Avi Tabib blocked Hanif's path. Like the September 11 hijackers, Hanif and his accomplice, Omar Khan Sharif, came from comfortable, middle-class backgrounds, in their case in Britain. They had not grown up in the slums of Gaza or Jenin, been beaten by Israeli soldiers or seen their homes demolished. Sharif did not complete his mission, and mystery surrounds his death: his body was washed up on the Tel Aviv shore several days later.

It is impossible to overstate the impact of suicide bombings on Israeli public opinion. If the intention of Islamic radicals is to sabotage the peace process and smash any consensus for compromise, they have succeeded. Suicide bombings have pulled Israeli public opinion substantially to the right, dramatically increased support for the fence that cuts off the West Bank and poisoned communal relations inside Israel for many years. In March 2002 alone there were nine suicide bombings, almost one every three days, killing seventy-eight people and injuring hundreds. Over the years, the bombers have honed their technique, to cause maximum death and injury, say security sources.

Bombers pack their explosives with nails and jagged shards of metal, and survivors often need repeated operations to remove dozens, sometimes hundreds, of pieces of shrapnel from their bodies. Shrapnel embedded very deep inside tissue is sometimes left, as it is too dangerous to extract. Once the bomb goes off, medical staff fall into a well-practised routine. Ambulances and paramedics rush to the scene to provide immediate first aid, coordinating with the local hospitals, who prepare their emergency rooms and operating theatres.

'Suicide bombers are a new kind of weapon,' explains Dr Moris Topaz, who has treated many victims. 'They are guided human missiles, bringing a huge amount of explosives to a specific target. They cause battlefield injuries, but in a civilian context. Most soldiers with these injuries would not survive, because of the distance to the hospital. But our medical services are very efficient—we do the minimum needed on the scene and rush the victims to hospital. We can have four teams within minutes working simultaneously in the operating room on a single patient,' he says, with a kind of weary pride in his voice. The general surgeon assesses the extent of the trauma and deals with chest and abdominal wounds; the orthopaedic surgeon focuses on limb and spinal injuries; the vascular surgeon closes the major blood vessels that are often severed, while the plastic surgeon deals with burns and soft tissue damage.

The human missile sometimes also carries a chemical and biological payload, says Dr Topaz. 'When the explosives detonate, the head and upper torso remain in one piece but the rest of the body is blown apart. The perpetrator's body fluids penetrate anyone nearby. This is exacerbated because the bombers usually choose an enclosed space, such as a bus or inside a building, so the blast is contained. In one case we removed a piece of the perpetrator's bone from a victim's limb.

In another we found a piece of bone in a victim's neck. Tests showed it contained hepatitis B, so the victim had to be vaccinated.' Dr Topaz treated many of the victims of the March 2002 attacks. The rows of casualties are seared into his memory. 'Kids, old people with their holiday clothes on, all appeared suddenly, dozens of them, just lying there on stretchers, waiting for help.'

Bars, hotels, shops and nightclubs are all protected by armed security guards, who check everyone going inside. But the seafront is open and crowded, providing good cover for would-be terrorists. On 1 June 2001, 21 were killed and 120 wounded by a suicide bomb outside the Dolphinarium nightclub, further up the coast from Mike's Place. Two days later a furious crowd of Israeli demonstrators attacked the Hasan Bey mosque and threw stones at the Abulafia bakery. Riot police were deployed to prevent the mob from rampaging through Jaffa. The Dolphinarium bombing was carried out by Said al-Khotari. His father then appeared on *Life is Sweet*, a Jordanian television show, to explain how he pacified Said's siblings after his death: 'We said he is a martyr—"Do not consider those who died for the sake of Allah dead, but alive and sustained by their God"—and we calmed the children. When they came from the television channel, the Abu Dhabi channel I think, or another channel, we told them: "We are willing to sacrifice our four children." Then our smallest child said: "Why can't I?!"'[5]

Israelis now take a stubborn pride in trying to live lives as normal as possible, says Dr Topaz. 'No society can bear a situation where there is no basic security, where you cannot feel safe when you send your kid on a bus to school or to the cinema. Suicide bombers are a constant threat—you don't know where or when it will happen. It's like something falling from the sky into the centre of Israel's cities. But even after an attack, people still go out to cafés, to football

matches. I think this is incredible.' The stress and tension caused by
suicide bombings are making many Israelis, both Arab and Jew, ill.
Jaffa's doctors report increases in heart-attacks, psychotic episodes,
outbursts of crying, panic attacks and depression. Many patients cannot bear to get on a bus and have developed a phobia about public
transport. Domestic violence is also increasing as husbands turn
their anger inward, against their wives.

Each time a bomb exploded, Khamis Abulafia despaired. Eventually he pulled his two sons out of school in Tel Aviv. The teachers were
supportive, but life in the playground had become intolerable. Once
again Khamis wrote an article for the newspaper *Maariv*, explaining
that Islam was a religion of mercy, not wanton killing, with rules for
waging war. 'My heart bleeds when I see these bombings. It makes me
very uncomfortable. I am part of the Palestinian people, and what is
happening to them hurts my soul, but I do not accept this. It is not
the right way. The Prophet Muhammad told his soldiers before they
went into battle, Do not harm pregnant women, elderly people, children, trees and animals. And if you take prisoners, deal with them
humanely.'

THERE IS NO fence dividing Jaffa from Tel Aviv. But Jews and
Arabs are instinctively turning inwards. Personal friendships are
stretched, sometimes almost to the breaking point, or are somehow
restructured. Michal Meisler-Yehuda, daughter of the sculptor Frank
Meisler, recounts how she was shopping in Jaffa together with her
baby son when she bumped into her old friend Yosi. He invited her
for a coffee. 'We went to a place at the Arab end of Yefet Street, just as
we had a hundred times before. For the first time, I did not feel safe.
Not because of Yosi, but I was thinking, What if there is a drive-by

shooting? We sat at the back, and I put the baby under the table. I realised that I do not have the right to put my baby in this kind of danger. Yosi had been shot at before.' Nothing happened, and Michal passed a pleasant, if slightly nervous, twenty minutes. 'Yosi is a nice man, whatever his business is. Since then I always say hallo when we meet, but I don't go for coffee. For me the innocence is gone.'

Michal does not take part in the continuing Jewish boycott of Arab Jaffa, and she still shops there. But she is the exception among her peers. 'To this day most of my Jewish friends do not buy from the Arab shops. Many of them won't even drive down Yefet Street any more. Recently I was in a humous restaurant with a friend. We were the only Jews—everyone else spoke Arabic. I felt safe because I have known the owner for ever, and he came out of the kitchen to say hallo. I saw an Arab guy I know on another table—he shouted at me in Hebrew: "Michal, what are you doing eating here? Don't you know Jaffa is Arab now?" He thought it was a joke, but it was a bad one.'

THE MUSLIM COMMUNITY leader in Ofer Aharoni's home was not joking when he gave his opinion about Ofer's and his friends' gentrification drive. Ofer's group spent years restoring Rabbi Hanina Street, a small lane behind the flea market, where the fine old Ottoman buildings had been piled high with debris. They cleared away the rubble, often by hand, and forced off the drug dealers and prostitutes. They commissioned architects to painstakingly restore the houses and lobbied the municipality to spruce up the surrounds. A small part of Jaffa's architectural heritage had been saved, but Ofer's guest was not happy. 'He told me that he would prefer that Jaffa would be home to junkies and whores, or that the city would be destroyed, rather than the Jews come and live here. He said that in my house. In a way I was glad that he said it. Now I know what he thinks. I don't have any personal feelings against him, but there are many Muslims who think like that.'

In Jaffa's zero-sum game of Arab-Jewish relations, even renovating a house was a political act. But like his father, Yoram, Ofer believes in straight talking. He is one of only two Jews in the street who hang out the Israeli flag on Independence Day. 'The other families don't want to "provoke" anything. I don't want to sound anti-Semitic, but the Jews always have this "don't make trouble" mentality. In my experience I think Arabs would rather talk to me than someone more left-wing, because I speak openly and frankly about what I think.' Ofer's home cost him $20,000. It is now an airy and spacious apartment spread over three floors, worth perhaps $500,000, and he lives there with his wife, Irit, and two young children, Gidion and Avigil. Ofer was a pioneer, risking his savings to live in a place that most Israeli Jews could not wait to escape from. But money was not his main motivation. 'I grew up in a small street in Tel Aviv, and we had a wonderful childhood. My dream was to make the same kind of place for my kids here in Jaffa. I believe, really, in my soul, that it is better to grow up in an area that is not homogenous. Here in Jaffa you have Jews, Arabs, Christians and Muslims. You have the Mediterranean culture, the Italian and French influences on the architecture. Everything is a big mix and I think that's great.'

Despite the mixed welcome Ofer and the renovators received, Rabbi Hanina Street is an organic part of Jaffa. But Old Jaffa did not live up to the hopes of those who saved it from the demolition balls. This was partly due to its geography, and partly because of the inherent contradictions of trying to construct an artists' quarter instead of letting one develop naturally. 'Old Jaffa never did become an area blossoming with art,' says Frank Meisler. 'It's nice to come to Jaffa, have lunch by the sea, experience a different kind of environment, but most gallery owners were in Tel Aviv and did not want to set up shop here. It's out of the way, and there is no passing trade. It was a well-intentioned idea. But the consequences are that there is almost no new generation of children who will live in Jaffa.' There are other problems, he explains. 'I own a house in Jerusalem, in the Yemin Moshe quarter. The criteria for buying there was that the buyer had to be an intellectual, a man of the spirit. One neighbour owns hotels, another a chain of bookmakers in Britain. So these are intellectuals— it means anyone with money,' he notes dryly. 'But the beauty of such intellectuals is that they maintain their homes. My upstairs neighbour in Jaffa is an artist who cannot even pay his alimony and has been repeatedly sent to prison for that. And he certainly can't retile his roof, which is the ceiling of my dressing room. For the last twenty-five years I have been paying for that while he sits and plays backgammon. So it's no joy having Van Gogh as a neighbour. It's nice to read a book about him, or admire his paintings in a gallery. But never have an artist next door.'

There are parallels between Old Jaffa and Frank's hometown of Danzig. He went back once, and like the Hammamis' visit to their house in Jebaliyyeh, it was a poignant journey. 'Danzig was levelled by the Russian artillery, and then they expelled the Germans. The Poles later rebuilt a few of the main streets as a showcase, in the Gothic and Hanseatic styles, but there were just props behind them, holding them up. We had lived around the corner at one time from one of the reconstructed streets. I could not see the entrance to our house, only the reconstructed façade of the nearby street.' Frank's childhood home had vanished. 'In both Old Jaffa and Danzig the original population has been kicked out. It was like walking through a film set. I took a trip on a tourist bus to the hinterland around the city. It was full of Prussian landowners, coming back for a last look. It was exactly like the Arab who came back after 1967 to see my neighbour's house and started to cry. There are squatters there, and squatters here.'

25

A Possible Future

Present Day

*When Israel competes in the Eurovision song contest or a
football match, we say, 'They got so many points.' But Amina
[Robyn] says, 'We got so many points.'*
Wedad Andraus, Robyn's aunt

Like Khamis Abulafia, the Andraus sisters—Suad, Wedad and
Leila—are caught between two worlds. They live in Israel, but
are not fully Israeli. They are Christian Arabs, but many of
their friends are either foreigners or Jewish. War heightens the contradictions of their lives. In 1973, when Israel's very survival seemed
threatened, they found themselves pulled strongly in opposite directions, says Wedad. 'We had good Jewish friends in the army. We worried about them, and some were pupils of mine. We did not want the
Egyptians to lose, and although Israel was fighting our people, we put
this aside because of the human contact we have with our Jewish
friends. We felt we were not with Israel, but with them. Nowadays we
usually do not discuss politics when we visit each other. We know
exactly what they think and they know what we think.'

Amin Andraus' children have all made successful careers. Leila is an administrator and Wedad a teacher at the Tabeetha School, while Suad is pro-consul at the British Consulate in Tel Aviv, where she has worked since 1964. In the 2001 New Year's Honours List, Suad was made a Member of the British Empire (MBE). The British ambassador, Sir Sherard Cowper-Coles, held a party for her at the embassy residence, where the guests included the pharmacist Fakhri Geday. It was all very reminiscent of the Mandate days she had heard so much about from her father, Amin. 'I am British pro-consul but I am not British, and I am a member of the British empire and there is no empire,' she quips. Her brother, Salim, also worked at the consulate for many years, as an accountant. All four chose to work in British or British-founded institutions, explains Wedad. 'We worked with the British because we would have felt like outsiders if we'd worked at Jewish institutions.' The Andraus family's world, of pre-1948 Jaffa, vanished in the *Nakba*, but they have adapted to the new one in which they live, says Suad. They are all involved in Jaffa life, and regularly attend baptisms, weddings and funerals among Jaffa's Christian community. But none of the sisters ever married, as after 1948 their potential partners were scattered across the Middle East and the rest of the world. Before he died in 1972, Amin Andraus told Salim to look after his sisters. 'He has done that to the letter, and we all rely very strongly on each other,' says Suad.

It is on the West Bank and in Ramallah, home to many of the old Jaffa families, that the traditions of pre-*Nakba* Palestine live on. Like Communist eastern Europe before the fall of the Berlin Wall in 1989, in some respects that way of life has been frozen in a time capsule. There are many benefits to this, including a greater respect for family and home and the traditions that give Arab society a rare cohesion in the modern world. Those paying family and social visits will dress up, the men usually wearing suits and ties, in contrast to the informality of an Israeli gathering. Guests are never allowed to pay for themselves in a restaurant. But modernisation, the breakdown of ethnic barriers and intermarriage between Jews and Arabs in Israel proper are generating a new and beneficial phenomenon, one that could yet help solve the Israeli-Palestinian conundrum. Behira Buchbinder, the Jewish resident of Ajami, argues that 'mixed marriages are the highest form of co-existence between Jews and Arabs.' One of Amin Andraus' neighbours once told him something similar, recalls Wedad. 'He said there is only one way you can solve this Arab-Jewish problem, which is to mix, to bring forward a new generation.'

That too could be part of the Andraus family's legacy to Jaffa. When Salim was forty he married Hillana, a Jewish woman from Romania. Marriages between Jews and Arabs are rare in Israel. Salim and Hillana have two children: Amin, who works as a lawyer in Tel Aviv, and his sister, Robyn (Amina), who works with under-privileged children. Both went to Tabeetha School. Suad and her sisters welcomed Hillana into the family, but worried about the religious and cultural divide and its effect on Salim's children. In fact Amin's and his sister's mixed background means they can move with ease in both Arab and Jewish society and have many friends in both. 'We are not fanatically political, but we would like to retain our Arab Palestinian identity,' says Suad. 'We keep Christmas and other Christian traditions in our house. Hillana is very good to us, and we are to her.'

WITH HER CLOSE-CROPPED black hair, modish clothes and fluent, accentless Hebrew, Robyn Andraus would fit in at any of Tel Aviv's trendy bars and cafés. Before graduating from a teachers' training college in creative education, Robyn studied cinema and media at

Tel Aviv University. She felt completely at home. 'I never felt an outsider there as a student, as I never based my identity on religion. The only place where I was expected to do that, by my peers, was at Tabeetha School. I couldn't do that, so that made me an outsider. But at home we got a little bit of everything—we spoke Hebrew and grew up in normal Israeli culture. Now I work with Arab people in Jaffa and I never feel an outsider, and I work with Jewish people in Tel Aviv and never feel an outsider.'

Like her grandfather Amin, Robyn was taught to be independent and resilient at an early age. Salim Andraus was the only Arab father she knew who allowed his daughter to stay overnight at a friend's house. Together with her brother, Amin, Robyn learnt judo, and she won the Israeli championship three years running before she was fourteen. 'Learning judo is not something that Arab girls normally do, rolling around on the floor with boys,' she says over coffee at Books and Coffee, on Yefet Street, Israel's only joint Jewish-Arab-owned café and bookshop. 'My parents took us to the competitions and sat there cheering us on.' Robyn, like Sami Abou-Shehade, is a regular at the café, one of the last places in Jaffa frequented by both Jews and Arabs.

Robyn works with several Jaffa voluntary and community groups, helping disadvantaged young people. Most of the volunteers are Jews and the disadvantaged children Arab, but many of the middle-class Jews who move to Jaffa do not engage with the local population. For Robyn, the divide is less between Arab and Jew than between rich and poor. Her grandfather's house is flanked on one side by new $500,000 apartments and on the other by one of the most run-down and overcrowded apartment blocks in Jaffa. Curiously—or not—once the luxury apartments were built, the municipality began to renovate

the exterior of the dilapidated block. 'There are mixed kindergartens, mixed schools and cultural events. The separation is more to do with money. Rich Arabs and rich Jews go to the same places, and the poorer ones don't. We grew up learning Arabic, Hebrew and English. We had a good education, and a much better chance in life. The kids down the road go to Arab schools where the way they teach Hebrew is atrocious and Arabic even worse. They are expected to cope with two languages and cannot read either. They don't have a chance.'

Robyn works with a group called Teenagers at Risk (TAR), and its programmes bring tangible results. TAR organised a year-long course for youngsters who had dropped out of school, covering basic literacy and a range of skills including computing, hairdressing and car mechanics. TAR had to request special permission for some of the students to attend, as they were under house arrest. 'These were youngsters who were breaking into cars and selling drugs. You would think that they would be too cynical to enjoy receiving a certificate that says "Well done, you can read". You could see how proud they were when they finished the course, like little kids who had worked really hard for something.' Jaffa's Arab community needs to do more to help itself, she says. One recent programme to train ten boys to be car mechanics received a disappointing response. The plan was for the boys to spend three days a week learning the trade and two at school. Arab garage owners were not much interested in helping. 'We know that when kids work, they do not steal. They don't steal to get rich, but to get basic things. You know when they have new jeans or shoes that they have stolen a car radio, for which they get about 80 shekels ($20). There are lots of garages owned by Arab people in Jaffa who could take more interest, but they don't understand that the delinquent kids are also part of this society.'

Robyn definitely does understand this, and she has staked out her place within Israel. 'Lots of young people have a big problem with their identity. They ask themselves, "What am I?" I am a mix, but I decided to enjoy it. I am not Jewish, I am not Christian. I am an Israeli. My mother tongue is Hebrew, which I speak better than English or Arabic. My social circle is Israeli. My best friend is Israeli. The Zionist way of thinking is that if you are Jewish you are Israeli, if you are not Jewish you are not. I reject that.' Like Igal Ezraty, the theatre director, Robyn says that Israel should become a citizens' state. 'My dad's generation says they are Palestinians who live in Israel. I say I am an Israeli. My generation was born after 1948, when being Palestinian was not an option. My dad's generation and we grew up in two different countries. Israel now is a big blend of people and there are many foreigners here, from all over the world. I don't think anyone should have the right of return, Jewish or Palestinian. They should be allowed to immigrate if they benefit the country. I was on a bus, listening to a Russian junkie complaining that he only came to Israel because the heroin is cheaper here. Every society has criminals, but we don't need to import them. Israel should become a normal society, and that is not such a big idea.'

Perhaps it is apt that the grandchildren of Amin Andraus, one of the great patriarchs of Jaffa, should provide a model for Israel's future. Robyn defines herself as Israeli, but her brother, Amin, identifies with his Palestinian heritage, and in a citizens' state, that would not matter. While Robyn is spirited and vivacious, Amin is quiet and watchful. He gives careful and considered answers to questions about himself, as befits a lawyer. 'I am not nationalistic by nature, neither for the Arab side nor the Jewish one. I am more humanistically inclined than political. I don't see myself as closer to a certain person

because he belongs to one of those groups. But while my mother is Jewish, she married a Palestinian and I grew up as a Palestinian. But I live in Israel and I have Israeli citizenship. It is complicated because Israel by definition is a Jewish state, and that excludes me. It is not a state of all its citizens, as some would like.'

Yet Israel is an open society, ruled by law, with an independent judiciary. A recent court decision ordered the government to move the route of the wall on the West Bank, in favour of the Palestinians. Two Arab judges have been appointed to the Supreme Court, one for a regular term. A court ruling in 2002 required the Tel Aviv municipality to add Arabic—an official language in Israel—to signposts even in areas where there is no Arab population. Amin explains: 'Israeli law is not an apartheid system, with laws saying whites go here, blacks go there. It is not on that level. The inherent discrimination in the legal system is well hidden. Studies show that Arab Palestinians coming before a judge usually receive longer sentences than Jews. It is not official, but it happens. The second main question is one of land ownership.' But here, too, the law is evolving. A recent ruling prohibited the state from discriminating against Arab citizens who wish to buy land. The question is, why do Israeli citizens have to go to the Supreme Court to buy property in their own country, merely because they are not Jewish?

THE ANDRAUS FAMILY are Israeli citizens, with recourse to the courts. Fadwa Hasna née, Hammami, is not. As a Palestinian living in East Jerusalem, she has little, if any, legal redress against the whims and caprices of Israeli officials. Fadwa is stateless. She does have an Israeli identity card, a necessity to live in her home, but it is not valid for travel abroad. If she wants to travel she must apply to the Israeli interior ministry for a laissez-passer to leave the country, an arduous and intentionally humiliating process. Once abroad she is always nervous that if she stays away too long, Israeli officials will question her right to return to Jerusalem. Electricity, water and local tax bills dating back years are all carefully preserved in a thick file, evidence of her residence in the city. Fadwa also has a Jordanian travel document, which must be renewed every few years. But she does not have a passport, citizenship or any official nationality. She could apply for a Palestinian passport, but if it were granted and she became a Palestinian national, she would forfeit her right to residency in Jerusalem. Life there resembles Joseph Heller's book *Catch-22*, inspired by Franz Kafka and edited by Ariel Sharon.

Before the *Nakba*, trains left Jaffa and Jerusalem for Cairo and taxis for Beirut and Damascus. Nowadays Fadwa can hardly go anywhere, especially since the start of the Al-Aqsa Intifada. Even Ramallah, the capital of the Palestinian territories, just north of Jerusalem, is off limits. 'Our world is getting smaller and smaller,' she says sadly. 'We used to go to Ramallah for dinner. We drove there in half an hour, and came back at midnight, but we cannot go there now. We cannot go to Bethlehem. Even if I want to go downtown to Jerusalem, I don't take the direct road. There are always roadblocks. Soldiers take your identity card number and search the car. When my husband was sick I had to rush him to hospital—he had cancer and he was bleeding. I was waiting at the roadblock for twenty minutes and I asked to pass. The soldier told me to get back in the car. He pointed his gun at me. I told him to come and see my husband, how ill he was. He told me to call an ambulance.' Ironically, the only place Fadwa can travel freely is within Israel. 'Sometimes we go shopping in West Jerusalem, but we feel we are not wanted there. They search you at the door, and make you feel that you are a bomber.'

Rema Hammami's world is shrinking too. Before Oslo, Rema drove to Gaza in an hour and a half, passing through the Israeli army checkpoints with a wave. After the accords were signed, Israel made it almost impossible to visit Gaza, and Rema has not been there for seven years. 'The only time I can see my friends from Gaza is when I go abroad, if we end up at a conference together. I used to throw New Year's Eve parties in Jerusalem and friends would come from everywhere, from Gaza and Nablus. That is unimaginable now.' The fifteen-mile journey between Rema's home in East Jerusalem and her office at Bir Zeit University, just outside Ramallah, used to take thirty-five minutes. There was only one checkpoint, at Ad-Dahiyeh in East Jerusalem, which was fairly relaxed. After the Al-Aqsa Intifada erupted in 2000, the checkpoint at Ad-Dahiyeh became much stricter. The Israelis put up a new checkpoint by the refugee camp at Qalandiya, just north of Jerusalem, and blocked the road completely at the village of Surda, north of Ramallah.

The simple process of trying to drive to and from work meant Rema had to negotiate a path through these three checkpoints twice a day. On the best days—these were rare—the journey took three times as long as it should, but once she spent five hours in her car. 'Qalandiya's main impact was to create a constant and massive snarled traffic jam for the thousands of Palestinian commuters needing to pass between the two cities every day,' she explains. 'Your car is stuck in the traffic with hundreds of others, and everyone is losing their tempers. Sometimes the soldiers would suddenly open fire over your heads, because the kids in the refugee camp were throwing stones at them.' Rema questions whether security, as Israel claims, is the real rationale for the checkpoints. 'Often when we finally reached the line of soldiers manning the checkpoint, they wouldn't even bother asking for our identity papers and just waved us through, as if their function was just to make us understand that they are in control of our destiny. Or I would wait hours for my turn, and then wait more while they chatted on their mobile telephones to their girlfriends. After a while, sitting in a line, waiting that long, begins to drive you mad. Now I have a phobia about lines and queues. Even if I am in a supermarket waiting to pay at the till, I get tense and nervous.'

At least Rema could drive through Qalandiya. At Surda, Israel erected an arduous 'walking checkpoint' to cut off Ramallah from its rural hinterland and the tens of thousands of Palestinians who depend on the city for everything from work to medical services. The Surda checkpoint also prevented the flow of people and traffic to Bir Zeit. Israeli army bulldozers destroyed the main road, then sealed it off at both ends with concrete blocks and mounds of rubble. Those wishing to pass through had to walk along the destroyed road until they reached the military post in the middle, where they would wait to be processed by the soldiers and then continue on foot, a two-kilometre journey in total. Israeli officials cited 'security considerations' as the justification for Surda and other roadblocks which do not control access in and out of Israel but are internal checkpoints within the West Bank. But the Israeli soldiers were more interested in flirting with young women than in checking for potential terrorists, says Rema. 'They harassed young men, and sexually harassed female students. They were always trying to start a conversation, asking for their identity cards and then saying things like, "Nice name—so what are you studying? Where do you live?" Our students are just trying to be like students anywhere—to get an education and have the basics of university life—and every day they are faced with soldiers pointing guns at them.'

In the first year of Surda's existence, the staff and students at Bir Zeit organised three peaceful marches against the checkpoint. Each time, in response, the Israeli authorities made it more restrictive, often blocking the road completely to prevent anyone reaching the university at all. There was little Rema could do about the Israelis' spite. Initially, when she saw a student being detained by Israeli soldiers, she tried to intervene. But that just made things worse. 'They became enraged, and would take it out on the students. It was clear, the soldiers' orders were to teach us that any resistance would backfire. Finally we learnt that if they stop someone you keep walking, for his sake and everyone else's. That was the worst, because you are already so powerless and they make you feel implicated as well.' In addition the Israelis opened and closed the checkpoints arbitrarily. Sometimes Rema passed through Qalandiya but Surda was closed. Or Surda would be closed while she was still at the university, and she would be stuck. 'That was the worst. We had to try and get back to Ramallah through the hills—twice they fired on us, hundreds of people scrambling through rocky hills just trying to get home.'

The checkpoint at Surda was eventually removed. But life did not get easier; new restrictions were imposed at Qalandiya, which is now surrounded by the security barrier, or the 'Apartheid Wall', as it is dubbed by Palestinians. The barrier has severed tens of thousands of Palestinians from their workplaces, from the cemeteries where their ancestors are buried, from their fields, their friends, even from their doctors and schools. 'Passing through Qalandiya is like running a gruesome marathon. You keep going and going, but one day I gave up. I could not wait any more,' says Rema. 'I parked my car, walked through and took a taxi on the other side. I stayed the night in Ramallah. When I came back, my car was not there.' Despite its UN number plates, it had been blown up by the Israeli army. Rema still makes the trek to Bir Zeit. 'People become very exhausted, and very stubborn. I will never leave Jerusalem. That would mean I have given in. But living like this takes a terrible toll. The standard of teaching at Bir Zeit has declined. We once had students from all over Palestine; now we are a local area university, because nobody can get to classes any more. Watching them build the wall at Qalandiya, you feel like you are watching them build your tomb, and all that is left is for them to put a lid on it.'

Meanwhile, Rema has found a new way to deal with the stresses of life under Israeli military occupation. With her Ph.D. on the social history of peasant women in Gaza finished, she is studying the ethnography of Israeli checkpoints. There is much to examine: the speed of transit, the attitude of the military, the differing treatment of those waiting depending on the age and sex of the Israeli soldiers, and so on. 'It was the only way I could try and turn things around. I didn't want to be a victim of the checkpoints any more, so I turned them into an object of study. What interests me the most is how the Palestinians here still stay human and make a life, despite the checkpoints and the occupation, which is extraordinary.' Qalandiya, although painstakingly slow, is comparatively civilised. Israel is sensitive about its international image, and Qalandiya is much more accessible to the foreign press based in Jerusalem. Israeli human rights activists monitoring the behaviour of the army often set up at Qalandiya. 'Because it is close to Jerusalem the Israelis try and put a better face on it,' says Rema. 'When we cross we usually look for the older men, the reservists, rather than the young conscripts. They try to be as humane as they can, in a very inhumane situation. But when the soldiers are not being observed, at checkpoints deeper in the West Bank, it is very different. The women soldiers are the worst, overcompensating for being women. This is not just in Israel, but any women in the military. We always try and avoid them.'

Palestinians argue that the route of the fence, deep inside the Green Line, is an ill-disguised land grab in preparation for Israel's new border after any possible peace deal, and that the daily humiliation of simply trying to get to work or school boosts support for the Islamists. Israelis argue that the security fence is a regrettable necessity, which has reduced terror attacks and suicide bombings by about 90 per cent. The fence, they say, can be dismantled when a final peace agreement is signed. For now it protects Israel from the suicide bombers. Their recruitment and support networks are based in the West Bank, as are the dispatchers who send them to their deaths in Israel. One dispatcher, now serving a life sentence in an Israeli prison, has admitted to recruiting potential bombers for Hamas at Bir Zeit University.[1]

Either way, the daily humiliation at the checkpoints as Palestinians try to go about their daily business is 'a breeding ground for hatred, and harms an innocent population in an inhumane manner', says one influential Israeli. In December 2004 he visited thirteen checkpoints together with activists from B'Tselem, the Israeli human rights group. He formed a 'very harsh impression', as he wrote in *Haaretz* newspaper.[2] Palestinians arrive at one checkpoint by car and must cross to the next one on foot, sometimes walking for several kilometres. Few humanitarian exceptions are made, if any. 'At one checkpoint we met four mothers with eight blind children aged between four and five who were walking to Nablus for medical treatment. It was a hair-raising sight to see the little blind children marching along, led by the women.' The Israeli soldiers cannot speak Arabic; they do not converse with the Palestinians and they do not smile. The human connection is 'expressed mainly in the giving of orders'. In addition, the checkpoints probably do not even work to prevent terrorist attacks, as 'every checkpoint can be bypassed'. These are the words of the retired general Shlomo Lahat, former mayor of Tel Aviv–Jaffa.

AS AN AMERICAN citizen, Rema's father, Hasan Hammami, can return to Israel and Jaffa whenever he likes. But his US passport brings problems as well as a measure of security. His name rings the first alarm. His place of birth, written in his passport, the second: Palestine. Then comes the barrage of questions, which he answers wearily but politely before his passport is stamped and he is waved through security. Hasan is going home, but to a country that does not really exist. The scraps of territory on the West Bank under Palestinian control are an almost-state, with a flag, a government, a people and a history, but this is not yet a nation in control of its own destiny. Hasan's Palestine is a land of memory as much as reality, kept alive by its diaspora scattered across the globe, the details of life before its destruction carefully recorded in books and memoirs, Web sites and Internet forums. By any standard, he has achieved much. He rebuilt his life in exile. He supported his family in their homes across the world. He and Barbara raised three fine daughters, Rema, Fawzia and Haifa. Hasan is a proud grandfather, active in inter-faith and community work in Punta Gorda, Florida. He and Barbara do not lack for material comforts. They have a lovely home, and they even had a yacht, before it was destroyed by Hurricane Charlie. Yet part of Hassan remains—and always will remain—a fifteen-year-old boy with a winning smile, frightened but determined, helping his parents, brothers and sisters scramble onto the boat at Jaffa's port in April 1948; a boy staring at the ochre sandstone buildings and Jaffa's seashore as they faded into a distant place and time.

'Why do I not feel fulfilled?' he asks. 'Is it because I feel like an outsider? Or because of my people's poor image? Maybe I am an overachiever and will never be fulfilled. But I know why. I have lost my home, but not my roots in Jaffa. I have lost my nation, but not my national cause. I have lost my nearness to my brothers, sisters, cousins, aunts and uncles, but not my deep family roots. All the money in the world, creature comforts, luxury holidays, respect and love from friends and neighbours can never replace this. The weight of the diaspora has been insidious, invisible but heavy. We missed most of the weddings of my brothers and sisters, the birth of their children. We never saw my nieces and nephews grow up, graduate, get married, have babies themselves. But worse, I realised that Fawzia, Rema and Haifa have grown up without these same roots. I tried to justify in my own mind that they were "citizens of the world", which has positive connotations but in reality no practical meaning. Exile is the common burden of both peoples, Arabs and Jews, which they need to unburden themselves of.' Yet Hasan looks not just back at the past but also to a better future. The answer, he says, is for both Jew and Arab to share the land, 'as equals in a free society which builds on the best of both, and replaces their fears with hope and dreams.'

Hasan's idealism is heartening, but neither the century of conflict nor the chronology of recent diplomacy between Israel and the Palestinians makes for optimistic reading. The 1993 Oslo Accords, the 2000 Camp David offer, the Road Map—none has achieved a genuine peace or brought the Palestinians meaningful statehood. Perhaps the time has come to focus not on politics but on the connection between people, and to build a new future from the bottom up, one also rooted in the past. On the wall of Shlomo and Mary Chelouche's home in Tel Aviv is a painting of Hajj Ibrahim Samarra, the Arab man who, as a lost boy in Jaffa over a century ago, was helped by the great patriarch Aharon Chelouche, and who in turn rescued the Chelouche family in the First World War. Perhaps Jaffa could yet be the laboratory for a new Israel, even a new Middle East, where Arab and Jew, Israeli and Palestinian, learn not necessarily to love one another but at least to live alongside each other in peace. A place where Ofer Aharoni is welcomed by his Muslim neighbours as he renovates his apartment, where Sami Albo can even enjoy the call to prayer of the *muezzin* and where Khamis Abulafia's sons may flourish at school in Tel Aviv. Where the Andraus sisters are able to discuss everything, even politics, with their Jewish friends, where the ghosts of Old Jaffa in Frank Meisler's house can be laid to rest and the Hammamis can finally come home to their house by the sea. Cynics on all sides may dismiss this as naive fantasy. It is, after all, barely two generations since the genocide of the Holocaust and the exile of the *Nakba*, the formative experiences in both peoples' recent history.

But as Theodor Herzl once said: 'If you will it, it is no dream.'

Afterword

few minutes' walk inland from my favourite seafront bench, past the Ottoman *kishle*, through Clock Tower Square, not far from the sites of Ahmad Hammami's fruit and vegetable shop and the Chelouche brothers' building supplies store, Eyal Ziv sits in his architect's studio listening to Jaffa's buildings. Eyal admits he is a man possessed—by the spirit of the city. 'I don't know where it comes from, this passion for Jaffa. It's something beyond me—you cannot hold it, you cannot control it. It tells you to do something and you do it. It sounds crazy, but I feel the Clock Tower is talking to me, saying, Please restore me. Or the gate to the mosque by the *kishle* and the nearby building. They are calling to me to renovate them, and I cannot refuse.'

Nor does he have to, for Eyal, an engaging and enthusiastic man in his early forties, is the architect in charge of Tel Aviv municipality's

renovation programme for Jaffa. Eyal grew up in Old Jaffa, near Frank
Meisler, in a house that his father bought in the late 1960s. After university and army service, he returned in 1988 and began work on renovating the flat that is now his studio. It was initially marked for
demolition, but after a two-year battle Eyal managed to save the
building and its neighbours. Beit Eshel Street is a classic late
nineteenth-century Jaffa construct, rows of shops with flats above
reached by a steep staircase that turns sharp right. Eyal's studio is a
fine high-ceilinged apartment with patterned floor tiles, tiles probably manufactured by the Chelouche brothers.

Together with his former partner, Rali Parto, Eyal completed the
renovation of the New Seray building, which was destroyed by the
Stern Group in January 1948. The Tel Aviv–Jaffa municipality and the
Ministry of Tourism have spent four million shekels ($960,000) on
the project. The New Seray's façade, windows, balconies and front pil-
lars have all been reconstructed with rigorous attention to detail. But
the long corridors which once housed Jaffa's municipal offices will not
be rebuilt. Instead, Baruch Peppermeister's neo-classical masterpiece
will eventually be transformed into a cultural and arts centre, which
Jaffa currently lacks, together with a public garden. Ron Huldai,
mayor of Tel Aviv, set up a group of architects with local connections
to work on renovating Jaffa. Several landmark buildings, including
the Clock Tower itself, have been restored. Eyal is now working on
Jaffa's disused train station, where decades ago Julia Chelouche and
her husband arrived from Haifa each year to spend the festival of
Passover with their relatives.

Rebuilding the New Seray—indeed, any of Jaffa—is not just a
question of architecture and construction techniques. Eyal met resistance when he wanted to restore a small gate between two shops that

leads off Clock Tower Square into the courtyard of Abou Nabout's Great Mosque. Several municipal officials told him that the mosque should pay, as the gate opened onto its property. Eyal disagreed. 'I told them that we are architects. We don't deal with religion, we deal with architecture. This is the history of Jaffa, of the city, and it doesn't matter whether it is Arab, Christian or Jewish. Anyway, if they want the tourists to come and to have nice things for them to look at, the tourists don't care who is the owner of the property.' Eyal's arguments worked and he got his budget.

Restoring relations between Jaffa's Jews and Arabs remained more complicated than renovating its buildings. In late summer 2005 Jaffa's Islamic leaders held an angry protest rally after a pig's head was thrown into the courtyard of the Hasan Bey mosque. Almost a century after it was built, the mosque was still the epicentre of Jaffa's struggle between Arab and Jew, just as its builder, the Turkish governor Jamal Pasha, had intended. Shin Bet quickly arrested two Jewish suspects, who said that they had wanted to disrupt the pull-out from the settlements in the Gaza Strip and the northern West Bank by triggering widespread riots. If so, they failed. Jaffa's Arabs did not riot. Instead they protested peacefully and announced plans to set up guard units at Islamic holy places in Jaffa and the nearby cities of Lod and Ramle.

Nor were the pull-outs from Gaza and the northern West Bank disrupted. Cynics dismissed the evacuation of about 9,000 settlers by the Israeli army as well-produced theatre, its stage directions agreed in advance by both Prime Minister Ariel Sharon and the settlers themselves. Despite much talk of bloody last stands and violent resistance, there was little of either. The army deployed water cannons, and the settlers threw eggs and stones and burnt car tyres.

When the soldiers broke through the barricades the settlers used passive resistance before being frogmarched away. There was much shouting and drama, but no real damage was done. Thus was the honour of all satisfied: Sharon could present himself as being forced to carry out a necessary but supposedly deeply painful operation for the national good, so strengthening his position among centrist voters. The settlers could parade their Zionist credentials before being rehoused and banking their compensation of around $200,000 or $300,000 per family. Meanwhile Israel retained control of Gaza's borders, airspace, water and electricity supplies.

Yet for all this, there was a sense among both Israelis and Palestinians that a line had been crossed, from which it was impossible to go back. There are no more Israelis in Gaza, and the neat European villas of the settlements of Netzarim and Neve Dekalim have been demolished to make way for high-rise housing to ease Gaza's overcrowding. The blue and white Israeli flag has been replaced by the red, black, white and green of Palestine. Ariel Sharon's Likud Party appeared set to split in two over the pull-out. Even the initially unsettling spectacle of Israeli soldiers forcibly removing Jews from synagogues somehow assumed a logic of its own. A precedent has now been set for further evacuations from the occupied West Bank. Gaza is now an independent Palestinian territory, so much so that several Arab governments have begun to pressure the Palestinian leadership to take back their refugees. Thus Arab unity and solidarity.

The Israeli departure from Gaza brought neither peace nor comfort to its inhabitants. It was also a missed opportunity. The settlers left behind an extensive network of computer-controlled modern greenhouses where they had grown tomatoes, strawberries and flowers, much of which was exported. These could have provided the basis for a thriving agricultural sector. Instead, within hours of the Israeli exodus Gaza's residents destroyed the greenhouses and stripped them of their glass, pipes and irrigation equipment. The remains were later bulldozed.

In January 2006 Hamas, the Palestinian Islamic movement, won national elections, defeating Fatah. The corruption, cronyism and incompetence that had so exasperated Hasan Hammami a decade earlier had only worsened over the years. Fatah had proved incapable of fostering either a functioning economy or civil society. Fatah's defenders argued that when Israel still controlled the Palestinian territories, no government could achieve much. The continuing Israeli land grab across the West Bank, the maze of checkpoints hindering the free movement of goods and people, Israel's armed incursions and the Palestinians' scepticism that they had any meaningful partner for peace all helped speed Hamas to victory. Hamas, as well as despatching suicide bombers to buses and restaurants in Israel, also ran an extensive social and welfare network of schools, orphanages and medical clinics.

Negotiations to form a National-Unity government between Hamas and Fatah broke down within weeks, and the first Islamic government took power in Gaza and the Palestinian territories. Hamas, like Fatah before it, proved unable to evolve from a liberation movement to a government. Hamas refused to recognise Israel, and its militants continued to fire rockets from the Gaza Strip into southern Israel. These attacks achieved nothing except to strengthen western and Israeli determination to isolate and eventually bring down the Hamas government. The international community imposed sanctions and Israel froze hundreds of millions of dollars of tax and customs revenues. Mired in their power struggle, Hamas and Fatah had no common vision of what might be best for the Palestinian people. Their only concern was consolidating their own power bases. By the end of

2006, a near civil war had erupted between rival Hamas and Fatah militias. Gunmen traded shots across Gaza and sporadic fighting spilled over into the West Bank. In just one day in January 2007 six people were killed. Palestinian society began to collapse. The prospect of a meaningful Palestinian state seemed more remote than ever.

Israel too was chastened. In January 2006 Prime Minister Ariel Sharon suffered a massive stroke from which he never recovered. He was replaced by Ehud Olmert, a lacklustre former mayor of Jerusalem. Olmert lacked both the experience and the confidence to provide the leadership Israel needed. In July 2006 fighters from the Iranian-sponsored Shia Hizbollah militia that controlled much of southern Lebanon fired rockets and mortars at towns and settlements in northern Israel. At the same time Hizbollah fighters crossed into Israel and abducted two soldiers. Israeli attempts to rescue its two fighters failed. Israel launched a ferocious bombardment of southern Lebanon and the southern suburbs of Beirut controlled by Hizbollah. Israel bombed Beirut international airport and destroyed much of southern Lebanon's infrastructure, including roads, bridges and electricity stations. Almost one million Lebanese were displaced and more than 1,400 lost their lives. Many were civilians, including numerous women and children. Israel blamed the casualties on Hizbollah, who it said was using civilians as human shields and firing from their homes.

In response Hizbollah fired waves of rockets into northern Israel, hitting towns and cities including Haifa, Hadera, Safed and Nahariya. The attacks were a massive psychological shock for Israel, whose heartland had not experienced such casualties since the war in 1948. Like the explosives used by suicide bombers, many of the rockets were filled with ball-bearings to maximise civilian casualties and injuries. Forty-three Israeli civilians and 119 soldiers were killed. Hundreds of thousands of civilians sought refuge for weeks in bomb shelters. The rockets did not discriminate between Arab and Jew: two Arab children were killed when a rocket hit Nazareth. Using the network of bunkers and tunnels they had constructed across southern Lebanon over the previous years, Hizbollah troops fought hard against the Israelis. These were a different calibre of soldiers from those Israel had faced in previous wars. Armed with state-of-the-art weapons, many provided by Iran and Syria, Hizbollah proved a deadly enemy. Its fighters destroyed Israeli tanks, disabled an Israeli naval gunboat and repeatedly ambushed Israeli troops. Human rights organisations accused both sides of committing war crimes by failing to distinguish between civilian and military targets. Many in Israel— and Lebanon—believe that the month of fighting in 2006 was merely the start of a long war between Israel and Hizbollah—even, by implication, Iran—that is only just beginning.

But if the regional picture was increasingly gloomy, there were signs that an increasing number of Israelis were recognising the price the Palestinians had paid for the establishment of the Jewish state. These developments could have profound implications on the future of both Israel and Jaffa. The Palestinian villages of Yalo and Imwas once stood not far from Latrun, on the road from Tel Aviv to Jerusalem. Emmaus was famed for its tradition of hospitality, and according to Christian tradition, Christ spent the night there after his resurrection. Like their neighbouring villages, Emmaus and Yalo were flattened by Israeli army bulldozers after the 1967 victory, and their inhabitants fled, mainly to Ramallah and Jordan. The land is now the site of the Jewish National Fund's Canada Park, a popular weekend picnic spot for Israeli families. The park's large exhibition, outlining the area's heritage, fails to record centuries of Palestinian history. Enter Zochrot, an Israeli organisation which keeps alive the memory of demolished Palestinian villages. Zochrot petitioned the High Court for the right to erect plaques commemorating Yalo and Emmaus. The JNF agreed. Finally Israel was beginning to admit that Palestine was not, after all, as the writer Israel Zangwill had claimed, 'a land without a people for a people without a land'.

Around this time members of the Knesset put forward several amendments to the Hatikvah, the national anthem, to make it—and, by definition, Israel—more inclusive to non-Jews. The first verse of the Hatikvah, which means 'hope', speaks of the 'Jewish soul yearn-ing deep in the heart' for Zion and Jerusalem. It is a purely Zionist song, in the late nineteenth-century sense of the word, calling for the redemption of the Jewish people through a return to the Holy Land. But Israeli politicians with greater foresight know that in the twenty-first century it is difficult, if not hypocritical, to call for civic loyalty from citizens, especially the substantial Arab community, when they are excluded by the state's most potent symbols. A parliamentarian from the centre-left secular Shinui Party proposed adding a verse in Arabic, another that the words 'Jewish soul' be changed to 'Israeli soul'. Nor are the calls for change confined to the left—one of the leading figures in the discussions is a senior Likud politician. A few words in the Hatikvah's lyrics could signpost Israel's future: a modern, secular democracy governed by politicians, or an obscurantist theoc-racy ruled by rabbis? Perhaps it is only after Israel has defined the type of state it wishes to be and has settled its relationship with its Arab minority that it will be able to make peace with the Palestinians.

Back in Beit Eshel Street, Eyal Ziv's studio also has a message. 'You cannot change history, or what has happened here. I don't know what will happen in the future, but I bought this house and for now I am the guardian of this house,' says Eyal. 'I am one resident in a long chain of residents, and the building will probably outlive me. But I did all I could to preserve it for future generations.' Eyal shows me a picture of a small, idyllic lagoon on the beach near Jebaliyyeh, where before the *Nakba* the Andraus and Hammami children watched the fishermen moor their boats. The lagoon no longer exists, but a modern beach promenade has been built nearby, where families stroll in the evenings.

Every Friday night at the other end of the city, Arab families crowd onto the Charles Clore Memorial Park, built over the rubble of Manshiyyeh, for a picnic. Children scamper on the beach; their parents and grandparents smoke and chat. The smell of coffee and sizzling kebabs mixes with the sharp tang of the sea, for the memory of Manshiyyeh outlives its reality—the memory, too, of those like Yosef Eliyahu Chelouche, who worked for co-existence between Jews and Arabs. Perhaps 50 per cent of Jaffa still exists as it did a century ago, Eyal explains: 'This is history, the destiny of the city. Its rulers all build and destroy, build and destroy. First the Turks, then the British and then the Israelis. Jaffa was a great Arab city, a Mediterranean city. Most but not all the Arabs are gone and you still have many of the buildings, but the street life, the smell, its special feel, are gone. We are starting not just to rebuild things but to try and connect them together again. Because Jaffa has to be the place where Jews, Muslims and Christians can connect, like they used to.'

Notes

1. A Battered Bride

1 http://www.jewishvirtuallibrary.org/jsource/History/haycraft.html
2 Central Zionist Archives, Jerusalem. File L3/483, testimonies to the Haycraft Commission.

2. Tel Aviv Is Born

1 Arthur Koestler, *Arrow in the Blue* (London, 1954), p. 113.
2 http://www.jewishvirtuallibrary.org/jsource/History/haycraft.html
3 Herzl did not invent political Zionism. The radical German-Jewish journalist Moses Hess, a contemporary of Karl Marx, had called for a Jewish homeland in *Rome and Jerusalem*, published in 1862. The first Jewish settlers in Palestine arrived decades before *The Jewish State* was written.
4 http://www.jewishvirtuallibrary.org/jsource/Zionism/herzlex.html
5 http://www.npr.org/news/specials/mideast/history/history1.html
6 http://www.kh-uia.org.il/Crisisnew/artical2002/english/180504english.html

7   http://www.nytimes.com/books/first/s/shlaim-wall.html

8   Joseph Roth, *The Wandering Jews* (London, 2001), p. 18.

9   Koestler, *Arrow in the Blue*, p. 113.

10 The word 'Aliyah' comes from the Hebrew term *a-alot*, meaning to 'go up', as in go up to the land of Israel, implying spiritual improvement as well as physical arrival. Those who leave Israel to live elsewhere are known as 'Yoredim', meaning those who go down, or descend. The First Aliyah lasted from 1882 to 1903, bringing 35,000 *olim*, immigrants, mainly from eastern Europe and Russia. The Second Aliyah lasted from 1904 to 1914, and brought 40,000 *olim* to Palestine, many of whom were inspired by socialism and socialist ideals. About half of all those who arrived in the First and Second Aliyahs left Palestine.

11 Ruth Kark, *Jaffa: A City in Evolution* (Jerusalem, 1990), p. 100.

12 Under the terms of the Capitulations, some foreign citizens, mainly from Europe, who resided in the Ottoman Empire were subject to the laws of their native countries. This granted them considerable autonomy in their personal and legal status. In response, Turkey gained favourable trade terms and export markets. France, for example, operated its own network of post offices across the Ottoman Empire, with branches in Beirut, Jerusalem and Jaffa. The system ended after the defeat of Turkey in World War I.

13 Kark, *Jaffa: A City of Evolution*, p. 116.

14 Mark Levine, *Overthrowing Geography: Jaffa, Tel Aviv and the Struggle for Palestine 1880–1948* (Berkeley, 2005), p. 119.

15 Modern-day Tel Aviv is a centre of the global sex-trafficking industry, its many brothels filled with young women from the former Soviet Union and eastern Europe.

16 Quoted in Levine, *Overthrowing Geography*, p. 322.

17 *Ibid.*, p. 119.

3. Jaffa Strikes

1   *Hajj* is the honorary title for one who has made the pilgrimage to Mecca.

2   *Inshallah* means 'by the will of Allah'.

3   Joachim Schlor, *Tel Aviv* (London, 1999), p. 191.

4   *Ibid.*, p. 189.

5   Tom Segev, *One Palestine, Complete* (London, 2000), p. 327.

6   See Aryeh Avneri, *Claim of Dispossession: Jewish Land Settlement and the Arabs, 1878–1948* (New Jersey, 1984), for a detailed discussion and analysis of pre-1948 Palestinian land sales to the Zionist movement.

7   Benny Morris, *Righteous Victims* (New York, 2001), p. 129.

8   *The Times*, 18 June 1936, p. 15.

9   Central Zionist Archive files, S25/9783.

10 Segev, *One Palestine, Complete*, p. 388. Such absurd territorial claims seem to be part of the nation-building process. During the Croatian war of independence in 1991 the author was dining in Zagreb and asked the waiter what he recommended for dinner. 'We have fish,' the waiter replied. 'What kind of fish?' 'Croatian fish,' the waiter snapped back.

11 Levine, *Overthrowing Geography*, p. 139.

12 *Ad-Difaa*, issue 2 February 1936. Quoted in Levine, *Overthrowing Geography*.

4. A Widening Divide

1   'The Brutification of Jaffa', by Onlooker of Palestine and Transjordan. CZA files S25/973.

2   *The Times*, 18 June 1936, p. 15.

3   Levine, *Overthrowing Geography*, p. 135.

4   Salim Tamari, 'The Vagabond Café and Jerusalem's Prince of Idleness', *Jerusalem Quarterly File*, Summer 2003.

5. Palestine Beckons

1   Quoted in Segev, *One Palestine, Complete*, p. 383.

2   'An Appeal to the English Soldiers'. CZA files S25/9783.

3   The split even carried on into the inferno of the Holocaust. During the Warsaw ghetto uprising in April 1943 the Revisionist Zionists formed their own

military organisation, which cooperated with the extreme nationalist wing of the Polish underground.

6. Days of Hunger

1 Segev, *One Palestine, Complete*, p. 436.
2 See the fascinating study by Orayb Aref Najjar: 'Falastin editorial writers, the Allies, World War II, and the Palestinian question in the 21st century', *Studies in Media & Information Literacy Education*, Vol. 3, Issue 4 (November 2003).
3 *Ibid.*

7. The White City Shines

1 Linda Grant, *When I Lived in Modern Times* (London, 2000), p. 71.
2 Pictures of Zaki Chelouche's buildings can be viewed at http://www .artlog.co.il/telaviv/14.html, also easily found with a search of his name.
3 http://www.etzel.org.il/english/ac07.html
4 Najjar, 'Falastin editorial writers . . .'

8. Jaffa Prepares for War

1 Najjar, 'Falastin editorial writers . . .'
2 http://www.Irgun.org.il/english/
3 Quoted in Meron Benvenisti, *Sacred Landscape: The Buried History of the Holy Land Since 1948* (Berkeley, 2000), p. 275.

9. *Al-Nakba*—The Catastrophe

1 Menachem Begin, *The Revolt* (London, 1983), p. 348.
2 Morris, *Righteous Victims*, p. 197.
3 *Ibid.*, p. 201.
4 Benny Morris, *The Birth of the Palestinian Refugee Problem, 1947–1949* (Cambridge, 1998), p. 47.

5   *Ibid.*, pp. 47–8.

6   *Ibid.*, pp. 46–7.

7   *Ibid.*, p. 97.

8   Ibrahim Abu-Lughod, 'After the Matriculation', http://www.palestinere
membered.com/Jaffa/Jaffa/Story194.html. Article first published in *Al-Ahram*
weekly.

9   Ibrahim Abu-Lughod, 'The War of 1948: Disputed Perspective and Outcomes', *Journal of Palestine Studies*, Vol. 18, No 2, Winter 1989.

10 Shukri Salameh, 'Cleansing Jaffa: A detailed eye-witness account',
http://www.palestineremembered.com.

11 Begin, *The Revolt*, pp. 352–3.

12 http://www.etzel.org.il/english/ac18.html

13 Morris, *The Birth of the Palestinian Refugee Problem*, p. 96.

14 Begin, *The Revolt*, p. 356.

15 *Ibid.*, p. 363.

16 Morris, *The Birth of the Palestinian Refugee Problem*, p. 101.

17 *Ibid.*

10. Jaffa Has New Masters

1   Meron Benvenisti, *Sacred Landscape*, p. 122.

2   It is a curious footnote of the 1948 war in Jaffa that the municipal records
until the end of the British Mandate no longer seem to exist. They are not at
the Tel Aviv municipal archives. Historians such as Mark Levine have also
been unable to locate them. They may have been destroyed in the bombing of
the New Seray in 1948 or removed by municipal officials who fled in April
1948. Some Palestinians believe they were captured and either destroyed or
locked away by the new Israeli authorities, to prevent any future claims over
land ownership.

3   Instructions to the Arab Population by the Commander of the Haganah, Tel
Aviv district, 13 May 1948. Copy provided by Suad Andraus.

4   http://www.mideastweb.org/thejewishstate.html

5   Morris, *Righteous Victims*, p. 219.

6 Jaffa Emergency Committee protest letter, 20 May 1948. Copy provided by Suad Andraus.

7 Amin Andraus letter, 10 June 1948. Copy provided by Suad Andraus.

8 Morris, *The Birth of the Palestinian Refugee Problem*, p. 141.

9 Amin Andraus letter, 5 July 1948. Copy provided by Suad Andraus.

10 Morris, *The Birth of the Palestinian Refugee Problem*, p. 63.

11 A detailed discussion of the causes of the Palestinian refugee exodus during 1948 is beyond the scope of this book. There are numerous books on the subject by both Jewish and Palestinian scholars, and I particularly recommend Benny Morris' authoritative work, *The Birth of the Palestinian Refugee Problem, 1947–1949*. Morris' work is a detailed, comprehensive study, thoroughly researched and referenced, and I have drawn on it often, especially in reference to events in Jaffa.

12 Ibrahim Abu-Lughod, 'The War of 1948: Disputed Perspective and Outcomes', *Journal of Palestine Studies*, Vol. 18, No. 2, winter 1989.

13 Morris, *The Birth of the Palestinian Refugee Problem*, p. 191.

14 Amin Andraus letter, 26 October 1948. Copy provided by Suad Andraus.

11. Sofia-by-the-Sea

1 Guy Haskell, *From Sofia to Jaffa* (Detroit, 1994) p. 149.

2 Benvenisti, *Sacred Landscape*, p. 142.

3 The Communist cause had little support in Palestinian society, which was overwhelmingly conservative and religious. But in the early years of the Israeli state it gained many Arab votes as it was not Zionist and defended the rights of the Palestinian minority, in stark contrast to the Labour Party.

4 Military rule was based on five regulations: 109, providing for the arrest of a person in a prohibited area; 110, providing for police supervision of a person for up to one year; 111, allowing administrative detention; 124, governing house arrest, and 125, permitting commanders to declare certain areas closed, requiring a permit for entry. Martin Gilbert, *Israel: A History* (London, 1998), p. 345.

5 The case of Al-Majdal, south of Jaffa on the coastal plain, is representative. Al-Majdal, site of the Biblical city of Ashkelon, had 10,000 inhabitants

before it was conquered in November 1948. Less than a quarter remained after the war ended, but by February 1950 the population had risen to over 2,300. The Israeli government wanted the Arabs out to make room for Iraqi Jewish immigrants. Al-Majdal's inhabitants were strongly encouraged to leave. Some were compensated. Al-Majdal was wiped from the map. The city of Ashkelon was (re)constructed on its ruins. The Majdal exodus excited no public debate or controversy. See Nur Masalha, *A Land Without A People: Israel, Transfer and the Palestinians 1949–96* (London, 1997).

6   Mark Mazower, *Salonica: City of Ghosts* (London, 2004).

7   Benvenisti, *Sacred Landscape*, p. 42.

8   Walid Khalidi (ed.), *All That Remains: The Palestinian Villages Occupied and Depopulated by Israel in 1948* (Washington, Institute for Palestine Studies, 1992), pp. 265–330.

12. Coming Home to Jaffa

1   Masalha, *A Land Without People*, p. 136.

2   Quoted in Masalha, *ibid.*, p. 135.

3   Handwritten copies of the five books of Moses inscribed on parchment, objects of veneration for Jews.

4   Morris, *The Birth of the Palestinian Refugee Problem*, p. 277.

5   *Ibid.*, p. 278.

13. New Lives

1   Rezso Kasztner was a Hungarian Zionist who negotiated with Adolf Eichmann in Budapest in 1944. Eichmann allowed 1,684 Jews to leave for Switzerland on a special train, after they had paid $1,000 each. Many were prominent community leaders and rabbis. They survived. The 'Kasztner Affair' caused enormous controversy and bitterness, especially among those who failed to get a place on the train. Kasztner moved to Israel and was shot dead outside his apartment in Tel Aviv in 1957 after a lengthy libel trial.

2   Tom Segev, *The Seventh Million* (New York, 1994), pp. 153–86.

3   The Kashubians are a Slavic people who live on the Baltic Sea shore. The German writer Günter Grass, with whom Frank went to school, is a Kashubian.

4   http://www.jewishvirtuallibrary.org/jsource/anti-semitism/egjews.html

14. Repopulating Jaffa

1   www.jewishvirtuallibrary.org/jsource/anti-semitism/morocjews.html

2   See "The Forgotten Refugees: The Causes of the Post-1948 Jewish Exodus from Arab Countries', by Philip Mendes, Latrobe University. Presented at the 14th Jewish Studies Conference in Melbourne, March 2002. http://www.labyrinth.net.au/~ajds/mendes_refugees.html

3   http://www.jewishvirtuallibrary.org/jsource/anti-semitism/egjews.html

4   http://www.en.wikipedia.org/wiki/Suez_Crisis

5   Segev, *The Seventh Million*, p. 349.

6   Tom Segev, *1949: The First Israelis* (New York, 1998), p. 160.

15. Saving Old Jaffa

1   From a guidebook to Israel by Joan Comay, published in 1962, quoted by Martin Gilbert in *Israel: A History*, p. 350. Ben-Gurion's foreword hailed what he called the 'dynamic quality of a new state turning deserts into gardens and welding heterogeneous immigrant groups into a sturdy nation'.

2   Segev, *The Seventh Million*, p. 327.

3   See note 1 for this chapter, above.

4   Quoted in Joachim Schlor, *Tel Aviv*, p. 206.

5   More usefully, the Sir Charles Clore Jewish-Arab Community Centre in Acre (an ethnically mixed port city to the north of Jaffa) supports mixed community and development projects.

6   Benvenisti, *Sacred Landscape*, p. 168.

7   Quoted in Benvenisti, *ibid.*, p. 199.

16. Six Days That Shook the World

1   Quoted in Gilbert, *Israel, A History*, p. 379.
2   http://www.jewishvirtuallibrary.org/jsource/anti-semitism/egjews.html
3   See the paper by Col. Warner D. Farr, 'The Third Temple's Holy of Holies, Israel's Nuclear Weapons', The Counter Proliferation Papers, Future Warfare Series No. 2, USAF Counter Proliferation Centre, September 1999. http://www.fas.org/nuke/guide/israel/nuke/farr.html
4   Morris, *Righteous Victims*, p. 301.
5   Gilbert, *Israel, A History*, p. 373.
6   *Ibid.*, p. 377.
7   Morris, *Righteous Victims*, p. 309.
8   Quoted in Gilbert, *Israel, A History*, p. 379.
9   *Ibid.*, p. 381.
10 http://www.aish.com/jewishissues/middleeast/Arab-Israeli_Conflict_3_Six _Day_War.asp
11 The Al-Aqsa mosque is the largest in Jerusalem, and can hold 5,000 worshippers. Muslims believe that the prophet Muhammad ascended to heaven from the site in 621, and it is the third holiest site in Islam. The mosque shares a supporting wall with the Western Wall of Solomon's Temple, the holiest site for Jews. There are frequent clashes at the site.

17. The Ghosts of Old Jaffa

1   http://www.palestineremembered.com/al-Ramla/Imwas/index.html

18. War, Once More

1   Ghassan Kanafani, 'Jaffa: Land of Oranges', translated by Mona Anis and Hala Halim. http://www.palestineremembered.com/Jaffa/Jaffa/Story153.html
2   Joseph Roth, *What I Saw: Reports from Berlin 1920–33* (London, 2003), pp. 66–67.
3   Quoted in the *Sunday Times*, 15 June 1969. The full extract is as follows: ' . . . asked whether the emergence of the Fedayeen (Arab guerrillas) is an impor-

tant factor in the Middle East, Mrs Meir replied: "Important, no. A new factor, yes. There was no such thing as Palestinians. When was there an independent Palestinian people with a Palestinian state? It was either southern Syria before the first World War and then it was a Palestine including Jordan. It was not as though there was a Palestinian people in Palestine considering itself as a Palestinian people and we came and threw them out and took their country away from them. They did not exist."'

4 http://www.en.wikipedia.org/wiki/Yom_Kippur_War
5 Morris, *Righteous Victims*, p 411–412.
6 *Ibid.*, p. 419.
7 *Ibid.*, p. 423.
8 *Ibid.*, p. 437.

19. Talking and Fighting

1 As told to the author, November 2004. Curiously, the Israeli diplomat named by the neighbour, contacted by the author, denied all knowledge of Said Hammami.
2 Abu Nidal obituary, David Hirst, *Guardian*, 20 August 2002.
3 Christopher Hitchens, 'The Terrorist I Knew', *Observer*, 25 August 2002.
4 Morris, *Righteous Victims*, p. 447.
5 Shlomo Argov remained permanently incapacitated until his death in February 2003.
6 Segev, *The Seventh Million*, p. 400.

20. Seaside Urban Sprawl

1 Quoted in Zvi Elhyani, Seafront Holdings, in 'Black to the sea' (Moria-Klein and Barnir eds.), Catalogue of the Israeli pavilion, 9th Biennale of Architecture, Venice, 2004, pp. 104–116.
2 Yosi is a pseudonym.
3 Elhyani, 'Black to the sea'.

21. Going Home to the Sea

1   Morris, *Righteous Victims*, p. 567.

2   According to the Israeli human rights organisation Be'tselem, Israeli security forces killed 1,095 Palestinians between December 1987 and December 1993. Tens of thousands of Palestinians were injured by rubber bullets, beatings and clubbings, while between 1987 and 1992, 119 Israelis—both military and civilian—were killed by Arabs in Israel itself and across the Green Line.

3   Morris, *Righteous Victims*, pp. 578–9.

4   http://www.amnesty.org/ailib/aireport/ar99/mde15.htm. See also media reports such as at: http//www.fas.org/irp/news/1999/01/990113-israel.htm

5   Morris, *Righteous Victims*, p. 601.

6   *Ibid.*, p. 606.

22. Gaza Comes to Jaffa

1   A report by the International Monetary Fund on economic conditions in the West Bank and Gaza, published in 2003, noted: 'Most of the laws passed by the PLC sat on the desk of President Arafat, and remained there for many years unsigned and therefore ineffective. Progress toward designing a new constitution stalled. The judicial process remained arbitrary and politically motivated. The fiscal process was perceived as extremely opaque, and liable to corruption.'

2   http://portal.telegraph.co.uk/news/main.jhtml?xml=/news/2004/10/31/waraf31.xml&sSheet=/news/2004/10/31/ixworld.html

3   Morris, *Righteous Victims*, pp. 637–8.

4   According to Jewish law, the site is actually forbidden to Jews, as the Temple Mount includes the unknown site of the Holy of Holies, an area of the Temple where only the high priest could enter. Muslims believe that Muhammad ascended to heaven from here, where the Dome of the Rock, with its famous gold dome, now stands. The Dome of the Rock is the centrepiece of a complex of Islamic buildings which includes the Al-Aqsa mosque.

5   Elias Canetti, *Crowds and Power* (London, 1998), pp. 58 and 73.

6   Statistics taken from 'Israel's Arab Minority', by Ori Nir. Lecture given at the Carnegie Endowment in April 2003.

7   Yossi Melman, 'Even the Shin Bet is Against Discrimination', *Haaretz*, 25 May 2004.

8   http://www.cbs.gov.il/statistical/arab_pop03e.pdf

9   The author's own experience confirms this. The son of one Arab interviewee declined to be interviewed, citing his unwillingness to draw the attention of Shin Bet.

23. Separation

1   Passover commemorates the Jewish exodus from Egypt. Jews are not permitted to eat any leavened bread during Passover, when all kosher bakeries close. The Israelites ate unleavened bread, known as *matzoh*, as they fled.

2   The author was struck by a conversation with one young Israeli, who explained that his personal ambition was to invite an Arab to his home for lunch. He explained that the only contact he had had with Arabs so far was during his military service on the West Bank, when he had been in their houses, albeit uninvited.

3   See also Samuel G. Freedman's article, 'Drama as a DMZ in Israel', *New York Times*, 1 August 2002.

4   See http://www.yeshgvul.org. Every year Yesh Gvul organises an alternative Independence Day celebration, to give a voice to marginalised social groupings, peace activists and Israeli Arabs.

5   The Jenin incursion triggered frenzied international media coverage, with reporters accusing Israel of slaughtering civilians en masse and conducting summary executions, allegations which were later disproven. Fifty-six Palestinians were killed, about half of whom were fighters. However, according to Human Rights Watch, the Israeli military committed grave breaches of the Geneva Convention in Jenin, as well as possible war crimes.

6   See Tom Segev's *Elvis in Jerusalem: Post-Zionism and the Americanization of Israel* (New York, 2003) for a fascinating discussion of this theme.

7   Or Aleksandrowicz makes several controversial claims of some interest to

devotees of Chelouche family history. Based on his interpretation of Yosef Eliyahu Chelouche's autobiography, *The Story of My Life*, he argues that the original Beit Chelouche was the second family house to be built outside Jaffa and was not constructed until 1893–4, which means it did not mark the foundation of Neve Tsedek. He also argues that Aharon Chelouche was not the only surviving male sibling of Avraham Chelouche, and that he had a brother called Yosef, who was included in the censuses of 1849 and 1855. There is a gravestone in Jaffa's Jewish cemetery inscribed for Yosef Chelouche, who died in 1865 at the age of twenty, says Aleksandrowicz. It is unclear why Yosef's existence would be denied by the rest of the family. In addition, family lore says Aharon Chelouche died in 1920, at the age of ninety-one, which means that he was born in 1829. But two Jewish censuses record his year of birth as 1840. Yosef Eliyahu Chelouche also mentions in his autobiography that the family originated in Morocco (not Algeria), and Aleksandrowicz says that Aharon Chelouche made the claim of originating in Oran to obtain French citizenship, which would offer considerable protection from the Ottoman authorities. All of this is disputed by Zvi Pomrock, who stands by the version of family history related here. Nothing can really be proved one way or the other. But the existence of the Chelouche family and all those family members included in this book is indisputable, as is their contribution to Neve Tsedek, Tel Aviv and Israel.

24. Islam on the March

1   The station has an excellent English-language website, http://english.aljazeera.net, and also broadcasts in English.

2   http://www.memri.de/uebersetzungen_analysen/themen/antisemitismus/as _almanar_18_12_03.html

3   Wagih Abou Zikra, a columnist for the government daily *Al-Akhbar*, wrote on 8 November 2002, 'Israel, and even most of the Jews of the world, carry out the *Protocols'* plan, whether they were written by the rabbis or not, whether the Jewish terrorists have read them or not.' See: http://www.memri.org/ bin/articles.cgi?Page=archives&Area=ia&ID=IA11302

4   Extracts can be viewed at: http://www.memritv.org/Search.asp?ACT=S9&
    Pi=275
5   http://www.memri.org/video

25. A Possible Future

1   http://www.worldpress.org/Mideast/1910.cfm
2   Shlomo Lahat, 'Breeding grounds for hatred', *Haaretz*, 3 January 2005.

Chronology

1909	Foundation of Jewish town of Ahuza Bayit, later Tel Aviv, outside Jaffa
1911	*Falastin* newspaper founded
August 1914	Start of First World War; Turkey allies with Germany and Austria-Hungary against Britain, France, Russia and others
January 1916	Britain and France sign the Sykes-Picot Agreement, drawing up new borders for the Middle East
Spring 1917	Turkish authorities expel Jews from Jaffa
November 1917	Britain issues the Balfour Declaration, expressing support for Jewish homeland in Palestine
Autumn–winter 1917	British forces under General Allenby capture Jerusalem, Tel Aviv and Jaffa; start of British rule over Palestine
1918	Muslim-Christian Arab association formed in Jaffa to oppose Zionism
1920	Haganah, Jewish self-defence organisation, founded in May
May 1921	Anti-Jewish riots in Jaffa; Tel Aviv given 'town council' status
1922	Areas of Jaffa annexed to Tel Aviv
July 1922	Britain given mandate to rule Palestine by League of Nations
August 1929	Further anti-Jewish riots in Jaffa and other cities in Palestine
1931	Irgun, right-wing Zionist militia, splits off from Haganah

1933	Arab demonstrations across Palestine against Jewish immigration
1934	Tel Aviv receives city status
April 1936	Arab Revolt begins against British
July 1936	British demolish large section of Old Jaffa
July 1937	Peel Commission recommends partition of Palestine into Jewish and Arab states; British outlaw Arab Higher Committee
1938	Woodhead Commission makes similar recommendations on partition
May 1939	British White Paper limits Jewish immigrants to Palestine to 75,000 over next five years
September 1939	Second World War begins; Haganah and Irgun work with British
1940	Avraham Stern splits from Irgun to form Stern Group (Lehi) to fight British
February 1944	Menachem Begin's Irgun militia relaunches operations against British
November 1944	Stern Group assassinates Lord Moyne in Cairo. Jewish Agency launches 'Hunting Season' against Irgun and Lehi members, with British
April 1946	Report of Anglo-American Commission of Inquiry recommends immigration of 100,000 Jews to Palestine
February 1947	Britain refers Palestine Mandate to United Nations

November 1947	United Nations votes to partition Palestine into Jewish and Arab states
November–December 1947	Fighting between Jewish and Arab militias; snipers fire between Tel Aviv and Jaffa
January 1948	Lehi blow up New Seray government building in Jaffa. Exodus of middle-class Arabs begins: soldiers of Arab Liberation Army start to arrive in Palestine
Winter –spring 1948	Fighting intensifies across Palestine. Jaffa's Arabs form defence guards
April 1948	Irgun and Lehi carry out massacre at Deir Yassin
Late April 1948	Irgun launches attack on Jaffa, triggering massive exodus of civilian population. Haganah's Operation Chametz campaign captures surrounding villages
9 May 1948	Jaffa Arab Emergency Committee writes to British authorities, declaring it an 'open city'
13 May 1948	British Mandate in Palestine ends. Jaffa surrenders to Haganah
14 May 1948	David Ben-Gurion declares establishment of State of Israel. Egyptian, Jordanian, Syrian and Iraqi troops invade, aided by other Arab states. Exodus begins of Jewish communities in Arab countries after riots and attacks
May 1948 –January 1949	First Arab-Israeli war; Palestinian *Nakba*, hundreds of thousands of refugees flee fighting
1950	Jaffa is merged with Tel Aviv
July 1952	Gamal Abdel Nasser takes power in Egypt

October —November 1956	Suez crisis. Israel invades Sinai peninsula, supported by Britain and France
1961	Trial in Jerusalem of Nazi leader Adolf Eichmann
May 1962	Execution of Adolf Eichmann
May 1964	Palestine Liberation Organization founded in Jerusalem
May 1967	Nasser deploys troops in Sinai, blockades Straits of Tiran. UN troops withdraw
5–10 June 1967	Six Day War—Israel defeats Egypt, Jordan and Syria, occupies Sinai, Gaza, West Bank, East Jerusalem and Golan Heights
August —September 1967	Khartoum conference; Arab states reject peace with Israel
September 1970	Nasser dies and is succeeded by Anwar Sadat
October 1973	Yom Kippur War—Egypt and Syria launch surprise attack on Israel, result is stalemate
April 1974	Israeli prime minister Golda Meir resigns, succeeded by Yitzhak Rabin
May 1977	Menachem Begin, former Irgun commander and leader of right-wing Likud Party, is elected prime minister, ending almost thirty years of Labour Party rule
November 1977	Egyptian President Anwar Sadat travels to Jerusalem
January 1978	Said Hammami, moderate PLO ambassador to London, is assassinated by Palestinian extremists
September 1978	Israel and Egypt negotiate peace accords at Camp David, overseen by President Jimmy Carter

March 1979	Israel signs peace treaty with Egypt, its first with an Arab neighbour
October 1981	President Sadat is assassinated by Islamic radicals in Cairo
April 1982	Israel withdraws from Sinai
June 1982	Israeli invasion of Lebanon
August 1982	Yasser Arafat and PLO leadership leave Beirut for exile in Tunis
September 1982	Christian militiamen murder hundreds of Palestinians at Sabra and Shatila refugee camps in Beirut
December 1987	The Palestinian Intifada, or uprising, erupts in West Bank and Gaza
January –February 1991	First Gulf War, as US-led force drives Iraq from Kuwait
October 1991	Middle East peace conference in Madrid
June 1992	Yitzhak Rabin elected Labour prime minister in Israel; secret negotiations continue between Israel and PLO
September 1993	Rabin and Arafat shake hands on White House lawn, sign Oslo Accords
July 1994	Rabin and King Hussein of Jordan sign peace treaty at White House
November 1995	Yitzhak Rabin is assassinated in Tel Aviv by right-wing Jewish fanatic
January 1996	First elections in Palestinian territories; Yasser Arafat elected president
January –March 1996	Hamas launches suicide bombing campaign inside Israel

November 1996	Benjamin Netanyahu wins election for Likud, appointed prime minister
May 1999	Labour leader Ehud Barak defeats Netanyahu in Israeli elections
July 2000	Barak and Arafat negotiate at Camp David, fail to reach agreement
September 2000	Ariel Sharon visits Temple Mount in Jerusalem, start of Al-Aqsa Intifada; Arabs riot in Jaffa and other cities in Israel
February 2001	Ariel Sharon wins election for prime minister, forms National-Unity government with Labour
March 2002	Israel army incursions into Palestinian cities, several re-occupied
January 2003	Ariel Sharon wins elections for Likud
April 2003	President Bush publishes 'Road Map' for peace between Israel and Palestinians
October 2004	Knesset approves Ariel Sharon's plan to disengage from Gaza Strip
November 2004	Yasser Arafat dies
January 2005	Mahmoud Abbas elected Palestinian president; Ariel Sharon forms National-Unity government with Labour Party
August 2005	Israel withdraws from Gaza
January 2006	Ariel Sharon suffers massive stroke
July 2006	Israel invades southern Lebanon

Bibliography

Books

Agnon, S. Y., *Only Yesterday*. Princeton and Oxford: Princeton University Press, 2000.

Aryeh, *Claim of Dispossession: Jewish Land Settlement and the Arabs, 1878–1948*. New Brunswick: Transaction Books, 1984.

Begin, Menachem, *The Revolt*. London: W.H. Allen, 1983.

Benvenisti, Meron, *Sacred Landscape: The Buried History of the Holy Land Since 1948*. Berkeley: University of California Press, 2000.

Bucaille, Laetitia, *Growing Up Palestinian: Israeli Occupation and the Intifada Generation*. Princeton and Oxford: Princeton, 2004.

Canetti, Elias, *Crowds and Power*. London: Phoenix Press, 2000.

Chacour, Elias, with Hazard, David, *Blood Brothers*. Grand Rapids: Chosen Books, 1984.

Chelouche, Yosef Eliyahu, *Reminiscences of My Life (1870–1930)*. Tel Aviv: Babel Publishers, 2005.

Dershowitz, Alan, *The Case for Israel*. Hoboken: John Wiley and Sons, 2003.

Gilbert, Sir Martin, *Jerusalem in the Twentieth Century*. London: Pimlico, 1997.

———, *Israel*. London: Transworld, 1998.

Glass, Joseph B. and Kark, Ruth, *Sephardi Entrepreneurs in Israel: The Amzalak Family 1816–1918*. Jerusalem: Magnes Press, The Hebrew University, 1991.

Goldberg, Rabbi David J., *To the Promised Land: A History of Zionist Thought*. London: Penguin, 1996.

Grant, Linda, *When I Lived in Modern Times*. London: Granta Books, 2000.

Grossman, David, *Sleeping on a Wire: Conversations with Palestinians in Israel*. New York: Picador, 2003.

——, *Death As a Way of Life: Despatches from Jerusalem*. London: Bloomsbury, 2003.

Guardia La, Anton, *Holy Land Unholy War: Israelis and Palestinians*. London: John Murray, 2002.

Ha-am, Ahad, *Selected Essays*. Jerusalem: Sefer ve Sefel Publishing, 2003.

Hameagel, Honi, *Balata Ballad*. Tel Aviv: Vilenski, 2003.

Haskell, Guy H., *From Sofia to Jaffa: The Jews of Bulgaria and Israel*. Detroit: Wayne State University Press, 1994.

Kark, Ruth, *Jaffa: A City in Evolution*. Jerusalem: Yad Izhak Ben-Zvi Press, 1990.

Keret, Edgar and El-Youssef, Samir, *Gaza Blues: Different Stories*. London: David Paul Books, 2004.

Khalidi, Walid (ed.), *All That Remains: The Palestinian Villages Occupied and Depopulated by Israel in 1948*. Washington: Institute for Palestine Studies, 1992.

Kidron, Peretz, (ed.), *Refusenik: Israel's Soldiers of Conscience*. London: Zed Books, 2004.

Koestler, Arthur, *Arrow in the Blue*. London: William Collins and Hamish Hamilton, 1954.

Laquer, Walter and Rubin, Barry (eds.), *The Israeli-Arab Reader: A Documentary History of the Middle East Conflict*. London: Penguin, 2001.

LeBor, Adam, *A Heart Turned East: Among the Muslims of Europe and America*. London: Little, Brown, 1997.

——, *Milosevic: A Biography*. London: Bloomsbury, 2002.

LeBor, Adam and Boyes, Roger, *Surviving Hitler: Choice, Corruption and Compromise in the Third Reich*. London: Simon and Schuster, 2000.

Levine, Mark, *Overthrowing Geography: Jaffa, Tel Aviv, and the Struggle for Palestine 1880–1948*. Berkeley: University of California Press, 2005.

Lewis, Bernard, *The Jews of Islam*. Princeton: Princeton University Press, 1984.

———, *What Went Wrong: Western Impact and Middle Eastern Response*. London: Orion, 2002.

Macfie, A. L., *The End of the Ottoman Empire*. London and New York: Longman, 1998.

Masalha, Nur, *A Land Without A People: Israel, Transfer and the Palestinians 1949–96*. London: Faber and Faber, 1997.

Mazower, Mark, *Salonica: City of Ghosts*. London: HarperCollins, 2004.

Meisler, Frank, *On the Vistula Facing East*. London: André Deutsch, 1996.

Morris, Benny, *The Birth of the Palestinian Refugee Problem, 1947–1949*. Cambridge: Cambridge University Press, 1997.

———, *Righteous Victims: A History of the Zionist-Arab Conflict, 1881–2001*. New York: Random House, 2001.

Nassar, Ibrahim and Nassar, Dr Majed, *Small Dreams: Fourteen Short Stories from Palestine*. Ramallah: Bailasan Design, 2003.

Oz, Amos, *The Hill of Evil Counsel*. London: Fontana, 1981.

———, *My Michael*. London: Flamingo, 1984.

Pearlman, Wendy, *Occupied Voices: Stories of Everyday Life from the Second Intifada*. New York: Thunder's Mouth Press/Nation Books, 2003.

Prescott, H. F. M., *Friar Felix at Large: A Fifteenth-Century Pilgrimage to the Holy Land*. New Haven: Yale University Press, 1950.

Rogan, Eugene L. and Shlaim, Avi (ed.), *The War for Palestine: Rewriting the History of 1948*. Cambridge: Cambridge University Press, 2001.

Roth, Joseph, *What I Saw: Reports from Berlin 1920–33*. London: Granta Books, 2001.

———, *The Wandering Jews*. London: Granta Books, 2001.

Sachar, Howard M., *A History of Israel From the Rise of Zionism to Our Time*. New York: Alfred A. Knopf, 1996.

Said, Edward W., *Orientalism: Western Misconceptions of the Orient*. London: Penguin, 1985.

Schlor, Joachim, *Tel Aviv*. London: Reaktion Books, 1999.

Segev, Tom, *The Seventh Million: The Israelis and the Holocaust*. New York: Hill and Wang, 1993.

————, *1949: The First Israelis*. New York: Owl Books, 1998.

————, *One Palestine, Complete: Jews and Arabs under the British Mandate*. London: Abacus, 2000.

————, *Elvis in Jerusalem: Post-Zionism and the Americanisation of Israel*. New York: Henry Holt, 2002.

Shehade, Raja, *Strangers in the House: Coming of Age in Occupied Palestine*. London: Profile Books, 2002.

————, *When the Bulbul Stopped Singing: A Diary of Ramallah Under Siege*. London: Profile Books, 2003.

Shipler, David K., *Arab and Jew: Wounded Spirits in a Promised Land*. New York: Penguin, 2002.

Shlaim, Avi, *The Iron Wall: Israel and the Arab World*. London: Penguin, 2000.

Stendel, Ori, *The Arabs in Israel*. Brighton: Sussex Academic Press, 1996.

Troen, S. Ilan, *Imagining Zion: Dreams, Designs and Realities in a Century of Jewish Settlement*. New Haven and London: Yale University Press, 2003.

Uris, Leon, *Exodus*. New York: Wings, 2000.

Websites

english.aljazeera.net

www.aish.com

www.amnesty.org

www.btselem.org

www.cbs.gov.il

www.etzel.org.il/english

www.fas.org

www.haaretzdaily.com

www.hrw.org

www.jewishvirtuallibrary.org

www.memri.org

www.merip.org

www.npr.org/news/specials/mideast/history/history1.html

www.nytimes.com/books

www.palestineremembered.com

www.timesonline.co.uk
www.en.wikipedia.org
www.worldpress.org
www.yeshgvul.org

Articles and Papers

Abu-Lughod, Ibrahim, 'The War of 1948: Disputed Perspective and Outcomes', *Journal of Palestine Studies*, Vol. 18, No. 2, winter 1989.

Aleksandrowicz, Or, 'The House of Aharon Chelouche: the Critical Account' and 'A Journey Towards a Forgotten Past', unpublished papers provided by the author, summarised and translated by Raz Segal.

Avishai, Bernard, 'Saving Israel from Itself: A Secular Future for the Jewish State', *Harper's*, January 2005.

Elhyani, Zvi, 'Seafront Holdings', in *Back to the Sea* (Moria-Klein and Barnir eds.), Catalogue of the Israeli Pavilion, 9th Biennale of Architecture, Venice, 2004.

Farr, Col. Warner D., 'The Third Temple's Holy of Holies, Israel's Nuclear Weapons', *The Counter Proliferation Papers, Future Warfare Series No. 2*, USAF Counter Proliferation Centre, September 1999.

Freedman, Samuel G., 'Drama as a DMZ in Israel', *New York Times*, 1 August 2002.

Giles, Frank, Interview with Golda Meir, *Sunday Times*, 15 June 1969.

Hammami, Rema, 'Intifada in the Aftermath', *Middle East Report Online*, 30 October 2001.

Hirst, David, Abu Nidal obituary, *Guardian*, 20 August 2002.

Hitchens, Christopher, 'The Terrorist I Knew', *Observer*, 25 August 2002.

Human Rights Watch, 'Jenin, IDF Military Operations', May 2002.

International Monetary Fund, 'West Bank and Gaza: Economic Performance and Reform under Conflict Conditions', Washington, DC, 15 September 2003.

Lahat, Shlomo, 'Breeding Grounds for Hatred', *Haaretz*, 3 January 2005.

LeBor, Adam, 'Archives Reveal Ruthless Settlers, Say New Historians', *Independent*, April 1998.

Melman, Yossi, 'Even the Shin Bet is Against Discrimination', *Haaretz*, 25 May 2004.

Menahem, Gila, 'Arab Citizens in an Israeli City: Action and Discourse in Public Programmes', *Ethnic and Racial Studies*, Vol. 21, Issue 3, May 1998.

Mendes, Philip, 'The Forgotten Refugees: The Causes of the Post-1948 Jewish Exodus from Arab Countries'. Presented at the 14th Jewish Studies Conference in Melbourne, March 2002.

Morris, Benny, 'A Fresh Look at Zionist Documentation of 1948', *Journal of Palestine Studies*, Vol. 24, No. 3, spring 1995.

Najjar, Orayb Aref, '*Falastin* editorial writers, the Allies, World War II, and the Palestinian Question in the 21st century', *Studies in Media & Information Literacy Education*, Vol. 3, Issue 4, November 2003.

Nir, Ori, 'Israel's Arab Minority'. Lecture given at the Carnegie Endowment, 30 April 2003.

Tamari, Salim, 'The Vagabond Café and Jerusalem's Prince of Idleness', *Jerusalem Quarterly File*, summer 2003.

Unpublished Memoirs

Chelouche, Julia, *The Tree and the Roots*.

Hammami, Hasan, *Memoirs*. Punta Gorda, US, 2004, 2005.

Acknowledgements

This book is testimony to the patience and courtesy of those whose lives are chronicled within: Khamis Abulafia; Sami and Ismail Abou-Shehade; Yoram, Ofer and Rina Aharoni; Sami Albo; Amin, Robyn, Leila, Salim, Suad and Wedad Andraus; Behira Buchbinder; the late Aharon and Shlomo Chelouche; Mary and Jacob Chelouche; Hasan, Barbara, Mustafa, and Rema Hammami; Fadwa Hasna, Fakhri Geday, Frank and Michal Meisler. Their willingness to spend so much time answering my questions, unearthing sometimes painful memories, brought depth and richness to the narrative. My thanks and gratitude go to all of them. I am especially grateful to Hasan Hammami for his detailed memoirs, written for this book, and to Rema Hammami and Fadwa Hasna. They took me to the Hammami family house in Jaffa, a memorable day which helped me understand Palestinian loss and exile. In Tel Aviv, Zvi Pomrock was an enthusiastic guide to the Chelouche family history and kindly showed me around Jaffa, while Frank Meisler's generous hospitality included several very enjoyable dinners. Edith Krygier gave me a copy of her mother Julia Chelouche's memoirs, which proved a rich resource.

In Israel I was lucky to find Raz Segal, through the help of Ruthi Vygodski at

Tel Aviv University. Raz worked with me throughout the project. His diligence, enthusiasm and assiduous research were invaluable. He not only helped find the families, but carefully answered a stream of questions about Jaffa and Tel Aviv, from arcane historical matters to the budget details of urban reconstruction projects. Thanks, Raz. Many others helped with their time and expertise, including Professor Shlomo Avineri, Igal Ezraty, Gloria Goldring, Ali Goughti, Asaf Ichilevich, Adib Jahashan, Baruch Krotman, Shlomo Lahat, Andre Mazzawi, Yoseph Nachmias, Professor Anita Shapira and Salim Tamari. I am especially grateful to Or Aleksandrowicz for translating several extracts from *Reminiscences of My Life*, the autobiography of Yosef Eliyahu Chelouche. Dr Mark Levine, of the University of California, generously sent me the manuscript of his incisive work, *Overturning Geography: Jaffa; Tel Aviv, and the Struggle for Palestine 1880–1948*, before publication. Ed Serotta's excellent website www.centropa.org, *Witness to a Jewish Century*, helped inspire the themes of this book. Yaron Kaldes, chief of Jaffa's detectives, took me on an illuminating drive around the city's back streets, while archaeologist Martin Peilstocker explained to me the workings of a dig. Paula Rakover-Kedem was a fascinating guide to Jaffa's history, while Zvi Schaham, Eyal Ziv and Yehuda Lebanoni also helped with their insights. Dr Moris Topaz shared his expertise in the physiological results of suicide bombings. Others, who asked not to be named, also shared their knowledge of such matters. In Jaffa, Arnon Amid and Dominic Canning made the Old Jaffa Hostel a welcome oasis.

The unfailing hospitality of the Tsafrir family—Karen, Yaron, Tal, Amit and No'am—proved true friendship does not fade over time and distance—especially at Yunis Restaurant, while in Jerusalem Guy Chazan was a warm and welcoming host. In Jerusalem I am grateful to the staff of the Central Zionist Archive, and to Hadassah Assouline and the staff of the Central Archive for the History of the Jewish People for their assistance. A generous grant from the Society of Authors—membership of which I recommend to all professional writers for its many services—helped finance my extensive trips to Jaffa. In London my thanks go to Patrick Bishop, Adrian Brown, Yigal Chazan, Rabbi David Goldberg, Ahmad Khalidi, Justin Leighton, Jenny Morgan, Omar Al-Qattan and Barbara Wyllie for their help and expertise, and to my brother Jason, for his diligent research in the British archives. In Budapest a trusty team of transcribers helped write up the many interviews: Agnes Csonka, Pablo Gorondi, Christian Jacobson and Kati Tordas, while my friends and colleagues Chris Condon, John Nadler, Olen Steinhauer and Mark Milstein were always morale boosters. So too were Robert, Zoltan and Zsuzsa Ligeti. *Köszönöm!*

Many thanks go as ever to my agents at MBA, Laura Longrigg, Susan Smith and David Riding, for their continuing support and inspiration. At Bloomsbury I am grateful to Bill Swainson, whose enthusiasm and thoughtful and considered input helped weave the stories of the families into a book. Pascal Cariss' editorial advice was invaluable at early drafts, as was Katharina Bielenberg's copy-editing later. I am grateful also to Ruth Logan and Sarah Marcus. My sincere thanks also to Alane Mason and Alex Cuadros at W. W. Norton and Company for their diligent editing and belief in this book. My colleagues at *The Times* foreign desk have been very supportive of a correspondent who did not always correspond much while working on this book. My thanks go especially to Roger Boyes, Martin Fletcher, Bronwen Maddox and Gill Ross, while Kelly MacNamara and Amanda Brewer deftly trawled *The Times'* archives.

This book is also rooted in many earlier visits to Israel and the Palestinian territories. I have fond memories of the six months I spent on Kibbutz Ramat Hashofet in 1980, where Esther Hakim was an enthusiastic teacher and guide, and where I first began to think about the complexities of Israel and Palestine. In 1998 I was commissioned by BBC Radio Five Live to travel to Israel and the Palestinian territories to make a series of programmes with Marina Salandy-Brown, which greatly increased my understanding of the conflict. As one door after another opened in Jaffa I gathered more material than I could include in this book, but all of those interviewed helped me to gain a deeper understanding of the city and its inhabitants. I am indebted to everyone who gave of their time, including Leon Alkalay, Yousef Asfour, Joseph Deek, Shlomo Gadav, Ilana Goor, Dr Adi Kassem, Dina Li, Abed Satal and Rifaat Turk. Doubtless there are those whom I have inadvertently omitted. To all, I say thank you for your time and knowledge, and that any mistakes are mine. Most of all, my love and gratitude go to my own family: my wife, Kati, for her unending support, Daniel Maurice and Hannah Lily, the biggest inspirations of all.

Permissions

For permission to reproduce copyrighted material the author and publishers gratefully acknowledge the following:

IBRAHIM ABU-LUGHOD, from 'The War of 1948: Disputed Perspectives and Outcomes', *Journal of Palestine Studies*, Vol. 18, no. 2, winter 1989, reproduced by permission of *Journal of Palestine Studies*. MERON BENVENISTI, from *Sacred Landscape* © 2000 by the Regents of the University of California, reproduced by permission of the University of California Press. LINDA GRANT, from *When I Lived in Modern Times*, reproduced by permission of Granta Books, London. GHASSAN KANAFANI (translation), from *Land of the Sad Oranges* © www.palestineremembered.com. ARTHUR KOESTLER, from *Arrow in the Blue*, permission granted by PFD on behalf of the Arthur Koestler Estate, published by Vintage, London. MIDDLE EAST MEDIA RESEARCH INSTITUTE, translations taken from: *The Diaspora*, television series broadcast on Al-Manar, Lebanon, 2003; *Knight without a Horse*, Egyptian television series, broadcast 2002; Palestine Television broadcast of sermons at Gaza main mosque, 3 August and 17 August; interviews with passers-by broadcast on Iqra channel, Saudi Arabia, 26 September 2004; *Life is Sweet*, broadcast on Jordanian television,

Index

Index

About the Author

Adam LeBor was born in London and read Arabic, international history and politics at Leeds University, graduating in 1983, and also studied Arabic at the Hebrew University of Jerusalem. He worked for several British newspapers before becoming a foreign correspondent in 1991. He has reported from thirty countries, including Israel and Palestine, and covered the Yugoslav wars for *The Times of London* and *The Independent*. Currently Central Europe correspondent for *The Times of London*, he also writes for the *Sunday Times*, *The Economist*, *Literary Review*, *Condé Nast Traveller*, the *Jewish Chronicle*, *New Statesman* and *Harry's Place* in Britain, and contributes to *The Nation* and the *New York Times* in the States. He is the author of seven books, including the best-selling *Hitler's Secret Bankers*, which was shortlisted for the Orwell Prize. His books have been published in nine languages. Visit him on the Web at www.adamlebor.com.